Lecture Notes in Computer Science   11910

More information about this series at http://www.springer.com/series/7409

Meikang Qiu (Ed.)

Smart Computing and Communication

4th International Conference, SmartCom 2019
Birmingham, UK, October 11–13, 2019
Proceedings

 Springer

Editor
Meikang Qiu ⃝iD
Columbia University
New York, NY, USA

ISSN 0302-9743   ISSN 1611-3349   (electronic)
Lecture Notes in Computer Science
ISBN 978-3-030-34138-1   ISBN 978-3-030-34139-8   (eBook)
https://doi.org/10.1007/978-3-030-34139-8

LNCS Sublibrary: SL3 – Information Systems and Applications, incl. Internet/Web, and HCI

This Springer imprint is published by the registered company Springer Nature Switzerland AG
The registered company address is: Gewerbestrasse 11, 6330 Cham, Switzerland

Preface

This volume contains the papers presented at SmartCom 2019: the 4th International Conference on Smart Computing and Communication held during October 11–13, 2019, in Birmingham, UK.

There were 286 submissions. Each submission was reviewed by at least 3 reviewers, and on average 3.5 Program Committee members. The committee decided to accept 40 papers.

Recent booming developments in Web-based technologies and mobile applications have facilitated a dramatic growth in the implementation of new techniques, such as cloud computing, big data, pervasive computing, Internet of Things, and social cyber-physical systems. Enabling a smart life has become a popular research topic with an urgent demand. Therefore, SmartCom 2019 focused on both smart computing and communications fields and aimed to collect recent academic work to improve the research and practical application in the field.

The scope of SmartCom 2019 was broad, from smart data to smart communications, from smart cloud computing to smart security. The conference gathered all high-quality research/industrial papers related to smart computing and communications and aimed at proposing a reference guideline for further research. SmartCom 2019 was held at Birmingham City University in the UK and its conference proceedings publisher is Springer.

SmartCom 2019 continued in the series of successful academic get togethers, following SmartCom 2018 (Tokyo, Japan), SmartCom 2017 (Shenzhen, China), and SmartCom 2016 (Shenzhen, China).

We would like to thank the conference sponsors: Springer LNCS, Birmingham City University, Columbia University, Beijing Institute of Technology, The Alliance of Emerging Engineering Education for Information Technologies, China Computer Federation, North America Chinese Talents Association, and Longxiang High Tech Group Inc.

September 2019
Meikang Qiu

Organization

General Chairs

Meikang Qiu	Columbia University, USA
Mark Sharma	Birmingham City University, UK

Program Chairs

Bhavani Thuraisingham	The University of Texas at Dallas, USA
Zhongming Fei	University of Kentucky, USA
Keke Gai	Beijing Institute of Technology, China

Local Chairs

Yonghao Wang	Birmingham City University, UK
Xiangyu Gao	New York University, USA

Publicity Chairs

Yuanchao Shu	Microsoft Research Asia, China
Han Qiu	Télécom ParisTech, France
Zhenyu Guan	Beihang University, China

Technical Committee

Jeremy Foss	Birmingham City University, UK
Cham Athwal	Birmingham City University, UK
Andrew Aftelak	Birmingham City University, UK
Yue Hu	Louisiana State University, USA
Aniello Castiglione	University of Salerno, Italy
Maribel Fernandez	King's College, University of London, UK
Hao Hu	Nanjing University, China
Oluwaseyi Oginni	Birmingham City University, UK
Alan Dolhasz	Birmingham City University, UK
Qianyun Zhang	Beihang University, China
Dawei Li	Beihang University, China
Bo Du	ZF Friedrichshafen AG, Germany
Cefang Guo	Imperial College London, UK
Thomas Austin	San Jose State University, USA
Aniello Castiglione	University of Salerno, Italy
Maribel Fernandez	King's College, University of London, UK
Zhiyuan Tan	Edinburgh Napier University, UK

William Campbell	Birmingham City University, UK
Xiang He	Birmingham City University, UK
Mohammad Patwary	Birmingham City University, UK
Peter Bull	QA Ltd, UK
Hendri Murfi	Universitas Indonesia, Indonesia
Zengpeng Li	Lancaster University, UK
Wenbo Shi	Inha University, South Korea
Pietro Ferrara	JuliaSoft SRL, Italy
Ke Miao	Mitacs Inc., Canada
Dalia El B. Abdelghany Ashmawy	Birmingham City University, UK
Xiaohu Zhou	Birmingham City University, UK
Kui Zhang	Birmingham City University, UK
Vitor Jesus	Birmingham City University, UK
Matthew Roach	Swansea University, UK
Chunhua Deng	Wuhan University of Science and Technology, China
Katie Cover	The Pennsylvania State University, USA
Shishank Shishank	Birmingham City University, UK
Jinguang Gu	Wuhan University of Science and Technology, China
Wei Cai	Chinese University of Hong Kong, Hong Kong, China
Junwei Zhang	Xidian University, China
Jue Wang	SCCAS, China
Hao Tang	City University of New York, USA
Md Ali	Rider University, USA
Paul Kearney	Birmingham City University, UK
Li Bo	Beihang University, China
Zijian Zhang	Beijing Institute of Technology, China
Meng Ma	Peking University, China
Cheng Zhang	Waseda University, Japan
Fausto Spoto	University of Verona, Italy
Song Yang	Beijing Institute of Technology, China
Lixin Tao	Pace University, USA
Rehan Bhana	Birmingham City University, UK
Ian A Williams (CEBE)	Birmingham City University, UK
Shaojing Fu	National University of Defense Technology, China
Agostino Cortesi	Università Ca' Foscari, Italy
Yunxia Liu	Huazhong University of Science and Technology, China
Yongxin Zhu	Chinese Academy of Sciences, China
Songmao Zhang	Chinese Academy of Sciences, China
Jongpil Jeong	Sungkyunkwan University, South Korea
Ding Wang	Peking University, China
Wenjia Li	New York Institute of Technology, USA
Peng Zhang	Stony Brook University, USA
Jeroen van den Bos	Netherlands Forensic Institute, The Netherlands
Ron Austin	Birmingham City University, UK

Wayne Collymore	Birmingham City University, UK
Haibo Zhang	University of Otago, New Zealand
Suman Kumar	Troy University, USA
Shui Yu	Deakin University, Australia
Emmanuel Bernardez	IBM Research, USA

Contents

A Survey of Deep Learning Applied to Story Generation

Chenglong Hou[1,2], Chensong Zhou[3], Kun Zhou[2], Jinan Sun[1(✉)],
and Sisi Xuanyuan[4]

[1] National Engineering Research Center for Software Engineering,
Peking University, Beijing 100871, China
{houchenglong, sjn}@pku.edu.cn
[2] School of Software and Microelectronics, Peking University,
Beijing 100871, China
1701210951@pku.edu.cn
[3] Potevio Information Technology Co., Ltd., Beijing, China
zhouchensong@potevio.com
[4] Department of Science and Technology of Shandong Province, Jinan, China
37762488@qq.com

Abstract. With the rapid development of deep learning in the fields of text abstraction and dialogue generation, researchers are now reconsidering the long-standing story-generation task from the 1970s. Deep learning methods are gradually being adopted to solve problems in traditional story generation, making story generation a new research hotspot in the field of text generation. However, in the field of story generation, the widely used seq2seq model is unable to provide adequate long-distance text modeling. As a result, this model struggles to solve the story-generation task, since the relation between long text should be considered, and coherency and vividness are critical. Thus, recent years have seen numerous proposals for better modeling methods. In this paper, we present the results of a comprehensive study of story generation. We first introduce the relevant concepts of story generation, its background, and the current state of research. We then summarize and analyze the standard methods of story generation. Based on various divisions of user constraints, the story-generation methods are divided into three categories: the theme-oriented model, the storyline-oriented model, and the human-machine-interaction–oriented model. On this basis, we discuss the basic ideas and main concerns of various methods and compare the strengths and weaknesses of each method. Finally, we finish by analyzing and forecasting future developments that could push story-generation research toward a new frontier.

Keywords: Story generation · Text generation · Deep learning

1 Introduction

A story is a series of real or fictional events that can be manifested in various forms, such as pictures, videos, or texts. Story generation refers to the search for story texts that meet the user constraints in an infinite text space. Probabilistic models for story

The original version of this chapter was revised: the last name of the author Sisi Xuanyuan had been misspelt. This has been corrected. The correction to this chapter is available at https://doi.org/10. 1007/978-3-030-34139-8_41

M. Qiu (Ed.): SmartCom 2019, LNCS 11910, pp. 1–10, 2019.
https://doi.org/10.1007/978-3-030-34139-8_1

generation are probability distributions that describe a stochastic process for generating a story. Research into story generation can be applied in the fields of education, entertainment, and transaction processing, such as providing writing suggestions for writers or providing a reasonable description of events for a group of pictures. The research can also be applied in the fields of virtual society and intelligent simulation, such as for automated generation of storylines in games.

Traditional automated story generation can be traced back to Meehan *et al.*, who used a TALE-SPIN system to automatically generate stories in the 1970s [1]. Early attempts in this field relied on intelligent planning, whose main idea was to transform story generation into a classical planning problem [2] in which the beginning of the story corresponds to the initial state of the plan, and the author's goal corresponds to the goal state of the plan. The actions taken by the main characters in the story correspond to those in the plan. The Interactive Storytelling System, developed by Cavazza of IVE Research Lab of Teesside University in the UK, is the representative work of this system [3]. Pizzi and Charles used heuristic search planning to generate stories and developed the EmoEmma system [4]. Lebowitz [5], Turner [6], Bringsjord and Ferrucci [7], Perez and Sharples [8], and Riedl and Young [9] also used story-generation methods based on intelligent programming. Early attempts in this field also included case-based reasoning (Gervas *et al.* [10]) or generalizing knowledge from existing stories to assemble new stories (Swanson and Gordon [11]).

Traditional story-generation methods are knowledge intensive and depend on an *a priori* domain model defined for the fictional world, including executable roles, locations, and actions [12]. Complex system design and domain knowledge are required, so traditional story-generation methods have some drawbacks, such as high labor costs and limited domains. However, deep learning can resolve these shortcomings, so the rapid development of deep learning has led to significant improvements in deep learning story-generation methods.

At present, the seq2seq model [13] is the basic model for story generation. It offers substantial advantages for machine translation, automated summarization, and other tasks, and the proposed attention model [14] has developed it further. However, difficulties remain in the application of story generation. First, producing coherent stories remains a challenge. Martin [15], Yao [17], Xu [21], Fan [20], and others have pointed out this problem and have used different models to solve it. Second is the problem of repeated generation. In the field of dialogue, Li pointed out that the seq2seq model tends to produce duplicate dialogue [16]. Accordingly, Yao *et al.* [17] argued that the seq2seq model had the same problem in story generation, so they proceeded to optimize it.

2   Story-Generating Probabilistic Models

Story-generating probabilistic models are probability distributions that describe a stochastic process for generating stories (i.e., they model *how* a story is written). Given training data D, an output story representation φ, and the possibly empty user constraints $C(\varphi)$, these models learn the probability distribution $P_D(\varphi|C(\varphi))$ and sample P_D to generate a story. In this work, we divide different models in the generation process according to the user constraints $C(\varphi)$. The user constraints $C(\varphi)$ include two parts: (1) whether constraints are static; in other words, whether a human-computer interaction exists in the process of generation, which means that the user constraints C (φ) will change dynamically as a function of human participation in the story-generation process. (2) For the strength of the user constraints, the important measure is whether the user constraints $C(\varphi)$ contain a complete storyline.

Theme-Oriented Models. When the user constraint $C(\varphi)$ is static; that is, no human-computer interaction exists in the process of story-generation, and the constraint (e.g., a theme word, a sentence, or some hints) is theme oriented and does not contain a complete storyline, P_D is reduced to a theme-oriented model.

Storyline-Oriented Models. When the user constraint $C(\varphi)$ is static and contains complete story plots, such as a set of pictures that have been given about the development of a storyline, an abstract description of the development of a storyline, or a specific story that needs an ending, P_D is reduced to a storyline-oriented model.

Human-Machine Interaction-Oriented Models. When the user constraint $C(\varphi)$ is dynamic, i.e., user constraint varies with human-computer interaction, P_D is reduced to a storyline-oriented model.

We divide the related work into theme-oriented models, storyline-oriented models, and human-machine-interaction–oriented models from the perspective of user constraints. Next, we compare and analyze the advantages and disadvantages of these three models.

2.1 Theme-Oriented Models

The theme-oriented model refers to a model in which the user constraint $C(\varphi)$ is static, which means that no human-computer interaction occurs in the process of story generation, and the constraint (e.g., a theme word, a sentence, or some hints) is theme oriented. It has the highest degree of openness, the weakest constraints on story generation, and the most difficulty to generate consistent, coherent, and vivid stories.

The theme-oriented model further guides the story through the context or keywords of the storyline development by using the hierarchical model, which can increase the long-distance dependence and make the story more coherent. The hierarchical model has been used in many fields; for example, Li *et al.* [30] learned to hierarchically embed words, sentences, and paragraphs and achieved good results; and Yarats and Lewis [31] used the hierarchical model in the field of dialogue. Although the following models are implemented differently, they are all based on the hierarchical model.

Hierarchical Neural Story Generation Model. Based on the work of Martin *et al.* [15], several subsequent researchers also adopted the hierarchical model. Fan *et al.* [20] proposed a hierarchical neural story-generation model, whose user constraint $C(\varphi)$ is $\emptyset$ (i.e., story generation is not constrained by users). The hierarchical neural story-generation model divides story generation into two steps: The first step is to generate the prompt to guide the direction of story generation, and the second step is to use the seq2seq model to generate a story according to the generated prompt. Experiments show that the hierarchical neural story-generation model achieves more coherent stories than the seq2seq model through hierarchical structure and the fusion mechanism.

Skeleton-Based Model. The user constraint $C(\varphi)$ of the skeleton-based model [21] is the beginning of the story (i.e., a sentence that expresses the theme of the story).

Sentences written by humans are closely linked, and the whole story is coherent and fluent. This is because humans advance the storylines and reorganize them into fluent sentences. The skeleton-based model is inspired by the fact that the connection between sentences is mainly reflected by key phrases, such as predicate, subject, object, etc. Other words (such as modifiers) are not only redundant for understanding semantic dependencies but also make for sparse dependency. Therefore, driven by the patterns of human writing, the skeleton-based model takes the phrases that express the critical meaning of sentences in story works as the skeleton and propose a skeleton-based model to promote the coherence of story generation. Unlike the traditional model of generating complete sentences at one time, the skeleton-based model first generates the most critical phrases, which is called the "skeleton." The skeleton is then extended to complete and fluent sentences. In addition, the skeleton in the model is not defined manually but learned through reinforced learning, which can make the generated story more coherent and consistent with the theme.

Planning-Based Model. The user constraint $C(\varphi)$ of the planning-based model [17] is a word (i.e., a word that expresses the theme of the story). According to Wang *et al.* [23] in the field of poetry creation and Mou *et al.* [24] in the field of dialogue, keywords are used as the main points to guide the generation. Inspired by the planning method applied in the field of dialogue [22] and narrative [9], the planning-based model realizes that story generation can be decomposed into two steps: the generation of the story plot and the generation of the story text based on the plot. Therefore, it proposes a planning-based story-generation framework that combines plot planning and story text generation to generate stories from titles. Obviously, this is similar to the skeleton-based model.

Multi-level Model. The user constraint $C(\varphi)$ of the multilevel model [25] is prompt. Although existing language models can generate stories with good local coherence, they have difficulty merging phrases into coherent plots, or even to maintain the consistency of roles throughout the story. One reason for this failure is that the language model generates the whole story at the word level, which makes it difficult for the model to capture storyline interactions above the word level. To solve this problem, Fan decomposes the problem into a series of easier sub-problems, from coarse grained to fine grained. These decompositions give three advantages: first, more abstract representations can be generated to solve the problem of modeling long-term dependencies; second, different models are allowed to solve different sub-problems with more pertinence; and third, data need not be labeled manually.

Upon analyzing these theme-oriented models, we find that they all use the idea of hierarchical structure. Whether planning, keywords, or action sequence, they all model the relationship of the storyline at a higher level than words and establish long-distance dependencies so that they get better results than with the seq2seq model in terms of story coherence and consistency.

2.2   Storyline-Oriented Models

For the storyline-oriented model, the user constraint $C(\varphi)$ is static, which means that no human-computer interaction occurs in the process of story generation, and the constraint contains complete story plots.

Model Based on a Group of Narrative Pictures. The user constraint $C(\varphi)$ of the model based on a group of narrative pictures is a set of sequential pictures that develops the storyline. Huang et al. [26] proposed the first dataset that gives a set of sequential pictures to generate stories. Wang and Chen [27] proposed a framework of adversarial reward learning to learn implicit reward functions from human demonstration and then optimized the strategy search of reinforcement learning by using the function after learning. Later, Kim et al. [28] proposed a global-local attention model to encode sequential pictures, focusing on the information between adjacent pictures. Huang et al. [29] proposed a hierarchical reinforcement learning method based on the work of Wang and Chen. High-level decoders generate semantic concepts for each image in turn to construct the planning, and low-level decoders use semantics to generate sentences for each image. This makes the results more consistent.

Model Based on Intermediate Semantic Representation. The user constraint $C(\varphi)$ of models based on intermediate semantic representation can be a set of abstract sentence representations, event representations, or specific event descriptions. Mostafazadeh et al. [32] proposed a novel semantic annotation framework to capture the temporal and causal relationships between events, which deepened the model's understanding of the story. Zhou et al. [33] assumed that news texts described in adjacent time periods had similar plot distributions and that news headlines and text shared similar plot distributions. These studies laid the foundation for generating stories from the intermediate semantic level. Jain et al. [34] generated stories based on a set of specific short text descriptions. Martin et al. [15] use their own method to preprocess text story data into an event sequence and then generate stories according to the event sequence. Tambwekar et al. [19] made advances in this regard. After analysis, the model based on intermediate semantic representation was closely related to the sub-task of the theme-oriented model based on the hierarchical structure. The hierarchical structure reuses the relevant results of the model based on the intermediate semantic representation.

Model for Generating Story Ending. The user constraint $C(\varphi)$ of the model for generating the story ending is a specific story that needs an ending. Generating the end of a story can be regarded as a sub-task of a story-generation task. Zhao et al. [35] tried to use reinforcement learning methods to generate story endings and achieved certain results. Guan et al. [18] proposed that generating reasonable endings for a given story is an important indicator of story understanding. This task requires not only understanding the scenario clues that play an important role in plot planning but also dealing with implicit common sense to deduce a reasonably coherent story ending. Generating the end of a story complements the task of story generation, which provides a new way of thinking about story generation.

2.3   Human-Machine Interaction-Oriented Models

The human-machine-interaction–oriented model refers to a model in which the user constraint $C(\varphi)$ is dynamic, which means that the user constraint varies with the human-computer interaction. The story-generation problem applied in real problems is more like a human-computer interaction problem than an algorithm problem.

Accordingly, Clark *et al.* [36] explored the machine-generated suggestions to stimulate the new ideas for the writer, which indicates that the human-machine inter-action is interesting and beneficial. Peng *et al.* [37] implemented an interface for writers to interact with computers to produce a coherent end. Goldfarb-Tarrant *et al.* [38] solved the shortcomings of previous human-machine-interaction systems in which users were not involved in the story-planning process. In their model, users can edit and modify the previous content, and control the diversity of the stories by adjusting the parameters. The human-computer interaction provides good prospects for applying story generation.

3   Comparison of Story-Generating Probabilistic Models

Comparative Analysis. Because of the inconsistency of datasets used for story generation and the lack of effective automated evaluation metrics, it is difficult to strictly compare the advantages and disadvantages of each model. In this paper, we sort some recent models and analyze from the perspective of whether the model focuses on coherence and consistency, vividness, and common sense or logical reasoning, as indicated in Table 1. The information given in Table 1 leads to the following conclusions:

Table 1. Comparison of story-generating probabilistic models.

Type	Reference	Coherence and consistency	Vividness	Common sense or logical reasoning
Theme-oriented models	Fan *et al.* [20]	√	—	—
	Xu *et al.* [21]	√	—	—
	Yao *et al.* [17]	√	—	—
	Fan *et al.* [25]	√	√	—
Storyline-oriented models	Wang *et al.* [27]	√	√	—
	Huang *et al.* [29]	√	√	—
	Jain *et al.* [34]	√	√	—
Human-machine interaction-oriented models	Guan *et al.* [18]	√	—	√
	Clark *et al.* [36]	√	√	—
	Goldfarb *et al.* [38]	√	√	—

(1) All models are concerned about coherence and consistency, because it is the basis of story generation. Only when it relates to the theme and the story is coherent can we explore the vividness and logical reasoning of the story on this basis.

(2) Only Guan *et al.* [18] explored the ability of common-sense judgment and logical reasoning at the end of the story, which reflects the fact that little research is available on this aspect at present, which is a direction worthy of study.

(3) Theme-oriented models focus mostly on coherence and consistency. Our analysis suggests that the theme-oriented model has difficulty producing a consistent and coherent story with the theme because of the lack of prior story planning. On this basis, adding vividness, common sense judgment, and logical reasoning will increase the complexity of the model.

Generally speaking, the theme-oriented model uses the idea of the hierarchical structure model to further guide the story generation by first generating the context or keywords of the storyline, thus increasing the long-distance dependence and making the story more coherent. Because the storyline-oriented model gives the context of the development of storyline, the model can focus on the vividness or logical reasoning of the story on the basis of ensuring coherence. The human-machine-interaction–oriented model is more concerned about the actual application scenarios and usage, and increasing interaction with people is its first consideration. Through analysis, story generation needs to unify multiple dimensions, including consistency, coherence, vividness, and reasonability. It remains a difficult problem to model the unification of these dimensions.

4 Challenges and Future Directions

The seq2seq model has made great progress in abstract text summarization, dialogue generation, and other fields but is unable to provide sufficient long-distance text modeling. Thus, it has difficulty solving problems for story generation, which requires long, coherent, and vivid stories. Specifically, the following four problems are manifested:

(1) *Consistency between story and theme.* Seq2seq models that generate stories often degenerate into language models. The story lacks a central idea and loses its consistency with the theme.

(2) *Coherence of story.* The stories generated from the seq2seq model often have no logical relationship, which means that the word order is chaotic and the reader does not know what is being expressed.

(3) *Diversity and vividness of story.* The story from the seq2seq model is not sufficiently novel because it tends to choose words with high frequency and high probability from the word probability distribution, rather than words with larger and more vivid meaning.

(4) *Common sense or logical reasoning of storyline.* Seq2seq models do not have common sense judgment and logical reasoning.

Although researchers have proposed a variety of hierarchical generation models to improve the seq2seq model, a big gap still remains between the generated stories and stories written by human beings. We thus propose the following possible research directions:

(1) *Story generation requires a unified modeling of dimensions such as coherence, consistency, vividness, and logical reasoning.* According to the comparative analysis of the previous section, the current model focuses on a single dimension and does not consider the multiple dimensions of story-generation requirements, which prevents the generated story from meeting the user needs in all dimensions. This drawback can be improved upon by implementing a unified multidimensional story-generation method.

(2) *Explore more specific planning processes such as narrative structure and entity relationship in the planning process.* Current models mainly use the method of extracting sentence keywords or sentence abstracts, which will lead to the loss of information. More specific representation and less loss of abstract representation can increase the coherence and diversity of generated stories.

(3) *Improve the metrics of automatic evaluation to better represent the multiple dimensions of story quality.* The current story-generation model relies on manual evaluation, which is not conducive to the optimization of a supervised learning model, making it difficult to compare the models in this field.

5   Conclusion

Research into automated story generation has been very active in recent years. According to the user constraint $C(\varphi)$ in the model $P_D(\varphi|C(\varphi))$, we divide models into theme-oriented models, storyline-oriented models, and human-machine-interaction–oriented models. Through comparative analysis, we obtain the focus of each model. Essentially, the behavior of story generation would be better described as a planning process rather than a process of sampling conditioned on observations. The theme-oriented model uses the hierarchical structure to describe the planning process, which allows it to generate coherent stories. The storyline-oriented model complements the theme-oriented model and adds vividness. Finally, the human-machine-interaction–oriented model focuses more on the interaction with people and applies them in real-world scenarios. This paper summarizes and analyses the latest methods to generate stories and highlights some promising directions for future research in the hopes of aiding researchers in related fields.

Acknowledgment. This work is supported by the National Key Research and Development Program of China (No. 2017YFB1400805).

References

1. Meehan, J.R.: TALE-SPIN, an interactive program that writes stories. IJCAI **77**, 91–98 (1977)
2. Zhu, F., Cungen, C.: A survey of narrative generation approaches. J. Chin. Inf. Process. **27** (3), 33–40 (2013)
3. Cavazza, M., Charles, F., Mead, S.J.: Character-based interactive storytelling. IEEE Intell. Syst. **17**(4), 17–24 (2002)
4. Pizzi, D.: Emotional planning for character-based interactive storytelling. Teesside University (2011)
5. Lebowitz, M.: Story-telling as planning and learning. Poetics **14**(6), 483–502 (1985)
6. Turner, S.R.: MINSTREL: a computer model of creativity and storytelling, pp. 1505–1505 (1994)
7. Bringsjord, S., Ferrucci, D.: Artificial Intelligence and Literary Creativity: Inside the Mind of Brutus, a Storytelling Machine. Psychology Press, Abingdon (1999)
8. Perez, R.P.Ý., Sharples, M.: MEXICA: a computer model of a cognitive account of creative writing. J. Exp. Theor. Artif. Intell. **13**(2), 119–139 (2001)
9. Riedl, M.O., Young, R.M.: Narrative planning: balancing plot and character. J. Artif. Intell. Res. **39**(1), 217–268 (2010)
10. Gervas, P., et al.: Story plot generation based on CBR. Knowl. Based Syst. **18**(4), 235–242 (2005)
11. Swanson, R., Gordon, A.S.: Say anything: using textual case-based reasoning to enable open-domain interactive storytelling. Ksii Trans. Internet Inf. Syst. **2**(3), 16 (2012)
12. Li, B., et al.: Story generation with crowdsourced plot graphs. In: National Conference on Artificial Intelligence, pp. 598–604 (2013)
13. Sutskever, I., Vinyals, O., Le, Q.V.: Sequence to sequence learning with neural networks. In: Neural Information Processing Systems, pp. 3104–3112 (2014)
14. Luong, T., Pham, H., Manning, C.D.: Effective approaches to attention-based neural machine translation. In: Empirical Methods in Natural Language Processing, pp. 1412–1421 (2015)
15. Martin, L.J., et al.: Event representations for automated story generation with deep neural nets. In: National Conference on Artificial Intelligence, pp. 868–875 (2018)
16. Li, J., et al.: Deep reinforcement learning for dialogue generation. In: Empirical Methods in Natural Language Processing, pp. 1192–1202 (2016)
17. Yao, L., et al.: Plan-and-write: towards better automatic storytelling. In: National Conference on Artificial Intelligence (2019)
18. Guan, J., Wang, Y., Huang, M.: Story ending generation with incremental encoding and commonsense knowledge. In: National Conference on Artificial Intelligence (2019)
19. Tambwekar, P., et al.: Controllable neural story generation via reinforcement learning. arXiv: Computation and Language (2018)
20. Fan, A., Lewis, M., Dauphin, Y.N.: Hierarchical neural story generation. In: Meeting of the Association for Computational Linguistics, pp. 889–898 (2018)
21. Xu, J., et al.: A skeleton-based model for promoting coherence among sentences in narrative story generation. In: Empirical Methods in Natural Language Processing, pp. 4306–4315 (2018)
22. Nayak, N., et al.: To plan or not to plan? Discourse planning in slot-value informed sequence to sequence models for language generation. In: Conference of the International Speech Communication Association, pp. 3339–3343 (2017)

23. Wang, Z., et al.: Chinese poetry generation with planning based neural network. In: International Conference on Computational Linguistics, pp. 1051–1060 (2016)
24. Mou, L., et al.: Sequence to backward and forward sequences: a content-introducing approach to generative short-text conversation. In: International Conference on Computational Linguistics, pp. 3349–3358 (2016)
25. Fan, A., Lewis, M., Dauphin, Y.: Strategies for structuring story generation. arXiv: Computation and Language (2019)
26. Huang, K., et al.: Visual storytelling. In: Proceedings of the 2016 Conference of the North American Chapter of the Association for Computational Linguistics: Human Language Technologies, pp. 1233–1239 (2016)
27. Wang, X., et al.: No metrics are perfect: adversarial reward learning for visual storytelling. In: Meeting of the Association for Computational Linguistics, pp. 899–909 (2018)
28. Kim, T., et al.: GLAC Net: GLocal attention cascading networks for multi-image cued story generation. arXiv: Computation and Language (2018)
29. Huang, Q., et al.: Hierarchically structured reinforcement learning for topically coherent visual story generation. In: National Conference on Artificial Intelligence (2019)
30. Li, J., Luong, T., Jurafsky, D.: A hierarchical neural autoencoder for paragraphs and documents. In: International Joint Conference on Natural Language Processing, pp. 1106–1115 (2015)
31. Yarats, D., Lewis, M.: Hierarchical text generation and planning for strategic dialogue. In: International Conference on Machine Learning, pp. 5587–5595 (2018)
32. Mostafazadeh, N., et al.: CaTeRS: causal and temporal relation scheme for semantic annotation of event structures. In: North American Chapter of the Association for Computational Linguistics, pp. 51–61 (2016)
33. Zhou, D., Guo, L., He, Y.: Neural storyline extraction model for storyline generation from news articles. In: North American Chapter of the Association for Computational Linguistics, pp. 1727–1736 (2018)
34. Jain, P., et al.: Story generation from sequence of independent short descriptions. arXiv: Computation and Language (2017)
35. Zhao, Y., et al.: From plots to endings: a reinforced pointer generator for story ending generation. In: International Conference Natural Language Processing, pp. 51–63 (2018)
36. Clark, E.A., et al.: Creative writing with a machine in the loop: case studies on slogans and stories. In: Intelligent User Interfaces, pp. 329–340 (2018)
37. Peng, N., et al.: Towards controllable story generation. In: Proceedings of the First Workshop on Storytelling (2018)
38. Goldfarb-Tarrant, S., Feng, H., Peng, N.: Plan, write, and revise: an interactive system for open-domain story generation. arXiv: Computation and Language (2019)

A Smart Roll Wear Check Scheme for Ensuring the Rolling Quality of Steel Plates

Kui Zhang[1,2], Xiaohu Zhou[3],
Heng He[1,2(✉)], Yonghao Wang[3], Weihao Wang[3], and Huajian Li[3]

[1] College of Computer Science and Technology,
Wuhan University of Science and Technology, Wuhan,
People's Republic of China
{zhangkui,heheng}@wust.edu.cn
[2] Hubei Province Key Laboratory of Intelligent Information
Processing and Real-Time Industrial System,
Wuhan, People's Republic of China
[3] Faculty of Computing, Engineering and the Built Environment,
Birmingham City University, Birmingham, United Kingdom
{xiaohu.zhou,weihao.wang,huajian.li}@mail.bcu.ac.uk,
yonghao.wang@bcu.ac.uk

Abstract. Roll surface wear morphology directly affects the surface quality of steel plates and even affects the texture composition of plates and strip steel products. Using image processing methods to judge the wear state of a roll is low cost, easy to operate, and easy to realize an automatic smart data processing system. In this paper, we propose a Smart Roll Wear Check (SRWC) scheme for ensuring the rolling quality of steel plates. In the SRWC scheme, roll surface images in different wear stages are analyzed, from which seventeen dimension features are extracted. At the same time, the fractal theory is introduced to explore the relationship between fractal dimensions and roll wear degree. The results show that four characteristic parameters, such as roundness, equivalent area circle radius, second moment and texture entropy, and the fractal dimension can be used as effective parameters to quantitatively judge roll wear state. Lastly, a back-propagation (BP) neural network model for recognition and judgment for roll wear is established. It provides an experimental test to show that the five parameters as a quantitative evaluation for roll wear morphology are effective. By processing the data on the images, the SRWC scheme can demonstrate whether the roll needs to get off mill in time, so as to avoid the hidden danger of safety and ensure the rolling quality of the steel plate.

Keywords: Roll wear · Image features · Fractal dimension · BP neural network · Image processing

---

This work was supported by the National Natural Science Foundation of China under Grant No. 61602351, 61802286.

M. Qiu (Ed.): SmartCom 2019, LNCS 11910, pp. 11–21, 2019.
https://doi.org/10.1007/978-3-030-34139-8_2

1 Introduction

Roll is an important part of rolling mills. The rolling mill makes use of the pressure produced by a pair or groups of rolls to mill the steel to produce plastic deformation [1, 2]. If damages of the surface are not found in time, it will affect the rolling size, shape quality and appearance of the steel sheet, reduce the corrosion resistance, wear-resistance and fatigue limit of the product, and even cause harm to personal safety [3]. Therefore, how to effectively detect the wear of roll is of great significance.

At present, in the industrial field, even in some large steelworks, the wear morphology recognition of roll surface is basically completed by manual. The roll must get off the machine, which is bound to affect the normal operation of production. And there is no unified standard for the identification of morphological defects. There are many external factors affect the worker's undefined judgment of morphological wear defects, which makes the identification results not objectively reflect the wear of roll surface. At the same time, in the traditional methods, there have great problems in the storage and the query of historical data of roll wear morphology. Therefore, it is urgent for a smart system to detect the wear degree of rollers in the industrial site, which can carry out automatic detection efficiently and accurately.

Currently, there are mainly two methods to quantitate metal surface roughness automatically. The one is using sensor technology, e.g. fiber optic ranging technology, light cutting technology, etc. [4, 5]. These technologies need special facilities, precision equipment, and even dedicated software. They are of high cost. Another is a technology basing on images processing technology. Images can be got by an ordinary camera and processed by image processing technology. The technology can be used widely in various industrial fields [6, 7].

Roughness measurements on a variety of steel surfaces and a textured magnetic thin-film disk have shown that their topographies are multi-scale and random. This spectral behavior implies that when the surface is repeatedly magnified, statistically similar images of the surface keep appearing. Therefore fractal characterization of surface topography is applied to the study of contact mechanics and wear processes [8]. It is a very worthy to study the image characteristics of oxide film morphology on roll surface, analyze the fractal law contained in it, and then extract the characteristic parameters used to reflect the wear degree of roll, and establish a quantitative model to detect the wear degree of the roll.

It is of great significance to deepen the study of roll wear mechanism and surface morphology by using image processing technology and fractal theory and to establish a quantitative model to characterize the wear morphology of roll surface and improve the automation level of the rolling process. In this paper, we propose a Smart Roll Wear Check (SRWC) scheme for ensuring the rolling quality of steel plates. In the SRWC scheme, six typical roll surface morphology images standing by different wear stages are selected. The contributions of this paper are as follows:

(1) The six images are preprocessed and converted into binary images, which can express the wear morphology features.

(2) Seventeen geometric features and texture features are extracted by using the image processing method. After analysis, four feature parameters are selected to express the wear degree of the roll.

(3) The fractal theory is introduced into the analysis of roll wear, and the relationship between fractal dimension and wear degree is analyzed, which shows that fractal dimension can be used as a parameter to characterize the wear degree of the roll.

(4) In order to verify the correctness of these conclusions, we design a roll wear pattern recognition system based on BP neural network. Six groups of data with five parameters are used as input to train the neural network, and then a set of data representing a certain wear degree is used to verify the system. The correct wear degree is obtained, which shows that the pattern recognition system is feasible.

Compared with the human eye observation method, this pattern recognition system has the advantages of automatically recognizing the wear degree of the roll, has a unified standard, and can be processed offline to find out in time whether the roll needs to get off the machine, so as to avoid the hidden danger of safety and ensure the rolling quality of the steel plate.

2 Image Preprocessing Methods for Roll Wear Morphology

2.1 Roll Wear Surface Morphology Images

In the rolling process of rolling mill, the roll is in a complex stress state. There have periodic thermal stress caused by contact heating between rolling piece and roll and by roll water cooling, and contact stress, shear stress and residual stress caused by the rolling load. According to the qualitative judgment of roll surface wear morphology, a grinding roll cycle can be divided into six stages listed in Table 1 and the according six images are shown in Fig. 1 [9, 10]. The images of these six typical stages lay the foundations for quantitative analysis of roll wear roughness degree.

Table 1. Roll wear surface morphology

Wear stage	Rolling tonnage	Describes of wear surface morphology
1st stage	200–600t	The silver-gray oxide film basically completely covers the roll surface. The roll morphology is smooth
2nd-stage	1000–1700t	The oxide film in the roll surface is still relatively complete, but the hemp surface begins to appear
3rd-stage	2000–2500t	There begins to appear fishbone peeling off with a small area
4th-stage	3200–4000t	The peelings of fishbone are evolved into scratches
5th-stage	4800–5100t	The quality of roll surface is further aggravating and a large number of friction scratches expand along the axis
6th-stage	>6400t	Scratches are connected into reticulated and massive peeling pits appear on the roll surface, at which time the roll must be repaired and ground to be used again

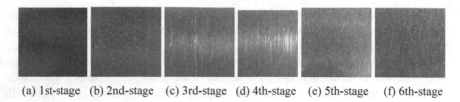

(a) 1st-stage   (b) 2nd-stage   (c) 3rd-stage   (d) 4th-stage   (e) 5th-stage   (f) 6th-stage

Fig. 1. Six typical stages of oxide film peeling in work roll

2.2   Image Preprocessing Methods

Here, image preprocessing does not consider the reason of image degradation, but selectively highlights the features of interest in the images, and attenuate the features of no need, that is, image enhancement. Image enhancement can be divided into spatial enhancement methods and frequency domain enhancement methods [11, 12]. The spatial enhancement method is to process the image directly in the space where the image is located, that is, to operate the pixel directly, including image gray transformation, image smoothing, and image sharpening. In this paper, the spatial enhancement method is used due to its simplicity.

Image Gray Transformation. Image gray transformation can display details needed in the image, so as to improve the visual effect of human beings. Gray transformation is divided into linear, piecewise linear, nonlinear and other gray transformation. In this paper, the linear gray transformation is used. Assuming that the gray range of the original image $f(x, y)$ is $[a, b]$, the gray-scale of the transformed image $g(x, y)$ is expected to be extended to $[0, 255]$, which can be realized by Eq. (1):

$$g(x, y) = \frac{255}{b - a}[f(x, y) - a] \tag{1}$$

This equation can make the underexposed image darker in the black part and whiter in the white part, thus improving the gray contrast of the image.

Image Smoothing. Image smoothing is to weaken or eliminate the high-frequency components of the image, enhance the low-frequency components of the image, and achieve the purpose of eliminating random noise in the image. Median filtering is a nonlinear removing noise method, which can keep the detail part of the image while eliminating the noise and preventing the edge part of the image from blurring. The principle is to use a sliding window with odd points and replace the value of the center point of the window with the median value of each point in the window. The window shape and size of the median filter template have a great influence on the filtering effect. The common median filter window is square with a size of 3×3.

Image Sharpening. The smooth processed image will inevitably cause the edge information of the image to be lost and become relatively blurred. If the edge information of the image is to be strengthened, the image should be sharpened. Image sharpening can eliminate or reduce the low-frequency component of the image so as to enhance the edge contour information in the image. It makes the gray value of the pixels other than the edge tends to be zero. The usual sharpening methods have the gradient method and the Laplacian operator. For roll wear morphology, the gradient method is preferred to the Laplacian operator method.

The Robert gradient operator is a commonly used gradient difference method, which can be expressed by Eq. (2):

$$\nabla G[f(x,y)] = |f(x,y) - f(x+1, y+1)| + |f(x+1, y) - f(x, y+1)| \qquad (2)$$

Image Segmentation. Image segmentation refers to the separation of meaningful objects from their background and the extraction of objects with different meanings in the image. It is a key step from image processing to image analysis. There are three kinds of traditional image segmentation methods: threshold-based segmentation method, region-based segmentation method and edge-based segmentation method [13]. The commonly used threshold processing is selecting a threshold to convert the image into a black and white binary image. In many cases, the gray value of the background is not constant, and the contrast between the object and the background also changes in the image. At this time, a threshold that works well in one area of the image may be very poor in other areas. In this case, it is appropriate to take the gray threshold as a function value that changes slowly with the position in the image. The adaptive threshold algorithm has large spatial complexity and time complexity but has strong anti-noise ability.

The above four steps of image enhancement have done to Fig. 1. Then the processed images are shown as Fig. 2. They are a series of binary images of roll wear morphology obtained by threshold segmentation, which is convenient for the feature extraction later.

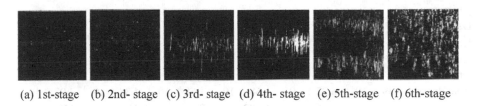

(a) 1st-stage   (b) 2nd- stage   (c) 3rd- stage   (d) 4th- stage   (e) 5th-stage   (f) 6th-stage

Fig. 2. Binary diagram of roll wear morphology

3   SRWC Scheme: Smart Roll Wear Check Scheme

3.1   Feature Extraction of Roll Wear Morphology Images

There are many features in the image. In the SRWC scheme, the features related to roll wear morphology contained in images will be extracted firstly, and then these features will be used to identify the degree of roll wear.

Image features can be either natural features that can be recognized by human vision, or certain abstract artificial defined features can be acquired or defined by measurement and processing of images [14]. Good object characteristics should have the characteristics of differentiability, reliability, independence, small quantity, and the low-dimensional space that can replace the high-dimensional image sample space. In roll wear morphology, the geometric features of the image can be used to describe the geometric shape of the defect and the texture feature can reflect the relationship between the defect regions.

From the image shown in Fig. 2, the thirteen geometric features are calculated, including boundary perimeter, defect area, rectangle, extension length, roundness, equivalent area circle radius, and invariant moment of Hu. M. K IM1–IM7. The results are shown in Table 2. After directly transforming images shown in Fig. 1 into gray-scale images, the four texture features are calculated, including the second moment, texture entropy, contrast, and correlation. The results are separately shown in Tables 2 and 3.

The changes regulation in geometric features and texture feature parameters after normalization in different wear stages are shown in Fig. 3. As can be seen from Fig. 3 (a), as the rolling process progresses, the boundary perimeter, defect area and equivalent area circle radius of roll wear defects increase gradually, and the increasing rate is fast at first, then slowly and then faster, which indicates that with the deepening of wear degree the defect range of surface morphology of roll is expanding, and the wear rate is also fast and then slow and then accelerated gradually. These are according to the characteristics of three dynamic stages of wear dynamics (self-organization stage,

Table 2. The geometric features parameters of images

Features parameters	1st-stage	2nd-stage	3rd-stage	4th-stage	5th-stage	6th-stage
Boundary perimeter	130	1317	6875	12546	27481	37913
Defect area	127	1208	6340	19820	26327	44875
Rectangle	2.6	3.97	1.27	0.477	0.992	1.22
Extension length	1	0.84	0.79	0.91	0.677	0.72
Roundness	$9.39 * 10^{-2}$	$8.75 * 10^{-3}$	$1.68 * 10^{-3}$	$1.58 * 10^{-3}$	$4.38 * 10^{-4}$	$3.92 * 10^{-4}$
Equivalent area circle radius	6.4	19.6	44.92	79	91.54	119
IM1	5.93	3.61	1.42	0.059	0.79	0.197
IM2	8.67	5.43	2.16	0.329	3.91	7.44
IM3	15.49	7.43	0.03	0.054	0.055	2.09
IM4	16.07	5.15	2.81	0.113	0.54	2.53
IM5	41.37	15.55	7.69	0.197	2.37	6.58
IM6	20.46	5.57	3.59	0.052	4.27	7.04
IM7	31.41	11.34	4.95	3.67	3.24	5.16

Table 3. The texture features parameters of the image

Features parameters	1st-stage	2nd-stage	3rd-stage	4th-stage	5th-stage	6th-stage
Second moment	0.0418	0.0241	0.0119	0.008	0.0053	0.0014
Texture entropy	12.455	14.69	16.86	18.62	19.04	22.56
Contrast	$6.44 * 10^6$	$7.678 * 10^6$	$7.68 * 10^6$	$7.97 * 10^6$	$8.62 * 10^6$	$9.55 * 10^6$
Correlation	$-5.06 * 10^3$	$-1.05 * 10^4$	$-1.83 * 10^4$	$-2.76 * 10^4$	$-2.67 * 10^4$	$-3.2 * 10^4$

chaos stage and system instability stage). As can be seen from Fig. 3(b), the change of roundness shows a decreasing trend, which indicates that the roll morphology becomes more and more complex. The rectangle shows the filling degree of the external rectangle of the wear defect, the extension length indicates the compactness of the defect area along the axis, and the curve changes show that the two parameters have no obvious change. Figure 3(c) reflects the changing trend of seven invariant moments. It can be seen from the diagram that the changes in these moments are similar, but there are no specific rules. From the curve change of Fig. 3(d), it can be seen that with the aggravation of roll wear, the image texture entropy and contrast change monotonously and incrementally. The texture entropy is a measure of image information. Larger entropy value means the roll has more fine textures, and the morphology is more complex. Greater contrast indicates that the texture is denser and clearer. It is known from Fig. 3(d) that the second-moment value is decreasing gradually, which means that the gray distribution of the image becomes gradually uneven. Correlation is a physical quantity used to represent the similarity between rows and columns in the gray symbiosis matrix. It is found that the variation range of this value is large, so it is not suitable to be used as a measure to judge the wear morphology of rolls.

From the above analysis, it can be seen that with the gradual deterioration of roll wear morphology, the geometric features and texture features of roll wear images change continuously. We can select the boundary perimeter, area, equivalent area circle radius, and roundness in the geometric features, and contrast, texture entropy and

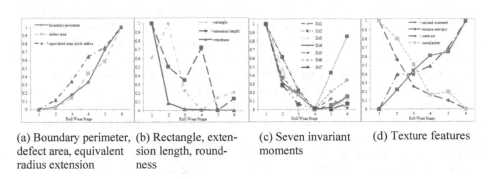

(a) Boundary perimeter, defect area, equivalent radius extension

(b) Rectangle, extension length, roundness

(c) Seven invariant moments

(d) Texture features

Fig. 3. Curves of geometry features and texture features

second moment in the texture feature as the quantitative indexes to determine the wear state of a roll. In the actual modeling process, considering that there have certain correlations between the attributes of some image feature parameters, in order to reduce the complexity of the model, it is necessary to reduce the attributes without losing the image information and remove some unrelated or unimportant image feature attributes. So the four image eigenvalues of roundness, equivalent area circle radius, second moment and texture entropy can be selected to quantitatively describe the wear morphology of the roll.

3.2   Fractal Behavior

Fractal phenomena are common in nature. In recent years, fractal geometry, as a nonlinear scientific theory, has been applied to the study of tribology. The surface change of roll is similar under the same wear state, which actually embodies fractal characteristics and contains rich fractal self-similar feature information [15].

In this paper, the fractal dimension of roll wear morphology is determined by the box dimension method. Table 4 shows the fractal dimensions of roll surface morphology under different wear stages corresponding to Fig. 2. The curve of the fractal dimension is shown as Fig. 4. The fitting coefficient in Table 4 is the correlation coefficient of straight-line fitting which further shows that the roll wear morphology has statistical fractal characteristics.

Table 4. The fractal dimension of different wear stages

Features parameter	1st-stage	2nd-stage	3rd-stage	4th-stage	5th-stage	6th-stage
Fractal dimension	1.2515	1.6428	1.5799	1.6333	1.8880	1.9614
Fitting coefficient	0.9778	0.9913	0.9970	0.9977	0.9992	0.9998

The fractal dimension reflects the irregularity of the surface profile, which is a similarity measurement parameter [16]. The larger the fractal dimension is, the more complex the surface morphology is. As can be seen from Fig. 4, with the increasing of roll wear, the fractal dimension increases rapidly at first, then almost keep unchanged, and at last increases gradually. This is mainly due to the fact that at the beginning of roll wear the roll surface is smooth and the dimension is low. With the wear going on, because of the mismatch between the roll and the contact surface between the roll and the strip, the roll surface will become relatively complex and rough, the micro surface area will increase, and the fractal dimension will increase rapidly. When entering the stable wear stage, the wear rate of the roll surface is basically constant, and the friction and wear behavior are in a stable and orderly state, the contact surfaces between the roll and the strip adapt to each other, and the fractal dimension is basically unchanged. While in the rapid wear stage, the relatively stable system before is broken, the roll wear rate increases rapidly, the roll surface morphology deteriorate and the fractal dimension increases gradually. As a result, the fractal dimension can be used as a parameter to measure roll wear morphology.

4 Recognition Model Based on Neural Network

Due to the excellent characteristics of a neural network in self-learning, self-organization, self-association and fault tolerance, an adaptive pattern recognition system with the ability of automatic selection can be established by the neural network [17]. In this paper, the surface wear defect recognizer based on error back-propagation (BP) neural network will be selected and studied.

Six sets of features parameters, including equivalent area circle radius, roundness, texture entropy, second moment, and fractal dimension, which are corresponding to the six wear stages, are selected as the input layer to construct a three-layer BP neural network. The number of hidden layer nodes is 8, and the number of output nodes is 1. The output constant represents the number of roll wear stages. The learning rate is 0.1. According to the data of Tables 1 and 2, the convergence result of the network is shown in Fig. 5. Figure 5 shows that the network achieves the goal of error of about 0.001 after 729 steps of learning, and the result converges.

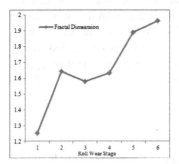

Fig. 4. The curve of the fractal dimension

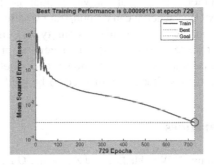

Fig. 5. Training results by BP neural network

In order to test the effectiveness of the trained network, the characteristic parameters in Table 5 are extracted from a roller image of 3100t rolling tonnage and used as the test sample input to the trained network. The output result is 3.8398, which is in good agreement with the actual situation.

Based on the above analysis, it is shown that it is effective and feasible to select the equivalent area circle radius, roundness, texture entropy, second moment, and fractal dimension as the quantitative parameters to measure the wear degree of a roll.

Table 5. Parameters for test

Equivalent area circle radius	Roundness	Texture entropy	Second moment	Fractal dimension
74	$6.26 * 10^{-4}$	17.32	$9.2 * 10^{-3}$	1.653

5   Conclusion

In this paper, we propose an SRWC scheme. In the SRWC scheme, firstly, the six roll images in deferent wear stages are preprocessing, and seventeen features parameters have been calculated, including geometry features and texture features. Based on the analysis and comparison of the feature parameters, four image feature parameters, namely, roundness, equivalent area radius, second moment and texture entropy, are extracted to reflect characteristics of the roll wear morphology.

Secondly, the fractal dimension of wear morphology image is calculated by the box dimension method, and the change law of fractal dimension of roll wear morphology is analyzed and explained. The results show that the morphology of roll wear shows good fractal characteristics, and the change of fractal dimension can be used to reflect the change of surface morphology in the roll wear process. The above works lay a foundation for the establishment of the roll wear morphology detection model.

Lastly, the BP network model is proposed which can be used to identify and predict the roll wear morphology. It provides an experimental test to show that the five parameters as a quantitative evaluation for roll wear morphology are effective. The SRWC scheme can demonstrate whether the roll needs to get off mill in time, so as to avoid the hidden danger of safety and ensure the rolling quality of the steel plate.

However, whether there is a general preprocessing process can be applied to all kinds of images containing noise, and whether the SRWC scheme will still be applicable to these images, will need to be studied in the later research.

References

1. Kong, X.W., Shi, J., Xu, J.Z., Wang, G.D.: Wear prediction of roller for hot mill during service. J. Northeast. Univ. (Natl. Sci.) **23**(8), 790–792 (2002)
2. Huang, Y.G.: Research of image feature and fractal on roll surface morphology in the wear process (轧辊磨损形貌图像特征及分形研究). Master thesis, Wuhan University of Science and Technology, Wuhan (2015)
3. Liu, X.L., Xu, C.G., Zhang, X.K.: Optimization technology of original surface roughness of rolls in cold continuous rolling mill. J. Iron Steel Res. (11), 888–893 (2018)
4. Song, F.: For the design of a reflective sensor system for the detection of roller. Electron. Test (5), 122–123 (2015)
5. Ge, Q.: Research on laser texturing roller surface roughness detection system using a light-section method (基于光切法的激光毛化轧辊表面粗糙度检测系统的研究). Master thesis, Huazhong University of Science and Technology, Wuhan (2011)
6. Chen, P.P., Su, L.H.: Detection of parallelism of hot rolling roll system based on embedded image processing. In: Proceedings of the 11th Annual meeting of China Iron and Steel, pp. 1–7. The Chinese Society for Metals, Beijing (2017)
7. Yang, G., Zhang, X.H., He, G.P., Huang, J.H.: Anomaly detection SVDD algorithm based on non-subsampled contoured transform. Autom. Instrum. **6**, 63–65 (2016)
8. Majumdar, A., Tian, C.L.: Fractal characterization and simulation of rough surfaces. Wear **136**(2), 313–327 (2016)
9. Lan, Y., Li, Y.H., Zhang, S.S.: Research of oxide film control on high chrome work roll surface in Maanshan Steel CSP. Chinese Metallurgy **21**(1), 33–37 (2011)

10. Li, L., Huang, Y.G., Zhang, K., Lv, X.Y., Li, B., Wu, X.D.: Image feature and fractal on roll surface morphology in the wear process. Iron Steel **50**(4), 98–103 (2015)
11. Gonzalez, R.C., Woods, R.E.: Digital Image Processing, 4th edn. Pearson Prentice Hall, Upper Saddle River (2017)
12. Hou, Q.L.: Investigation on the technology of tool wear detection based on machine vision (基于机器视觉的刀具检测技术研究). Master thesis, Shandong University, Shandong (2018)
13. Lee, J.H., Kim, Y.S., Kim, S.R.: Real-time application of critical dimension measurement of TFT-LCD pattern using a newly proposed 2D image-processing algorithm. Opt. Lasers Eng. **1**, 558–569 (2008)
14. Zhai, J.H., Zhao, W.X., Wang, X.Z.: Research on the image feature extraction. J. Hebei Univ. (Natl. Sci. Ed.) **29**(1), 106–112 (2009)
15. Meng, H.D., Liu, L.: Study on steel slag grinding characteristics. Iron Steel **45**(2), 28 (2010)
16. Ge, S.H., Zhu, H.: Fractal of Tribology (摩擦学的分形). Mechanical Industry Publishing House, Beijing (2005)
17. Cui, Z.M., Li, Y.L., Ying Chen, Y.: Surface structure and fractal dimension calculation of pore in low silicon sinter. Iron Steel **49**(9), 10–14 (2014)

An Improved Prediction Model
for the Network Security Situation

Jingjing Hu[✉], Dongyan Ma, Liu Chen, Huaizhi Yan,
and Changzhen Hu

School of Computer, Beijing Institute of Technology, Beijing 100089, China
{hujingjing, yhzhi, czhoo}@bit.edu.cn,
836198858@qq.com, 519866998@qq.com

Abstract. This research seeks to improve the long training time of traditional methods that use support vector machine (SVM) for cyber security situation prediction. This paper proposes a cyber security situation prediction model based on the MapReduce and SVM. The base classifier for this model uses an SVM. In order to find the optimal parameters of the SVM, parameter optimization is performed by the Cuckoo Search (CS). Considering the problem of time cost when a data set is too large, we choose to use MapReduce to perform distributed training on SVMs to improve training speed. Experimental results show that the SVM network security situation prediction model using MapReduce and CS has improved the accuracy and decreased the training time cost compared to the traditional SVM prediction model.

Keywords: Network security situation · Prediction · SVM · Acceleration

1 Introduction

Cyber security situation prediction plays a vital role in the field of network security. It can predict the network environment, improve the security of the network environment, and prevent impending network security incidents [1, 7]. However, there exist many network data attributes and huge amounts of data. Every day, massive amounts of data are generated, which poses a huge challenge to the use of algorithms [8]. The amount of massive data increases the training time of the machine learning algorithm, and reduces its efficiency. The space-time cost of the algorithm has a profound impact on the establishment of the network security prediction model.

Many algorithms have been applied to the prediction of network security situation, including artificial neural networks, clustering algorithms, association analysis, and support vector machines [2, 3].

The support vector machine (SVM) classifies the data set via the VC dimension theory and the structural risk minimization theory based on statistical learning [4]. SVMs exhibit good performance in processing high-dimensional numbers and small sample data sets [5]. However, for data sets with large sample sizes, the SVM processing speed is slower than other machine learning algorithms, which is unfriendly to predict network security situation with huge amount of data. So the parallelization method is proposed to train the support vector machine. This paper uses MapReduce to

M. Qiu (Ed.): SmartCom 2019, LNCS 11910, pp. 22–33, 2019.
https://doi.org/10.1007/978-3-030-34139-8_3

parallelize the SVMs. MapReduce passes the data fragment to the mapper function for parallel processing, and then uses the reduce function to obtain the final result.

In order to improve the prediction accuracy of the SVM, the Cuckoo Search (CS) algorithm is used to optimize the parameters [6, 11]. There are many other parameter optimization algorithms for SVM, including the grid search algorithm [12, 13], particle swarm optimization algorithm [14], etc. Of the available algorithms, the CS has global convergence, can find the global optimal solution of parameters, has fewer control parameters, and has higher versatility and robustness.

In summary, this paper proposes a cyber space security situation prediction model based on MapReduce and SVM (MR-SVM). The MapReduce method is used to parallelize the SVMs, and the effectiveness and prediction accuracy of the method are quantitatively analyzed by experimentation. Compared to the results of a traditional SVM network security situation prediction method, the feasibility of the model is verified.

Main research content of this paper is divided into six sections. The first section introduces the current methods of cyber space security situation prediction, and proposes a network security situation prediction model based on MapReduce and SVM. The second section establishes the prediction model and outlines the steps of establishing the prediction model proposed in this paper. The third section introduces MapReduce distributed training and describes the parallel method used in the paper. The fourth section introduces the SVM classification and the SVM classification algorithm used in this paper. The fifth section describes the SVM parameter selection process and algorithm. The sixth section is the analysis of the experimental results, which describes the data set selected by the experiment and the experimental verification of the MapReduce and SVM network security situation prediction models proposed in this paper.

2 Building a Predictive Model

The network security situation prediction process based on MapReduce and SVM algorithm is presented in Fig. 1.

The cyber security situation prediction process is mainly divided into the following steps:

(1) Obtain a network security data set, select a training set and testing set;
(2) Upload the data set to HDFS, schedule it by MapReduce, and parallelize the SVM;
(3) The data stored in HDFS is used as the data set of the SVM. The RBF kernel function is selected in the SVM. Define the SVM parameter value interval and step size, and apply the CS combined with the ten-fold cross-validation method for parameter optimization;
(4) Use the parameters obtained in the third step to determine the SVM cyber security situation prediction model, and test the model;
(5) Determine whether the prediction result satisfies the termination condition. If it is true, obtain an optimized support vector machine prediction model; otherwise,

return to the third step to continue optimizing the model, the termination condition is that the model prediction accuracy reaches a predetermined threshold or the number of cycles exceeds a preset maximum number of cycles;

(6) The parallel SVM is reduced to obtain the cyber security situation prediction model.

In supervised machine learning, data sets are usually divided into training sets and testing sets, in which training sets are used to optimize model parameters, and a high-precision network security situation prediction model is obtained. Testing sets are required to check whether the prediction model has the promotion ability. In this model, n training sets are needed: n data sets are obtained by sampling data sets containing massive data, n support vector machine models are trained by n data sets. Finally, the support vector machine prediction results are reduced. This results in the final cyber security situation prediction model. When using the training set to train the

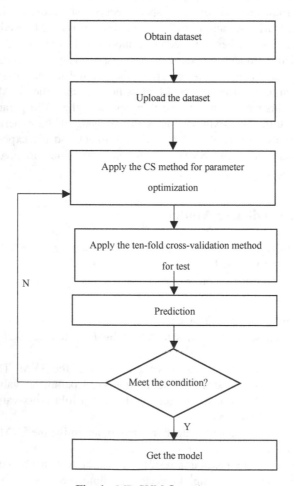

Fig. 1. MR-SVM flow chart.

SVM classifier, the SVM parameter optimization method uses the CS combined with the ten-fold cross-validation to obtain the SVM classifier with high classification accuracy.

The selection and parallelization of the basic classifier is the core of the network security situation prediction. The MapReduce-SVM (MR-SVM) network security situation prediction model proposed in this chapter consists of two parts. The first part uses MapReduce for data parallelization, and the second part uses SVM to perform classification predictions. The core algorithms of the model and the reasons for the algorithm selection are detailed i the following.

3 MapReduce Distributed Training

MapReduce is a programming model for parallel computing of large data sets [9, 10]. 'Map' and 'Reduce' are their main functions. It is implemented to specify a 'Map' function to map a set of key-value pairs into a new set of key-value pairs, and to specify the concurrent 'Reduce' function to ensure that each of the mapped key-value pairs shares the same key group.

(1) Once a MapReduce program starts, MRAppMaster will start first. After the MRAppMaster starts, the number of required maptask instances is calculated according to the number and size of the network security data sets uploaded at this time, and then the corresponding number of maptask processes is started.

(2) After the maptask process starts, data processing is performed according to the given data slice range. The main flow is:
   A. Use the specified input format to get the RecordReader to read a data set,
   B. Pass the input data set to the customer-defined map() method, perform SVM training, and collect the KV pairs output by the map() method into the cache;
   C. the KV in the cache is sorted according to the K partition and then overflows to the disk file.

(3) After MRAppMaster monitors all maptask process tasks, it starts the reducetask process and tells the reducetask process what range of data to process.

(4) After the reducetask process starts, several maptask output result files are obtained according to the location of the data to be processed as notified by MRAppMaster, and then maptask output result files are re-merged and sorted locally. Then, according to the KV of the same key as a group, the 'Reduce' method is called to predict the prediction result. The result is reduced and the result KV of the operation output is collected, then the customer-specified output format is called to output the result data to the external storage.

4 SVM Classification

First, the work flow chart of the network security situation classification SVM is introduced, as shown in Fig. 2. $X_i, i \in [1, n)$ is the sample point entered, which is a piece of data in the training set $X_i, i \in [1, n)$ input into the kernel function $K(x_i, x)$. In this paper, the kernel function $K(x_i, x)$ selects the radial basis kernel function and finally passes the decision function sgn().

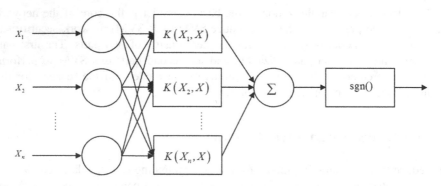

Fig. 2. SVM work process.

Using the network security training set to train the SVM, the two optimal parameters of the SVM are obtained, i.e. the classification hyperplane is determined, and the SVM model establishment process ends. The process of prediction is to input the test set into the trained SVM classifier and make a decision through the decision function. If the input data falls within the safe space determined by the optimal classification hyperplane function, the output result of the SVM classifier is marked as +1, i.e. the network connection corresponding to the data is determined to be safe. If the classification of the input data is in the unsafe space as determined by the hyperplane function, it is marked as −1 in the output result of the SVM classifier, i.e. the network connection corresponding to the data is determined to be unsafe.

The sample points of the network security data set usually have outliers, as illustrated in Fig. 3. This situation is called approximate linear separability. If the original steps to search are followed, a classification hyperplane that can separate the two types of sample points cannot be found, and the problem cannot be solved.

In order to solve the above problem, it is necessary to introduce slack variables in the classifier. $\xi_i(\xi_i \geq 0, i = 1, 2, \cdots, n)$ The slack variable is used to describe the outliers, and is a non-negative value. A penalty factor is introduced to evaluate this loss, indicating the degree of emphasis on outliers during training, and the outliers are also called loss points.

After introducing the penalty factor and the slack variable, the objective function is as shown in Eq. (1).

$$\psi(w, \xi) = \frac{1}{2}w^T w + C \sum_{i=1}^{n} \xi_i \tag{1}$$

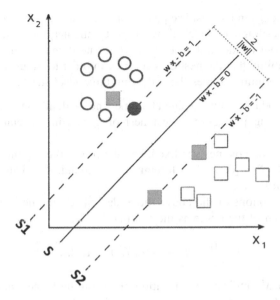

Fig. 3. SVM which has outlier.

For the actual data, the training process of the SVM is to solve the optimization problem of (2)

$$\begin{cases} \min\left\{ \frac{1}{2}\|\omega\|^2 + C\sum\limits_{i=1}^{n} \xi_i \right\} \\ s.t. y_i(\omega^T \gamma(x_i) + b) \geq 1 - \xi_i, i = 1, 2, \cdots, n \end{cases}, \ \xi_i \geq 0 \qquad (2)$$

In Eq. (2), C is the penalty coefficient, ξ_i is a relaxation variable, ω is a vector orthogonal to the classification hyperplane, b is a deviation term, and $\gamma(x)$ is a kernel function used by the SVM. In this model, $\gamma(x)$ is a radial basis kernel function. The result of solving the above optimization problem is the final decision function, as shown in Eq. (3).

$$f(x) = \text{sgn}\left(\sum_{i=1}^{n} \lambda_i y_i K(x_i, x) + b \right) \qquad (3)$$

5 SVM Parameter Selection

Cuckoo Search (CS) is used for the SVM algorithm. It combines the ten-fold cross-validation method for parameter optimization, including penalty factor C and kernel function parameters g.

Normally, large cuckoos remove one or more eggs from a host before they lay their own eggs in the nest. In order not to be discovered by the host, the cuckoos ensure that the number of new eggs in the nest is equal or similar to the number that was removed. Once the cuckoo nestlings are hatched by the foster mother, the foster mother's own chicks are pushed out of the nest so that the foster nestlings are raised. This greatly increases the probability that the nestlings survive. In order to simulate the habit of the cuckoo, the CS algorithm assumes the following three ideal states:

(1) Each cuckoo produces only one egg at a time, and randomly selects a nest to store;
(2) During the nesting process, the best nest of eggs will be retained to the next generation;
(3) The number of available nests is fixed, and the probability of finding foreign eggs in the nest is P, $P \in [0, 1]$. If a foreign bird is found, the owner of the bird re-establishes a bird's nest.

Under the assumptions of the above three ideal states, the update formula of the position and path of the CS is as the Eq. (4):

$$x_i^{(t+1)} = x_i^t + \alpha \oplus L(\lambda), \, i = 1, 2, \ldots, n \qquad (4)$$

In the equation, $x_i^{(t)}$ indicates the position of the i-th bird's nest in the t-generation nest, $\oplus$ is point-to-point multiplication, and α is a step control amount that is used to control the search range of the step size, and its value obeys a normal distribution. Finally, $L(\lambda)$ is the Levi random search path, and the random step size is the Levi distribution.

The algorithm of the CS is described as follows.

Algorithm 2: CS algorithm

Input:the fitness function $f(X)$,the population size n ,the maximum discovery probability P ,the maximum iteration number MaxGeneration

Process:

---

1. Initialize the position of n nests, $X_i(i = 1,2,3,\ldots,n), X_i = (x_1, x_2)$;
2. While($t <$ MaxGeneration$\|$ Minimum error requirement not met) do
3. Select the correct rate of the SVM for the test set as the fitness function, and calculate the function value of each X_i;
4. Record the optimal function value and update other X_i;
5. Calculate the fitness function value for the updated X_i,compare it with the optimal function value, and if it is better, update the current optimal X_i;
6. Compare random numbers $r \in [0 , 1]$ with P, if $r > P$, Then randomly change X_i^{t+1} , else stay X_i^{t+1}.Finally retain the best set of bird nest locations X_i;
7. end while

Output: Optimal position X_i

The CS optimization range is 0.1–150, the population size is 20, the maximum discovery probability P is 0.25, and the maximum iteration number is 20. The SVM classification accuracy rate is selected as the fitness function. The values of the parameters and the highest accuracy of the SVM are obtained, and the optimal classification hyperplane function is calculated. Finally, the SVM classifier is trained by the above steps. When the normalization operation is involved, it is mapped to [0, 1].

The experimental process of k-fold cross-validation is

Algorithm 3: k-fold cross-validation

Input: Dataset

Process:

---

1. Divide the dataset into k subsets ;

2. while(model < k) do

3. Select one of the subsets as the test set in sequence, and the remaining k-1 subsets as the training set ;

4. Training to obtain network security situation prediction model ;

5. end while

Output : Average of the accuracy of k prediction models

The model is verified by a ten-fold crossover method. The training set is divided into 10 subsets. Under the parameters determined by the CS algorithm, each subset is tested once. After 10 trials, 10 experiments are calculated to determine the average classification accuracy as a fitness function for evaluating the parameters of the group.

6 Experimental Simulation and Results Analysis

This section will verify the MR-SVM model. The KDD dataset is from an intrusion detection assessment project conducted by the US Department of Defense's Advanced Planning Agency (DARPA) at the MIT Lincoln Laboratory. The experimental data set in this chapter was selected from the KDD dataset. Considering the characteristics of MapReduce and SVM algorithms, the experiment is divided into the following two parts: (1) Parallelized support vector machine. The purpose of this part of the experiment is to optimize the parameters for the two key parameters existing in the MR-SVM algorithm, train the SVM and perform reduction, and find the optimal network security situation prediction model under the experimental data set. (2) The purpose of the second part of the experiment is verifying the feasibility of the model. Verification is conducted by comparing the prediction results of the MR-SVM model with the prediction results of traditional SVM model.

6.1   Experimental Data Set

The experimental data uses the KDD (Data Mining and Knowledge Discovery) data set of an intrusion detection assessment project conducted by MIT Lincoln Laboratory [15]. It contains 2 data sets. A detailed description of the data characteristics is provided in Table 1. This chapter selects the ICMP protocol data in the KDD data set for test.

6.2   Model Validation Experiment

In order to verify the performance of the proposed model, a 10-fold cross-validation (10-fold CV) was used in the experiment. First, the training set was randomly divided into 10 subsets. For each experiment, one of the subsets was used as the test set, and the remaining nine subsets were used as the training set. Each subset was used once as a test set, so a total of 10 validation experiments were performed. After the completion of 10 experiments, the average of 10 experiments of each indicator was used to evaluate the performance of the model.

Table 1. KDD dataset.

Basic feature	Specific feature	Time_based feature	Host_based feature
duration	hot	count	dst_host_count
protocol_type	num_failed_logins	srv_count	dst_host_srv_count
service	logged_in	serror_rate	dst_host_same_srv_rate
flag	num_compromised	srv_serror_rate	dst_host_diff_srv_rate
src_bytes	root_shell	rerror_rate	dst_host_same_src_port_rate
dst_bytes	su_attempted	srv_rerror_rate	dst_host_srv_diff_host_rate
land	num_root	same_srv_rate	dst_host_serror_rate
wrong_fragment	name_file_creations	diff_srv_rate	dst_host_srv_serror_rate
urgent	num_shells	srv_diff_host_rate	dst_host_rerror_rate
	name_access_files		dst_host_srv_rerror_rate
	name_outbound_cmds		
	is_hot_login		
	is_guest_login		

This paper uses four indicators to evaluate the performance of the model, namely accuracy, precision, recall, and F-measure values (harmonic average of precision and recall) [16]. The recall rate indicates the ratio of the number of unsafe connections detected to the actual number of connections. The precision indicates the ratio of the number of unsafe connections to the actual number of connections. The F value is the harmonic average of the precision and recall, which has achieved a compromise between recall and precision. SVM parameter optimization is achieved with a CS combined with ten-fold cross-validation.

6.3   Experimental Results and Analysis

Based on the above selection parameters, the experimental results are the best prediction results of the MR-SVM model. The different SVM models are compared against the four evaluation indicators. LTSA is a nonlinear manifold learning method for dimensionality reduction of high-dimensional data, and can maintain the inherent features and structure of the original data, which can improve the classification efficiency of support vector machines. The prediction results are provided in Table 2.

Table 2. The prediction of SVM, CS-SVM, LTSA-SVM and MR-SVM.

Algorithm	Accuracy	Precision	Recall	F-measure
SVM	94.73%	86.54%	48.39%	62.07%
LTSA-SVM	95.01%	80.60%	58.06%	67.5%
CS-SVM	95.97%	90.48%	61.29%	73.08%
MR-SVM	96.16%	88.41%	65.69%	74.31%

Table 3 provides a comparison of the time efficiency between CS_SVM and MR-SVM.

Table 3. The cost of time.

Algorithm	Time (ms)
CS_SVM	11078932
MR-SVM	1655501

The following Figs. 4, 5, 6 and 7 describe the performance of SVM, CS-SVM, LTSA-SVM and MR- SVM under different size data sets:

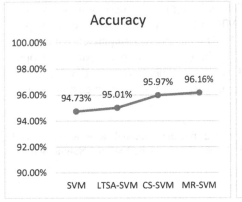

Fig. 4. The comparition of accuracy   Fig. 5. The comparition of precision

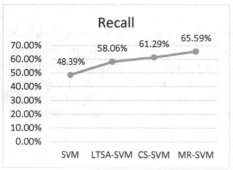
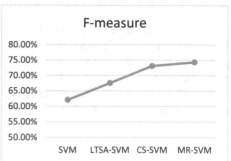

Fig. 6. The comparison of recall   **Fig. 7.** The comparison of F-measure

It is evident from the above figures that the SVM model using the CS algorithm is superior to the traditional SVM model in terms of all four indicators. The experimental results illustrate two aspects: on the one hand, when other conditions are the same, the parallelization of the SVM is more efficient than the traditional SVM model; on the other hand, the CS algorithm can be suitable to address the SVM parameter optimization problem, as it improves the four indicators.

The algorithm proposed in this paper can solve the problem of the binary classification of data sets with more data. The MapReduce method reduces the training cost of SVM by parallelizing the SVMs. The speedup of the model is 6.69. The CS algorithm solves the problem of parameter optimization of SVM, because it can find the optimal solution for this global problem.

7   Conclusions

This paper proposes a SVM network security situation prediction model MR-SVM. The model shows that it effectively reduces the training time of SVM and improves the accuracy of network security situation prediction. Using the CS algorithm proposed in this paper, the prediction accuracy of the MR-SVM network security situation prediction model increases. This paper selects KDD data set for comparison experiment between the traditional SVM, the SVM using the CS algorithm for parameter optimization, LTSA-SVM, and the MR-SVM. The experiments proved the MR-SVM model can effectively solve problem of rapid increase of SVM training cost associated with increases of data volume.

Acknowledgements. This work has been supported by the National Key Research and Development Program of China (Grant No. 2016YFB0800700) and the National Natural Science Foundation of China (Grant No. 61772070).

References

1. Fan, Z., Xiao, Y., Nayak, A.: An improved network security situation assessment approach in software defined networks. Peer-to-Peer Netw. Appl. **12**, 295–309 (2017)
2. Hao, H., Hongqi, Z., Yuling, L.: Quantitative method for network security situation based on attack prediction. Secur. Commun. Netw. **2017**, 19 (2017)
3. Zhao, D., Liu, J.: Study on network security situation awareness based on particle swarm optimization algorithm. Comput. Ind. Eng. **125**, 764–775 (2018)
4. Ding, S., Cong, L., Hu, Q., Jia, H.: A multiway p-spectral clustering algorithm. Knowl.-Based Syst. **164**, 371–377 (2019)
5. Ding, S., Zhang, N., Zhang, X.: Twin support vector machine: theory, algorithm and applications. Neural Comput. Appl. **28**, 3119–3130 (2017)
6. Ding, S., Zhu, Z., Zhang, X.: An overview on semi-supervised support vector machine. Neural Comput. Appl. **28**, 1–10 (2017)
7. Guan, Z., Zhang, Y., Wu, L.: APPA: an anonymous and privacy preserving data aggregation scheme for fog-enhanced IoT. J. Netw. Comput. Appl. **125**, 82–92 (2019)
8. Li, Y., Hu, J., Wu, Z.: Research on QoS service composition based on coevolutionary genetic algorithm. Soft. Comput. **22**, 7865–7874 (2018)
9. Madani, Y., Erritali, M., Bengourram, J.: Sentiment analysis using semantic similarity and Hadoop MapReduce. Knowl. Inf. Syst. **8**, 413–436 (2018)
10. Bendre, M., Manthalkar, R.: Time series decomposition and predictive analytics using MapReduce framework. Expert Syst. Appl. **116**, 108–120 (2018)
11. Zhu, H., Qi, X., Chen, F.: Quantum-inspired cuckoo co-search algorithm for no-wait flow shop scheduling. Appl. Intell. **49**, 791–803 (2019)
12. Bhat, P.C., Prosper, H.B., Sezen, S.: Optimizing event selection with the random grid search. Comput. Phys. Commun. **228**, 245–257 (2018)
13. Kong, X., Sun, Y., Su, R.: Real-time eutrophication status evaluation of coastal waters using support vector machine with grid search algorithm. Mar. Pollut. Bull. **119**, 307–319 (2017)
14. Vijayashree, J., Sultana, H.P.: A machine learning framework for feature selection in heart disease classification using improved particle swarm optimization with support vector machine classifier (2018)
15. https://download.csdn.net/download/xiqianwei7030/10389510
16. Fernandes, S.E.N., Papa, J.P.: Improving optimum-path forest learning using bag-of-classifiers and confidence measures. Pattern Anal. Appl. **22**(2), 703–716 (2019)

A Quantified Accuracy Measurement Based Localization Algorithm for Autonomous Underwater Vehicles

Xiao Yu[1], Kunqing Wang[2(✉)], Quanxin Zhang[2], and Yuanzhang Li[2]

[1] School of Computer Science and Technology,
Shandong University of Technology, Zibo 255000, China
yuxiao8907118@163.com

[2] School of Computer Science and Technology, Beijing Institute of Technology,
Beijing 100081, China
282522085@qq.com, {zhangqx,popular}@bit.edu.cn

Abstract. A quantified accuracy measurement based AUV localization algorithm which employs cooperation among multiple AUVs is proposed. With cooperative communication, AUVs with high location accuracies can help to improve the localization accuracy of AUVs with currently low location accuracies. The average updating time via GPS and deviation distance are measured. Simulation results show that the proposed localization algorithm improves the localization accuracy and reducing the location updating frequency for AUVs. Besides, it helps to prolong the AUV lifetime.

Keywords: AUV · Localization · Acoustic · Coordinates · Deviation

1 Introduction

Autonomous Underwater Vehicle is usually an indispensable tool for this sort of tasks, where high risks like pollution and radioactivity make it unrealistic for human activities.

The most essential advantage of AUV is the autonomous navigation, which makes it ideal for missions including seabed mapping and undersea resource locating [1]. However, these applications usually require an AUV to provide its current location. Without localization capability, the applicability of AUV will be significantly degraded.

The AUV localization system is quite different from terrestrial localization system. The GPS signal cannot be used in underwater environment because the radio cannot be propagated well in water [2, 3]. Therefore, the AUV cannot be localized via GPS system. In fact, the AUVs or the nodes of UWSN (Underwater Wireless Sensor Network) depend on acoustic system for communication [4]. The acoustics bandwidth is narrow and its propagation delay is huge compared with the radio signal [5]. Meanwhile, the AUV localization is more difficult since the acoustic propagation speed is highly dynamic due to the influence of water depth, temperature, current and salinity [6, 7].

© Springer Nature Switzerland AG 2019
M. Qiu (Ed.): SmartCom 2019, LNCS 11910, pp. 34–41, 2019.
https://doi.org/10.1007/978-3-030-34139-8_4

In the past, the collaborative localization among AUVs is not the research focus because the AUV is expensive and only single or few AUVs were used for application each time. The main AUV localization technology is remote control via acoustic localization system, such as LBL (Long Baseline), SBL (Short Baseline), and USBL (Ultra Short Baseline) etc. [8–10]. There are also other localization systems which utilize techniques similar to GPS localization, such as buoy localization [11] on the surface or anchor localization [12] on the seabed. But there are some shortages of these technologies. For example, the acoustic remote-control system must be utilized within a certain distance and the acoustic signals would be weakened greatly if there are obstacles between the controller and the AUV. As the price of AUV is decreasing, it becomes practical to use a larger number of AUVs for specific applications, which motivates us to develop a collaborative localization algorithm among multiple AUVs.

2 Quantified Accuracy Measurement Based Localization Algorithm - QuAMeL

2.1 Algorithm Overview

The real time coordinate deviation caused by navigation equipment error and water current is usually unknown and therefore the current coordinate accuracy can be highly dynamic. Given the critical importance of the coordinate accuracy, we propose an accuracy index α to reflect the current coordinate accuracy of an AUV:

$$\alpha = \left(1 - \frac{t_n - t_{lu}}{N * t_{ui}}\right) * \left(1 - \frac{d_{(u,t)}}{d_{(u,lu)} + d_{(u,t)}}\right) \tag{1}$$

The coordinate that is just calibrated by GPS has the highest accuracy index which is $\alpha = 1$. The accuracy index of an AUV will be decreased with the increase of its underwater navigation time since the coordinate deviation is accumulated and enlarged. The accuracy index is designed to reflect the synthesized influence, where here t_n is current time, t_{lu} the last coordinate updated time of this AUV, N is a positive integer modulus, t_{ui} is the defined coordinate updating time interval, $d_{(u,t)}$ is the distance between navigation coordinate and updated coordinate after coordinate is updated and its initial value is 0, $d_{(u,lu)}$ is the Euclidean distance of the locus between the current and the previous coordinate updated position and it can be calculated by the two updated coordinate. We set $d_{(u,lu)} = 1$ when $d_{(u,t)} = 0$ to avoid division by zero (which will occur when the AUV is just put into the water or the AUV wants to hold its position) and the $d_{(u,lu)}$ will be set to Its actual value when $d_{(u,t)} \neq 0$. The first part of formula (1) in the first parentheses Lowers the accuracy index while the AUV navigates under-water, which accounts for the accumulative deviation caused by the navigation equipment inaccuracy. The second part of formula (1) in the second parentheses is the synthesized influence to accuracy index, which is caused by the navigation equipment and current. The accuracy index will drop down faster if ratio of the synthesized deviation distance $(d_{(u,t)})$ and the locus between the current and the previous coordinate updated position $(d_{(u,lu)})$ is larger. The second part of the formula (1) belongs to posterior value based on the current coherent property since it is influenced by the previous locus and its essence is to predict the current synthesized deviation according to previous deviation.

2.2   Initial Status

A destination coordinate is set into each AUV and the AUV goes to the target area for working autonomously (The returning coordinate can be set as another target area if it needs for the AUVs to go back autonomously after finish working). The accuracy index is highest when the AUVs are just put into the water since they can get the GPS signal on surface, which means all the initial αs are 1.

2.3   The Underwater Navigation Status

The AUVs depend on the navigation equipment for localization when they navigate towards the target area underwater. The accuracy index is adjusted according to formula (1).

2.4   Broadcast Coordinate and Accuracy Index Information

Each AUV broadcasts its coordinate and accuracy index periodically. The AUVs whose accuracy indices are below the threshold will not broadcast their coordinate and accuracy index to save the acoustic bandwidth. The AUVs receiving the coordinates and accuracy index from their neighbors calculate the distance (d) between themselves and the neighbors who broadcast the information according to the TOA (Time of Arrival) and the acoustic speed [13]. The received information will be ignored if d is larger than a predefined neighbor distance. This prevents an AUV from setting coordinates for a too far away neighboring AUV since the acoustic signal travelling a long distance is prone to error. The neighbor coordinate, accuracy index and the distance between them are recorded into the neighbor list if d is shorter than the defined neighbor distance threshold. An entry in the neighbor list will expire after a certain time period and be discarded if not updated timely.

2.5   Coordinate and Accuracy Index Update

The coordinate and accuracy index of one AUV will be updated when its accuracy index is below the accuracy threshold or there are at least three neighbors' accuracy indexes higher in the neighbor list. Therefore, the coordinate is updated in three situations.

A. One AUV's accuracy index is below the accuracy threshold. One AUV searches its neighbor list firstly if its accuracy index is below the accuracy threshold. The three neighbors with the highest accuracy indices are selected. This AUV gives up updating its coordinate via neighbors if the third highest accuracy index in the neighbor list is lower than this AUV's current accuracy index and in this case, the AUV tries to go to the surface to search the GPS signal. Its accuracy index is set to 1 if its coordinate is updated by GPS. Otherwise the AUV tries to update its coordinate and accuracy index via MTL (Modified Triangle Localization).

Suppose the AUV's (node A) coordinate to be localized is (x, y) and the coordinates of the three reference AUVs (node A_1, A_2, A_3) for localizing node A are (x_1, y_1), (x_2, y_2), (x_3, y_3) and their corresponding accuracy index are α, α_1, α_2, α_3, where $\alpha_1 \geq \alpha_2 \geq \alpha_3 > \alpha$. The distances between A and A_1, A_2, A_3 are d_1, d_2, d_3. The traditional triangle localization equations are:

$$\begin{cases} (x - x_1)^2 + (y - y_1)^2 = d_1^2 \\ (x - x_2)^2 + (y - y_2)^2 = d_2^2 \\ (x - x_3)^2 + (y - y_3)^2 = d_3^2 \end{cases} \tag{2}$$

The solution should be the only intersection point of three circles. The Eq. (2) is modified to increase the probability of getting solution as follows:

$$\begin{cases} (x - x_1)^2 + (y - y_1)^2 = d_1^2 \\ (x - x_2)^2 + (y - y_2)^2 = d_2^2 \\ d_3^2 * \lambda_3 \leq (x - x_3)^2 + (y - y_3)^2 \leq d_3^2 * (2 - \lambda_3) \end{cases} \tag{3}$$

There may be unique solution, no solution or multi solutions for Eqs. (3). 1. If there is a unique solution, then we can use that solution to update the coordinate of A. 2. If there are multi solutions, then we use $\min\left\{\left|\left((x - x_3)^2 + (y - y_3)^2 - d_3^2\right)\right|\right\}$ to update the coordinate of A. Then the accuracy index of A is set to α_3. 3. Node A will stop updating its coordinate via MTL if there is no solution for Eq. (3) and go to the surface to get the GPS signal. Its accuracy index is set to 1 in such case.

B. One AUV's accuracy index is higher than threshold but there are at least three neighbors in its neighbor list whose accuracy indexes are higher than its accuracy index. This AUV will try to update its coordinate via MTL. It updates its coordinate and accuracy index if there is a solution for Eq. (3) or, it adjusts its accuracy index according to formula (1) if there is no solution for Eq. (3).

C. One AUV's accuracy index is higher than threshold and there are not at least three neighbors in its neighbor list whose accuracy indexes are higher than its accuracy index. This AUV will continue to work and navigate underwater and adjust its accuracy index according to formula (1).

3   Features of the Algorithm

3.1   The Updating Process of Coordinate and Accuracy Index

Each working AUV performs the initialization, navigation, accuracy index adjustment, coordinate and accuracy index broadcasting and the updating process. The process is shown in Fig. 1.

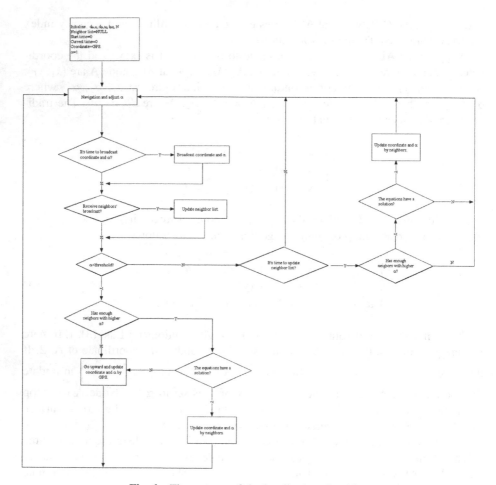

Fig. 1. The process of the localization algorithm

4 Performance Evaluation

4.1 Simulation Settings

The general simulation settings are as follows: (1). The initial deployment area is 1 km*1 km. (2). The initial deployment mode is random deployment. (3). Modulus N = 1. (4). The AUV number is from 1 to 300/500. (5). The synthesized navigation deviation randomly varies from 0 to 10%. (6). t_{ui} is 100 s. (7). The defined distance of neighbor is from 200 m. (8). Accuracy index threshold is 0.9. (9). The average velocity of AUV is 8 knots. (10). Each result is the average value of 1000 tests.

The Kinematic model in [21] is applied as the mobility mode in simulation. The current field is assumed to be a superposition of a tidal and a residual current field. The tidal field is assumed to be a spatially uniform oscillating current in one direction and the residual current field is assumed to be an infinite sequence of clockwise and anticlockwise rotating eddies. The dimensionless velocity field in the kinematical model can be approximated as

$$\begin{cases} V_x = k_1 \lambda v \sin(k_2 x) \cos(k_3 y) + k_1 \lambda \cos(2k_1 t) + k_4 \\ \qquad V_y = -\lambda v \cos(k_2 x) \sin(k_3 y) + k_5 \end{cases} \quad (4)$$

where V_x is the speed in the X axis and V_y is the speed in the Y axis. $k_1, k_2, k_3, \lambda, v$ are variable which are closely related to environment factors such as tides and bathymetry. These parameters will change with different environments. k_4, k_5 are random variables. In our simulations, we assume k_1, k_2 to be random variables which are subject to normal distribution with π as mean values and the standard derivations to be 0.1π. k_3 is subject to normal distribution with 2π as mean value and the standard derivation to be 0.2π. λ is subject to normal distribution with 3 as the mean value and 0.3 as the standard derivation. v is subject to normal distribution with 1 as the mean value and 0.1 as the standard derivation. k_4, k_5 are random variables which are subject to normal distribution with 1 as mean value and 0.1 as standard derivations.

4.2   The Average Updating Times via GPS

A. The influence of AUV density on average updating times via GPS

The average updating time via GPS decreases with fluctuation along with the increase of the AUV number. There are more neighbors in the neighbor list with higher accuracy index which can be utilized for updating along with the increment of the AUV number. So

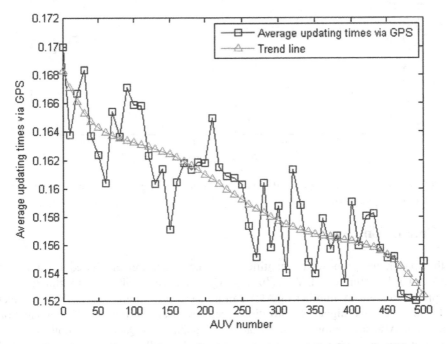

Fig. 2. The influence of AUV density on average updating times via GPS

the AUVs prefer to update their coordinate and accuracy indexes via neighbors other than going upward to surface to get the GPS signal. Then the average updating times via GPS drops down and the AUV can spend more time working underwater (Fig. 2).

B. The influence of accuracy threshold on average navigation deviation distance and updated deviation distance.

The AUV number in this simulation is 200. Both the average navigation deviation distance and the updated deviation distance decline along with the increment of the accuracy threshold, which means that the coordinate deviation can be controlled by the accuracy threshold. On the other hand, the updated deviation is always smaller than the navigation deviation with different accuracy thresholds, which again verifies the effectiveness of QuAMeL. As the accuracy threshold grows larger, coordinate update frequency also increases (Fig. 3).

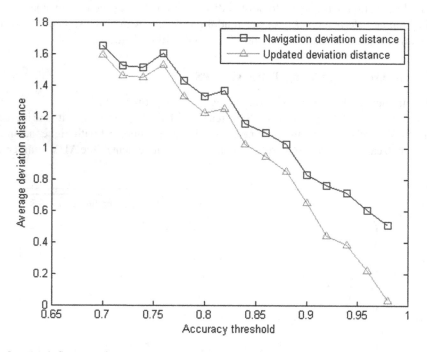

Fig. 3. The influence of accuracy threshold on average navigation deviation distance and updated deviation distance

5 Conclusion

In this paper, we propose a Quantified Accuracy Measurement based Localization (QuAMeL) algorithm for AUV localization. QuAMel is a distributed algorithm that can be applied to arbitrary number of AUVs in the network. Simulation results show that QuAMeL achieves higher localization accuracy than on-board AUV navigation equipment. Also simulations demonstrate the adaptability of QuAMeL to both accuracy threshold and the number of AUVs in the network. It is fully distributed with no central controller and adaptive to a wide range of AUV number. The result of simulation shows that the accuracy index can reflect the change trend of coordinate accuracy and the coordinate with high accuracy index can be distributed among the AUV network.

Acknowledgement. This work has been supported by the National Natural Science Foundation of China (No. U1636213, 61876019, 61772070).

References

1. Williams, S.B., Pizarro, O., Mahon, I., Johnson-Roberson, M.: Simultaneous localisation and mapping and dense stereoscopic seafloor reconstruction using an AUV. In: Khatib, O., Kumar, V., Pappas, G.J. (eds.) Experimental Robotics, vol. 54, pp. 407–416. Springer, Heidelberg (2009). https://doi.org/10.1007/978-3-642-00196-3_47
2. Liu, L., Zhou, S., Cui, J.-H.: Prospects and problems of wireless communication for underwater sensor networks. Wirel. Commun. Mob. Comput. **8**(8), 977–994 (2008)
3. Heidemann, J., Ye, W., Wills, J., Syed, A., Li, Y.: Research challenges and applications for underwater sensor networking. In: Proceedings of the IEEE Wireless Communications and Networking Conference, vol. 1, pp. 228–235 (2006)
4. Whitcomb, L., Yoerger, D.R., Singh, H., Howland, J.: Advances in underwater robot vehicles for deep ocean exploration: navigation, control, and survey operations. In: Hollerbach, J.M., Koditschek, D.E. (eds.) Robotics Research, pp. 439–448. Springer, London (2000). https://doi.org/10.1007/978-1-4471-0765-1_53
5. Stojanovic, M., Preisig, J.: Underwater acoustic communication channels: propagation models and statistical characterization. IEEE Commun. Mag. Underwater Wirel. Commun. **47**(1), 84–89 (2009)
6. Stojanovic, M.: On the relationship between capacity and distance in an underwater acoustic communication channel. ACM SIGMOBILE Mob. Comput. Commun. Rev. **11**(4), 34–43 (2007)
7. Akyildiz, I.F., Pompili, D., Melodia, T.: Underwater acoustic sensor networks: research challenges. Ad Hoc Netw. **3**(3), 257–279 (2005)
8. Singh, H., et al.: An integrated approach to multiple AUV communications, navigation and docking. In: OCEANS '96. MTS/IEEE. Prospects for the 21st Century. Conference Proceedings, 23–26 September 1996, vol. 1, pp. 9–64 (1996)
9. Curcio, J., et al.: Experiments in moving baseline navigation using autonomous surface craft. In: OCEANS, 2005. Proceedings of MTS/IEEE, vol. 1, pp. 730–735 (2005)
10. Matos, A., Cruz, N., Martins, A., Pereira, F.L.: Development and implementation of a low-cost LBL navigation system for an AUV. In: OCEANS '99 MTS/IEEE. Riding the Crest into the 21st Century, vol. 2, pp. 774–779 (1999)
11. Austin, T.C., Stokey, R.P., Sharp, K.M.: PARADIGM: a buoy-based system for AUV navigation and tracking. In: OCEANS 2000 MTS/IEEE Conference and Exhibition, vol. 2, pp. 935–938 (2000)
12. Chandrasekhar, V., Seah, W.K., Choo, Y.S., Ee, H.V.: Localization in underwater sensor networks - survey and challenges. In: WUWNet 2006 Proceedings of the 1st ACM International Workshop on Underwater Networks, pp. 33–40 (2006)
13. Chitre, M., Shahabudeen, S., Freitag, L., Stojanovic, M.: Recent advances in underwater acoustic communications & networking. In: OCEANS 2008, 15–18 September 2008, vol. 2008-Suppl., pp. 1–10 (2008)
14. Beerens, S.P., Ridderinkhof, H., Zimmerman, J.: An analytical study of chaotic stirring in tidal areas. Chaos Solitons Fractals **4**, 1011–1029 (1994)

An Improved Assessment Method
for the Network Security Risk

Jingjing Hu$^{(\boxtimes)}$, Shuangshuang Guo, Fankun Meng, Dongsheng Hu,
and Zhiyu Shi

School of Computer, Beijing Institute of Technology, Beijing 100089, China
hujingjing@bit.edu.cn, 18838969867@163.com,
baimu0214@163.com, hu1305573709@gmail.com,
shizhiyubit@163.com

Abstract. Network security risk assessment is very important to improve the network security. The existing network security risk assessment method based on HMM is not enough to estimate the network risk, because some methods manually set model parameters or calculate the overall network risk only using the host node. Therefore, a network security risk assessment method based on improved Hidden Markov Model (I-HMM) is proposed. Firstly, the observation sequence acquisition of the model is optimized by calculating the quality of the sampling period alarm. Secondly, the model parameters are improved through the learning algorithm. Finally, the reliability and accuracy of the network security risk measurement are increased by introducing the network node correlation. The final results by the simulation experiment shows that the network security risk assessment method based on I-HMM has certain applicability, can accurately reflect the security risk status of the network, and can distinguish the influence degree of different hosts on network risk.

Keywords: Assessment model · Risk · Network security · Hidden Markov Model

1 Introduction

While the network brings great convenience to people, it is accompanied by many security issues [1]. Security incidents emerge one after another [2]. It is essential to conduct network security risk assessment. The network security risk assessment is a precaution in the face of an attack, or it can control the spread of adverse consequences to reduce losses when the attack occurs [3].

Under the guidance of some security risk assessment standards at home and abroad [4], many researchers have proposed a variety of operational network security risk assessment methods. Evaluation methods based on HMM were also proposed [5, 6], many experts and scholars have done a lot of research on HMM and applied it to the analysis of network security risks [7, 8]. However, the results of the network risk assessment through these algorithms are inaccurate due to model parameters set manually, or the overall network risk calculated only with the host node.

© Springer Nature Switzerland AG 2019
M. Qiu (Ed.): SmartCom 2019, LNCS 11910, pp. 42–52, 2019.
https://doi.org/10.1007/978-3-030-34139-8_5

To solve the issue above, the network security risk assessment method based on I-HMM uses the alarm quality and learning algorithm, which calculates the network security risk value from two dimensions: host layer and network layer. The experiment proves that the method can accurately show the security risk status of the network, reflect the network risk trend in a timely and intuitive manner, and distinguish the influence of different hosts on the network risk.

2 I-HMM Model Parameters

2.1 Observed Sequence Acquisition

Quality of Alert (QoA) [9] refers to the degree of threat to the security status of the system. This article uses the alert frequency, alert criticality and alert severity to calculate the alert quality. Using the analytic hierarchy process, we establish a hierarchical analysis model shown in Fig. 1. The judgment matrix is

$$A = \begin{bmatrix} 1 & \frac{1}{2} & \frac{1}{4} \\ 2 & 1 & \frac{1}{3} \\ 4 & 3 & 1 \end{bmatrix}$$

The weight vector W = (0.1365, 0.2385, 0.625). AF, AC, and AS are standardized to obtain the same range of values [1, 4] to balance the effects of each attribute.

The calculation formula for QoA is:

$$QoA = [AF, AC, AS] \cdot W^T \tag{1}$$

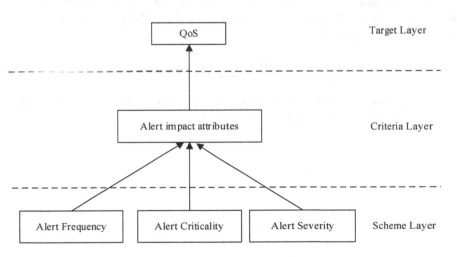

Fig. 1. Alarm quality hierarchy.

In each acquisition cycle, the highest quality alarm is selected as the observation vector of HMM. Through the value of alarm quality, the observation vector is mapped to four levels as 1, 2, 3 and 4 by formula 2.

$$V_t = \begin{cases} 1 & 0 \leq QoA < 1 \\ 2 & 1 \leq QoA < 2 \\ 3 & 2 < QoA \leq 3 \\ 4 & 3 < QoA \leq 4 \end{cases} \tag{2}$$

2.2 Parameter Estimation Algorithm

In order to avoid that the manual set parameters of HMM depend on expert experience, this paper adopts the revaluation formula of Baum-Welch algorithm [10].

$$\bar{\pi} = \xi_1(i) \tag{3}$$

$$\overline{a_{ij}} = \sum_{t=1}^{T-1} \xi_t(i) \Big/ \sum_{t=1}^{T-1} \xi_t(i) \tag{4}$$

$$\overline{b_{jk}} = \sum_{t=1, O_t = v_k}^{T} \xi_t(i) \Big/ \sum_{t=1}^{T} \xi_t(j) \tag{5}$$

$\xi_t(i)$ is the probability of the Markov chain in the S_i state at time t.

3   Calculation of Network Security Risk Value

The network security risk is divided into direct risk (DR) and indirect risk (IR). It is necessary to consider the network node association (NNC) between the nodes [11, 12]. DR is calculated by Eq. 6.

$$DR = \sum_{i=1}^{n} \rho_t w_i, \tag{6}$$

ρ_t is the probability distribution of the network security state of the host at time t, which is calculated by the algorithm in Table 1.

Table 1. Network security state probability calculation algorithm.

Algorithm Network Security State Probability Calculation
Input: observation vector O_t at time T, parameter $\lambda = (N, M, A, B, \pi)$ of HMM model.

Output: probability $\rho_t(i)$ of the network in various security states S_i at time T.

If $T=1$ then

    For $i=1$ to N do

        $\alpha_1(i) = \pi_i b_i(O_1)$

        $\rho_1(i) = \frac{\alpha_1(i)}{\sum_{i=1}^{N} \alpha_1(i)}$

    End for

    Else

    For $i=1$ to N do

        $\alpha_t(i) = b_i(O_t) \sum_{j=1}^{N} \alpha_{t-1}(j) a_{ij}$

        $\rho_t(i) = \frac{\alpha_t(i)}{\sum_{i=1}^{N} \alpha_t(i)}$

    End for

For the IR, find the node associated with host h denoted as $h_1, h_2, \ldots h_N$. Determine the NNC relationship type $W_{h_k,h}$ of the host h.

$$W_{h_k,h} \in \{W_1, \ldots, W_7\}, \quad \sigma(W_{h_k,h}) \in \{1.0, 0.7, 0.5, 0.3, 0.2, 0.1, 0.8\} \tag{7}$$

1. For each node, the risk value at a certain time t is denoted as $R_{h_k}, 1 \leq k \leq N$, the influence magnitude on the risk value of the host h by each node in the NNC relationships is denoted as $\Delta R_{h_k}, 1 \leq k \leq N$.

$$\Delta R_{h_k} = \sigma(W_{h_k,h}) \cdot R_{h_k}, 1 \leq k \leq N \tag{8}$$

2. Calculate the value of IR_h

$$IR_h = \max\{\Delta R_{h_k}\} = \max\{\sigma(W_{h_k,h}) \cdot R_{h_k}\}, 1 \leq k \leq N \tag{9}$$

3. Calculate overall risk value
   The weighting function f(x) is selected to weight the DR and IR parts [13].

$$f(x) = 4(x - 0.5)^3 + 0.5, x \in [0, 1] \tag{10}$$

$$R_h = [1 - f(x)]DR_h + f(x)IR_h = [1 - f(\sigma(W_{h_k,h}))]DR_h + f(\sigma(W_{h_k,h}))IR_h \tag{11}$$

Finally, the risk calculation of the entire network is calculated by Eq. 12.

$$\overline{R} = \sum_{h=1}^{N} v_h R_h / N \tag{12}$$

4   Experimental Results and Analysis

4.1   Experimental Environment Construction

The topology of the experimental network environment is shown as follows (Fig. 2):

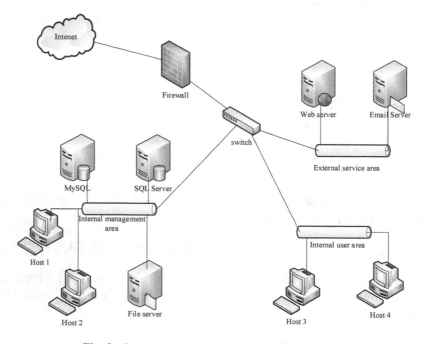

Fig. 2. Experimental network environment topology.

Use the vulnerability scanning tool Nessus to scan the nodes in the network [14], and obtain the vulnerability information in the network.

4.2   Experimental Data Collection and Processing

In the experiment, Nagios is used to monitor the service status, Ntop detect network traffic, Nessus scan for vulnerabilities in the system, and Snort collect IDS intrusion alarm information. Use IDS Informer to simulate an attack.

The 10 attack files [15] in the IDS Informer attack library were selected, and the events with the priorities low, medium, high, and low and medium mixed were sent in turn. The attack lasted for two hours and a total of 1500 packets were sent.

Three Dimensions Indicators Obtained. This paper describes the state of network security from three dimensions, which are the basic operation of the network, vulnerability and threat.

In the basic operation dimension indicator, the quantified value of the host asset is calculated by Eq. 13.

$$AssetValue = log_2\left[\left(a \times 2^C + b \times 2^I + c \times 2^A\right)/3\right] \tag{13}$$

To reduce the error of direct assignment, the formula uses weighted logarithmic averaging to assign value to asset confidentiality (C), integrity (I), and availability (A) by splitting each attribute into association and criticality. a, b, c are three constants between 0 and 3, and a + b + c = 3.

$$HostState = AssetValue + Ser\_Score \tag{14}$$

$$NetworkState = 0.5 * AF + 0.3 * PF + 0.2 * BAR \tag{15}$$

AF is the average flow and PF is the peak flow.

$$c_h = HostState + NetworkState \tag{16}$$

$$c_h = c_h * e^{V\_Score} \tag{17}$$

V_Score is the comprehensive quantitative evaluation of the vulnerability dimension.

The asset assignment is shown in Table 2.

Table 2. Asset assignment.

X_C	Y_C	X_I	Y_I	X_A	Y_A
2	3	2	3	4	3
C = 3		I = 3		A = 5	
AV = 4.1					

Through the method of asset assignment, the asset value of the web server is AV = 4.1.

Using 5 min as an acquisition cycle, the index data related to the Web server in the system are collected. The host state index is calculated by Eq. 14. The network state index is calculated by Eq. 15. The host importance is calculated by Eq. 17, and the observation value is obtained by the above method. The specific values are shown in Table 3.

Table 3. Measurement values of each dimension indicator.

Number	Host Status Index	Network Status Index	Host Importance	Observations
1	5.1	0.421	13.44	1
2	5.1	0.247	13.02	2
3	5.1	0.269	13.07	1
4	6.1	0.619	16.36	3
5	6.1	0.639	16.41	2
6	5.1	0.378	13.34	1
7	7.1	0.514	18.54	2
8	6.1	0.765	16.72	2
9	6.1	0.523	16.13	3
10	6.1	0.681	16.51	3
11	5.1	0.783	14.33	2
12	7.1	0.609	18.77	4
13	6.1	0.572	16.25	4
14	5.1	0.663	14.03	2
15	6.1	0.742	16.66	2
16	5.1	0.359	13.29	2
17	5.1	0.603	13.89	1
18	5.1	0.476	13.58	2
19	5.1	0.445	13.5	2
20	5.1	0.429	13.46	1
21	7.1	0.373	18.2	4
22	5.1	0.793	14.35	4
23	6.1	0.522	16.12	4
24	5.1	0.582	13.84	3

Model Parameter Training. Adopt the model parameters setting method proposed in Reference 9, the state transition matrix T is set as follows.

$$T = \begin{vmatrix} a_{GG} & a_{GR} & a_{GB} & a_{GC} \\ a_{RG} & a_{RR} & a_{RB} & a_{RC} \\ a_{BG} & a_{BR} & a_{BB} & a_{BC} \\ a_{CG} & a_{CR} & a_{CB} & a_{CC} \end{vmatrix} = \begin{vmatrix} 0.839 & 0.15 & 0.009 & 0.002 \\ 0.005 & 0.972 & 0.02 & 0.003 \\ 0.004 & 0.017 & 0.975 & 0.004 \\ 0.004 & 0.017 & 0.125 & 0.854 \end{vmatrix}$$

The probability distribution matrix O of the observation vector is shown as follows.

$$
O = \begin{vmatrix} b_G(1) & b_G(2) & b_G(3) & b_G(4) \\ b_R(1) & b_R(2) & b_R(3) & b_R(4) \\ b_B(1) & b_B(2) & b_B(3) & b_B(4) \\ b_C(1) & b_C(2) & b_C(3) & b_C(4) \end{vmatrix} = \begin{vmatrix} 0.8999 & 0.02 & 0.08 & 0.0001 \\ 0.6699 & 0.25 & 0.08 & 0.0001 \\ 0.7350 & 0.10 & 0.16 & 0.005 \\ 0.8000 & 0.04 & 0.11 & 0.05 \end{vmatrix}
$$

Initial state probability distribution matrix π is shown as follows.

$$
\pi = \begin{vmatrix} \pi_G & \pi_R & \pi_B & \pi_C \end{vmatrix} = \begin{vmatrix} 1 & 0 & 0 & 0 \end{vmatrix}
$$

Risk weight vector w_i is shown as follows.

$$
w = \begin{vmatrix} w_G & w_R & w_B & w_C \end{vmatrix} = \begin{vmatrix} 0 & 25 & 50 & 100 \end{vmatrix}
$$

The hmmlearn package of python is selected to estimate and optimize the model parameters. The final model parameters are as follows (Tables 4, 5 and 6).

Table 4. Transfer matrix T value.

$T = (a_{ij})_{4\times4}$			
3.63190764e−001	6.36809236e−001	0.00000000e+000	1.81695936e−193
3.80665022e−019	8.53700689e−001	7.18750673e 002	7.44242435e−002
7.12826312e−054	3.15114032e−029	7.22297840e−001	2.77702160e−001
2.60148289e−192	2.03116851e−001	1.50830068e−004	7.96732319e−001

Table 5. Observation matrix O value.

$O = (b_{ij})_{4\times4}$			
1.00000000e+00	3.40579686e−18	0.00000000e+00	0.00000000e+00
3.20507971e−01	6.79492029e−01	4.12880218e−43	3.73716043e−45
1.41177553e−10	4.49498092e−01	5.50501908e−01	2.98541604e−22
1.11024649e−12	8.87255135e−05	1.70831007e−01	8.29080267e−01

Table 6. Initial state probability distribution π value.

π			
1	0	0	0

Finally, the convergence curve of $P(O|\lambda)$ is shown in Fig. 3.

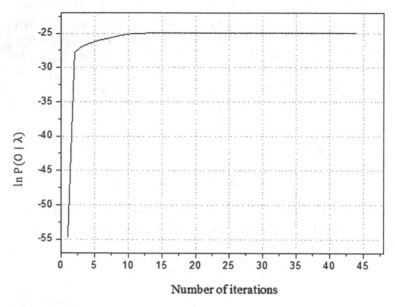

Fig. 3. Convergence curve of $\ln P(O|\lambda)$ with increasing number of iterations.

It can be seen from the figure that when the iteration reaches 35 times, the value of $\ln P(O|\lambda)$ has converged and there is no obvious change. The model obtained at this time is close to the optimal, and the best correspondence is obtained between the observation sequence of the model and implicit network security states.

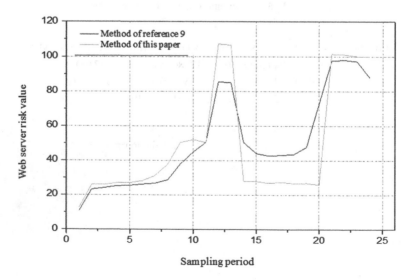

Fig. 4. Web server risk value changes.

Algorithm Performance Comparison. Compare the risk value change of the Web server calculated by the method proposed by Reference 9 and I-HMM method.

As can be seen from Fig. 4, in the overall trend, the security risk values of the web server calculated by the two methods are the same. In the 8th, 12th, and 13th sampling periods, it can be clearly seen that the difference between the risk values obtained by the two methods is large, and the rate of change is also significantly different. It indicates that after the introduction of the node correlation, the change of the risk value of host 1 correlated with web server can significantly affect the risk status of the web server, making the risk change of the web server more obvious. Between the 14th and 20th sampling periods, the security risk value obtained by using the method in this paper is obviously lower than that of the comparison method. Corresponding to the specific attack scenario, it can be found that the attack degree at this time is mostly 2. The risk status of the first five sampling cycles should be similar, so the risk value obtained by the I-HMM method of this paper is more in line with the actual situation.

The network security risk value of the experimental network changes as shown in Fig. 5.

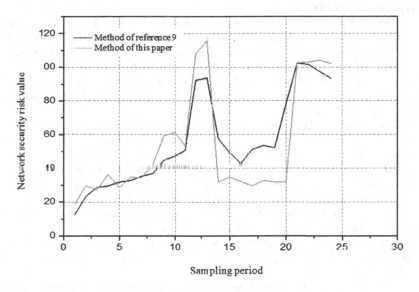

Fig. 5. Network security risk value changes.

When measuring the overall cybersecurity risk value, the overall trend of the two methods is consistent, and the risk changes are basically the same. However, in comparison, the I-HMM method in this paper is more obvious in the rate of change. This is because the association of the nodes is introduced. The indirect risk and relative importance of the nodes are considered.

5 Conclusion

We redefine alarm quality, optimize the acquisition of observation sequences, and use the Baum-welch algorithm to learn the model parameters to improve the acquisition of parameters. Considering the NNC, we introduce the association of network nodes. The results show that, compared with the previous method, the sensitivity of the I-HMM method is higher and the dynamic change perception is stronger. The fluctuation of the risk value is more obvious than the original method. And it can also distinguish the influence degree of different hosts on the network risk.

References

1. Guang, K., Guangming, T., Xia, D.: A network security situation assessment method based on attack intention perception. In: 2016 2nd IEEE International Conference on Computer and Communications (ICCC). IEEE (2016)
2. Kun, W., Hui, Q., Haopu, Y.: Network security situation evaluation method based on attack intention recognition. In: International Conference on Computer Science & Network Technology. IEEE (2016)
3. Samy, G.N., Shanmugam, B., Maarop, N.: Information security risk assessment framework for cloud computing environment using medical research design and method. Adv. Sci. Lett. **24**(1), 739–743 (2018)
4. Li, S., Bi, F., Chen, W.: An improved information security risk assessments method for cyber-physical-social computing and networking. IEEE Access **6**, 10311–10319 (2018)
5. Li, X., Zhao, H.: Network security situation assessment based on HMM-MPGA. In: International Conference on Information Management, pp. 57–63. IEEE (2016)
6. Hamid, T., Al-Jumeily, D., Hussain, A.: Cyber security risk evaluation research based on entropy weight method. In: 2016 9th International Conference on Developments in eSystems Engineering (DeSE). IEEE (2016)
7. Huang, K., Zhou, C., Tian, Y.C.: Application of Bayesian network to data-driven cyber-security risk assessment in SCADA networks. In: 2017 27th International Telecommunication Networks and Applications Conference (ITNAC), pp. 1–6 (2017)
8. Liu, S., Liu, Y.: Network security risk assessment method based on HMM and attack graph model. IEEE/ACIS International Conference on Software Engineering, Artificial Intelligence, Networking and Parallel/Distributed Computing, pp. 517–522. IEEE (2016)
9. Xi, R.-R., Yun, X.-C., Zhang, Y.-Z.: An improved quantitative evaluation method for network security. Chin. J. Comput. **38**(4), 749–758 (2015)
10. Pietras, M., Klęsk, P.: FPGA implementation of logarithmic versions of Baum-Welch and Viterbi algorithms for reduced precision hidden Markov models. Bull. Pol. Acad. Sci. Tech. Sci. **65**(6), 935–947 (2017)
11. Wang, Z., Lu, Y., Li, J.: Network security risk assessment based on node correlation. J. Phys.: Conf. Ser. **1069**(1), 012073 (2018)
12. Li, Y., Liu, S., Yu, Y.: Analysis of network vulnerability under joint node and link attacks. Mater. Sci. Eng. Conf. Ser. **322**(5), 052052 (2018)
13. Wangen, G.: Information security risk assessment: a method comparison. Computer **50**(4), 52–61 (2017)
14. Doynikova, E., Kotenko, I.: CVSS-based probabilistic risk assessment for cyber situational awareness and countermeasure selection. In: Euromicro International Conference on Parallel, Distributed and Network-Based Processing, pp. 346–353. IEEE (2017)
15. Coffey, K., Smith, R., Maglaras, L.: Vulnerability analysis of network scanning on SCADA systems. Secur. Commun. Netw. **2018**(4), 1–21 (2018)

A High-Performance Storage System Based with Dual RAID Engine

Jingyu Liu[1], Jinrong Zhang[1,3], Juan Li[1], and Lu Liu[2(✉)]

[1] School of Artificial Intelligence, Hebei University of Technology,
Tianjin, China
[2] School of Computer Science and Technology, Beijing Institute of Technology,
Beijing, China
liulu@bit.edu.cn
[3] Peng Cheng Laboratory, Center for Quantum Computing,
Shenzhen 518055, China

Abstract. With the advent of the 5G, more and more applications use cloud storage to store data. Data becomes the cornerstone of the development of smart society. At the same time, these data have the characteristics of uneven generation rate, large write demand and low read requirement. The dynamic change of load during data storage has new requirements for storage architecture. This paper proposes a storage system that allocates strips in real time based on current load changes. Based on the traditional RAID layout, a dual-engine based high-performance storage system (DSH) is proposed. This system uses software and hardware co-processing architecture to implement strip allocation and address calculation. The strip allocation functions using software and the verification algorithm is implemented by hardware transfer to the FPGA through PCIE. Through experimental analysis shows that the DSH algorithm has a great advantage in saving CPU computing resources and saving disk energy consumption in the dynamic load storage environment.

Keywords: Disk array · Dynamic load · Energy-efficient storage · Co-design

1 Introduction

With the advent of the artificial intelligence era [1], the storage devices are becoming larger and larger, and storage requirements are becoming complex and varied [2]. Data storage in different scenarios has become a research hotspot, and storage systems's main goal is to save system performance and reduce energy consumption while keeping storage secure [3].

For the file filing system [4], Liu [5] et al. proposed an energy-saving disk array S-RAID5 system [6], which can greatly reduce the energy consumption of the disk array under the premise of meeting performance requirements. However, the partial parallel data of the S-RAID5 algorithm's layout is static, suitable for smoother workloads, and has poor adaptability to strong fluctuating loads [7] or sudden loads. In response to this problem, Sun [8] and others proposed the DPPDL algorithm to implement dynamic

© Springer Nature Switzerland AG 2019
M. Qiu (Ed.): SmartCom 2019, LNCS 11910, pp. 53–62, 2019.
https://doi.org/10.1007/978-3-030-34139-8_6

allocation of strips. When the load is small, a small number of disks are opened, and when the load is large, multiple disks are opened.

Researchers mostly use the RAID5 [9] source code architecture in the Linux kernel to implement the prototype system, that is, calculate the stripe address, read the disk data fill strips, XOR the stripe, fill the strip, submit the bio, and write to the disk. In the architecture, the XOR calculation of the stripe consumes a large amount of CPU computing module resources, which imposes a great burden on the entire monitoring system.

For this problem, this paper proposes a high-performance storage system based on dual engine. The system adopts the software and hardware co-design of dynamic load. In the low-level layout, the system uses the hot and cold tree structure to manage the disk space, according to the currently open disk and the number of times the disk has been used in the past is striped. According to different application scenarios applicable to software and hardware respectively, the algorithm adopts a software and hardware co-processing architecture, and implements functions such as strip allocation and address calculation using software, and transfers the XOR check algorithm of the disk to the FPGA [10] through PCIE [11]. Implementation, this layout greatly saves CPU computing resources and disk power consumption.

2   DSH Implementation

2.1   Software Algorithm Implementation

The underlying data layout of the DSH algorithm should satisfy the following conditions:

(1) Dynamically adjust the strip size.
(2) Reduce the generation of strip fragments.
(3) Lower disk switching frequency.
(4) Equal disk usage time.
(5) There is no conflict in deleting data.

Choosing the right strip is necessary for monitoring the system's energy saving. For the best disk scheduling, the existing hot and cold tree structure is used to record the existing disk strips. There are three things to consider when choosing the right strip:

(1) Use an already open disk (hot disk), unless you need more disks than you have opened, you need to open a new disk.
(2) All open disks are found from disks (cold disks) that are rarely used in the address space and are used if found.
(3) If you can't find it, split the strip with the largest number of disks.

Assume that 6 disks constitute the underlying DSH layout. The initial state of the hot and cold tree is shown in Fig. 1.

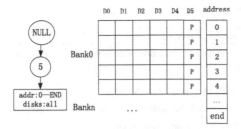

Fig. 1. Initial state of cold/hot tree

In order to find the most suitable strip, use the following flow chart to select the strip. If the number of requested disks is larger than the number of disks that have been opened, the number of open disks is insufficient. You need to open a new disk. In this case, the second type of cold disk is used first. The level method calculates and splits the strips. If there is exactly the required strip in the hot and cold tree and the number is greater than 1, then the first method of calculating the cold disc priority is used to calculate and select the strip, otherwise the second method of calculating the cold disc priority is adopted. The specific flow chart is shown in Fig. 2.

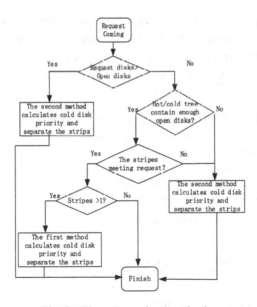

Fig. 2. Flow chart of strip selection

Algorithm 1 details:

algorithm 1 First priority calculation method
（1） Nth gradient priority number: A collection of disks with the same priority, which is ranked nth from high to low.
（2） Average priority = 100 / number of requested disks;
（3） Priority granularity = (the disk free address / all free addresses) * average priority;
（4） if(request_disks<=first gradient priority number)
（5）　First gradient priority = average priority
（6）　Second Gradient Priority = Average Priority -　Second Gradient Priority　　Granularity
（7）　else if (request_disks = first gradient priority +...+ Nth gradient priority)
（8）　First Gradient Priority　= Average Priority + First Gradient Priority Granularity
（9）　...
（10） N-1th gradient priority = average priority + n-1th gradient priority granularity
（11） Nth gradient priority = (100-(first gradient　total priority +...+nth gradient total priority))
（12） Nth gradient priority number
（13） n+1th gradient priority = nth gradient priority - n-1th gradient priority granularity
（14） n+2 gradient priority = n+1th gradient pr iority - n+2 gradient priority granularity
（15）　...
（16） After calculating the priority of the cold disk, the　strip that satisfies the situation is traversed from the beginning. If the priority is 100%, the strip　is directly selected, otherwise the strip with the highest priority is selected after all calculations are completed.
（17） Updating the hot and cold tree structure

The second method of calculating the priority is to split the required strips (including the opened disks) from the maximum number of strips.

Algorithm 2 details:

algorithm 2 Second priority calculation method
（1）　Striping the maximum number of disks
（2）　Calculate the cold disk priority of all disks
（3）　Select all open disks at first
（4）　Then choose the unopened cold plate priority from high to low.

We assume that there are 6 disks to form the DSH bottom layer layout, and the data with a load of 3 is initially stored. The subsequent load changes are 3, 5, 4, 3, 2, 1. The change of hot and cold trees is shown in Fig. 3.

With the disk allocation algorithm, we started thinking about the disk reclamation process. When there is no strip of 5 disks in the hot and cold tree, the disk reclamation process begins, and the oldest data is deleted in turn until a strip with 5 disks appears. This deletion ensures that there is enough disk strips to meet the maximum load when the maximum load comes in, and the cold disk allocation disk algorithm is preferred beforehand to facilitate the creation of the largest disk strip as early as possible during the reclamation operation. Assume that the recovery is performed once in the following figure. The change of the hot and cold trees is shown in Fig. 4.

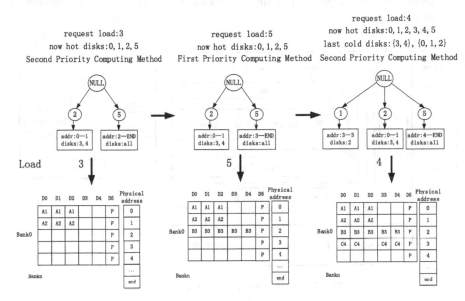

Fig. 3. Layout change of cold/hot tree

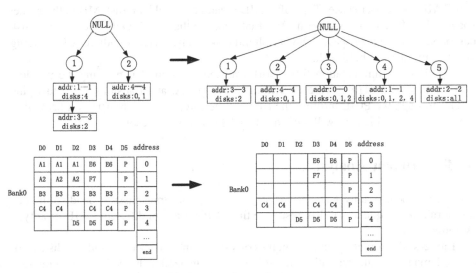

Fig. 4. Recycling strip layout

2.2 DSH Communication Framework

In order to make the MD module and FPGA in the Linux kernel communicate, the open source riffa driver source code is modified into the kernel module, so that it can pass the data that needs to be verified in the kernel to the FPGA through the PCIE interface for XOR calculation, dual engine. The high-performance storage system framework is shown in Fig. 5.

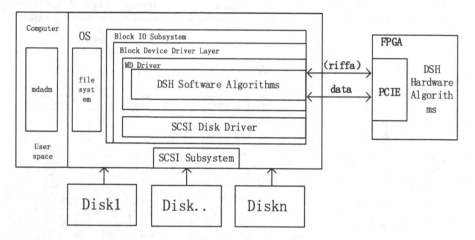

Fig. 5. DSH communication framework

The traditional software RAID architecture first uses the MDADM tool to create a soft RAID in the user space. The soft RAID creates a virtual hard disk MD in the kernel space. The MD combines several disks that make up the RAID. Only one md hard disk can be seen in the user space. The peripheral disk can be accessed indirectly by reading and writing the md hard disk.

The DSH communication framework transfers the step of generating the verification data in the DSH software algorithm to the FPGA, and transmits the data to the FPGA through the PCIE through the riffa architecture, and then transmits it back after the calculation. This step will save a lot of CPU and GPU resources.

3 Experiment Analysis

This experiment mainly tests the energy consumption, transmission bandwidth (different random, sequential ratio), response time, CPU usage of different RAID prototype systems.

Large-scale storage systems usually consist of hundreds or thousands of disks. For ease of management, the entire storage system is generally divided into several sub-storage systems that consist of multiple disks and a RAID structure. In order to test the performance and energy saving effect of the DSH system, a DSH prototype system is built under the MD (Multiple Device driver) module under the Linux 4.40 kernel.

The DSH prototype system uses 5 disks to form a DSH prototype system, and the DSH in-band data block. The size is 64 KB. The experimental results are applicable to large-scale monitoring of storage systems.

The system uses a commonly used NILFS (New Implementation of a Log-structured File System) file system, which is a file system based on a log format. The system writes data in a sequential write manner and always writes to the disk head until the logical storage space. Rewrite the deleted data only when it is full. This file system is suitable for continuous storage systems such as video surveillance and archive backup.

IOMeter is the most widely used tool for testing IO subsystems. It uses IOMeter to perform write performance tests on DSH systems under the load of 90% continuous data and 10% random data. In contrast, three storage systems of the same configuration of S-RAID5 and DPPDL were built for testing.

As shown in Fig. 6, when the request length is 16 KB to 512 KB, the SRAID5 transfer rate is faster than DPPDL and DSH. This is because SRAID5 always opens two disks. When the request length is small, DPPDL and DSH only need to open one disk. Therefore, the SRAID5 transmission rate is greater than the DPPDL and DSH transmission rates. When the request length is greater than 1024 KB, since the DSH and DPPDL algorithms open more disks due to the larger load, the transfer rate is greater than the SRAID5 algorithm, and since the SRAID 5 always opens two disks, the transfer rate remains unchanged.

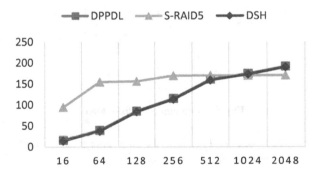

Fig. 6. Comparison of transmission rate

As shown in Fig. 7, since the DSH algorithm transfers the XOR computing portion of the most CPU-consuming resources to the FPGA, the CPU usage of the algorithm is the lowest, which is basically the CPU usage under the system idle state. The S-RAID5 algorithm always turns on only two disks, and its address conversion method is very simple. Its main CPU usage is used in the read-and-write verification algorithm, so its CPU utilization is maintained at about 10%. The DPPDL algorithm uses CPU resources because of the need to split strips in real time. The parity check algorithm of address translation and read rewriting uses CPU resources, so its CPU utilization increases with the increase of load. When the load is greater than 1024 KB, all The disk is in the on state. When the system reaches full load, the write operation becomes the entire write, and the CPU resource usage rate remains stable.

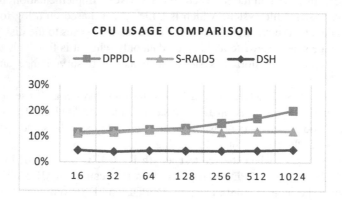

Fig. 7. Comparison of CPU usage

The load in real life is dynamically changing, for which we simulate the load versus time graph, as shown in Fig. 8.

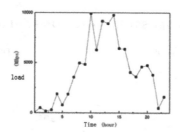

Fig. 8. Simulation of disks load

Under the simulated load in Fig. 8, a 24-hour energy consumption comparison chart is obtained, as shown in Figs. 9, respectively.

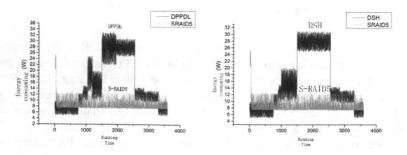

Fig. 9. Energy consumption comparison of DPPDL, DSH and S-RAID5

As can be seen from the figure, the S-RAID5 algorithm has stable energy consumption because it has a simple striping strategy and its number of open disks is fixed.

The DPPDL algorithm is relatively random when selecting strips, and does not consider the feature of using open disks as much as possible. Therefore, in some cases where the load is relatively balanced, sudden increase in power consumption may occur.

The DSH algorithm reasonably considers the use of an already opened disk. Compared to the DPPDL algorithm, its energy consumption changes steadily as the load changes.

4 Future Work

In this paper, a high-performance storage system based on dual engine is proposed in the dynamic load storage application scenario. The system uses dynamic and hard collaborative architecture (DSH) dynamic load storage. Compared with S-RAID5 and DPPDL, DSH uses hot and cold trees to dynamically allocate strips according to real-time load, calculate storage address, perform exclusive-OR check calculation with FPGA, save resources of CPU computing module, and save energy in data storage process. In further research work, all the RAID algorithms in this paper can be transferred to the FPGA to further save system resources. In order to move the software operations such as the logical address to the calculation part of the physical address to the RAID card, the ZYNQ series is required. The FPGA is used as a RAID card. The ZYNQ series FPGA integrates the ARM processor and FPGA logic resources, and can transplant the Linux operating system into the FPGA.

References

1. Meng, X., Ci, X.: Big data management: concepts, techniques and challenges. J. Comput. Res. Dev. **50**(01), 146–169 (2013). (in Chinese)
2. Chen, P.M., Lee, E.K., Gibson, G.A., et al.: RAID: high-performance, reliable secondary storage. ACM Comput. Surv. **26**(2), 145–185 (1994)
3. Luo, S., Zhang, G., Wu, C., et al.: Boafft: distributed deduplication for big data storage in the cloud. IEEE Trans. Cloud Comput. (2015)
4. Barroso, L.A., Hlzle, U.: The Datacenter as a Computer: An Introduction to the Design of Warehouse-Scale Machines. Synthesis Lectures on Computer Architecture. Morgan & Claypool Publishers, San Rafael (2009)
5. Macko, P., Ge, X., Kelley, J., et al.: SMORE: a cold data object store for SMR drives. In: Proceedings of 34th Symposium on Mass Storage Systems and Technologies (MSST), vol. 35, no. 7, pp. 343–352 (2017)
6. Jie, W., Yu, H., Zuo, P., et al.: Improving restore performance in deduplication systems via a cost-efficient rewriting scheme. IEEE Trans. Parallel Distrib. Syst. **19**(7), 121–132 (2019)
7. Xiao, W., Ren, J., Yang, Q.: A case for continuous data protection at block level in disk array storages. IEEE Trans. Parallel Distrib. Syst. **20**(6), 898–911 (2009)

8. Gurumurthi, S., Sivasubramaniam, A., Kandemir, M., et al.: DRPM: dynamic speed control for power management in server class disks. In: Proceedings of the 30th Annual International Symposium on Computer Architecture, pp. 169–179. IEEE, San Diego (2003)
9. Papathanasiou, A.E., Scott, M.L.: Energy efficient prefetching and caching. In: Proceedings of the Annual Conference on USENIX Annual Technical Conference, pp. 24–37. ACM, Boston (2004)
10. Carrera, E.V., Pinheiro, E., Bianchini, R.: Conserving disk energy in network servers. In: Proceedings of International Conference on Supercomputing, pp. 86–97. CiteSeer (2003)
11. Zhu, Q., Chen, Z., Tan, L., et al.: Hibernator: helping disk arrays sleep through the winter. ACM SIGOPS Oper. Syst. Rev. **39**(5), 177–190 (2005)

An Universal Perturbation Generator for Black-Box Attacks Against Object Detectors

Yuhang Zhao[1], Kunqing Wang[1], Yuan Xue[1], Quanxin Zhang[1],
and Xiaosong Zhang[2($\boxtimes$)]

[1] School of Computer Science and Technology, Beijing Institute of Technology,
Beijing 100081, China
zhaoyuhang1027@163.com, 282522085@qq.com, xueyuan_1007@163.com,
zhangqx@bit.edu.cn
[2] Department of Computer Science and Technology, Tangshan University,
Tangshan 063000, China
zxs0224@163.com

Abstract. With the continuous development of deep neural networks (DNNs), it has become the main means of solving problems in the field of computer vision. However, recent research has shown that deep neural networks are vulnerable to well-designed adversarial examples. In this paper, we used a deep neural network to generate adversarial examples to attack black-box object detectors. We trained a generation network to produce universal perturbations, achieving a cross-task attack against black-box object detectors. We demonstrated the feasibility of task-generalizable attacks. Our attack generated efficient universal perturbations on classifiers then attack object detectors. We proved the effectiveness of our attack on two representative object detectors: Faster R-CNN based on proposal and regression-based YOLOv3.

Keywords: Deep learning · Adversarial attack · Adversarial example

1 Instruction

In the field of computer vision, deep learning has become the main technology to solve problems such as image classification, object detection, and semantic segmentation. With the continuous development of deep learning technology and the continuous improvement of computing resources, people are gradually applying deep learning to security fields, such as mobile phone face recognition and ATM facial recognition.

However, recent studies have shown that deep learning models are highly susceptible to small perturbations. Szegedy et al. [13] first proposed the vulnerability of deep learning models in the field of image classification, that is, adding carefully created perturbation can cause the image classifier to misclassify input

© Springer Nature Switzerland AG 2019
M. Qiu (Ed.): SmartCom 2019, LNCS 11910, pp. 63–72, 2019.
https://doi.org/10.1007/978-3-030-34139-8_7

images with extremely high confidence, while the same perturbation can fool multiple image classifiers.

Since Szegedy et al. [13] proposed that the image classifier based on deep neural network has a problem against the adversarial samples, it has caused considerable research heat, and the corresponding attack and defense methods have emerged. Goodfellow et al. [4]proposed that the linear distribution of the deep learning model in high-dimensional space leads to the possibility of the existence of the adversarial examples. Then he proposed the FGSM (Fast Gradient Sign Method) attack method, which uses the gradient descent method to minimize the loss function to generate adversarial example. The perturbation is indistinguishable to human eyes, and the input images can be correctly classified by the image classifiers with high degree of confidence. The adversarial examples are misclassified by the image classifier, but the human eye can still correctly recognize them. In addition, relevant scholars have also proposed attack methods such as Box-constrained L-BFGS [13], FGSM [4], BIM [5], ILCM [5], JSMA [11], C&W [2], Deepfool [9], MI-FGSM [3], One Pixel Attack [12], and Decision-Based Attack [1].

There are many types of attack methods. According to the purpose or expectation of the attack, it can be divided into targeted attack and non-targeted attack. Targeted attack means that the attacker hopes that the image classifier can misclassify the adversarial example into a certain incorrect class specified by the attacker. And non-targeted attack means that the attacker hopes that the image classifier can just misclassify the adversarial example. According to the attacker's knowledgement to the model, it can be divided into white-box attacks and black-box attacks. In the white-box state, we know all the information of the image classifier, such as the structure and parameters of the classifier, the training set when the model is trained, and so on. But in the black-box state, we can't know the internal information of the image classifier and the dataset used during training. We can only get the adversarial example according to the input and output of the classifier by query. In addition, The state of the gray-box is somewhere in between. We can get the training data and the structure of the classifier used in the training process, but the specific parameters of the classifier can not be obtained. According to the type of perturbation, it can be divided into universal perturbation attacks and image-dependent perturbation attacks. The universarial perturbation is fixed and does not change with the change of the input image, and the image-dependent perturbation vary with the input images. At present, there are more than ten attack methods in the field. The white-box attack methods include Box-constrained L-BFGS [13], FGSM [4], BIM [5], ILCM [5], C&W [2], DeepFool [9], JSMA [11], I-FGSM [7], MI-FGSM [3], etc.; black-box attack methods include One Pixel Attack [12], Alternative Model Attack [6,14], and Decision-Based Attack [1].

The main contributions of this work can be summarized as follows:

- We succeed implementing the attack on object detectors with a universal perturbation.

– We confirm the feasibility of cross-task attacks from image classification tasks to object detection tasks.

The rest of our paper is organized as follows: we introduce some related works for adversarial attacks such as Universal adversarial perturbation and Fast Feature Fool Attack in Sect. 2. Next, We describe the threat model and introduce some notations in Sect. 3. In the next section, we propose our approaches to generate universal perturbations and attack object detectors. After that, the setup and results of our experiments will be presented in Sect. 5. Finally, we draw the conclusions of our entire work.

2 Related Work

In the real world, we usually have no knowledge to target model's architecture, hyper-parameters and dataset used during training, so we hope to find a universal perturbation that can fool object detectors. In addition, We not only hope that can we generate perturbations faster, but also hope that the generated perturbations have better attack effects.

2.1 Universal Adversarial Perturbation

Moosavi-Dezfooli et al. [8] first proposed the concept of universal perturbation in the article "Universal adversarial perturbation". Their experiments have shown that adding a fixed-size general perturbation to the original image can have a deceptive effect on the pre-trained image classifier.

By studying their papers, we found that this method actually superimposes multiple image-dependent perturbations and then crops them to obtain general perturbations. The perturbation still needs to take the original image as input during the generation process, so the perturbations generated by their method are not universal perturbation in the true sense. And most importantly, it can not be used to attack object detectors.

2.2 Fast Feature Fool

In the article "Fast Feature Fool: A data-independent approach to universal adversarial perturbations", Mopuri et al. [10] proposed a method that does not rely on the original images to generate perturbation. They add perturbation to the input to affect the feature extraction of the next layer, the cumulative effect will lead to a wrong prediction in the last layer.

However, a large number of experiments have proved that although obviating the need of training data, Mopuris' method is not as effective as Moosavi-Dezfoolis' method. And it can't be used to attack object detectors either.

3   Threat Model

Deep learning technology has achieved great success in the field of computer vision. In the object detection field, DNNs are used to detect objects in the input images. In our work, we attempt to add small perturbation which is imperceptible for human to input images that can fool DNN classifier to classify the objects in the input images to any incorrect class or hidden the bounding boxes. In the next, we will introduce some popular object detectors and declare some notations that will be frequently used in later sections.

As we all know, YOLOv3 is the most popular one-stage object detectors now, it can detect objects in real time. YOLO means "you only look once", that is, the objects' location processes and classification processes are completed in one step. YOLO returns the locations of bounding boxes and the categories of bounding boxes at the output layer to achieve one-stage. In this way, YOLO can achieve 45 frames per second of computing speed, fully meet the real-time requirements.

Before YOLOv3, Faster R-CNN is the state-of-the-art detector at that time. It detects objects in a two-stage way, firstly, the region proposal networks judge whether the candidate frame is the target, then classify which class it belongs to. The entire network can share the feature information extracted by the convolutional neural network, which saves computational cost and solves the problem that the Fast R-CNN algorithm generates candidate frames in a slow way.

We mainly judge the performance of perturbation from two aspects. One is attack success rate, which we will introduce in the next. The other is the norm of the perturbation which is added to the original image, we use L_∞ in our experiments where p-norm is defined as:

$$\|x\|_p = (\sum_{i=1}^{n} |x_i|^p)^{\frac{1}{p}}. \tag{1}$$

4   Approaches

In this section, we will introduce the main process of how to refine previous work and firstly propose to use universal adversarial perturbation to attack object detector. This section contains two parts that separately introduce the generation process of the universal adversarial perturbation and how to use the transferability of the perturbation to attack object detector across tasks.

4.1   Generation Process of Universal Perturbation

In order to solve the above problems, we use a generative model to generate universal perturbation. For the generation process of the universal perturbation, we send the random vector $Z \in [0,1]^n$ sampled from the uniform distribution $U \in [0,1]^n$ into the generator G to generate the disturbance p, To satisfied the size of the perturbation in the range we specified, the perturbation p is multiplied by the scaling factor $min(1, \frac{L_{\infty} maximum}{||G(Z)||_{\infty}})$ so that we obtain the scaled perturbation. Then we add the perturbation to the original image x and crop it to get the adversarial example x'. In addition, we clip the adversarial example to the size of 224×224 in order to satisfy the input size requirement of the VGG16 model. The image classifier F predicts the adversarial example and outputs the prediction label l. Finally, the cross-entropy loss function H is used to measure the prediction label l and the least-likely label l_t, and the parameters of the generator model are continuously updated by back propagation, so that we can get a universal perturbation generator. The loss function is defined as follows:

$$Loss = log(H(F(x'), l_t)). \tag{2}$$

In addition, in Fig. 1, we describe the flowchart of this method in detail.

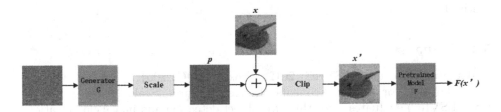

Fig. 1. Flowchart of the universal perturbation generation process.

In our experiment, use a neural network as a generator. For the architecture of the generator, there are usually two structures to choose: U-Net and ResNet. There is a jump connection in the generator of the U-Net structure, for an n-layers network, the i_{th} layer and the $(n - i)_{th}$ layer will be connected by jump connection, and each jumper will also connect the feature channel of the i_{th} layer and the $(n - i)_{th}$ layer, so that it can avoid the information bottleneck of the input data after several layers of downsampling. Another one is ResNet architecture, a residual block is used in the generator of the ResNet structure, and the shortcut connection structure in the residual block connects the input layer to the subsequent layer, and the latter layer only needs to learn the residual. There are problems of information loss during the information transmission process in convolutional layers and the fully connected layers. After using the shortcut connection structure, the accuracy degradation can be avoided while the number of neural network layers is increased. So in this article, we choose the ResNet structure for the perturbation generator.

The generator first convolves the input random vector, then performs a transposition convolution operation to generate a perturbation image. The transposition convolution operation can be understood as a deconvolution operation, but it is not a true deconvolution operation.

4.2   Attack Against Object Detectors

In order to prove whether the perturbation is transferable across tasks and dataset, we need to add the perturbation generated in the previous section to images in Pascal VOC 2007 and MS COCO 2014 datasets. Because the size of perturbation is smaller than the size of images in the Pascal VOC 2007 and MS COCO 2014 dataset, there are two ways to add the perturbation to the images: resizing the perturbation to the size of the images, or piling up the perturbation and then clip it to the size of the images.

5   Evaluation

We conduct two sets of experiments against Faster R-CNN and YOLOv3. In the next subsections, we will show our experimental results and evaluate our methods.

5.1   Setup

Datasets. We use ILSVRC 2012, Pascal VOC 2007, and MS COCO 2014 datasets for our experiments. ImageNet Large Scale Visual Recognition(ILSVRC) evaluates algorithms for object detection and image classification at large scale. ILSVRC 2012 dataset is a subset of ImageNet dataset, which is a large scale hierarchical image database.MS COCO 2014 dataset is a large scale objection detection, segmentation, and captioning dataset, which contains 80 classes of targets. Pascal VOC 2007 contains 20 classes of targets. And we don't do any cropping operations for images in this dataset. The size of each image is scaled to the range of (-1,1) to make the process of training generator more convenient.

Target Model Architectures Selection. In our experiments, we choose VGG16 as our target model to generate perturbation because of its powerful black box attack ability. And the adversarial examples generated based on the VGG-16 model have stronger generalization and robustness than the adversarial examples generated based on other models. In addition, we aim at Faster R-CNN and YOLOv3 to verify the transferability of the perturbation.

Hyper-Parameters. We use the SGD optimizer with a learning rate of 0.0002 and a momentum of 0.9 to train all the perturbation generation models. In our experiment, we use the cross-entropy function as the loss function. In addition, we set the epoch to 10, the training batch to 13, and the testing batch to 5.

Experiment Environment. We use the pytorch 0.4.1 framework on the Linux system to conduct all the experiments. In addition, we perform our experiments across two Nvidia GeForce GTX 1080 GPUs with 8 GB memory each.

5.2 Success Rate

Attacks Against YOLOv3. Firstly, we resize the perturbation generated using the top ten classes of the imagenet dataset to the size of the input image in Imagenet dataset. And during the training process of the perturbation generator, we set $L_\infty = 10$, $L_\infty = 15$, $L_\infty = 20$, $L_\infty = 25$ respectively to observe the attack effect. Here the attack success rate is defined as follows.

$$attack\ success\ rate = \frac{N_e + N_h}{N_i} \tag{3}$$

Where N_e is the number of objects that are classified incorrectly, N_h is the number of objects that are hidden, and N_i is the number of objects in the input images.

From the experimental results we can see that the attack success rate is the highest when $L_\infty = 20$, so in the next experiment in the case of $L_\infty = 20$, we use the first 20, first 40, first 60, first 80, first 100 classes of the ImageNet dataset to train the perturbation generator respectively. Subsequently, we perform resize operation and pile-up operation on the generated perturbations to add them to the input images. And the attack success rate is shown in Table 1. Figure 2 depicts the perturbation added to different input images.

Table 1. Non-targeted universal perturbation attack effect against YOLOv3

$L_\infty = 20$	First 20 classes	First 40 classes	First 60 classes	First 80 classes	First 100 classes
Resize	15.89%	30.77%	28.85%	28.85%	30.77%
Pile-up	15.89%	35.58%	34.62%	28.85%	40.38%

To get more powerful and robust universal perturbations, we used all of the classes in ImageNet dataset to train the perturbation generator. Table 2 show the attack success rate and Fig. 3 depicts the perturbation added to different input images.

Table 2. Non-targeted universal perturbation attack effect against YOLOv3

$L_\infty = 20$	Resize	Pile-up
Attack success rate on YOLOv3	37.70%	40.98%

Fig. 2. We used the first 100 classes in ImageNet dataset to train the perturbation generator. The top line are input images, the second line are adversarial examples with resized perturbation, and the bottom line are adversarial examples with pile-up perturbation.

Fig. 3. Attacks against YOLOv3 model when $L_\infty = 20$. The top line are input images, the second line are adversarial examples with resized perturbation, and the bottom line are adversarial examples with pile-up perturbation.

Table 3. Non-targeted universal perturbation attack effect against Faster-RCNN

$L_\infty = 20$	Resize	Pile-up
Attack success rate on Faster R-CNN	37.50%	81.25%

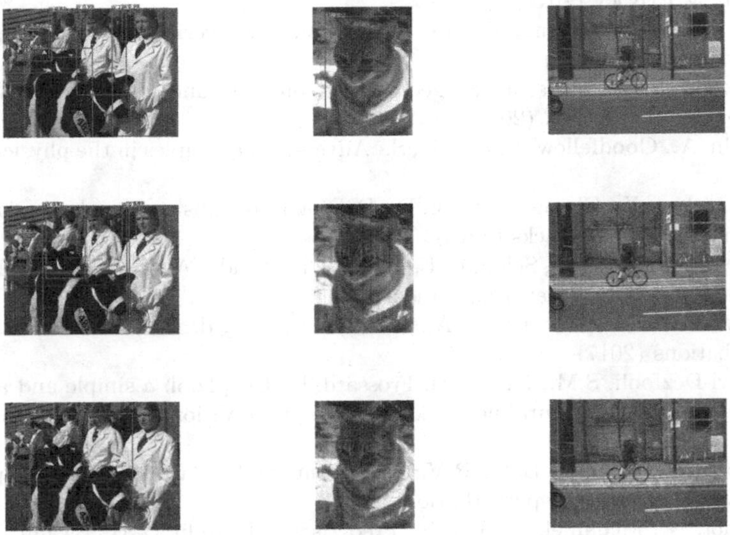

Fig. 4. Attacks against Faster R-CNN model when $L_\infty = 20$. The top line are input images, the second line are adversarial examples with resized perturbation, and the bottom line are adversarial examples with pile-up perturbation.

Attacks Against Faster R-CNN. We also attack Faster R-CNN on Pascal VOC 2007 dataset, the universal perturbation is generated across 1000 classes images in ImageNet dataset too. Table 3 shows the attack success rate and Fig. 4 depicts the perturbation added to different input images.

6   Conclusions

In this paper, we proposed a cross-task universal perturbation attack against black-box object detectors. We trained a deep neural network to generate universal perturbations on the classifier, then use the generated perturbation to attack black-box object detectors. We finished experiments on two representative object detectors: Faster-RCNN based on proposal and regression-based YOLOv3. We demonstrated the efficiency and transferability of the universal perturbation generated by our attack. We also demonstrated the feasibility of cross-task attack in the field of computer vision, contributing to the security of deep neural networks.

Acknowledgment. This work is supported by National Natural Science Foundation of China (No. 61876019 & U1636213).

References

1. Brendel, W., Rauber, J., Bethge, M.: Decision-based adversarial attacks: reliable attacks against black-box machine learning models (2017)
2. Carlini, N., Wagner, D.: Towards evaluating the robustness of neural networks. In: Security & Privacy (2017)
3. Dong, Y., Liao, F., Pang, T., Hu, X., Zhu, J.: Discovering adversarial examples with momentum (2017)
4. Goodfellow, I.J., Shlens, J., Szegedy, C.: Explaining and harnessing adversarial examples. Comput. Sci. (2014)
5. Kurakin, A., Goodfellow, I., Bengio, S.: Adversarial examples in the physical world (2016)
6. Liu, Y., Chen, X., Chang, L., Song, D.: Delving into transferable adversarial examples and black-box attacks (2016)
7. Madry, A., Makelov, A., Schmidt, L., Tsipras, D., Vladu, A.: Towards deep learning models resistant to adversarial attacks (2017)
8. Moosavi-Dezfooli, S.M., Fawzi, A., Fawzi, O., Frossard, P.: Universal adversarial perturbations (2017)
9. Moosavi-Dezfooli, S.M., Fawzi, A., Frossard, P.: DeepFool: a simple and accurate method to fool deep neural networks. In: Computer Vision & Pattern Recognition (2016)
10. Mopuri, K.R., Garg, U., Babu, R.V.: Fast feature fool: a data independent approach to universal adversarial perturbations (2017)
11. Papernot, N., Mcdaniel, P., Jha, S., Fredrikson, M., Celik, Z.B., Swami, A.: The limitations of deep learning in adversarial settings. In: IEEE European Symposium on Security & Privacy (2016)
12. Su, J., Vargas, D.V., Kouichi, S.: One pixel attack for fooling deep neural networks. IEEE Trans. Evol. Comput. (2017)
13. Szegedy, C., et al.: Intriguing properties of neural networks. Comput. Sci. (2013)
14. Tramr, F., Papernot, N., Goodfellow, I., Dan, B., Mcdaniel, P.: The space of transferable adversarial examples (2017)

A Brief Survey on Cyber Security Attack Entrances and Protection Strategies of Intelligent Connected Vehicle

Zhao Wang[1], Yanqi Wang[2(⊠)], Yanan Zhang[2], Yangyang Liu[2],
Chao Ma[2], and Haijun Wang[2]

[1] Auto Standardization Research Institute,
China Automotive Technology and Research Center Co., Ltd., Tianjin, China
[2] Automotive Data Center, China Automotive Technology and Research Center
Co., Ltd., Tianjin, China
adc_wangyanqi@163.com

Abstract. The Intelligent Connected Vehicle (ICV) related to the communication of the stakeholders has become a large and open ecosystem. From the automobile ecosystem, it can be found that there are many attack entrances everywhere, which will bring a lot of risks and threats. In this work, we have summarized the seven major attack entrances of automobile cyber security, and proposed the corresponding six key protection strategies of intelligent and connected vehicle.

Keywords: Intelligent Connected Vehicle · Vehicle ecosystems · Automobile cyber security · Attack entrance · Protection strategy

1 Introduction

The automobile is a complex network communication system and it has a complex electronic information system, covering many information and communication technologies. So, the vehicle ecosystem is large and complex. But now, with the rise of Intelligent Connected Vehicles (ICVs) and mobile travel services, the vehicle ecosystem has been further expanded, including technology, services, infrastructure providers and smart cities. The four subversive technology trends – Electrification, Autonomous driving, Diverse mobility, and Connectivity – will transform a typical vertically integrated automotive value chain into a more complex, and more horizontally structured ecosystem. Everyone will be more dependent on the vehicle ecosystem in the future, especially when car companies use in-vehicle interconnection services to achieve personalized vehicle configuration. There are some similarities between the vehicle ecosystem and the cyber-physical system, which has three typical layers, namely the application layer, transmission layer, and perception layer [1].

While the rapid development of in-vehicle information systems is improving information technology, information security issues are becoming increasingly prominent. The way vehicles are subject to hacking is also being refurbished. The number of Trojans and virus variants continues to rise, threatening the driving safety of

© Springer Nature Switzerland AG 2019
M. Qiu (Ed.): SmartCom 2019, LNCS 11910, pp. 73–82, 2019.
https://doi.org/10.1007/978-3-030-34139-8_8

drivers' lives and property. It was first occurred in 2010 that attacking on the car information systems [2]. As the scope of application of the ICV continues to expand, cyber security also attacks continue to increase. Information tampering, virus intrusion and other means have been successfully applied by hackers in cyber-attacks on smart cars [3], which has aroused great concern from all walks of life.

This paper mainly focuses on automobile security based on the vehicle ecosystem. And we obtained the attack entrance of the ICV by means of testing the vehicle and other simulation investigation and research. Then, we summarize the key strategies of vehicle cyber security protection, which can be used as a reference in the design and manufacture of automobiles to improve the overall information security level of automobiles.

2   Vehicle Connectivity Ecosystem

In the digital age, the degree of global connectivity has increased, making people more connected, and the automotive industry has undergone the same transformation. With the rise of ICV and mobile travel services, the traditional ecosystem of vehicles has been further expanded to include technologies, services, infrastructure providers and smart cities to make vehicles an interconnected system. Vehicle ecosystems can be broadly classified into 4 broad categories that are terminal equipment, cloud platforms, third party service, and communication and network transmission as Fig. 1 shown.

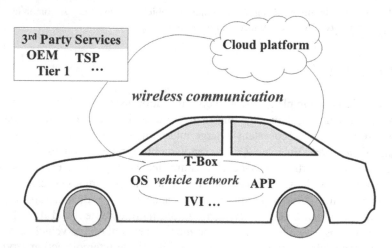

Fig. 1. The diagram of vehicle ecosystem. It contains terminal equipment, cloud platforms, third party service, and communication and network transmission.

The terminal equipment layer will always be used as a third-party interface that can be used to create services and applications. It contained inside car and outside car two parts. The equipment inside vehicle include the operating system (OS), semiconductor chip, T-Box, IVI, On Board Diagnostics (OBD), mobile application (APP), vehicle

APP, and so on. People has more directly interactions with the OS, mobile APP and vehicle APP in the vehicle ecosystem terminal equipment. In many use cases, other advanced technologies such as artificial intelligence and blockchain are also used in those equipment. The external infrastructure includes road test equipment, road conditions, sensor device, traffic conditions, weather conditions, and the others which may affect the vehicle.

The core of the cloud platforms is the connectivity platform, which consists of the vehicle and the 3rd part services. Cloud technology also provides a platform for users and vehicles to share information. It can get and share data and information through the vehicle includes precise positioning of the vehicle, vehicle health and climatic conditions. Such data sources will be connected to the cloud platforms, which requires technical support for cellular networks such as 4G, and will be implemented in the future using 5G communication networks. Users and vehicles can communicate in real time, and can obtain vehicle maintenance information in a timely manner. Vehicle service reservations are smarter and more convenient. In the future, the use of cloud storage will realize the sharing of information between vehicles and people, vehicles and vehicles, vehicles and infrastructure, laying the foundation for optimizing travel, improving efficiency and realizing smart life, and building a more complete intelligent ecosystem and intelligence.

In the development of new technologies in the automotive industry, more and more new players have emerged as the third-party service, such as internet and software companies, sensor manufacturers, and travel service providers. And data management and maintenance can also be outsourced to third-party organizations. These new players form a new automotive ecosystem with traditional vehicle manufacturers and component suppliers. They may represent business (e.g. legal, communications, purchasing) and technical organizations (e.g. engineering, IT) within original equipment manufacturers (OEMs), suppliers, and other automotive stakeholders. The OEM, telematics service provider (TSP), Tier1, suppliers, and other automotive industry stakeholders have played a role include product cybersecurity managers, support staff, crisis managers, executives, legal counsel, and product managers in vehicle cyber security. So, it is better to find and fix issues in vehicle ecosystems that with the help of a variety of internal and external stakeholders.

The communication in vehicle ecosystem includes in-vehicle communication and V2X communication such as vehicle to cloud communication, vehicle to infrastructure communication, and vehicle to human communication. The in-vehicle communication mostly contains CAN bus, LIN bus, FlexRay bus, and MOST bus. All data transactions in the vehicle are made through the gateway. A vehicle gateway that can communicate through various protocols is installed in the vehicle. The V2X communication contained 4G, LTE-V, WIFI, Bluetooth, USB, OTA, dedicated short range communications (DSRC), on board diagnostics (OBD), etc. DSRC is an efficient wireless communication technology that enables the identification and two-way communication of moving targets in high-speed motion in a small area (usually tens of meters), such as the "vehicle-road" and "vehicle-vehicle" of the vehicle two-way communication. It transmits image, voice and data information in real time, to connect vehicles and roads organically. ODB can monitor the working status of the engine electronic control system and other functional modules of the vehicle in real time during the running of the vehicle.

From the vehicle ecosystem, we can find it is very widely, cantinas the numerous stakeholders, and has a lot of ways of communication. Therefore, the risks and threats faced by the vehicle are numerous and ubiquitous, so the information security of cars has a long way to go.

3   Attack Entrances of Vehicle Cyber Security

Any device connected to the Internet may be vulnerable to hackers. While enjoying the convenience of the network, we must also face the "dark side" of the network—the information security threat, which is not immune to the automotive industry. To ensure the cybersecurity of the vehicle, based on the car's ecosystem, we simulated the attack entrances for vehicle cybersecurity and came up with the following common attack portals.

3.1   Smartphone APP

Smartphones are network communication tools that are often used by car users. APP on smartphones can be freely distributed, downloaded and installed, and there are many types of APP, including many automotive-oriented APP, which may have low reliability and poor security. Such characteristics, hackers through the loopholes, through the smart phone, making the vehicle information system, navigation system abnormal, or eavesdropping on the user's conversation record and the driver's personal privacy information [4]. When a user uses a smartphone, it means that the entire vehicle is connected to the outside network. Therefore, hackers crack the smart phone through the external network, the purpose is to interfere with the in-vehicle information system and launch a vicious attack on the vehicle under high speed.

3.2   Electronic Control Unit (ECU)

Inside the car, each ECU communicates with each other via a CAN bus in a multi-stage interconnection, which not only significantly improves processing efficiency and stability, but also means that control of the entire car can be obtained from any interface. More importantly, the ECUs of the high-end models on the market have the learning function of recording data during driving. In addition, this learning function is also widely used in engines, ABS anti-lock braking systems, four-wheel drive systems, transmission systems, active suspension systems, hydraulic control systems and other systems controlled by ECUs, which makes the ECU get more and more information. The attacker uses the distributed ECU to control multiple systems of the vehicle, precisely because each ECU is connected to the CAN bus, and from the engine ECU to the airbag ECU, these ECU control systems are in the same level relationship. Once the attacker cracks the CAN bus system, and all the control system ECUs face a large security risk.

3.3 Vehicle Network

The controller in the vehicle mainly relies on the vehicle network to transmit messages, including the MOST bus responsible for multimedia communication, the CAN bus responsible for transmitting control information, and the LIN bus responsible for the central locking system. In theory, any controller on the CAN, MOST, and LIN buses can send commands to any other controller. Therefore, any controller that suffers from a bus attack poses a substantial threat to the vehicle communication network. Especially the security for T-BOX, ECU and other important parts, the vehicle network is the last line of defense.

3.4 T-BOX

T-BOX is the communication gateway of intelligent networked vehicles, that almost all communication like 4G, Wi-Fi, OTA and vehicle remote communication are all completed by T-BOX. So, it has played an important role in intelligent and connected vehicle. The main threat of the T-BOX is the attack of middlemen. The attacker hijacks the T-BOX session and listens to the communication data through pseudo base stations and DNS hijacking. For example, in an embedded system, the T-BOX-hardware layer UART debug interface can be used to enter the uboot for firmware upgrade, as the Fig. 2 shows.

```
=> md.b 14008000 10000
14008000: 00 00 a0 e1 00 00 a0 e1 00 00 a0 e1 00 00 a0 e1    ................
14008010: 00 00 a0 e1 00 00 a0 e1 00 00 a0 e1 00 00 a0 e1    ................
14008020: 02 00 00 ea 18 28 6f 01 00 00 00 00 c8 95 4e 00    .....(o.......N.
14008030: 00 90 0f e1 99 04 00 eb 01 70 a0 e1 02 80 a0 e1    .........p......
14008040: 00 20 0f e1 03 00 12 e3 01 00 00 1a 17 00 a0 e3    . ..............
14008050: 56 34 12 ef 00 00 0f e1 1a 00 20 e2 1f 00 10 e3    V4........ .....
14008060: 1f 00 c0 e3 d3 00 80 e3 04 00 00 1a 01 0c 80 e3    ................
14008070: 0c e0 8f e2 00 f0 6f e1 0e f3 2e e1 6e 00 60 e1    ......o.....n. .
14008080: 00 f0 21 e1 09 f0 6f e1 00 00 00 00 00 00 00 00    ..!...o.........
14008090: 00 00 00 00 00 00 00 00 00 00 00 00 00 00 00 00    ................
140080a0: 0f 40 a0 e1 3e 43 04 e2 02 49 84 e2 6b 00 00 eb    .@..>C...I..k...
140080b0: 5b 0f 8f e2 4e 1c 90 e8 1c d0 90 e5 01 00 40 e0    [...N.........@.
140080c0: 00 60 86 e0 00 a0 8a e0 00 90 da e5 01 e0 da e5    ................
140080d0: 0e 94 89 e1 02 e0 da e5 03 a0 da e5 0e 98 89 e1    ................
140080e0: 0a 9c 89 e1 00 d0 8d e0 01 a8 8d e2 00 50 a0 e3    .............P...
140080f0: 01 a9 8a e2 0a 00 54 e1 1e 00 00 2a 09 a0 84 e0    ......T...*.....
14008100: 70 90 8f e2 09 00 5a e1 1a 00 00 9a 09 ac 8a e2    p.....Z.........
14008110: ff a0 ca e3 6c 50 4f e2 1f 50 c5 e3 00 00 4f e1    ....1PO..P....O.
```

Fig. 2. Extract the kernel from uboot.

3.5 In-Vehicle Infotainment (IVI)

IVI is an in-vehicle integrated information processing system based on a vehicle-mounted bus system and Internet service. It can be divided into four hierarchical categories, hardware layer, application layer, system layer and communication layer. Each layer may be subject to information security attacks, such as interfaces, chips and

USB of hardware layer, and system applications, third-party applications as well as some sensitive information in the application layer. IVI enables a wide range of applications including 3D navigation, real-time traffic, IPTV, assisted driving, fault detection, vehicle information, body control, mobile office, wireless communications, online-based entertainment and TSP services, which greatly enhances the level of vehicle electronics, networking and intelligence.

3.6   Cloud Platform

The cloud platform serves as a bridge between the vehicle and the owner for remote control communication. Vehicle-cloud communication plays an important role in the safety of vehicle networking, and it has become the main entrance of vehicle network attack. The vehicle networking service platform is generally based on cloud computing technology, so it is also easy to introduce the security problems of the cloud computing itself into the platform, such as operating system vulnerability threats, virtual resource scheduling problems, SQL injection, password security, and more. Figure 3 shown the attackers used the cloud platform HeartBleed vulnerability to attack the vehicle.

```
0000:  02 40 00 20 2F 63 6F 6E 66 69 67 2F 70 77 74 6F   .@. /config/pwto
0010:  6B 65 6E 5F 67 65 74 3F 73 72 63 3D 79 65 6D 61   ken_get?src=yema
0020:  69 6C 69 6D 61 70 26 74 73 3D 31 33 39 36 39 35   ilimap&ts=139695
0030:  39 32 35 38 26 6C 6F 67 69 6E 3D 68 6F 6C 6D 73   9258&login=holms
0040:  65 79 37 39 26 70 61 73 73 77 64 3D               ey79&passwd=
0050:        6 73 69 67 3D 4E 37 64 72 70                 &sig=N7drp
0060:  68 45 4A 53 6E 77 50 5A 69 62 34 39 34 39 55 33   hEJSnwPZib4949U3
0070:  51 2D 2D 20 48 54 54 50 2F 31 2E 31 0D 0A 48 6F   Q-- HTTP/1.1..Ho
```

Fig. 3. Attackers can use the HeartBleed vulnerability of the cloud platform to directly read server data, including user's cookies and even plaintext accounts and pass-words.

3.7   Wireless Communication

To prevent physical attacks, vehicles have many functions that are completed through wireless networks. For example, smart key, tire pressure detection system, road shop communication and other devices use short-range wireless communication, which opens the door for hackers to intercept information content.

4   Protection Strategies of Vehicle Cyber Security

The complex application scenarios and technologies of the intelligent and connected of vehicles make it have more security risks. So, the comprehensive measures are needed to protect them [5, 6]. Based on above security attack entrances, we put forward several relevant and common protection strategies, which are OBD firewall, encrypted transmission, system protection, firmware hardening, application hardening, and code obfuscation [7, 8].

4.1 OBD Firewall

The OBD firewall is used to isolate message and information injected into the bus through the OBD port and isolate the internal network information. If abnormal conditions are found, the specific fault is determined according to a specific algorithm, and it is stored on the memory in the system in the form of diagnostic trouble codes (DTC). The useful information obtained after the system self-diagnosis can help the repair and maintenance of the vehicle. The maintenance personnel can use the original instrument of the original vehicle to read the fault code, so that the fault can be quickly located to facilitate the repair of the vehicle and reduce the manual diagnosis time.

4.2 Encrypted Transmission

Encrypted transmission is a technical means used to transmit data on the internet to prevent data from being stolen, falsified and forged, etc., and to ensure that data is transmitted securely over the Internet.

The method of encrypted transmission mainly uses encryption technology, digital signature technology, time stamp, digital voucher technology, and so on. The most commonly used technology is secure layer protocol like SSL and TLS. The SSL/TLS protocol provides client and server authentication, data integrity, and information confidentiality to client-server applications over the Internet based on transport protocol (TCP/IP), both at the server and client. Implementation support. The goal is to provide users with secure communication services for the Internet and corporate intranets.

Currently, for SSL/TLS, an attacker can perform a man-in-the-middle attack by forging a certificate. In order to prevent the generation of man-in-the-middle attacks and encrypt the transmitted data, the certificate must be authenticated in both directions. Two-way authentication which requires another certificate to be sent to the client for verification, is the client verification server certificate, and the server also needs to verify the client's certificate.

4.3 System Protection

Customized installation of professional protection software can effectively protect the normal and safe operation of the intelligent system used by the car's IVI and T-Box. For some common IVI, T-Box and system intrusion methods, the protection software can be divided into four major modules: Virus killing, Equity detection, Vulnerability detection, and Communication flow detection.

The virus killing module most rely on cloud virus databases. The cloud virus database is used to analyze and scan the suspicious program and the behavior is checked and killed, and the sensitive operation of the application is monitored in real time. And using the cloud virus database we can establish the virus signature database, which can scan the application by the signature code.

Equity detection module establish a blacklist of privilege software to detect the installed application, dynamically detect the behavior of the application to temporarily raise the right, and stop it in time.

Vulnerability detection module can regularly obtain vulnerability information of system kernel and system application, and update it in time.

Communication flow detection module establish a communication whitelist, monitor all traffic data communicated with the system, and filter all suspicious data outside the whitelist.

4.4 Firmware Hardening

Firmware is the software that is the most basic and bottom-level work of a system. In hardware devices, firmware is the soul of hardware devices, and it determines the function and performance of hardware devices. To harden the firmware, we can encrypt the chip, and increase the difficulty of firmware extraction.

4.5 Application Hardening

Application hardening allows adding programs that require hardened protection. In the way of detecting the application running state, it intercepts the behavior of the program and prevents malicious programs from exploiting the vulnerability of the application to damage the computer.

Reinforcement can protect its core code algorithm to a certain extent, improve the difficulty of cracking, piracy, and secondary packaging, and alleviate attacks such as code injection, dynamic debugging, and memory injection.

4.6 Obfuscated Code

Obfuscated code, also known as flower instruction, converts the code of a computer program into a functionally equivalent, but difficult to read and understand form of behavior. Identifier confusion is to rename the package name, class name, method name and variable name in the source program, replace it with a meaningless identifier, making the decompiled code more difficult to analyze.

Code obfuscation can be used for program source code or for intermediate code compiled by the program. There are three common ways to confuse code, rewriting various elements in the code, disrupt the format of the code, and using the code obfuscation tool. Rewriting various elements in the code, such as variables, functions, and class names, into meaningless names makes it impossible for the person reading the book to guess its purpose. Rewrite some of the logic in the code to make it functionally equivalent, but more difficult to understand. Disrupting the format of the code means first converting some of the more critical string variables into hexadecimal arrays or Unicode encodings, and then restoring them to strings when used. This can avoid the disassembled code is easy to be analyzed and understood by the cracker, so that the cracker analysis cost increases.

Use the code obfuscation tool to enhance the difficulty of the reverse. It provides 3 protection modes: control flow flattening, spurious control flow, and instruction replacement. Control flow flattening is to convert control statements such as if, while, for, and do in C, C++, or Java code into switch branch statements without changing the function of the source code. The spurious control flow confuses each basic code block, creating a new conditional jump code block that jumps to the real basic block or another code block containing the garbage instruction, the original basic code block. Will also be cloned and populated with randomly selected spam commands. Instruction substitution does not change the original control flow of the function, but replaces ordinary arithmetic and Boolean operations with more complex operations. When several equivalent sequences of instructions are available, it will randomly select one to replace (Fig. 4).

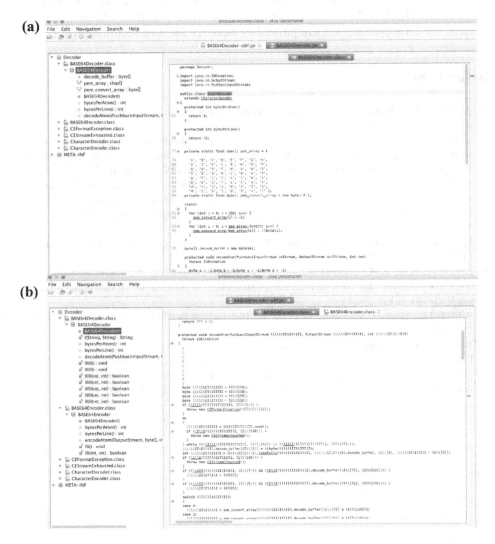

Fig. 4. Identifier confusing instantiation in code obfuscation. The (a) is before the confusion, and the (b) is after confusing, the confusion can increase the analysis difficulty of the decompiled code.

5 Conclusion

In general, the protection measures for ICVs cyber security are not only reflected in the hardware and software requirements of the vehicle, but also reflected in the requirements of communication and cloud. Only by doing cybersecurity protection measures in the entire automobile ecosystem, can we cope with various possible cyber security issues and ensure the cyber security of ICVs as much as possible

This paper outlines the vehicle attack entrance and protection strategies, analyzes the common attack methods and potential security threats for automobiles, and summarizes the corresponding vehicle protection measures for each security threat.

References

1. Ashibani, Y., Mahmoud, Q.H.: Cyber physical systems security: analysis, challenges and solutions. Comput. Secur. **68**, 81–97 (2017)
2. Chen, L.W., Syue, K.Z., Tseng, Y.C.: A vehicular surveillance and sensing system for car security and tracking applications. In: Proceedings of the 9th ACM/IEEE International Conference on Information Processing in Sensor Networks (IPSN 2010), pp. 426–427 (2010)
3. Okul, Ş., Aydin, M.A., Keleş, F.: Security problems and attacks on smart cars. In: Boyaci, A., Ekti, A.R., Aydin, M.A., Yarkan, S. (eds.) International Telecommunications Conference. LNEE, vol. 504, pp. 203–213. Springer, Singapore (2019). https://doi.org/10.1007/978-981-13-0408-8_17
4. Wolf, M., Weimerskirch, A., Wollinger, T.: State of the art: embedding security in vehicles. EURSIP J. Embed. Syst. **16**(1) (2007)
5. Lee, C.H., Kim, K.H.: Implementation of IoT system using block chain with authentication and data protection. In: 2018 International Conference on Information Networking (ICOIN), pp. 936–940. IEEE (2018)
6. Alfred, J.R., Sidorov, S., Tsang, M.C., et al.: In-vehicle networking. U.S. Patent Application 15/270,957, 22 March 2018
7. Wroblewski, G.: General method of program code obfuscation (2002)
8. Pizzolotto, D., Fellin, R., Ceccato, M.: OBLIVE: seamless code obfuscation for Java programs and Android apps. In: 2019 IEEE 26th International Conference on Software Analysis, Evolution and Reengineering (SANER), pp. 629–633. IEEE (2019)

Hierarchically Channel-Wise Attention Model for Clean and Polluted Water Images Classification

Yirui Wu[1,2], Yao Xiao[2], and Jun Feng[1(✉)]

[1] College of Computer and Information, Hohai University, Nanjing, China
{wuyirui,junfeng}@hhu.edu.cn
[2] National Key Lab for Novel Software Technology, Nanjing University,
Nanjing, China
1600151467@qq.com

Abstract. Water image classification is challenging because clean water images of ocean or river share almost the same properties with images of polluted water. Inspired by the significant power of Convolutional Neural Network (CNN) in extracting various features for classification, we intend to utilize CNN to classify clean and polluted water images based on quantity of channel-wise and multi-layer CNN-extracted features. Since not all features are informative for water image classification, a dynamic feature attention scheme that utilize the properties of channel-wise and multi-layer is necessary to achieve robust and accurate results. In this paper, we propose a novel hierarchically channel-wise attention model for clean and polluted water images classification. The proposed model dynamically modulates context with multi-layer feature maps in a local and global sense, constructing a representative combination of features to boost classification performance. Experimental results on a latest water image dataset (reporting 71.2% in accuracy) with several comparative methods demonstrate the effectiveness and robustness of the proposed model incorporating CNN for water image classification.

Keywords: Hierarchical attention model · Channel-wise CNN feature · Multi-layer CNN feature · Channel-wise attention module

1 Introduction

Rapid economic development, large growth of population and over exploitation of nature resources may result in serious pollution of water ecosystem, *e.g.*, river, lake and sea, if not instantly monitoring, controlling and abating pollution. In the last decade, water pollution monitoring system based on cloud and big data system [7,13] is established by manually water sampling and laboratory analysis. However, there is an obvious time-delay with such low efficient monitoring strategies. Realtime monitoring sudden and large-scale pollution outbreaks thus have gained a lot of interests from researchers and government.

© Springer Nature Switzerland AG 2019
M. Qiu (Ed.): SmartCom 2019, LNCS 11910, pp. 83–92, 2019.
https://doi.org/10.1007/978-3-030-34139-8_9

Fig. 1. Architecture of the proposed water pollution monitoring system, where we can notice the proposed hierarchically channel-wise attention model classifies the inputting captured water images into clean and polluted categories with 10 subcategory labels.

Due to the developments of surveillance cameras and drones, researchers can gather a quantity of water images from different locations for further analysis [6,12]. With Captured water images, researchers try to classify them into clean and polluted water images. Moreover, they recognize subcategories of clean and polluted water images, such as fountain, lake, ocean, river for clean water images, fungus, dead animals, industrial pollution, oil and rubbish for polluted water images [11]. By constructing such water pollution monitoring system as shown in Fig. 1, researchers could real-time monitor and report sudden pollution breaks. However, images captured by drones and surveillance cameras generally suffer from reflecting, low contrast and poor quality, which makes analyzing water images more complex and challenging [2].

To solve this problem, this work focuses on classification of clean and polluted water images to enhance water pollution monitoring system. Researchers have proposed several methods for water image detection in literature. Early, Rankin *et al.* [9] proposed a method for water body detection based on sky reflections, which finds similarity between intensity values of pixels. However, it's designed to detect water body in wide-open areas but not different types of water pollution. Prasad *et al.* [5] proposed quadcopter based stagnant water identification, which utilizes the combination of colors and optical flow for classification. Recently, Mettes *et al.* [3] proposed water detection through spatio-temporal invariant descriptors, which uses probability-based classification for extracted features. However, the descriptors used in this method require high contrast images with clear object shapes to achieve better results.

Inspired by the significant performance of deep learning architectures, researchers intend to utilize such an architecture to discover distinguish features for water image classification. For example, Qi *et al.* [8] proposed to explore deep learning architectures for feature extraction and studying texture property of scene images. Note that this method is developed for scene image classification including water images considered as scenes. Recently, Zhao et al. [14] propose a spectral−spatial feature based classification framework that jointly uses dimension reduction and Convolutional Neural Network (CNN) features for scene classification, including water body images as well. However, these two methods utilize mature deep learning structures without proper modifications to finetune them for classification of clean and polluted water images, which result in a low precision and recall performance. In fact, classification of clean and polluted water images is actually an ambiguous category-level classification problem with high intra variations and less inter variations, so that these methods are not robust and accurate to classify with a limited size of training dataset. In other words, these methods are not qualified to search for highly representative features for robust and correct classification with a relatively small dataset. Expanding and tapping the potentials on searching for representative features with deep learning architectures is one of the appropriate ways to solve the problem.

Considering that a convolutional layer consisting of different channel filters scans the input image and output a feature map, each 2D slice of the output 3D feature map essentially encodes the spatial visual responses raised by a filter channel, where the filter performs as a pattern detector, *i.e.*, lower-layer filters detect lowlevel visual cues like edges and corners while higher-level ones detect high-level semantic patterns like parts and object. By stacking the layers, a CNN extracts image features through a hierarchy representation of visual abstractions. Therefore, CNN image features are essentially channel-wise and multi-layer. However, not all the features are representative and informative for classification of water images. Therefore, we propose a channel-wise aware hierarchical attention model, which automatically focuses on discriminative and channel-wise features for classification of water images.

In this paper, we build our work on former channel-wise attention module by regarding it as an attention gate scheme and further construct a hierarchical attention model to search highly representative channel-wise features for classification of clean and polluted water images. We have made the following two main contributions in this work.

- To the best of our knowledge, this is first hierarchically channel-wise aware attention model designed based on CNN architectures for classification of water images.
- A hierarchically channel-wise attention model is carefully designed to take account the channel-wise and multi-layer CNN features.
- The proposed hierarchical attention model is powerful and easy to implement to discover the fundamental and discriminative patterns for ambiguous classification problem, so that it could be easily transformed to solve other similar questions.

2 The Proposed Method

In this section, we describe the proposed method by channel-wise attention module, hierarchically channel-wise attention model and design of objective function.

2.1 Channel-Wise Attention Module

In this subsection, we introduce a channel-wise attention module as a lightweight gating mechanism, which is specially designed to model channel-wise

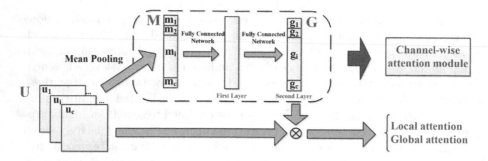

Fig. 2. Structure of the proposed channel-wise attention module, which is utilized to describe local and global channel-wise attention.

relationships between feature maps and will be further utilized in a local and global manner to construct the hierarchal attention model. We show the structure of proposed channel-wise attention module in Fig. 2. Inspired by [4] which considers the attention problem as the sequential decision process of how an agent interact with a visual environment, the "interaction level" for the proposed channel-wise attention module is essentially described by weights assigned to each feature channel. Specifically, let's suppose an input feature map $U = [u_i; i = 1, ..., c]$, where u_i represents the ith channel of U and c is the total number of feature channels. Since each of the learned convolutional filters operate with a local receptive field to compute features and couldn't exploit contextual information outside of this region [1], we propose to utilize mean pooling operator to collect the contextual information into a channel descriptor, which could be represented as

$$m_i = \frac{1}{W \times H} \sum_{j=1}^{W} \sum_{k=1}^{H} u_i(j, k), \tag{1}$$

where W and H are width and height of u_i. M consists of m_i and is defined as the channel descriptor.

To make full use of information collected in M, we follow the idea of "interaction level" to construct the weighting scheme G. As shown in Fig. 2, the proposed channel-wise attention module is composed of two fully-connected layers and two corresponding nonlinear activation functions, which could be represented as

$$g_i = Nor(sig(W_2 \eta(W_1 m_i + b_1) + b_2)), \tag{2}$$

where function $sig()$, $Nor()$ and $\eta()$ refer to sigmoid, normalization and ReLU functions respectively, W_1 and W_2 are the learnable parameter matric, and b_1 and b_2 are the bias vectors. The reason to adopt such structure for module constructing lies in two facts, $i.e.$, firstly the designed structure must be capable of learning a highly nonlinear interaction between channels, and secondly, it must allow multiple channels to be emphasised opposed to one-hot activation. The

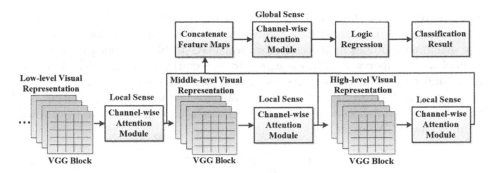

Fig. 3. The illustration of hierarchically channel-wise attention model for classification of clean and polluted water images.

resulting weight vector $\{G = g_i; i = 1, ..., c\}$ thus leads to the attention on informative channel features, where Fig. 2 explains how the channel-wise attention module works with

$$\tilde{u}_i = u_i \otimes g_i \tag{3}$$

where $\otimes$ represents the element-wise multiplication.

2.2 Hierarchically Channel-Wise Attention Model

We adopt the popular VGG-16 network to modify it for classification of clean and polluted water images. VGG-16 is pre-trained on Imagenet dataset and achieves highly efficient results for visual category classification. Built on VGG16, we propose to fine-tune it incorporating with the proposed hierarchically channel-wise attention model for accurate and task-specified classification based on training sets of real data collecting from sensors. Figure 3 gives the overview of the proposed method, where we construct two levels of channel-wise attention module to describe channel-wise attention in both local and global sense. The reason of building hierarchically channel-wise attention lies in the fact that low-level and middle-level features could be representative for ambiguous category-level classification problem. Take classification of water images as an example, texture, one of the most important low-level features, is the determined feature to recognize water surface polluted by oil, which has been proved by [10]. However, the decay effect of gradients and semantic abstraction of higher layers in neural network may ignore the importance of low-level or middle-level features. Based on these considerations, we regard the proposed hierarchically channel-wise attention model as an option to emphasize the low-level and middle-level features for ambiguous category-level classification problem.

As shown in Fig. 3, the local channel-wise attention weights are built as a function of the lth CNN channel feature $U_{k,l}$ output by the kth vgg block and then work with it as

$$\tilde{U}_{k,l} = U_{k,l} \cdot \Phi(U_{k,l}) \tag{4}$$

where Φ represents the channel-wise attention module described in the last subsection, and $\cdot$ is element-wise multiplication. We build such local channel-wise attention modules at the end of several VGG-16 blocks, which utilizes the channel-wise property of CNN features to automatically focuses on discriminative and representative features for classification in a local sense. After constructing local level of attention, we concatenate feature maps $\tilde{U}_{k,l}$ output by local attention modules and utilize a channel-wise attention module to work with the multi-layer CNN features:

$$\begin{cases} \tilde{U}_k = [\tilde{U}_{k,l}], l = 1, ..., c \\ \hat{U}_k = \tilde{U}_k \cdot \Phi(\tilde{U}_k) \end{cases} \tag{5}$$

where function $[\cdot]$ represents transforming and concatenating different size of matric into a single vector. In fact, such global channel-wise attention module utilizes the multi-layer property of CNN features to emphasize the representative ability of low and middle layers of visual cues, which is particularly effective for ambiguous category-level classification problem. Based on $\hat{U}_k$, we apply average pooling operation and classier of logical regression to achieve the final classification results.

2.3   Design of Objective Function

Constrained by the objective function, the pre-trained VGG-16 CNN network and the hierarchically channel-wise attention model can be jointly trained to implicitly learn the model. We thus formulate the final objective function of the hierarchically channel-wise attention network with a regularized cross-entropy loss for a training sample as

$$Loss = -\sum_{i=1}^{n} y_i \log P_{y_i} + \lambda_1 \|W_N\|_2 + \lambda_2 \|B_N\|_2 \tag{6}$$

where n is the number of groundtruth labels. If the training sample belongs to the ith class, then $y_i = 1$ and $y_j = 0$ for $j \neq i$. P_{y_i} indicates the probability that the sample is predicted as the ith class. The second and third regularization item with L2 norm is to reduce overfitting of the networks, where B_N consists of bias values and W_N denotes the connection matrix (merged to one matrix here) in the networks, including W_1, W_2 in Eq. 2 and other parameter matrices in the adopted VGG-16 modules. We set $\lambda_1 = e^{-4}$ and $\lambda_2 = e^{-5}$ by experiments. Note that we use the back-propagation to minimize the $Loss$ function.

3   Experiments

Since there is no benchmark dataset for clean and polluted water image classification in literature, we follow [11] to utilize their collected dataset. Their dataset consists of 1000 water images, includes images from standard videos of different water images [3] and internet sources, such as Google, Bing and Baidu. Their clean water image class is classified as four sub-classes, namely, Fountain, Lakes, Oceans and Rivers. Similarly, the polluted water image class is labeled with six sub-classes, namely, Algaes, Dead animals, Fungus, Industrial pollution, Oils and Rubbish. In summary, the considered dataset in this paper is complex with high intra variations and less inter variations.

During experiments, we adopt 750 images as training set and others as testing set to perform experiments. We use 4-fold cross validation to evaluate classification with measurements of precision, recall and f-score. The proposed model is trained within 150 epoches by defining batch size as 64. The initial learning rate of the logic regression layer and other layers are settled as $5e^{-3}$ and $5e^{-4}$, respectively. To make the convergence faster and more stable, we adopt a trick that all the learning rate values will be divided by 10 when the validation accuracy begins to decrease.

Table 1. Comparison of overall classification performance with the proposed method, Wu et al. [11] and Mettes et al. [3].

Method	Clear water				Polluted water				Total accuracy
	Precision	Recall	F-score	Accuracy	Precision	Recall	F-score	Accuracy	
Proposed	**0.65**	**0.69**	**0.67**	**66.4%**	**0.65**	**0.67**	**0.66**	**73.6%**	**71.2%**
Without attention	**0.65**	**0.69**	**0.67**	63.2%	0.60	0.64	0.62	65.6%	69.2%
Wu et al. [11]	0.52	0.52	0.52	52.0%	0.44	0.45	0.44	59.2%	51.2%
Mettes et al. [3]	0.30	0.30	0.30	41.6%	0.07	0.16	0.10	35.2%	20.0%

To show the superiority of the proposed method to the existing method, we adopt [11] and [3] for comparison. [11] explores Fourier transform based features to extract texture properties of clean and polluted water images. We implement their proposed method following their recently published paper to perform further analysis. Since [3] is proposed to explore spatio-temporal information for water body detection in video, we create duplicate images for single input image to run this method on the dataset. To evaluate the performance of the proposed and existing methods, we adopt standard measures, namely, Recall, Precision, F-score and Accuracy, which can be formulated as $Precision = \frac{TP}{TP+FP}$, $Recall = \frac{TP}{TP+FN}$, $F-score = \frac{2*Precision*Recall}{Precision+Recall}$, $Accuracy = \frac{TP+TN}{TP+TN+FP+FN}$ where True Positive (TP) is the number of images labeled correctly and belongs to the positive class, True Negative (TN) is the number of images labeled correctly and belongs to the negative class, False Positive (FP) and False Negative (FN) are the numbers of images labeled incorrectly in the positive class and negative classes separately.

Quantitative results and confusion matrices of the proposed and existing methods are reported in Table. 1 and Fig. 4, respectively. Note that we report the results of recall, precision and F-measure for clean, polluted water images (with

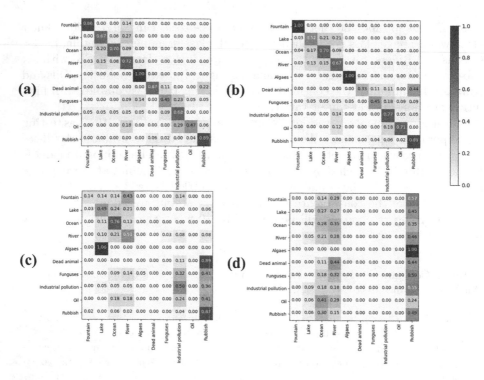

Fig. 4. Confusion matrices on classification for 10 classes of clean and polluted water images, where (a)–(d) refer to result of the proposed method, the proposed method without attention, [11] and [3], respectively.

four and six classes) and accuracy for total water images (with ten classes) in Table. 1. We can be seen that the average accuracy performance of the proposed method is the best compared to the existing methods. The main reason of [3] to get poor results is that the descriptors used in [3] are not robust to classify clean and polluted water images. In fact, [3] is initially designed to perform water detection in videos and requires high contrast and clear object shapes to get higher accuracy. The presence of irregular objects in polluted images, such as rubbish, oil and dead animals, thus leads to poor classification results. [11] takes advantages of HSV and Fourier spectrum to extract distinguish features in frequency domain to overcome the shortages of irregular objects, which results in a much better performance than [3].

Quantity of complex patterns of clean and polluted water images are hard to classify with a single manually designed feature. This could be proved by Fig. 4(c), where misclassification rate of dead animal to rubbish is as high as 0.89 and meanwhile correctness rate of rubbish is as high as 0.87. The reason to achieve good performance for rubbish and bad performance for dead animal is the high sensitivity and effectiveness of the manual designed feature for rubbish other than dead animals. Furthermore, the small inter-class variations between rubbish and dead animals and high intra-class variations of rubbish make the

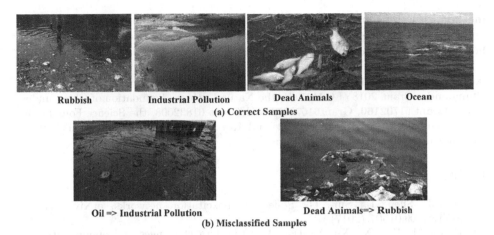

(a) Correct Samples

(b) Misclassified Samples

Fig. 5. Samples of correct and misclassified classification results of clean and polluted water images achieved by the proposed method.

classification more difficult. We thus propose to encode channel-wise and multi-layer 3D feature maps in CNN as pattern detectors to perform ambiguous classification. High performance of the proposed with or without attention in Table. 1 and Fig. 4 prove the efficiency and robustness of the deep learning structure. By designing channel-wise and hierarchical attention model, we further involve features to automatically focus on informative and multi-level visual abstractions. It's obvious that the proposed hierarchial attention model improves performance in classification of clear water images. This is due to the highly visual resemblance of sub-classes of clear water images, which requires low-level features to assist the classification. However, utilizing low-level features might bring noise to classification with clear inter-class variations, which results in a bit decrease in recall of classification of polluted water images.

Sample qualitative results of the proposed method for correct and misclassified water images are shown in Fig. 5(a) and (b), respectively. From the correct samples, we can notice the proposed method is robust enough to classify clean and polluted water images correctly. For misclassified water images, we can clearly view the main difficulty of the task, *i.e.*, small inter-class variations, especially between oil and industrial pollution, dead animals and rubbish. Moreover, unbalance numbers of training samples promote to wrong results as well, since the number of collected rubbish images in dataset is much larger than that of dead animals. Therefore, there is a scope for future work to overcome this issue.

4   Conclusion

In this paper, we propose a novel hierarchically channel-wise attention model incorporating with CNN structure for clean and polluted water images classification. Experimental results on a latest water image dataset with several comparative methods demonstrate the effectiveness and robustness of the proposed method for water image classification. Our future work includes the explorations on implementing the proposed method in water pollution monitoring system to help instantly monitor, control and abate water pollution.

Acknowledgment. This work was supported by National Key R&D Program of China under Grant 2018YFC0407901, the Natural Science Foundation of China under Grant Grant 61702160, Grant61672273 and Grant 61832008, the Science Foundation of Jiangsu under Grant BK20170892, and Key R&D Program Projects in Jiangsu Province under Grant BE2015707.

References

1. Hu, J., Shen, L., Sun, G.: Squeeze-and-excitation networks. arXiv preprint arXiv:1709.01507 (2017)
2. Khan, M., Wu, X., Xu, X., Dou, W.: Big data challenges and opportunities in the hype of industry 4.0. In: Proceedings of IEEE International Conference on Communications, pp. 1–6 (2017)
3. Mettes, P., Tan, R.T., Veltkamp, R.C.: Water detection through spatio-temporal invariant descriptors. Comput. Vis. Image Underst. **154**, 182–191 (2017)
4. Mnih, V., Heess, N., Graves, A., Kavukcuoglu, K.: Recurrent models of visual attention. In: Proceedings of NIPS, pp. 2204–2212 (2014)
5. Prasad, M.G., Chakraborty, A., Chalasani, R., Chandran, S.: Quadcopter-based stagnant water identification. In: Proceedings of Fifth National Conference on Computer Vision, Pattern Recognition, Image Processing and Graphics (NCVPRIPG), pp. 1–4 (2015)
6. Qi, L., Chen, Y., Yuan, Y., Fu, S., Zhang, X., Xu, X.: A QoS-aware virtual machine scheduling method for energy conservation in cloud-based cyber-physical systems. World Wide Web, pp. 1–23 (2019)
7. Qi, L., et al.: Finding all you need: web APIs recommendation in web of things through keywords search. IEEE Trans. Comput. Soc. Syst. **6**(5), 1063–1072 (2019)
8. Qi, X., Li, C.G., Zhao, G., Hong, X., Pietikäinen, M.: Dynamic texture and scene classification by transferring deep image features. Neurocomputing **171**, 1230–1241 (2016)
9. Rankin, A.L., Matthies, L.H., Bellutta, P.: Daytime water detection based on sky reflections. In: Proceedings of ICRA, pp. 5329–5336 (2011)
10. Santana, P., Mendonça, R., Barata, J.: Water detection with segmentation guided dynamic texture recognition. In: Proceedings of IEEE International Conference on Robotics and Biomimetics (ROBIO), pp. 1836–1841 (2012)
11. Wu, X., Shivakumara, P., Zhu, L., Lu, T., Pal, U., Blumenstein, M.: Fourier transform based features for clean and polluted water image classification. In: Proceedings of International Conference on Pattern Recognition (2018)
12. Xu, X., Liu, Q., Zhang, X., Zhang, J., Qi, L., Dou, W.: A blockchain-powered crowdsourcing method with privacy preservation in mobile environment. In: IEEE Transactions on Computational Social Systems (2019)
13. Xu, X., Zhang, X., Gao, H., Xue, Y., Qi, L., Dou, W.: Become: blockchain-enabled computation offloading for iot in mobile edge computing. In: IEEE Transactions on Industrial Informatics (2019)
14. Zhao, W., Du, S.: Spectral-spatial feature extraction for hyperspectral image classification: a dimension reduction and deep learning approach. IEEE Trans. Geosci. Rem. Sens. **54**(8), 4544–4554 (2016)

Energy-Efficient Approximate Data Collection and BP-Based Reconstruction in UWSNs

Yuanyuan Liu[1], Xiaohui Wei[1], Lina Li[1,2], and Xingwang Wang[1(✉)]

[1] College of Computer Science and Technology, Jilin University, Changchun, China
liuyuanyuan16@mails.com, {weixh,xww}@jlu.edu.cn, linal11@mails.jlu.edu.cn
[2] Economics and Management Cadres College of Jilin Province, Changchun, China

Abstract. Approximate data collection that has been extensively studied in Terrestrial Wireless Sensor Networks (TWSNs) can be leveraged in underwater scenarios. However, it is challenging to balance between energy cost and data quality because timely quality feedback strategies applicable in TWSNs may not be suitable for underwater scenarios constrained by long acoustic delay.

Faced with high-frequency packet failure, we first formulate the problem of selecting the minimum sensing node set into a minimum m-dominating set problem that is known to be NP-hard, and then propose a heuristic Center-based Active Sensor Selection (CASS) algorithm for approximate data collection with the consideration of node correlation and residual energy. With the computing ability of the cloud, Belief Propagation (BP) is utilized to infer missing data. Evaluation based on real-world datasets shows our proposed approximate collection strategy can reduce 60% more energy cost with little accuracy loss.

Keywords: Underwater wireless sensor network · Approximate data collection · Data quality · m-dominating set

1 Introduction

Underwater data collection is of great significance for underwater exploration applied in various fields, such as environment monitoring for pollution detection or disaster prediction [1]. Underwater Wireless Sensor Networks (UWSNs) are increasingly applied for (near) real-time data monitoring and collection due to the cooperative communication capabilities by acoustic, optical or electromagnetic wireless techniques [2]. As the rapid development of the Internet of Things (IoTs), the explosive growing data brings dual challenges for efficient data collection to achieve low energy consumption while ensuring data quality.

Supported by National Natural Science Foundation of China (NSFC) (Grant No.61772228).

M. Qiu (Ed.): SmartCom 2019, LNCS 11910, pp. 93–104, 2019.
https://doi.org/10.1007/978-3-030-34139-8_10

It is known that the propagation speed for an acoustic link is about 1,500 meters/sec, which is five orders of magnitude lower than that of a radio link. Hence, underwater acoustic communication in UWSNs consumes much higher energy cost than terrestrial radio communication. Recharging and replacing battery for underwater sensors is also difficult, and data retransmission designed in dedicated transfer protocols cause extra energy cost. To alleviate the usage of limited power, approximate data collection is an efficient scheme to optimize energy consumed for sensing and communication. Approximate strategies aim to only transmit partial data to represent all of the data, and in this case we do not need to set all sensor to work or deliver every raw sensing value.

Moreover, it is acknowledged that the collected data in the adjacent temporal or same spatial regions are high-correlated. The correlation feature of sensing data enables us to approximately collect data by mathematical prediction models (e.g., least mean square [3], Compressive Sensing (CS) [13]). However, these methods are efficient for simple scenarios or with some preconditions. For instance, CS-based methods assume the measurement matrixes are sparse [4], which may not be practical in some WSN scenarios. As the connection of cloud and IoT systems, more statistical learning models, such as belief propagation (BP) [6], can be used to exploit complicated correlations where the process of data inference/prediction is transferred from nodes to the clouds.

First, we model the problem of selecting sensing sensors as a process of constructing a most representative dominating set taking both the residual energy and node correlation into account. It's known that data transmission in UWSNs is prone to high-frequency data loss affected by harsh underwater environments (e.g., ambient noise, packet failure) that may lower the quality of the collected data and cause failure prediction or analysis. To assure data quality, the sensor selection should assure sufficient data are collected at the initial sensing phase. To address the problem, we utilize the idea of fault-tolerant nodes where the sensor selection problem is converted as a minimum m-dominating problem, which is known to be NP-hard [5]. With the pre-learning correlation information in the center, we propose a heuristic-based sensor selection algorithm where the node with largest weights are greedily selected as a dominating node. Here the node weight is defined by modeling the combined factor of energy cost and node influence.

With the computing ability of cloud resources, data inference, evaluation and improvement are performed at the end of each cycle. For missing data, we use a well known algorithm, BP [6], to perform inference by a graphical model. Using BP is efficient and it has the ability of integrating multiple correlations (e.g, temporal, spatial, multivariate) to provide high inference accuracy. The contributions of this paper are the following:

(1) we first model the sensor selection problem in UWSNs as a multi-objective optimization problem, and propose a heuristic sensor selection algorithm to solve the problem.

(2) By modeling temporal, spatial and data correlation, we use Belief Propagation (BP) algorithm to infer uncollected and missing data.

(3) Experiments with real-world data are conducted to validate the efficiency of our approximate sensor selection and data reconstruction strategies.

2 Problem Formulation

Assume there are $S = \{s_1, s_2, \cdots, s_n\}$ sensors, and the i-th sensor s_i is anchored at the location coordinate $l_i = [l_i^x, l_i^y, l_i^z]$. All data collected by the sensor network can be written as $\mathbb{D}$, which corresponds to an approximate dataset, $\widehat{\mathbb{D}}$. We then use a graph $G = (V, E)$ to model the sensor network, where V means the vertex set of sensor nodes, and E means the set of edge.

Given a data collection task with C cycles, let x_i^c be a binary decision variable. $x_i^c = 1$ if sensor s_i is selected at cycle c, and $x_i^c = 0$ otherwise. Let $E_r(i)$ be the residual energy of sensor s_i and $E_c(i)$ be the energy cost of s_i if it is selected in a cycle. At the end of each cycle, the cloud-based center uses collected data to deduce the missing data. Denoted the inference error as $\mathcal{E}_c(\mathbb{D}, \widehat{\mathbb{D}})$, we need to compare it with the specified error constraint ϵ.

Considering the tradeoff between data quality and energy consumption, we dynamically select a subset of sensor nodes with the objective of maximizing residual energy and the constraint of quality requirements. Except for the energy cost, it is also desired to choose most representative nodes by which uncollected data can be well estimated. Intuitively, the selection strategy gives priority to those nodes that are highly associated with their neighbors. Here we define the node influence, denoted as NI, to represent the extent how the node affects other nodes. Our second objective is to max the total node influence:

Hence, we model a multi-objective optimization problem for the sensor selection:

$$\text{Objective} \quad \max \quad \sum_{c=1}^{C}\sum_{i=1}^{S} E_r(i) \cdot x_i^c, \quad \sum_{c=1}^{C}\sum_{i=1}^{S} NI(i) \tag{1}$$

$$\text{Subject to} \quad E_r(i) - E_c(i) \cdot x_i^c \geq E_{thr}, \quad \forall i \in n; \ \forall c \in C \tag{1a}$$

$$\mathcal{E}_c(\mathbb{D}, \widehat{\mathbb{D}}) \leq \epsilon, \quad \forall c \in C \tag{1b}$$

Constraint (1a) means that the consumed energy cannot exceed its low threshold. The value of $E_c(i)$ depends on the size of dataset, $\widehat{\mathbb{D}}_i$, collected by node s_i. In our scenario, we assume the transmission path of a deployed node is fixed so that we can estimate $E_c(i)$ by data size. Let p_i^{in} and p_i^{out} be the energy consumption of sensor s_i on transmitting and receiving through acoustic channels, respectively. There is:

$$E_c(i) = p_i^{out} + \sum_{k \in path(i)} (p_k^{in} + p_k^{out}) \tag{2}$$

where p_i^{out} or p_i^{in} can be estimated using Urick Propagation Model [7] that includes two acoustic propagation mechanisms. One is cylindrical spreading for the shallow water (depth ≤ 100 m) and the other is spherical spreading for the deep water. In our paper, we consider the energy consumption of the second case.

Constraint (1b) requires the overall error should not exceed the predefined error bound. In TWSNs or other IoT-based networks (e.g., crowdsensing), it's feasible to construct a real-time feedback mechanism to ensure data quality with the high speed communication [4]. In the mechanism, the decision maker will select more sensors to send collected data if the current estimated quality does not satisfy the predefined requirement. However, the mechanism is not practical for underwater networks, which is constrained by long propagation delay. To ensure the data quality, the selected sensors need to provide sufficient collected data as possible in the initial collection cycle.

When combining the usage of dominating set in wireless networks, the problem can be further converted into the problem of constructing a minimum dominating set based on learning correlation information. Compared with communication in TWSNs, data loss in underwater transmission is much more frequency as mentioned in Sect. 1. Inspired by the construction of fault-tolerant virtual backbone in WSNs, we formulate the problem of sensor selection into a minimum m-dominating set problem. The selected node subset has a certain degree of redundancy to alleviate the effect of data loss caused by routing failure on the inference quality. The quality constraint (1b) is converted to the expression of m-dominating set:

$$x_i^c + \frac{1}{m} \sum_{j \in N(i)} x_j^c \geq 1, \quad \forall i \in n; \ \forall c \in C \tag{3}$$

where Eq. (3) requires unselected sensors are represented by at least m selected sensors. Before making selection decisions, there is an off-line learning to obtain the initial setting of m by historical collected data [8]. The value of m also depends on the loss rate of the final collected data where we consider the average loss rate.

3   Approximate Data Collection

In this section, we propose a greedy sensor selection algorithm for approximate data collection. First we make correlation analysis that are used to evaluate the node influence and construct graph model in BP inference.

3.1   Correlation Analysis

We introduce temporal-spatial correlations commonly used in modeling sensor networks, and also consider the correlation of multi-dimensional parameters [4]:

(1) *Temporal correlation*: The correlation between the observation at time t and $t - 1$ can be defined as:

$$\psi_i^t(t, t - 1) \triangleq exp\left(-\frac{(d_i^t - d_i^{t-1})^2}{\sigma_i^2}\right) \tag{4}$$

(2) *Spatial correlation*: Generally, the closer two sensors, the more similar collected data are. We compute the Euclidean distance between two nearby sensors to model their spatial correlations. Similarly, the normalized function with range [0,1] is:

$$\psi^{dis}(i, j) \triangleq exp\left(-\frac{\|l_i - l_j\|_2}{\sigma_{ij}^2}\right) \tag{5}$$

where $\|l_i - l_j\|_2 = \sqrt{(l_i^x - l_j^x)^2 + (l_i^y - l_j^y)^2 + (l_i^z - l_j^z)^2}$. The parameters σ_i^2, σ_{ij}^2 can be learned from training data.

(3) *Data correlation*: In heterogeneous IoT networks, generally sensing data are multivariate. For instance, underwater environmental parameters include temperature, salinity, conductivity. Let d_i, d_j be the data vectors of sensors s_i and s_j in different dimensions and the cosine similarity between two vectors is:

$$\psi^{da}(i, j) \triangleq \frac{d_i \cdot d_j}{\|d_i\| \cdot \|d_j\|} \tag{6}$$

The off-line phase utilizes historical data to learn the node correlation $\psi(i, j)$. Here we jointly consider the distance and data similarity with its neighbors:

$$\psi(i, j) = \alpha \cdot \psi^{dis}(i, j) + (1 - \alpha) \cdot \psi^{da}(i, j) \tag{7}$$

where $\alpha \in [0, 1]$ is a tradeoff factor to adjust the weight between the spatial and data correlations.

Modeling NI. The main idea is to model the impact of the node on other neighbor nodes where we consider the interaction between nodes:

$$NI(i) = \sum_{j \in N(i)} \psi(i, j) \left(\frac{\psi(i, j)}{\sum\limits_{k \in N(j)} \psi(k, j)}\right) \tag{8}$$

Algorithm 1. Centralized Active Sensor Selection in UWSNs (**CASS**)

Input : E_{thr}, $E_r(i)$, m;
Output: a node set with *selected* status;

1 Initialize dominant value $Dom = m$ for each node, add all node in *pending* list;
2 Compute node influence $NI(i)$ using Eq. (8);
3 Update $E_r(i)$ and compute $w(s_i)$ for each sensor node s_i according to Eq. (9);
4 Descending sort $w(s_i)$;
5 **while** *pending is not empty* **do**
6      $j = \arg \max \{w(s_i)|i \in pending\}$;
7   Delete node j from *pending*;
8   Modify the status of node j as *selected* and $Dom(j) = 0$;
9   **for** *all neighbor nodes* $k \in N(j)$ **do**
10 | $Dom(k) \leftarrow Dom(k) - 1$;
11   **end**
12   **if** $Dom(k) == 0$ **then**
13 | Mark node k as *unselected*, delete node k from *pending*;
14   **end**
15 **end**
16 **return** *selected* node set

3.2 Centralized Active Sensor Selection Algorithm (CASS)

To solve the optimization problem of Eq. (1), the two objectives, energy cost and node correlations, are put together to represent the selection priority:

$$w(s_i) = \beta \cdot e^{-\frac{E_{thr}}{E_r(i)}} + (1 - \beta) \cdot NI(i) \tag{9}$$

where $\beta \in [0, 1]$ determines the proportion of two objectives in the weight function.

Although the distributed algorithm is flexible, it requires the pre-learning of priori knowledge is operated by sensors and each node needs to store historical data about itself and its neighbors. Considering the limited storage and computing resources, we make the sensor selection strategy determined by the center. The heuristic-based algorithm (CASS) greedily search nodes based on their weights. In the algorithm description, the status of sensor node can be divided into three types: *selected, pending, unselected*. Correlated parameters are updated, including $NI(i)$, $E_r(i)$, and $w(s_i)$. Based on the estimated energy cost and pre-learning node correlations, the algorithm calculates nodes' weights and sort the weights in descending order. In each round, the algorithm chooses the node with a largest weight in the *pending* list as the dominator node and add it into *selected* set. At the moment, its neighbors are dominated at least one node, so the dominant value of neighbors is reduced by one. If the dominant value after minus is 0, the node can be dominated by m nodes and marked as *unselected*. The algorithm ends when the *pending* list is empty. At last, all nodes are marked as *selected* or *unselected*.

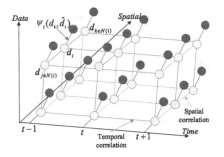

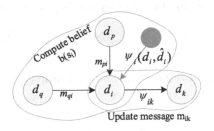

Fig. 1. The constructed MRF graph model.

Fig. 2. The illustration of iterative message update and belief computation.

4 Data Reconstruction by Belief Propagation

In this paper, using BP aims to infer measurements about uncollected data as well as missing data caused by packet failures.

4.1 Belief Propagation

Before introducing BP algorithm, we first import a graphical model known as Markov random fields (MRF) [6] to represent the correlations between sensing data. Figure 1 shows a MRF graph model with undirected edges that illustrates both temporal and spatial correlation defined in Sect. 3.1. We use the white node to represent a hidden data value (true value) and the blue node to represent the observation, respectively denoted as d_i, $\hat{d}_i$. The edge between two hidden nodes i and j means that they have statistical dependencies, encoded by the potential function ψ_{ij}. The dependency between the observation node is expressed by the evidence function ψ_i. Based on the Hammersley-Clifford theorem, we can jointly infer the hidden information using the joint probability distribution function:

$$P(S) = \prod_i \psi_i(d_i, \hat{d}_i) \prod_{ij} \psi_{ij}(d_i, d_j) \tag{10}$$

The basic principle of BP is to compute the margin probability distribution of each hidden node by a message passing algorithm. The message from node i to j is updated based on the local neighbor information, which is defined as

$$m_{ij} \propto \int \psi_i(d_i, \hat{d}_i)\psi_{ij}(d_i, d_j) \prod_{k \in N(i), k \neq j} m_{ki}(d_i) \tag{11}$$

where m_{ki} represents the incoming message from the neighbors of node i except for node j. The message update is an iteration process where messages from previous iteration are the input of computing the current message in each iteration. BP performs message update until Eq. (11) converges after enough or pre-set iterations. Thus, the estimated marginal probabilities (*belief*) of each node is computing by all neighbors's passing messages and the local belief, that is

$$belief(d_i) = \psi_i(d_i, \hat{d}_i) \prod_{k \in N(i)} m_{ki}(d_i) \tag{12}$$

Figure 2 shows the belief propagation process where we illustrate the case of message update between s_i and s_k and belief computation of s_i.

4.2   Data Inference Using BP

From the process of belief computation formulated in Eqs. (10)–(12), we first need to estimate the potential functions and evidence function. When corresponding to the constructed graph showed in Fig. 1, the potential function is modeled by spatial, temporal and also data correlations. The evidence function depends on the difference between the observed and true readings.

The temporal potential function refers to Eq. (4) according to the correlation analysis of Sect. 3.1. We combine the spatial and data function using Eq. (7) that jointly considers data correlation from distance and data similarity. Taken together, the potential function is:

$$\psi_{ij}(d_i, d_j) = [\psi_i^t(t, t-1), \psi(i, j)] \tag{13}$$

For the evidence function $\psi_i(d_i, \hat{d}_i)$, the correlation between the true reading and observation can be defined based on Gaussian Kernel [9]:

$$\psi_i(d_i, \hat{d}_i) = exp\left(-\frac{(d_i - \hat{d}_i)^2}{\sigma_i^2}\right) \tag{14}$$

where the state of data missing need to be considered separately. If data is missing, the evidence function is set a constant [8] , i.e., $\psi_i^e(d_i, \hat{d}_i) = 1$, for all observations $\hat{d}_i$ where missing data mean uncollected, collected but missing during transmission.

5   Evaluation

We now evaluate the performance of our proposed approximate data collection strategy. In the underwater network simulation, sensors are randomly deployed in a 3D grid space of 3.33 km × 3 km × 200 m , which is divided with a number of 6 × 5 × 5 (Latitude × longitude × depth). The data transmission rate is set 2000 bit/s. The initial energy is 100 J and the low energy threshold is 10 J. The powers of receiving and sending data are 0.03 W, 0.67 W, respectively.

5.1   Experiment Setup

Datasets. We use real-world datasets collected from Global Argo Dataset Index and Query System [10] as original datasets. We consider both the data collection simulation for one-dimensional and multi-dimensional data. We download datasets gathered at 123^oE–126^oE, 21^oN–24^oN from January 2005 to December 2012 that record the information including timestamp, depth, longitude and latitude. We also select heat content data that has the same latitude-longitude and time period with the first temperature datasets.

Comparison Algorithms and Methods. To evaluate the performance of CASS, we compare it with several baseline algorithms: (1). *Random*, sensor nodes are selected randomly at each collection cycle. (2). *Max Degree (MD)*, each time the method selects nodes with largest out degree as the dominate node. (3). *Max Energy-Degree coefficient (MED)*, we consider the combined influence between the residual energy and out degree ,which is considered in [11]. (4). *No approximation*, we also simulate data collection process with all senors active. To evaluate the performance of data inference, we compare BP inference with *KNN* [12] ($K = 6$), *Compression Sensing(CS)* [13] and *Gaussian process (GP)* [14].

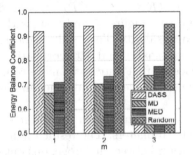

Fig. 3. The comparison of energy balance coefficients.

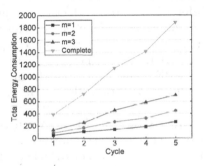

Fig. 4. Total energy consumption during 5 cycles.

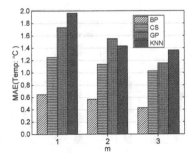

Fig. 5. Missing value inference error for Temperature

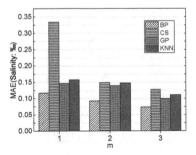

Fig. 6. Missing value inference error for Salinity

5.2   Performance Analysis

Energy Consumption Analysis. We compute the energy balance coefficient to evaluate the network lifetime that has significant impact on the network performance. The equation is $\sum_{i\in\{selected\}} \frac{E_r(i)}{E_{avg}\cdot|selected|}$. Figure 3 shows the comparison of balance coefficients. Among these methods, CASS is much better than ME and MED and is close to the random selection method. The reason is that CASS considers the tradeoff between residual energy and node influence by modeling temporal-spatial as well as data correlations, which helps to choose active nodes of each cycle more evenly while MED tends to select nodes with larger degrees. To show the energy saving with approximate data collection, Fig. 4 shows the total energy consumption with the increasing collection cycle. The experiment simulates five-cycle data collection task with different dominating sets. The total energy cost with CASS is less than $1/6$ of the complete data collection when setting $m = 1$ and less than $1/3$ when setting $m = 3$.

Approximate Inference Analysis. Then we evaluate the performance of the BP inference methods with other common methods (KNN, CS, GP) introduced in Sect. 5.1 using the metric of mean absolute error. Figures 5 and 6 show the missing value inference errors for temperature and salinity. The results indicate BP outperforms other methods. With the temporal-spatial and data correlations in the MRF graph structures, the inference process of BP integrates more comprehensive information. Hence, BP can perform more accurate inference in our settings.

Figure 7 shows the MAE (Mean Absolute Error) comparison for the missing value inference with multivariate correlated parameters. The result further validates the advantage of BP where the correlation between heterogenous data contributes to the inference of multi-dimensional data. Other methods only consider temporal or/and spatial correlations and do not exploit the inherent data correlations that is significant especially for high-correlated data. Figure 8 shows the error comparison with and without considering data correlation when using

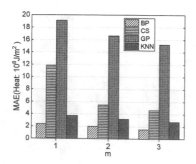

Fig. 7. Missing value inference error for heat content

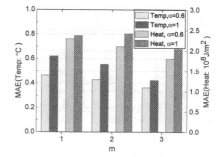

Fig. 8. MAE comparison with and without data correlation ψ^{da}

BP to simultaneously estimate missing data about temperature and heat content. When setting $m = 2$, the mean error decreases by 23.8% for temperature and 13% for heat. The results also verify the analysis of data correlations can improve inference accuracy.

6 Conclusion

In this paper, we propose an energy-efficient approximate data collection strategy in UWSNs. To design efficient data collection strategy, the specific features of underwater scenarios, long propagation delay and high-frequency packet failure, cannot be ignored. Taking these features into account, we formulate the sensor selection problem as a minimum m-dominating problem and design a heuristic distributed algorithm by integrating two factors of energy cost and node correlations. Then missing values are inferred with the belief propagation method. The simulation results with real-world ocean datasets validate the effectiveness of our proposed approximate strategy.

References

1. Heidemann, J., Stojanovic, M., Zorzi, M.: Underwater sensor networks: applications, advances and challenges. Philos. Trans. R. Soc. A Math. Phys. Eng. Sci. **370**(1958), 158–175 (2012)
2. Garcia, M., Sendra, S., Atenas, M., Lloret, J.: Underwater wireless ad-hoc networks: a survey. In: Mobile Ad hoc Networks: Current Status and Future Trends, pp. 379–411 (2011)
3. Wu, M., Tan, L., Xiong, N.: Data prediction, compression, and recovery in clustered wireless sensor networks for environmental monitoring applications. Inf. Sci. **329**, 800–818 (2016)
4. He, S., Shin, K.G.: Steering crowdsourced signal map construction via bayesian compressive sensing. In: IEEE INFOCOM 2018-IEEE Conference on Computer Communications, pp. 1016–1024. IEEE (2018)
5. Dai, F., Wu, J.: On constructing k-connected k-dominating set in wireless networks. In: 2005 Proceedings of the 19th IEEE International Parallel and Distributed Processing Symposium, p. 10. IEEE (2005)
6. Yedidia, J.S., Freeman, W.T., Weiss, Y.: Understanding belief propagation and its generalizations. Exploring Artif. Intell. New Millennium **8**, 236–239 (2003)
7. Etter, P.C.: Underwater Acoustic Modeling and Simulation. CRC Press, Boca Raton (2018)
8. Bijarbooneh, F.H., Du, W., Ngai, E.C.-H., Fu, X., Liu, J.: Cloud-assisted data fusion and sensor selection for Internet-of-things. IEEE Internet Things J. **3**(3), 257–268 (2016)
9. Takeda, H., Farsiu, S., Milanfar P., et al.: Kernel regression for image processing and reconstruction. Ph.D. dissertation, Citeseer (2006)
10. An, Y., Li, C., Wang, G., Zhang, R., Wang, H.: User's manual of global Argo dataset index and query system (version 1.0)", p. 11 (2012)
11. Hong, Z., Pan, X., Chen, P., Su, X., Wang, N., Lu, W.: A topology control with energy balance in underwater wireless sensor networks for IoT-based application. Sensors **18**(7), 2306 (2018)

12. Pan, L., Li, J.: K-nearest neighbor based missing data estimation algorithm in wireless sensor networks. Wirel. Sens. Netw. **2**(02), 115 (2010)
13. Kong, L., Xia, M., Liu, X.-Y., Wu, M.-Y., Liu, X.: Data loss and reconstruction in sensor networks. In: Proceedings IEEE INFOCOM, pp. 1654–1662. IEEE (2013)
14. Yen, H.-C., Wang, C.-C.: Cross-device Wi-Fi map fusion with gaussian processes. IEEE Trans. Mob. Comput. **16**(1), 44–57 (2016)

I2P Anonymous Communication Network Measurement and Analysis

Likun Liu[1]([✉]), Hongli Zhang[1], Jiantao Shi[1], Xiangzhan Yu[1],
and Haixiao Xu[2]

[1] Harbin Institute of Technology, Harbin HRB, China
liulikun@stu.hit.edu.cn,
{zhanghongli,shijiantao,yuxiangzhan}@hit.edu.cn
[2] Jilin University, Changchun CC, China
haixiao@jlu.edu.cn

Abstract. The I2P (Invisible Internet Project) network is a low-latency anonymous network composed of I2P routers based on garlic routing, which is mainly to protect privacy and prevent tracking, such as evading censorship and hiding whistle-blowers. As opposed to well-known and well-research Tor network, I2P aims to organize itself and distribute its anonymity. To our best knowledge, the study of I2P measurements is still insufficient. Thus, this paper proposed a novel method to measure I2P anonymous network nodes, including passive measurement and active measurement, and designed a local I2P node analysis system. Through experiments, we collected 16040 I2P nodes and analyzed properties including country distribution, bandwidth distribution and FloodingFill node attributes.

Keywords: Anonymous communication network · I2P · Network
Measurement · Network security · Smart Communication

1 Introduction

Network security has attracted more and more attention in recent years, such as cloud security [1], Internet of Things security [2, 3] and mobile security [4]. To anonymous communications over the Internet is a very active field. Anonymous network communication system is designed to provide anonymous network communications services that users cannot be identified by third-party entities. There are three aspects of anonymous communication: sender anonymity, recipient anonymity, and relationship anonymity. Anonymous communication is also a double-edged sword. The normal users can protect their personal privacy through anonymous communication system, while the malicious users can also use the anonymous communication system to carry out some illegal activities. For example, the DDOS attack is implemented through anonymous communication, and it is very difficult to trace the source.

TOR and I2P are well-known anonymous network. TOR aims to allow users to access the Internet anonymously and allows them to access restricted or blocked services. I2P is quite similar to TOR Project [5]. I2P is designed to protect messages inside

© Springer Nature Switzerland AG 2019
M. Qiu (Ed.): SmartCom 2019, LNCS 11910, pp. 105–115, 2019.
https://doi.org/10.1007/978-3-030-34139-8_11

its network, so the access is granted to all participants. To gather facts about the structure and size of the I2P network, this paper makes the following contributions:

1. We proposed a combined measurement method, which includes passive measurement and active measurement. In this approach, passive measurement can collect most nodes, while active measurement is its complement, and its input is the result set of passive measurement. This combination greatly reduces the number of missing nodes in a single measurement.
2. According to the measurement results, we analyzed the I2P network from six aspects including key space distribution, subnet, country distribution, bandwidth distribution, software version distribution, and FloodingFill node attributes.
3. We discussed the vulnerability of I2P network and proposed a security optimization scheme.

2   Related Work

Onion Routing, which has a significant effect in establishing low-latency communication system. The sender only knows the address information of the next hop. The intermediate node only knows the address information of the previous hop and the next hop. Each node on the transmission path has only partial node information. In this way, the identity of both parties to the communication is hidden. On the basis of Onion Routing, another kind of routing method is Garlic Routing [2], which is employed by I2P anonymous communication system. I2P anonymous communication system adopts Garlic Routing [6] to construct dark network. Many anonymous services are installed in the belly of I2P system, such as eepsite, torrent (I2P snark), and anonymous email (susimail). The garlic packets can carry multiple packets each time. I2P anonymous communication system [7–14] implements the communication through a tunnel mechanism, and Ye et al. [15] considered the user's preferences, they proposed two user-oriented node selection algorithms to meet the individual demands of specific user. But in the onion routing [10, 11], the data link is full-duplex, the sent and received data are transmitted in the same link. For Garlic Routing, when the party wants to send information, it first creates an outbound tunnel and sends the information to the inbound tunnel of the receiver. Therefore, participants in the network can set the length of their tunnels to make the balance of anonymity, latency, and bandwidth.

In order to measure the size of the I2P anonymous communication network, Liu et al. [12] presented an empirical measurement, and Zincir-Heywood et al. [13] focused on factors for measuring anonymity services. However, the measurement of nodes has been going on for several years, with the change of network environment, new measurement methods and data are necessary. Recently, Hoang et al. [16] measured some properties of I2P network. Using the collected data, they examined the blocking resistance of I2P against a censor that wants to prevent access to I2P using address-based blocking techniques. Nevertheless, I2P node measurement relies only on passive measurement. Thus, this paper proposed a measurement method that a combination of active acquisition and passive acquisition, and passive results can be applied as an active input. We analyzed the results from multiple perspectives after measurement.

Although I2P can communicate anonymously, researchers can still find its vulnerability. An I2P monitoring study [17], to identify published I2P applications and characterize the usage of I2P network, showed that web servers and file-sharing clients accounted for a great proportion. Herrmann et al. [18] presented an attack to deanonymization based on peer selection, that the adversary controlled nodes by launching a DoS attack to force target to choose peers. Recently, an USB side-channel attack on Tor [19] was proposed, which is also effective for I2P anonymous network.

In addition to the security issues discovered by these researchers, this paper analyzed the remaining vulnerability of I2P from three aspects, including brute-force attack, collusion attack and heavy traffic attack. After that, we provided theoretical countermeasures.

3 I2P Network Node Measurement

3.1 System Architecture

The I2P network node measurement analysis system is mainly used to measure I2P nodes, analyze the network characteristics and node attributes. The system is mainly composed of two subsystems, one is a node measurement capture subsystem, and the other is a node attribute analysis subsystem. The system architecture is shown in Fig. 1.

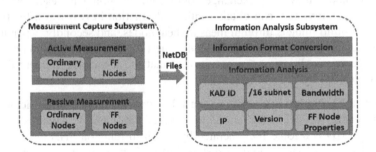

Fig. 1. System architecture

Node measurement capture subsystem: there are two measurement methods which are active measurement and passive measurement. Each measurement covers ordinary node (also called router node) and FF (FloodingFill) node.

1. Active measurement can capture I2P node by setting the value of "donotincludePeers". The capture system sends DLM (DataBaseLookupMessage) to the known FF node in local database, and then obtains the node from the reply packet. And then, measure these acquired nodes.
2. Passive measurement can capture I2P node by setting the value of "router.floodfillParticipant". If true, the local node is disguised as a FF node, and false is an ordinary node. It collects information of other ordinary nodes that communicate with the local node or exchange routing information. Finally, the collected nodes

are saved to the local Network Database for analysis of their node attributes. Network Database, also known as NetDB, built on top of Kademlia, which stores two kinds of information: Routers and LeaseSets. To observe FloodFill router, we add a FloodFill Routers to the NetDB.

Node attribute analysis subsystem: extract and preprocess the acquired data from the captured node above, and analyze data from six aspects, Key Space distribution, country distribution, distribution of IP addresses on the/16 subnet, bandwidth distribution, distribution of I2P software version and FloodFill node attribute. Finally, it is expressed in the form of a web page HTML, and the daily average value of the data is converted into a monthly attribute value.

3.2 Measurement Capture Subsystem

- **Passive Measurement**

Passive measurement can set the measurement node as ordinary node and FF node to measure traffic. We deploy multiple I2P measurement nodes to collect information at same time. The collected information served as the initial node library for active measurement.

Running as an Ordinary I2P Node: When an I2P node communicates with a measurement node, they will exchange routing information with each other. More specifically, this subsystem can obtain routing information in two ways. Firstly, other nodes want to build tunnels through measurement nodes, and secondly, when the local route is update, measurement node will send request of building tunnels to other nodes. The convergence condition of the operation is that the local measurement data table remains stable.

Running as a FF Node: Each node in the I2P network contains an ID (identity key) and a rID (routing key). The ID is used to mark its own identity, which is fixed in its life cycle. The rID is a route ID generated by the Hash function SHA256 (ID + date), that is used to calculate the logical distance of each node in the Kad network. To prevent the Sybil attack, all the I2P network nodes will recalculate the rID every 24 h and publish their own information to the closest FF node. Thus, running a FF node can be used as a way to collect I2P nodes. In addition, the communication between any two nodes starts with the exchange of the router information. Therefore, the deployed FF node can acquire any node information that interacts with it.

I2P networks often choose nodes with higher bandwidth as FF nodes, and it takes a period of interaction for a newly started node to switch to FF node. Therefore, if we simply run an I2P node and wait for it become a FF node, a higher bandwidth and a certain amount of time are necessary. Fortunately, in the I2P software configuration file router.config, a configuration statement can be added "router.floodfillParticipant =

true", which forces the I2P node to run in FF mode to collect routing nodes in the I2P network.

- **Active Measurement**

Active measurement is a supplement to passive measurement, whose result set is an input of active measurement. There are two steps: query FF nodes and query router node. For query progress, there are three type packet, DLM (DatabaseLookupMessage) is query request packet, DSM (DatabaseStoreMessage) and DSRM (DatabaseSearchReplyMessage) are query reply packets. The query type depends on a field in DLM called "dontIncludePeers", and which package to reply depends on the match result of FF node. If information matches, reply DSM, else DSRM carries three nodes with the shortest XOR distance.

According to the data published on I2P website, there are about 30000 ordinary nodes, since the FF peers is about 6% of all the ordinary nodes.

According to KAD routing algorithm, one peer prefers to store nearest peers in the ID space. For nearer ID zones, the crawler crawls every zones. For further ID zones, it only crawls the 2^x th zones. We construct a XOR distance prefix list. For FF peers, the list contains $(5 + 32)$ prefix, and for ordinary routers the list contains $(8 + 128)$ prefix. The algorithm 1 describes a crawling method for FF node, while the algorithm 2 for ordinary node.

Algorithm 1: ActiveCrawlFF	
input	InitialPeerSet (The peer set collected by passive methods).
1.	FFPeerSet ← InitialPeerSet
2.	QureyPeerSet ← FFPeerSet
3.	**While** QureyPeerSet is not empty **do**
4.	p ← QureyPeerSet.next();
5.	**For** i ← 1 to 37 **do**
6.	q ← p xor prefix[i];
7.	send DatabaseLookup(q) message for FF peers to p;
8.	**If** (received DatabaseSearchReplyMessage[k] message within timeval) **then**
9.	**If** k is not in FFPeerSet **then**
11.	FFPeerSet.insert(k);
12.	QureyPeerSet.insert(k);
13.	**Endif**
14.	**Endif**
15.	**Endfor**
16.	QureyPeerSet.delete(p);
17.	**Endwhile**
18.	return FFPeerSet

Algorithm 2: ActiveCrawlRouter	
input	FFPeerSet (collected by Algorithm 1).
1.	RouterSet ← ∅
2.	QureyPeerSet ← FFPeerSet
3.	**While** QureyPeerSet is not empty **do**
4.	p ← QureyPeerSet.next();
5.	**For** i ← 1 to 136 **do**
6.	q ← p xor prefix[i];
7.	send DatabaseLookup(q) message for routers to p;
8.	**If** (received DatabaseSearchReplyMessage[k] message within timeval) **then**
9.	**If** k is not in RouterSet **then**
11.	RouterSet.insert(k);
12.	**Endif**
13.	**Endif**
14.	**Endfor**
15.	QureyPeerSet.delete(p);
16.	**Endwhile**
17.	return RouterSet

3.3   Information Analysis Subsystem

There is a lot of information available in the I2P node information. The measurement capture subsystem collects the following information.

1. Number of active nodes: In the NetDB entry, the current number of active nodes can be estimated.
2. Number of nodes in each country: The IP address of the node can be used to confirm the specific address of the running I2P node.
3. Number of FF nodes: In NetDB, the capacity code of published node information assists to identify FF node.
4. The version of the I2P software.
5. The shared bandwidth of each I2P node.
6. Transmission protocol used by data packets.

Table 1. Measurement data.

Time	NetDB	Routers	FloodFill routers	Known leaseSets
09:00	49	4856	29	1930
10:00	136	4599	82	4696
11:00	154	4622	88	5190
12:00	166	4635	92	5893
13:00	177	4635	93	5790
14:00	179	4635	93	5768
15:00	196	4766	100	6236
16:00	267	4777	170	10725
17:00	280	4777	172	10495
18:00	294	4877	177	11177
19:00	308	4915	184	11365
20:00	311	5162	186	11758
21:00	333	5583	202	13421
22:00	345	5583	205	13891
23:00	356	5583	212	14167

Table 1 shows the results of the node analysis program on December 15, 2018. The analysis program runs every 30 min for an analysis. It indicates that the largest known router number of the FF node on the day is 5583, the number of local FF nodes is 212 which accounts for 3.8%, and the total set of leasesets is 14,167. There were 356 NetDB entries at the time. In terms of time, I2P user activity increased rapidly at 11:00, 15:00, 18:00 and 20:00, which can reveal the temporal regularity of I2P user activity in coarse-gained way. For further detailed analysis, pay attention to the next section.

4 Experiments and Analysis

4.1 Experiments Environment

All of the software used in this paper is running on a Windows 10 64-bit system with an Intel(R) Core(TM) i5-3230 M processor, 1 TB hard disk, and 8 GB memory. We borrowed the open source I2P project [8], modified and compiled open source code [9]. And we deployed three measurement nodes in different regions. Finally, a total of 16,040 nodes were collected in this experiments.

Like all other P2P networks, I2P anonymous communication system considers the problem that users cannot connect to I2P network when it first starts the software. To solve it, I2P uses bootstrapping to learn the latest routeInfo, which is known as "re-seeding". The reseeding is that the router fetches a copy of NetDB entries from other sources including regular websites or another router. All known routerInfo files are contained in this copy which is a zip archive. After the system starts, the reseeding is especially helpful as the system has no knowledge about the network at this moment and needs to learn other routerInfo as fast as possible. Knowing the bootstrapping mechanism of I2P, an Internet-scale censorship system can disable the I2P boot-strapping process by blocking access to the reseed servers. The I2P developers have foreseen the situation and update the software to allow for manual reseeding. In fact, the blocking is validated by measuring the reseeding server provided in I2P project. Based on the experiments, we analysis the nodes from three aspects described respectively which are country distribution, bandwidth distribution and FF node attribute.

Based on the experiments, we analysis the nodes from three aspects described respectively in the following sections, which are country distribution, bandwidth distribution and FF node attribute.

4.2   Country Distribution

To map all collected nodes to their respective countries, this paper adopted MaxMind's GeoIP2 [20] database to finish the mapping. We randomly selected 250 I2P nodes and labeled them on Google Maps, as shown in Fig. 2. It clearly reflects the geographic distribution of I2P nodes in the world. North America and Europe are the most anonymous users, followed by Australia. In Asia, there are fewer nodes in Japan, Korea, Hong Kong and India. In particular, few clients use I2P anonymous commu-nication services in China Mainland with a large number of Internet users. This may be due to three reasons. Firstly, most users do not care about privacy. Secondly, these users use VPS to combine IP multiplexing, and thirdly, it may be because of the GreatWall restrictions.

Fig. 2. Geographic distribution of 250 I2P nodes.

4.3   Bandwidth Distribution

After the node in the I2P network started, a bandwidth flag is set according to the network environment. The estimated shared bandwidth flag is indicated by one of seven available letters: K, L, M, N, O, P. The scope of the flag is defined as follows:

$$K \leq 12KBps$$

$$12KBps < L \leq 48KBps$$

$$48KBps < M \leq 64KBps$$

$$64KBps < N \leq 128KBps$$

$$128KBps < O \leq 256KBps$$

$$256KBps < P \leq 2000KBps$$

$$X > 2000KBps$$

We classify the collected I2P nodes according to their bandwidth flags. The classification results are shown in Table 2. Among them, the N-type is the most dominant in the network, accounting for 37%, followed by the O-type, accounting for 29%. Because O-type nodes and P-type nodes have large bandwidth, these two types nodes are most likely to become high-speed nodes, which is more likely to build customer tunnel. Compared with Tor anonymous network, I2P has larger traffic and slower speed. With the increase of network bandwidth in the world, this explains why N-type accounts for largest proportion, not P-type or X-type. Bandwidth Distribution of I2P nodes.

Table 2. Bandwidth distribution of I2P nodes.

Type	N	O	L	P	M	K
Rate(%)	37	29	18	14	2	0

4.4   FloodingFill Node Attribute Analysis

For each FF node, there is an attribute "netdb.knownRouters" in the routerinfo file. This attribute indicates the number of other nodes that this FloodingFill node stores. We parse DLM packets and record the routing information in netdb.knownRouters. Figure 3 shows the approximate distribution of netdb.knownRouters. The average of netdb.knownRouters is 3464, the maximum is 5049 and the minimum is 1077. The larger the number of records, the larger the bandwidth of the node.

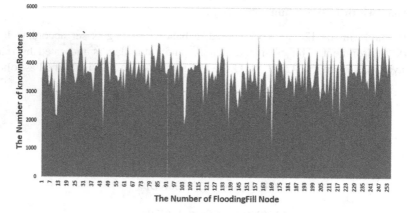

Fig. 3. Number of knownRouters for FloodingFill nodes.

5   Conclusions

Anonymous networks can provide secure, non-tracked P2P connections and can also resist censorship, which is a hotbed for hackers, and I2P network is an important one. In order to grasp I2P network and trace the source of attacks, it is essential to measure the network. This paper designed a system that can perform anonymous node measurements and analysis of measurement results. For the former, we proposed a combined measurement method that are active measurement and passive measurement. For the latter, data analysis is performed from three aspects, including country distribution, bandwidth distribution and FloodFill node attributes.

Acknowledgement. This work was supported by National Key Research & Development Plan of China under Grant 2016QY05X1000, and National Natural Science Foundation of China under Grant No.61771166.

References

1. Gai, K., Qiu, L., Chen, M., Zhao, H., Qiu, M.: SA-EAST: security-aware efficient data transmission for its in mobile heterogeneous cloud computing. ACM Trans. Embed. Comput. Syst. **16**(2), 1–22 (2017)
2. Gai, K., Qiu, M.: Blend arithmetic operations on tensor-based fully homomorphic encryption over real numbers. IEEE Trans. Ind. Inf. **14**(8), 3590–3598 (2017)
3. Gai, K., Qiu, M., Ming, Z., Zhao, H., Qiu, L.: Spoofing-jamming attack strategy using optimal power distributions in wireless smart grid networks. IEEE Trans. Smart Grid **8**(5), 2431–2439 (2017)
4. Gai, K., Choo, K.K.R., Qiu, M., Zhu, L.: Privacy-preserving content-oriented wireless communication in internet-of-things. IEEE Internet Things J. **5**(4), 3059–3067 (2018)
5. The onion router (tor) project, official website. https://www.torproject.org/
6. Zantout, B., Haraty, R.: I2P data communication system. In: Proceedings of ICN, Citeseer, pp. 401–409 (2011)

7. Qiu, H. Noura, H. Qiu, M. Ming, Z., Memmi, G.: A user-centric data protection method for cloud storage based on invertible DWT. IEEE Transactions on Cloud Computing (2019)

8. T. I. Project.: The invisible internet project. https://geti2p.net/

9. I2p source code. https://github.com/i2p/i2p.i2p

10. Conrad, B., Shirazi, F.: A survey on tor and I2P. In: Ninth International Conference on Internet Monitoring and Protection (ICIMP), pp. 22–28 (2014)

11. Liu, Z., Liu, Y., Winter, P., Mittal, P., Hu, Y.C.: Torpolice: towards enforcing service-defined access policies for anonymous communication in the tor network. In: 2017 IEEE 25th International Conference on Network Protocols (ICNP), pp. 1–10 (2017)

12. Liu, P., Wang, L., Tan, Q., Li, Q., Wang, X., Shi, J.: Empirical measurement and analysis of I2P routers. J. Netw. 9(9), 2269–2279 (2014)

13. Zincir-Heywood, K.S.A.N.: Weighted factors for measuring anonymity services: a case study on tor, jondonym, and I2P

14. Shahbar, K., Zincir-Heywood, A.N.: Effects of shared bandwidth on anonymity of the I2P network users. In: 2017 IEEE Security and Privacy Workshops (SPW), pp. 235–240 (2017)

15. Ye, L., Yu, X., Zhao, J., Zhan, D., Du, X., Guizani, M.: Deciding your own anonymity: user-oriented node selection in I2P. In: IEEE Access, vol. 6, pp. 71350–71359 (2018)

16. Hoang, N.P., Kintis, P., Antonakakis, M., Polychronakis, M.: An empirical study of the I2P anonymity network and its censorship resistance. In: Proceedings of the Internet Measurement Conference (IMC), pp. 379–392 (2018)

17. Timpanaro, J.P., Isabelle, C., Olivier, F.: Monitoring the I2P network. Ph.D. dissertation, Inria (2011)

18. Herrmann, M., Grothoff, C.: Privacy-implications of performance-based peer selection by onion-routers: a real-world case study using I2P. In: Fischer-Hübner, S., Hopper, N. (eds.) PETS 2011. LNCS, vol. 6794, pp. 155–174. Springer, Heidelberg (2011). https://doi.org/10.1007/978-3-642-22263-4_9

19. Yang, Q., Gasti, P., Balagani, K., Li, Y., Gang, Z.: Usb side-channel attack on tor. Comput. Netw. 141, 57–66 (2018)

20. Maxmind-geoip2. https://www.maxmind.com/

Plot Digitizing over Big Data Using Beam Search

Zhanyang Xu, Haoyang Shi, and Xihua Liu$^{(\boxtimes)}$

Nanjing University of Information Science and Technology, Nanjing 210044, China
562871618@qq.com, shylocksyang@gmail.com, liuxihua710@gmail.com

Abstract. In recent years, scholars have proposed different plot digitizing algorithms. Shen proposed a node-based algorithm, which used the topological structure to correct the clarity of the curve to some extent but could not separate the different curve segments. Shi proposed the tracking of sparse pixel traversal, which only applicable to the solid curve and cannot recognize the dotted curve. This paper studies a digital image processing problem for digitizing plot images, in which contains multiple curves and noise. The objective is to completely digitizing the data from the plot images, whether dotted curves or solid curves, and resists interference such as coordinate axes and other noises. A mathematical programing model is presented to describe the problem. One heuristic procedure based on beam search is developed aiming at quickly seeking optimal or near-optimal solutions. Computational experiments show that the proposed algorithm perform well, which was statistically whether identical or better than other approaches.

Keywords: Curve detection · Hough transform · Beam search

1 Introduction

Literatures usually contain non-trivial plots, especially material properties or experimental results. In scientific research, it is prominent to digitize these graphs and convert the graphs into data for comparison with new experimental results sometimes, such as vectorization of graphs in engineering design. Through the scanner and other digital equipment, scanning the images into the prototype format. Then the data points are repainted by manual processing to derive the vectorized plot image. However, the manual processing takes too long, and there may be exits too much noise and insufficient definition in the original curve image, which results in a large difference between the vectorized data and the original data.

To digitize plots in images computationally, feature curve algorithms occupy the market. Kai proposes a method reconstructs feature curves from the intersections of developable strip pairs which approximate the regions along both sides of the features [3]; Bronstein proposes feature curve correspondences to provide flexible abstractions of semantically similar parts of non–isometric shapes

© Springer Nature Switzerland AG 2019
M. Qiu (Ed.): SmartCom 2019, LNCS 11910, pp. 116–125, 2019.
https://doi.org/10.1007/978-3-030-34139-8_12

[2]; Marina proposes a method based on a novel generalization of the Hough transform technique able to identify and localize [10].

There exist more or less problems in the methods mentioned above, such as differentiate the solid curve and the dotted curve. In this paper, we proposed a new method to digitize plot over big data using beam search. We hypothesize a mathematical programming model to denote this problem. With respect to each pixel point in an image, most likely to have two states – part of curves or hindrances. We need to purge hindrances, retain curves, differentiate different curve and fit the curve to data sets based on specific conditions. For all the pixel points $Z_i(x, y)$ in the image file, we need to find a set of point U_t. For each pixel point $Z_{t_i}(x, y)$ in the set U_t, satisfying the largest conditional probability that all the points are on the same plot I, as Eq. 1 shows:

$$\begin{cases} Z_{t_i}(x, y) = 1 \\ Z_{t_i} \in U_t \\ P(Z_{t_1}^{<1>}, Z_{t_2}^{<2>}, \ldots, Z_{t_i}^{<i>}) = \arg\max_I P \end{cases} \tag{1}$$

We divide the above procedure into six methods step by step, Greyscale and Binarization, Distill plot region, Exclude sub lines, Denoise, Abstract plots and Derive plot data. Previous research we have done before [7–9,14,15] has indicated that the convenience with big data. Therefore, we create a ground truth alignments based on GLDAS big data set [1], apply the alignments to compare result between different methods.

2 Methods

As is shown in Fig. 1, we used the following methods to obtain the results we want step by step. Each method has its input and output, where Image File represent the specific file to digitizing plot, $M_i(i = gs, R, S, L, D)$ represent the reminder matrix after processing each method, U_t represent the collection list which contains ever plot's collection in the form of pixels points, Data File represent the data which store in format.

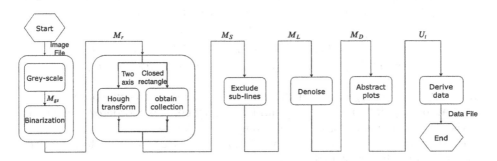

Fig. 1. The flow chart of the algorithm

2.1   Grey-Scale and Binarization

As Eq. 2 show, here we choose to define each pixel point's value in the image with I_{rgb} while addressing plot images [5]. This way we can quantify the value of the pixel point.

$$I_{rgb} = (F_R, F_G, F_B) \qquad (2)$$

where F_R represents the red channel value of the specific point's red channel, F_G represents the green channel value of the specific point's red channel, F_B represents the red channel value of the specific point's red channel. Subsequently, we use handy theorems to calculate the corresponding gray-scale value I_{gs} for I_{rgb} computationally, with respect to metadata's SRGB space type or linear space type.

While plots usually appear as the darker components of the image, entailing the differentiating of the plot part and the noise part from the gray scale value matrix M_{gs}. We set the Grey level of I_{gs} to m, using a fast threshold segmentation method [13] to calculate the threshold t of each image.

$$F(x) = \begin{cases} 1 & \text{if x} < \text{t} \\ 0 & \text{otherwise} \end{cases} \qquad (3)$$

After the threshold t has been obtained, we address the binarization of each gray-scale value I_{gs} from the matrix M_{gs} based on the truncation equation as Eq. 3. After the binarization, we obtain the reminder matrix M_r, the sole value is 0 or 1. Thus, we have completed the binarization of the RGB image, which is convenient for subsequent processing.

2.2   Distill Plot Region

As a standard plot image, there are generally two coordinate axes of the horizontal axis and the vertical axis exist. Which denotes that the image has two straight lines in both horizontal and vertical directions, equivalents to the two points collections exist both x direction and y direction in the matrix M_r. Here we use the Hough transform [12] to detect the line and we detect the maximum value and the minimum value from U_x, U_y as Eq. 4 shows:

$$\begin{cases} x_{min} = \min(x_{x1}, x_{x2}, \ldots, x_{xn}), x_{max} = \max(x_{x1}, x_{x2}, \ldots, x_{xn}) \\ y_{min} = \min(y_{y1}, y_{y2}, \ldots, y_{yn}), y_{max} = \max(y_{y1}, y_{y2}, \ldots, y_{yn}) \end{cases} \qquad (4)$$

where x_{x1}, x_{x2} and x_{xn} represent the unordered sequence of x-axis coordinate values of all pixel points in U_x, y_{y1}, y_{y2} and y_{yn} represent the unordered sequence of y-axis coordinate values of all pixel points in U_y. We use $x_{min}, x_{max}, y_{min}, y_{max}$ to differentiate the substantive region of plot from image as Eq. 5 shows, for the purpose of distilling plot region.

$$M_S = M_r(x_{min} : x_{max}, y_{min}, y_{max}) \qquad (5)$$

where M_S represents the matrix equivalent to the substantive region of plot in the image. The Hough transform method is suitable for most images, but the time complexity of Hough transform is $O(N^3)$, therefore the processing speed is slow. There is a special case where the plot's region is included by the closed rectangle, equivalents to the rectangle collection U in the matrix M_r, whose boundary value equals one. We describe the rectangle region by the following Eq. 6.

$$U_m = \max\left(crad(U_1), crad(U_2), \ldots, crad(U_n)\right), U_i \in I_t \tag{6}$$

where $crad(U_1), crad(U_2)$ and $crad(U_n)$ represent the length of the unordered sequence from the collection U_i in the matrix M_r, i represents the number of collections and U_i represents the connected region. We use the following algorithm which sparked by Image segmentation algorithm [4] to obtain these collections.

First, we create a matrix M_v to record the visit of each point and a stack S_v to save the point which used in the following steps.

Second, we set i to one, select point P_{begin} from M_v, which satisfy the following Eq. 7.

$$P_{begin}(x, y) \in M_r, x = \min\left(x_1, x_2, \ldots, x_n\right) \tag{7}$$

where x_1, x_2 and x_n represent the unordered sequence of abscissa value from every point in the matrix M_r whose value equals one. Then we push point P_{begin} into stack S_v and set $M_v(P_{begin}(x), P_{begin}(y))$ to one, for the purpose of marking the visit in matrix M_r about the point P_{begin}.

Third, we pop point P_{top} from stack S_v and create point collection array U_i, in order to store the neighborhood of each reminder point. Then we push each point P_i from point P_{top} 'S 8-connectedneighborhood matrix $M_{top} = \begin{bmatrix} P_1 P_2 P_3 \\ P_4 P_{top} P_5 \\ P_6 P_7 P_8 \end{bmatrix}$ into stack S_v and the point collection array U_i, which satisfy the following condition Eq. 8:

$$\begin{cases} M_v(x, y) = 0 \\ P_i(x, y) = 1 \\ P_i \in M_{top} \end{cases} \tag{8}$$

Then we set the value of point $M_v(x, y)$ to one in the visit matrix M_v and loop this step ceaselessly until satisfy the following condition Eq. 9:

$$crad(S_v) = 0 \tag{9}$$

The Eq. 9 represent that the sound collection U_i contains P_{begin} has been found, then we increment the value i by one and push the collection U_i to the collection list L_u.

Fourth, Repeat the second step and the third step until there are no black points which haven't been visited in the image, equivalent to no point $P(x, y)$ in matrix M_r matches the following condition Eq. 10:

$$\begin{cases} P(x, y) = 1 \\ V_t(x, y) = 0 \end{cases} \tag{10}$$

Fifth, we distill the collection U_m from the collection list $L_u = U_1, U_2, \ldots, U(I-1)$, which satisfy the following condition Eq. 11:

$$\begin{cases} U_m \in L_u \\ crad(U_m) = \max\left(crad(U_1), crad(U_2), \ldots, crad(U_{I-1})\right) \end{cases} \tag{11}$$

where $crad(U_1), crad(U_2)$ and $crad(U_{I-1})$ represent the length of the unordered sequence from the collection U_i in the list L_u, which denotes that the collection U_m represent the largest connected region i n the image relatively. Then we detect the maximum value and the minimum value from U_m, which satisfy the following condition Eq. 4.

Then we use $x_{min}, x_{max}, y_{min}, y_{max}$ to abstract the substantive region of plot from image as Eq. 12:

$$M_S = M_r(x_{min} : x_{max}, y_{min}, y_{max}) \tag{12}$$

where M_S represents the matrix equivalent to the substantive region of plot in the image.

2.3 Exclude Sub-lines

With respect to the matrix M_S distilled in method Distill plot region, still exists hindrances such as coordinate axes, tick marks and grid lines in the matrix. We use the following algorithm to denoise the hindrances:

First, there is an exclusive feature exists in coordinate axes, scale lines, grid lines which refer to the perpendicular to the x direction or the y direction in a conservative plot image. So, we scan the plot region matrix M_S row by row, column by column, push the point $P(x, y)$ into the black point list L_p. If the number of black points in a row or a column is greater than the threshold γ_{line}, which is equivalent to the condition $crad(L_p) > \gamma_{line}$, we presume the black point $P(x, y)$ in the black point list L_p to be the hindrances [11].

Second, we need to differentiate the point of intersection from the plot and the hindrances. With respect to each point $P(x, y)$ in the point list L_p, we create the n-connectedneighborhood matrix $M_c = \begin{bmatrix} P_1 \ldots P_N \\ \vdots \ddots \vdots \\ P_{N^2-N} \ldots P_{N^2-1} \end{bmatrix}$, for the purpose of marking each neighbor from point $P(x, y)$.

Third, we distill the point $P_i(x_i, y_i)$ relative to the point $P(x, y)$ horizontally or vertically from the matrix M_c, which equivalents to the following conditions Eq. 13.

$$\begin{cases} P_i(x_i, y_i) \in M_c \\ x_i = x \parallel y_i = y \end{cases} \tag{13}$$

Fourth, we set the value of these points in the matrix M_c to zero, set the value of $P(x, y)$ in the matrix M_c to zero, in order to remove the interference. Then we derive the number S_{black} of points $P_i(x_i, y_i)$ whose value equals one in the matrix M_c. If the number S_{black} is greater than the threshold $\gamma_{crossover}$, we presume the point $P(x, y)$ to be the intersection point on the plot, otherwise set the value of the point $P(x, y)$ in the matrix M_S to zero.

After performing the few steps as we described above, we obtain the reminder matrix M_L without sub-lines.

2.4   Denoise

We use the fuzzy similarity-based filter [10] to denoise the remainder noise points in the matrix M_L. We detect each point $P(x, y)$ in the matrix M_L, starting with the point $P(0, 0)$, create 8-connectedneighborhood matrix $M_{8-connected} = \begin{bmatrix} P_1 P_2 P_3 \\ P_4 P P_5 \\ P_6 P_7 P_8 \end{bmatrix}$. Then we derive the number S_{black} of points $P_i(x_i, y_i)$ whose value equals one in the matrix $M_{8-connected}$. If the number S_{black} less than the threshold γ_{salt}, we presume the point $P(x, y)$ to be the remainder noise point. Then we set the value of each reminding noise point's value to zero. Consequently, we obtain the reminder matrix M_D.

2.5   Abstract Plots

After the above preconditions, we detect the start point $P_{start_i}(x, y)$ from each plot L_i, which satisfy the following condition Eq. 14:

$$\begin{cases} x \rightarrow \min (x_1, x_2, \ldots, x_n) \\ y \rightarrow \max (y_1, y_2, \ldots, y_n) \parallel \min (y_1, y_2, \ldots, y_n) \end{cases} \tag{14}$$

where x_1, x_2 and x_n represent the unordered sequence of x-axis coordinate values of all points in plot L_i, $y_t(t \in [1, n])$ represent the unordered sequence of y-axis coordinate values of all points in plot L_i. Then we detected the end point y_1, y_2 and y_n which satisfy the following condition Eq. 15:

$$\begin{cases} x \rightarrow \max (x_1, x_2, \ldots, x_n) \\ y \rightarrow \max (y_1, y_2, \ldots, y_n) \parallel \min (y_1, y_2, \ldots, y_n) \end{cases} \tag{15}$$

where x_1, x_2 and x_n represent the unordered sequence of x-axis coordinate values of all points in plot L_i, y_1, y_2 and y_n represent the unordered sequence of y-axis coordinate values of all points in plot L_i.

If we start from $P_{start_i}(x, y)$ and detect the points $P_{start_i}, P_{i1}, P_{i2}, \ldots$, P_{in}, P_{end_i} from the matrix M_S, which stabilize the conditional probability $\arg\max_i P$ favorably, we resume the points P_{i1}, P_{i2} and P_{in} to be the most likely identification of plot L_i. Here we propose the following algorithm using beam search method [6] to abstract the points $P_{start_i}, P_{i1}, P_{i2}$ and P_{in}, P_{end_i}.

First, we select a certain value B as the Beam Width to indicate the result of selecting the maximum condition probability $P_{max}B$ each time. Then we set $i + 1 \rightarrow i$, where i represent the total of plots. Afterwards, we create a point list B_i, set variable $0 \rightarrow i$ and select B connected areas as the candidate result collection list U_0 for plot L_i, which start with the point P_{start_i}, equivalent to find B clusters of P_{start_i} in the portion region. If the size of list U_0 is less than B, we inference there is no more residual plots and terminal this algorithm.

Second, if value $t * w$ less than the maximum of x-axis in matrix M_S, we split matrix M_S with the threshold μ to matrix $M_{f_t} = M_S(t * w : t * w+, :)$ and create the collection list B_{i_t}. Otherwise, we assume that the number of remainder points on plot L_i in matrix M_{f_t} equals zero. Then we assign points $P_{start_i}, P_{i1}, P_{i2}$ and P_{end_i} from the first collection in U_{t-1} as the points in the plot i, push them into collection L_i and turn to the first step.

Fourth, we consider the conditional probability results for each collection C_k in the collection list B_{i_t} with the candidate result collection list U_{t-1}, whose procedure is proposed as following: Initially, we detect point $P_S(x_s, y_s)$ in collection C_k, which satisfy the following condition Eq. 16:

$$y \rightarrow \max(y_1, y_2, \ldots, y_n) \tag{16}$$

where y_1, y_2 and y_n represent the unordered sequence of y-axis coordinate values of all points in collection C_x. Afterwards, we detect point $P_N(x_N, y_N)$ from each collection C_{t-1_B} in the collection list U_{t-1}, satisfy the following condition 17:

$$x_N \rightarrow \max(x_1, x_2, \ldots, x_n) \tag{17}$$

where x_1, x_2 and x_n represent the unordered sequence of x-axis coordinate values of all points in collection C_{t-1_B}.

Eventually, we calculate Euclidean metric $L_{NS} = \sqrt{(x_N - x)^2 + (y_N - y)^2}$ [12] between the specify point $P_N(x_N, y_N)$ and point $P_S(x_s, y_s)$. We assume that the smaller the value L_{NS} is considered, the higher the conditional probability of the connected region C_k as the next part of the plot i in matrix $M(f_x)$ which contains the collection C_{t-1_B}.

Fifth, after assigning $B * K$ conditional probability in the fourth step, we consider the B-highest conditional probability results for each collection in the previous result collection $U(t - 1)$ as the next result collection U_t. Which is equivalent to that we detect the B collection C_k, whose probability results $P(U_x, U_{i_{t-1}}^{<t-1>}|i)$ equals $P(U_x, U_{i_{t-1}}^{<t-1>})P(U_{i_{t-1}}^{<t-1>})$, push each point in collection C_k into the highest-conditional-probability-related collection C_{t-1_B}. After exploiting the collection list U_t, we set $t + 1 \rightarrow t$ and turn to the second step.

2.6 Derive Data

With respect to each point collection L_i, we use the following method to derive plot data. First, we create the data list D_i, detect the start point

$P_{start_i}(x_{start_i}, y_{start_i})$ and the end point $P_{end_i}(x_{end_i}, y_{end_i})$, which match the following condition 18:

$$\begin{cases} x_{start_i} \rightarrow \max(x_1, x_2, \ldots, x_n) \\ x_{end_i} \rightarrow \min(x_1, x_2, \ldots, x_n) \end{cases} \tag{18}$$

where x_1, x_2 and x_n represent the unordered sequence of x-axis coordinate values of all points in point collection L_i.

Second, we loop variable X from the value x_{start_i} to the value x_{end_i}, retrieve each point $P(x, y)$ in collection L_i whose x-axis value equals x. Then we take the mean y-axis value y_{mean_X} of such points, assume (X, y_{mean_X}) as the data point intrinsically. Afterwards, we push $P_x(x_{actual}, y_{actual})$ into data list D_i, which matches the following condition:

$$\begin{cases} x_{actual} = \frac{X}{L_{x-axis}} * (X_{end} - X_{start}) * X_{scale} + X_{start} \\ y_{actual} = \frac{y_{mean_X}}{L_{y-axis}} * (Y_{end} - Y_{start}) * Y_{scale} + Y_{start} \end{cases} \tag{19}$$

where L_{x-axis} represents the length of x-axis in matrix M_S, X_{end} represents the value of the end point on the x-axis, X_{start} represents the value of the beginning point on the x-axis, X_{scale} represents the graduation value of x-axis, L_{y-axis} represents the length of y-axis in matrix M_S, Y_{end} represents the value of the end point on the y-axis, Y_{start} represents the value of the beginning point on the y-axis and Y_{scale} represents the graduation value of y-axis.

Third, export the data list D_i as the prototype file.

3   Results

Firstly, we download GLDAS data set from EARTH DATA(https://disc.gsfc. nasa.gov/), which date range from 2000-01-01 to 2019-05-31. Then we generate big data set F using python(https://www.python.org/) with the Matplotlib library(https://matplotlib.org/), which use random dishes. The total of the data is 1,101,600+.

Second, we choose Gehre's method as algorithm A, Kai's method as algorithm B, Bronstein's method as algorithm C, the method we propose above as algorithm D. Then we compare the averange result in run time, number of curves differentiate.

We abstract 100,000 images from the big data set F to compare the running time of the four algorithms in the target with different number of curves.

As Fig. 2 shows, In the case where the number of curves is 1, the four algorithms run at the same time. When the number of curves reaches five, the speed of algorithm B decreases significantly. When the number of curves reaches ten, the running time of algorithm C opens the gap with algorithms A and D. Algorithms A and D still share the analogous run time until the number of curves reaches 20.

Then We compare the number of curves differentiated using the four algorithms.

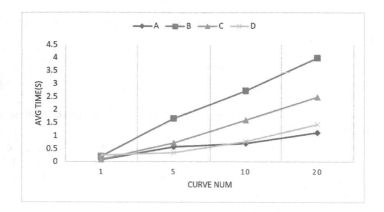

Fig. 2. The average result of algorithm running time

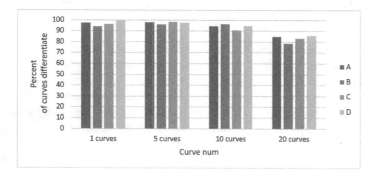

Fig. 3. The average percent result of the curves each algorithm differentiated

As Fig. 3 shows, When the number of curves is 1, the recognition effect is basically the same, and the recognition effect of algorithm D is better. When the number of curves comes to five, the recognition effects of the four algorithms are similar. When the number of curves increases to ten, the recognition effect shows a significant decline, and the recognition effect of algorithm C is poor. When the number of curves reaches twenty, the recognition effect is further reduced, algorithm D is better.

4   Discussions

After algorithm simulation, it is not difficult to see that the proposed algorithm has state of the art on plot digitization in the current research background, and the time complexity can also meet the requirements of big data processing. If the algorithm is applied to the mobile field, it can meet the needs of ordinary users for real-time tasks. Subsequent work will continue to improve the algorithm, improve processing speed and recognition accuracy, and extend the algorithm to more complex images.

References

1. Fang, H., Beaudoing, H.K., Teng, W.L., Vollmer, B.E., et al.: Global land data assimilation system (GLDAS) products, services and application from NASA hydrology data and information services center (HDISC) (2009)
2. Gehre, A., Bronstein, M., Kobbelt, L., Solomon, J.: Interactive curve constrained functional maps. In: Computer Graphics Forum, vol. 37, pp. 1–12. Wiley Online Library (2018)
3. Lee, K.W., Bo, P.: Feature curve extraction from point clouds via developable strip intersection. J. Comput. Design Eng. 3(2), 102–111 (2016)
4. Lei, X., Ouyang, H.: Image segmentation algorithm based on improved fuzzy clustering. Clust. Comput. 1–11 (2018)
5. Liu, C., Chen, X., Wu, Y.: Modified grey world method to detect and restore colour cast images. IET Image Process. 13(7), 1090–1096 (2019)
6. Ow, P.S., Morton, T.E.: Filtered beam search in scheduling. Int. J. Prod. Res. 26(1), 35–62 (1988)
7. Qi, L., Chen, Y., Yuan, Y., Fu, S., Zhang, X., Xu, X.: A QoS-aware virtual machine scheduling method for energy conservation in cloud-based cyber-physical systems. World Wide Web 1–23 (2019)
8. Qi, L., et al.: Finding all you need: web APIs recommendation in web of things through keywords search. IEEE Trans. Comput. Soc. Syst. 6(5), 1063–1072 (2019)
9. Qi, L., et al.: Structural balance theory-based e-commerce recommendation over big rating data. IEEE Trans. Big Data 4(3), 301–312 (2016)
10. Torrente, M.L., Biasotti, S., Falcidieno, B.: Recognition of feature curves on 3D shapes using an algebraic approach to hough transforms. Pattern Recogn. 73, 111–130 (2018)
11. Tripta, F.A., Kumar, S.B.A., Saha, T.C.S.: Wavelet decomposition based channel estimation and digital domain self-interference cancellation in in-band full-duplex OFDM systems. In: 2019 URSI Asia-Pacific Radio Science Conference (AP-RASC), pp. 1–4. IEEE (2019)
12. Wei, Q., Feng, D., Zheng, W.: Funnel transform for straight line detection. arXiv preprint arXiv:1904.09409 (2019)
13. Xie, D.H., Lu, M., Xie, Y.F., Liu, D., Li, X.: A fast threshold segmentation method for froth image base on the pixel distribution characteristic. PloS One 14(1), e0210411 (2019)
14. Xu, X., Dou, W., Zhang, X., Chen, J.: EnReal: an energy-aware resource allocation method for scientific workflow executions in cloud environment. IEEE Trans. Cloud Comput. 4(2), 166–179 (2015)
15. Xu, X., Liu, Q., Zhang, X., Zhang, J., Qi, L., Dou, W.: A blockchain-powered crowdsourcing method with privacy preservation in mobile environment. IEEE Trans. Comput. Soc. Syst. 1–13 (2019)

Trust-Aware Resource Provisioning for Meteorological Workflow in Cloud

Ruichao Mo[1], Lianyong Qi[2], Zhanyang Xu[1,3], and Xiaolong Xu[1,3(✉)]

[1] School of Computer and Software,
Nanjing University of Information Science and Technology, Nanjing, China
njuxlxu@gmail.com
[2] School of Information Science and Engineering, Qufu Normal University,
Qufu, China
[3] Jiangsu Collaborative Innovation Center of Atmospheric Environment
and Equipment Technology (CICAEET), Nanjing University of Information Science
and Technology, Nanjing, China

Abstract. Cloud computing centers are becoming the predominant platform of offering high-performance computing services based on high-performance computers. However, enabling meteorological workflow that requires real-time response is still challenging due to uncertainty in the cloud, once the computing nodes in the cloud are down, the tasks deployed on the cloud will not be completed in time. To address this problem, an optimal cloud resource for the downtime tasks provisioning method (ODPM) is proposed by formulating a programming model. The ODPM method can select the appropriate migration strategy for the tasks on the compute node to achieve the shortest workflow completion time and load balancing of the compute center compute nodes. A large number of experimental are conducted to verify the benefits brought by ODPM.

Keywords: Cloud computing · Trust-aware · Meteorological workflow · NSGA-II

1 Introduction

Cloud computing has been evolved over a decade to support Industrial Internet of things (IIoT) with credible, concurrent and universal access to high-end calculating capabilities, and it has ability to satisfy the demands of IIoT application execution which need to analysis large-scale data [1,2]. As an important branch in IIoT, the meteorological department has large-scale data increasing at a daily growth rate of 12 TB. Meanwhile, meteorological applications (e.g., prediction of natural disasters, synchronization of information, etc.) require huge physical resources and sufficient computing power for the execution to store and analyze datasets collected [3,4]. Thus, cloud computing is fully leveraged to accommodate the meteorological services and data [5].

© Springer Nature Switzerland AG 2019
M. Qiu (Ed.): SmartCom 2019, LNCS 11910, pp. 126–135, 2019.
https://doi.org/10.1007/978-3-030-34139-8_13

Meteorological services are complex, which need excellent performance in different aspects such as real-time, accuracy, predictability, etc. in different applications. As a key technology for process coordination and tasks scheduling, the workflow is employed to provide a complete framework that breaks down and integrates the overall meteorological services [2,4,6,7]. The inter relations between tasks of data-intensive meteorological applications are represented in a breeze by workflow model which defines variety parameters to realize the automation of entire process [8]. Therefore, meteorological workflow is able to coordinate a series of data-intensive tasks which contain a wide variety of large-scale data to realize the efficient execution of the complicate meteorological services [9].

Although cloud computing offers tremendous opportunities to response to various demands of meteorological services, there are still some issues need to be addressed during the deployment of meteorological workflows in cloud platform. On the one hand, load balance should be considered when meteorological workflows are being executed [10]. By optimizing load balance, all compute nodes work in a stable state, which is advantageous to improve the efficiency of cloud computing. Moreover, optimizing load balance also reduces the possibility of the single-point failure in the implementation of meteorological workflows, thereby improving the fault-tolerance of the cloud.

On the other hand, there are many factors that may give rise to server downtime such as overwhelming of server, unreasonable applications and so on [11]. When any one of the computing nodes fails, all sorts of consequences (e.g., data loss, extension of the makespan, performance degradation, etc.) will arise. To solve the problem of data loss, reliability replication with workflow which is an important software fault tolerance technology to meet reliability requirements is employed in cloud. However, a suitable offloading method is needed to solve the problem of the makespan which affect the efficiency of meteorological workflows.

In order to improve the quality and efficiency of meteorological services, various meteorological applications are abstracted into workflows which have excellent performance in organizing the tasks. These meteorological workflows are deployed on cloud computing platforms to be executed efficiently. Once a computing node fails, the offloading of meteorological tasks is needed to ensure the fault-tolerance. However, due to the complexity of data-intensive meteorological workflows, it is difficult to balance the load balance and the makespan in random offloading. Therefore, there is still a challenge to optimize the load balance and the makespan. For addressing this challenge, an offloading method that is beneficial to dynamic resource provisioning with fault tolerance is proposed.

Specifically, the main contributions of this paper are the following:

- Virtual Layer 2 (VL2) network topology is exploited to erect the meteorological cloud infrastructure. In addition, the meteorological workflow model, the fault task recovery time model and the fault task recovery load balancing model were designed.
- Use Non-dominated Sorting Genetic Algorithm II (NSGA-II) to find the solution set of the fault task offloading strategies with the shortest meteorological workflow makespan and load balance for all computing nodes in the cloud.

- Use Simple Additive Weighting (SAW) and Multiple Criteria Decision Making (MCDM) to find the best fault task offloading strategy from the solution set.
- A large number of experimental results obtained by multiple comparison experiments with Benchmark, BFD and FFD demonstrate the effectiveness of ODPM.

The outline of this paper is as follows. A VL2 based meteorological cloud platform is described in Sects. 2. In Sect. 3, a multi-objective optimization offloading model for the downtime task is built. A Downtime task Offloading Method(ODPM) is proposed in Sect. 4. The performance of ODPM, simulation details and results are conducted in Sect. 5. The related work of this paper is given in Sect. 6. In Sect. 7, we conclude this paper and look ahead to the future.

2   A VL2 Based Meteorological Cloud Platform

Figure 1 shows a VL2 based meteorological cloud platform. In this framework, different departments of Meteorological Administration (e.g., the Satellite Meteorological Center, the Meteorological Information Center and Subordinate meteorological bureau, etc.) deploy numerous task mirror nodes and computing nodes according to actual needs, and all computing nodes and task mirror nodes in the same meteorological department are connected to the same switch at the TOR layer. In addition, in order to ensure meteorological data communication between the two meteorological departments, the TOR layer switch to which they belong will be connected to the same aggregation layer switch. Meanwhile, the switches at the aggregation layer are connected to all intermediate switches to ensure data communication among all meteorological departments in the network. [12,13].

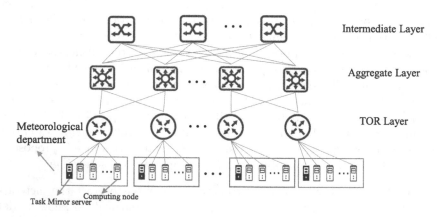

Fig. 1. A VL2 based meteorological cloud platform

3 System Model and Problem Formulation

3.1 Recovery Time Model

To recover these fault tasks $wt_i(1 < i < m)$ and the data generated by their parent tasks need to be acquired. Then, these fault tasks will be restarted on other computing nodes. However, it takes time for the offloading target computing nodes to acquire the data from different computing nodes, and these times cannot be ignored in the cloud. In this case, the recovery time $RT_i(1 < i < m)$ of the fault task wt_i is calculated by

$$RT_i = rt_i^s + rt_i^m + rt_i^f, \tag{1}$$

where rt_i^s denotes the startup time of task wt_i on other nodes in the cloud, rt_i^m denotes the time for downloading the mirror of task wt_i from the task mirror nodes, and rt_i^f represents the longest time to get data from parent tasks.

Suppose that wt_i is to be restarted at $p_i^s(1 < i < l)$, then p_i^s needs to download the mirror of wt_i and the data required for the execution of wt_i from different computing nodes. According to the VL2 network topology we described above, assume that the data required to restart wt_i includes the task mirror and the data from their parent task, which are stored in $p_a^m(1 < a < k)$ and p_j^s respectively. The relationship between p_i^s and p_a^m is expressed by ξ. There are three cases of ξ: (a) $\xi = 0$ means that p_i^s and p_a^m are in the same TOR; (b) $xi = 1$ represent that p_j^s and p_a^m are not in the same TOR switch and aggregation switch, but in the same intermediate switch. Besides, the relationship between p_i^s and p_j^s is also expressed by ξ, and the situation of ξ is consistent with the discussion above.

Assume that the mirror size of the fault task t_i is d_i^m, in this case, the fault task mirror of t_i transmission time is deduced by

$$rt_i^m = \begin{cases} 2 \cdot d_i^m/w_{st}, \text{if } \xi = 0, \\ 2 \cdot (d_i^m/w_{st} + d_i^m/w_{ta}), \text{if } \xi = 1, \\ 2 \cdot (d_i^m/w_{st} + d_i^m/w_{ta} + d_i^m/w_{au}), \text{if } \xi = 2, \end{cases} \tag{2}$$

where w_{st} is the bandwidth of two nodes in the same TOR, w_{ta} is the bandwidth between TOR switch and aggregation switch, and w_{au} is the bandwidth between the aggregation switch and intermediate switch.

After the task mirror transmission is completed, the task execution needs to get data from their parent tasks. Suppose that t_j is a parent task of t_i, nd the data size from t_j is d_j^f, he transmission time $rt_{i,j}^f$ between t_i and t_j is measured by

$$rt_{i,j}^f = \begin{cases} 2 \cdot d_i^f/w_{st}, \text{if } \xi = 0, \\ 2 \cdot (d_i^f/w_{st} + d_i^f/w_{ta}), \text{if } \xi = 1, \\ 2 \cdot (d_i^f/w_{st} + d_i^f/w_{ta} + d_i^f/w_{au}), \text{if } \xi = 2. \end{cases} \tag{3}$$

A task in a workflow may have serval parent tasks, so restarting the fault task requires getting data from parent tasks, but getting data from their parent tasks are done simultaneously with multiple paths, therefore, when calculating the data acquisition time, the longest transmission time is selected as the time required for the recovery task, so the longest time required to transfer data from parent tasks is measured by

$$rt_i^f = \max_{t_j \in q(t_i)} \{rt_{i,j}^f \mid i \in [1,n], j \in [1,n]\}. \tag{4}$$

3.2 Load Balance Model

In order to keep the load balance of the computing nodes in the cloud, the appropriate offloading computing nodes should be selected to restart these fault tasks. Assume that the virtual machine size required to complete the task t_i is vm_i. In addition, the average utilization of each computing node is represented by μ_i, which is calculated by

$$\mu_i = \frac{1}{c_i} \sum_{i=0}^{n-1} \sigma(t_i) \cdot vm_i, \tag{5}$$

note $\sigma(t_i)$ as a flag to estimate whether the task t_i is deployed on $p_b(1 < b < l)$, which is measured by

$$\sigma(t_i) = \begin{cases} 1, \text{if } t_i \text{ runs on } p_b, \\ 0, \text{otherwise.} \end{cases} \tag{6}$$

Let $\overline{\mu}$ be the average resource utilization of the computing node, which is measured by

$$\overline{\mu} = \frac{1}{n} \sum_{i=0}^{n-1} \mu_i. \tag{7}$$

Finally, the load balance of the cloud is deduced by

$$U = \frac{1}{n} \sum_{i=0}^{n-1} (\mu_i - \overline{\mu})^2. \tag{8}$$

3.3 Problem Formulation

In this paper, the fault task offloading problem for meteorological workflow in the cloud is focusing on optimizing the makespan of the meteorological workflow and load balance of the cloud. Thus, the problem to be solved is defined by

$$min D', U. \tag{9}$$

$$s.t. \forall \sigma(t_i) = 1 p_b \in P^s, \tag{10}$$

$$\sum_{i=1}^{n} \sigma(t_i) \cdot vm_i \leq c_i. \tag{11}$$

4   A Downtime Task Offloading Method

The fault tasks offloading problem to be solved in this paper is a multi-objective optimization problem, which is to make the shortest makespan of the meteorological workflow and maintain the load balance of the computing nodes in the cloud. NSGA-II is a non-dominant genetic algorithm with an elitist strategy that be able to well solve the problem of fault tasks offloading.

4.1   Fitness Function and Constraints

In the case of the fault task offloading, the fitness of the problem solution is related to the trade-off between the makespan D of the meteorological workflow and the load balance U of the computing nodes in the cloud. Besides, the constraints are given in Eqs. 10 and 11, representing the normal computing nodes to which the task is offloaded and ensure that the capacity of the offloaded computing nodes is greater than the computing resources needed for the down task.

4.2   Genetic Operator

In the genetic algorithm, the crossover operation is a process in which two pairs of parent chromosomes exchange parts of their genes in a way that creates two new offspring individuals, which inherit good genes from their parent chromosomes and form their own unique genotypes, increasing the diversity of the population. In this paper, the multi-point crossover method is used to generate possible offloading strategies for down tasks.

4.3   Iteration

I n the iteration process of NSGA-II, the parent population H_o generates the child population Q_o through the selection and mutation, then merges all the individual from the parent population and the child population into R_o. The algorithm first selects the appropriate individuals from R_o through non-dominated sorting, then selects N individuals to form new populations N individuals to form new populations H_{t+1} by crowding distance sorting. The iteration process of NSGA-II stops after the result converges. The current population will form a solution set, which is called Pareto optimal solution.

4.4   Optimal Offloading Strategies Acquiring

In fact, multiple solutions which represent the offloading strategy of the down tasks may be generated by NSGA-II. Thus, in order to get the optimal solution, SAW and MCDM are implemented to select the optimal solution from multiple solutions.

With SAW and MCDM, the utility value of each solution is calculated, and the solution with the maximum utility value will be selected as the offloading strategy of the down task. Assume that E_D^i and U_χ^i represents the values of the two objective function of x_i. In addition, ρ_1 and ρ_2 indicates the weight of workflow completion time and load balancing indicators respectively. E_D^{max}, E_D^{min}, U_χ^{max} and U_χ^{min} indicates the maximum and minimum values of the two objective functions respectively. Thus, the utility value θ_i of X_i is calculated by

$$\theta_i = \rho_1 \cdot \frac{E_D^{max} - E_D^i}{E_D^{min} - E_D^i} + \rho_2 \cdot \frac{U_\chi^{max} - U_\chi^i}{U_\chi^{min} - U_\chi^i} \tag{12}$$

5   Experimental Results and Analysis

In this section, our proposed algorithm ODPM is evaluated. We first briefly describe the basic parameter settings of the experiment. Then, we describe the meteorological workflow used in this experiment. In order to evaluate the performance of ODPM, three comparison methods are selected. Finally, we analyze and conduct the results of the experiment.

5.1   Result and Discussion

In order to illustrate the performance of our proposed algorithm ODPM, we select three commonly used task migration algorithms for comparison, i.e., Benchmark, First Fit Decreasing (FFD), and Best Fit Decreasing (BFD).

Comparison of the Meteorological Workflow Makespan. In this paper, the makespan of the meteorological workflow is the key evaluation criterion for evaluating the offloading method of the fault tasks. After the failure of the computing nodes, the shorter the makespan of the meteorological workflow is, the better the fault tolerance performance of the cloud is. In our experiment, we first select five fault tasks to add to the fault task set, then add two fault tasks to the down task set each time. The experimental results of the Benchmark, BFD, FFD, and ODPM are shown in Table 1. Compared with the other three methods, the offloading strategy found by ODPM makes the meteorological workflow makespan significantly better than other methods.

Table 1. Comparison of the makespan by Benchmark, BFD, FFD, ODPM

Method name	Task number					
	3	5	7	9	11	13
Benchmark	70	76.0008	78	57	54.001	47.0014
BFD	78	70.0003	70.0008	21.0017	76.0007	78
FFD	78	78	50.0012	43	57.0006	33.0003
ODPM	49.00049	37.0011	34.0021	26.0036	24.003	21.0023

Comparison of Load Balance. Load balance is also an important evaluation criterion for the fault task offloading method. On the one hand, maintaining load balancing of all computing nodes could improve the performance of the cloud. On the other hand, when all computing nodes in cloud maintain load balancing status, the risk of computing nodes down is reduced. In our experiment, the smaller the value of load balance variance is, the better the load balance of computing nodes. In Table 2, the offloading strategies found in Benchmark, BFD and FFD make the load of the computing nodes in the cloud worse than the ODPM.

Table 2. Comparison of the load balance by Benchmark, BFD, FFD, ODPM

Method name	Task number					
	3	5	7	9	11	13
Benchmark	0.10631	0.10772	0.11147	0.1269	0.12484	0.12621
BFD-F	0.10868	0.11534	0.12181	0.13281	0.14155	0.15193
FFD-F	0.10868	0.11584	0.12176	0.13025	0.14559	0.15599
ODPM	0.09801	0.10345	0.11008	0.11136	0.12149	0.12389

6 Related Work

The completion of meteorological services (e.g., weather forecast, natural disaster warning, etc.) requires to utilize vast computing resources [14]. In order to meet the computing demends, the meteorological department realized the efficient execution of meteorological services by constructing a meteorological cloud platform with powerful computing performance, high flexibility and reliability. [15,16].

Due to the complexity of meteorological services, it is necessary to model the services into meteorological workflows, which could ensure the meteorological service processed more effectively with the capabilities of the powerful computing and processing in cloud. However, the computing nodes in the cloud have the possibility of downtime, which would cause errors during the execution of the meteorological workflow [17]. Aiming to optimize the operation of the meteorological workflow, several methods and models with fault tolerance have been investigated in [18,19], to name a few.

Ostermann et al. used case scenarios for a wide range of applications from operations to research based on cloud computing and grid computing [5,20]. Asvija et al. introduced the MM5 meteorological model as a supporting framework for computing grid workflows [18]. Chen et al. proposed a set of models for weather forecasting and an excellent example for the design and implementation of meteorological data workflows that have been running for many years

[19]. Ostermann et al. successfully executed meteorological applications on distributed computing infrastructure and showed that meteorological applications can be executed using Grid and Cloud resources [21].

There are a few studies consider that fault tolerance is indispensable in cloud platform. Aiming to improve fault tolerance of the cloud, a dynamic resource provisioning method based on NSGA-II is proposed in this paper, which optimizes the makespan of the meteorological workflow and ensure load balance of all computing nodes in the cloud when the computing node errors occur. Moreover, obvious achievementhas obtained in this paper.

7   Conclusion and Future Work

In this paper, to improve the fault tolerance of cloud, we proposed a dynamic resource provisioning method (ODPM) based on NSGA-II which is used to find the resource provisioning for fault task strategy that satisfies both the minimum meteorological workflow completion time and the load balancing of all compute nodes in the cloud. Then, we use SAW and MCDM to find the optimal migration strategy. A large number of experiments were conducted to verify the effectiveness of ODPM.

In future work, we will try to apply ODPM to real meteorological workflow scenarios.

Acknowledgment. This research is also supported by the National Natural Science Foundation of China under grant no. 61702277, no. 61702442, no. 61672276. Besides, this work was supported by the National Key Research and Development Program of China (No. 2017YFB1400600).

References

1. Maenhaut, P.-J., Moens, H., Volckaert, B., Ongenae, V., De Turck, F.: Resource allocation in the cloud: from simulation to experimental validation. In: 2017 IEEE 10th International Conference on Cloud Computing (CLOUD), pp. 701–704. IEEE (2017)
2. Xie, X., Yuan, T., Zhou, X., Cheng, X.: Research on trust model in container-based cloud service. Comput. Mater. Continua **56**(2), 273–283 (2018)
3. Botta, A., De Donato, W., Persico, V., Pescapé, A.: Integration of cloud computing and internet of things: a survey. Future Gener. Comput. Syst. **56**, 684–700 (2016)
4. Zhang, J., Xie, N., Zhang, X., Yue, K., Li, W., Kumar, D.: Machine learning based resource allocation of cloud computing in auction. Comput. Mater. Continua **56**(1), 123–135 (2018)
5. Wu, Q., Ishikawa, F., Zhu, Q., Xia, Y., Wen, J.: Deadline-constrained cost optimization approaches for workflow scheduling in clouds. IEEE Trans. Parallel Distrib. Syst. **28**(12), 3401–3412 (2017)
6. Xu, X., Dou, W., Zhang, X., Chen, J.: EnReal: an energy-aware resource allocation method for scientific workflow executions in cloud environment. IEEE Trans. Cloud Comput. **4**(2), 166–179 (2015)

7. Duan, R., Prodan, R., Li, X.: Multi-objective game theoretic schedulingof bag-of-tasks workflows on hybrid clouds. IEEE Trans. Cloud Comput. **2**(1), 29–42 (2014)
8. Qi, L., et al.: Structural balance theory-based e-commerce recommendation over big rating data. IEEE Trans. Big Data **4**(3), 301–312 (2016)
9. Qi, L., Chen, Y., Yuan, Y., Fu, S., Zhang, X., Xu, X.: A QoS-aware virtual machine scheduling method for energy conservation in cloud-based cyber-physical systems. World Wide Web **4**(3), 1–23 (2019)
10. Li, Z., Ge, J., Hu, H., Song, W., Hu, H., Luo, B.: Cost and energy aware scheduling algorithm for scientific workflows with deadline constraint in clouds. IEEE Trans. Serv. Comput. **11**(4), 713–726 (2015)
11. Chaisiri, S., Lee, B.-S., Niyato, D.: Optimization of resource provisioning cost in cloud computing. IEEE Trans. Serv. Comput. **5**(2), 164–177 (2011)
12. Greenberg, A., et al.: Vl2: a scalable and flexible data center network. In: ACM SIGCOMM Computer Communication Review, Vol. 39, pp. 51–62. ACM (2009)
13. Rankothge, W., Le, F., Russo, A., Lobo, J.: Optimizing resource allocation for virtualized network functions in a cloud center using genetic algorithms. IEEE Trans. Netw. Serv. Manage. **14**(2), 343–356 (2017)
14. Xia, Z., Wang, X., Sun, X., Wang, Q.: A secure and dynamic multi-keyword ranked search scheme over encrypted cloud data. IEEE Trans. Parallel Distrib. Syst. **27**(2), 340–352 (2015)
15. Xu, X., Liu, Q., Zhang, X., Zhang, J., Qi, L., Dou, W.: A blockchain-powered crowdsourcing method with privacy preservation in mobile environment. IEEE Trans. Comput. Soc. Syst. 340–352 (2019)
16. Sadooghi, I., et al.: Understanding the performance and potential of cloud computing for scientific applications. IEEE Trans. Cloud Comput. **5**(2), 358–371 (2015)
17. Liu, J., Pacitti, E., Valduriez, P., Mattoso, M.: A survey of data-intensive scientific workflow management. J. Grid Comput. **13**(4), 457–493 (2015)
18. Asvija, B., Shamjith, K., Sridharan, R., Chattopadhyay, S.: Provisioning the MM5 meteorological model as grid scientific workflow. In: 2010 International Conference on Intelligent Networking and Collaborative Systems, pp. 310–314. IEEE (2010)
19. Chen, X., Wei, M., Sun, J.: Workflow-based platform design and implementation for numerical weather prediction models and meteorological data service. Atmos. Clim. Sci. **7**(03), 337 (2017)
20. Qi, L., et al.: Finding all you need: web APIs recommendation in web of things through keywords search. IEEE Trans. Comput. Soc. Syst. 337–351 (2019)
21. Ostermann, S., Prodan, R., Schüller, F., Mayr, G.J.: Meteorological applications utilizing grid and cloud computing. In: 2014 IEEE 3rd International Conference on Cloud Networking (CloudNet), pp. 33–39. IEEE (2014)

Do Top Social Apps Effect Voice Call? Evidence from Propensity Score Matching Methods

Hao Jiang[1], Min Lin[2], Bingqing Liu[1(✉)], Huifang Liu[2], Yuanyuan Zeng[1(✉)], He Nai[1], Xiaoli Zhang[1], Xianlong Zhao[3], Wen Du[4], and Haining Ye[2]

[1] School of Electronic Information, Wuhan University, Wuhan, China
{jh,liubbq,zengyy,naihe,Xiaoli}@whu.edu.cn
[2] China United Telecommunications Co., Ltd., Guangzhou, China
{linmin23,liuhf67,yehn1}@chinaunicom.cn
[3] Beijing Smart Chip Microelectronics Co., Ltd., Beijing, China
zhaoxianlongbj@163.com
[4] Shanghai DS Communication Equipment Co., Ltd., Shanghai, China
duwen@dscomm.com.cn

Abstract. The various mobile social APPs greatly enrich the way people communicate with each other. It has been argued that the use of mobile social APPs may influence user mobile phone call behaviour, as more and more people are used to using mobile social APPs for voice or video calls. Although mobile social APPs has penetrated into every aspect of our daily lives, so far there is no convincing research showing how the mobile social APPs influence the use of traditional mobile phone calls. Based on the potential outcomes model, we use the potential outcomes model to study the causal effects of the frequent use of mobile social APPs on mobile phone calls. The propensity score matching method is performed for bias adjustment. Moreover, the sensitivity analysis is conducted to test whether the results remained robust in the presence of hidden biases. The results suggest statistically significant positive effects of frequent use of Wechat on traditional mobile phone calls. But for QQ, we found that frequent use of QQ reduces mobile phone calls. The conclusion provides a new theoretical feature for business package recommendation, namely, the frequency of mobile social APPs. For WeChat users who use WeChat frequently, they are more inclined to provide business package containing high call duration, and for QQ users who use QQ frequently, they are more inclined to provide business package containing low call duration, which further enriches the method of business package recommendation.

Keywords: Mobile social APPs · Mobile phone calls · Causal influence · Propensity score matching

© Springer Nature Switzerland AG 2019
M. Qiu (Ed.): SmartCom 2019, LNCS 11910, pp. 136–149, 2019.
https://doi.org/10.1007/978-3-030-34139-8_14

1   Introduction

The latest data released by QuestMobile showed that mobile social users in China reached 1.104 billion by February 2019. As an emerging Internet technology and communication channel, mobile social APPs have an ever-increasing impact on people's work and life [19]. From the "on the phone" to "on-line chat", social APPs such as WeChat and QQ have enriched the way people communicate. However, the rapid development of various online social calls. Compared with Internet telephony, the signal is more stable when communicating using mobile phone calls. It is more efficient to make a phone call when the network is in poor condition. APPs did not completely replace traditional mobile phone. Both social APPs and smart-phones are important communication methods for comsumers, so it is meaningful for business cooperation to explore the relationship between social APPs and traditional voice.

Frequent use of mobile social APPs may have two effects on using phones for voice calls. One view is that mobile social APPs can increase interaction between people [15,17]. However, it is also argued that mobile social APPs make people's expressions more fragmented and symbolized [20], and more and more people are unwilling to call or receive calls because it is mandatory and immediate.

This paper aims to assess the causal effects of frequent use of WeChat and QQ on mobile phone calls respectively. In this paper, The WeChat, QQ visit and offline call data records provided by China Unicom are used for empirical research. Based on the potential outcomes framework, we use the propensity score matching method to "control" the confusion that may occur when evaluating the effect, to get an accurate estimate of the impact of frequent use of WeChat and QQ on mobile phone calls.

The rest of this paper is organized as follows. The ralated work is discussed in Sect. 2. Section 3 introduces the data and model which used to analyse, and Sect. 4 evaluates and analyses experimental Results. Finally, the paper is concluded in Sect. 5.

2   Related Work

The mobile Internet has developed rapidly and gradually penetrated into people's lives and all aspects of work. With the rapid development of 3g, 4g or even 5g technology, the network is in our pockets. More and more people are inseparable from mobile phones. At the same time, the birth of many mobile social APPs has greatly enriched the way people communicate, and the connection between people is becoming more and more convenient and close. Many scholars begin to explore the impact of mobile social Apps on people's real life [7].

Althoff et al. [1] studied the impact of social APPs on online and offline behavior of users. By analyzing the online and offline behavior of 6 million users in 5 years, the paper concludes that social networks can significantly increase users' online and offline activities. Based on the study on the household survey data from Italy, Sabatini et al. [14] found that the use of SNS social networking sites (SNS) has a negative effect on social trust.

There is also a considerable part of the literature on the impact of social APPs on physical health and mental health [11,16]. In studies [9,10], the scholars found a slight positive effect of social APPs on health behavior change. Burke et al. [4] conducted a longitudinal study of 1,200 Facebook users and analyzed a series of behaviors on Facebook (such as likes, private messages, comments, etc.). Her conclusion is that social APP alone does not make people feel unhappy and lonely, but some of its functions and features can easily adversely affect users.

Also, the relationship between online social network based on social APPs and offline social network has been studied by some researchers [6]. Reich et al. [2,12] found a moderate overlap between teenagers' closest online and offline friends, which indicated that the online context is used to strengthen offline relationships. Using Facebook users as a research sample [5], the researchers found that the size and scope of social networks on mobile social APPs are similar to offline social networks.

These findings provide a better understanding of how mobile social APP affects user engagement behavior and provides guidance for improving the design of the APP. However, in the work of studying the impact of mobile social APPs on people's behavior, most of them need to be completed through the assistance of tracking surveys or questionnaires. user behavior is often affected by many variables. In some empirical studies, the author did not consider the existence of selectivity bias. Without controlling the selection biases, the conclusions obtained by calculating the correlation coefficients are often not convincing.

3   Data and Model

3.1   Data Source and Description

The empirical analysis is based on the information records of mobile phone users in Jiangmen city provided by China Unicom operators. The data covers some basic user information. including user's age, gender, and job type. In addition, due to the operator's billing requirements, the user behavior information will be stored when the user uses the mobile phone, including the Internet content records, mobile phone calls records. First, the paper analyzes the behaviors of users using WeChat, QQ by using the APPs visit records in April and May, 2018 from mobile phone users.

In order to study how the frequent use of mobile social APPs affects users' use of mobile phone calls, we first select the users whose records of daily access APP exceed the median of that day as the experimental group users. Users in the experimental group are users with frequent use of mobile social App behavior. According to the research need, the users age, gender [16,17], and job type are selected as covariate to control the user's own basic situation. The package fee and voice call fee paid by user in early month are selected as covariate to control the user's original voice call demands. In order to reflect the situation of the user's mobile phone call, we select the number and duration of voice calls, the sizes of calling and called user as the dependent variables. The specific variable definition is selected as shown in Table 1.

Table 1. Variable definitions

Type	Name	Definition
Covariate	Age	Age of mobile user
Covariate	Sex (F)	Sex of mobile user (0: Female 1: Male)
Covariate	Job (X)	Job type of user (range: 0–9)
Covariate	Rent	Monthly basic package fee paid by user (Unit: yuan)
Covariate	Voice rent	Monthly basic voice fee paid by user (Unit: yuan)
Covariate	PS	Propensity score (range: 0–1)
Dependent variable	Call times	Monthly total voice call numbers of times
Dependent variable	Calling times	Monthly active call out numbers of timesJob type of user
Dependent variable	Call dur	Monthly voice call duration (Unit: minitues)
Dependent variable	Calling num	Monthly call out numbers of user
Dependent variable	Calling num	Monthly call in numbers of users

3.2 Basic Assumptions

Assumption 1: Stable Unit Treatment Value Assumption. In our analysis, the individual under tested is smartphone user. We assume that the causal effects of frequent use of mobile social APPs on individuals using mobile phone voice calls are consistent and stable. It is also assumed that mobile users do not interfere with each other. Generally, users who do not often use mobile social APPs are not affected by other users who frequently use them. Generally speaking, the user's Internet behavior preference is related to the individual, and the personal behavior does not affect other people's online or phone voice call behavior. Therefore, the stable unit treatment value assumption is reasonable.

Assumption 2: Ignorable Treatment Assignment Assumption. To ensure the assignment is random when a mobile user is assigned to the experimental or control group, other variables that make the difference between the experimental group and the control group should be excluded. Equation (1) is the mathematical expression of the assumption.

$$(Y^1, Y^0) \perp Z \tag{1}$$

The symbol $\perp$ indicates independence, that is, the assignment variable Z must be "joint" independent of all functions that take the potential result as a parameter. The Eq. (1) is also called strong ignorable treatment assignment assumption, which is a necessary assumption for reliable cause-and-effect conclusions. In actual study, it is impossible to find two people who are exactly the same in all aspects. Other personal factors may be overlooked when studying the impact of frequent use of mobile social APPs on mobile phone calls. For example, users who frequently use social APP may use mobile phone calls more frequently than control groups due to their differences in personal or original social circles. In this case, we can't clearly know how the mobile social APP influence phone voice calls. In our analysis, we control as much as possible the covariate that may affect the assignment and experimental results. Equation (2) shows the mathematical expression under this condition.

$$(Y^1, Y^0) \perp Z | X \tag{2}$$

Unlike the requirement of Eqs. (1), (2) relaxes the condition. The probability that a user is assigned to an experimental group or a control group does not need to be strictly equal, only needs to be equal under the condition of controlling the covariate.

Assumption 3: Balance and Overlap of Covariates. The covariates we select in this experiment include the user's age, gender, job type, the basic package fee and voice fee paid by the user at the beginning of the month. The distribution of these variables in the experimental and control group must be balanced and overlapped. Typically, the voice call fee paid by user of the experimental group in early month is higher than that of the control group. That is, the user's original demand for voice call is the reason for the difference between the two user groups of phone voice calls in that month. In this paper, we determine whether the distribution of the covariates between two user groups after matching was balanced by comparing the covariates' mean and the standardized mean difference. The SMD (standardized mean difference) is calculated as Eq. (3).

$$\delta = \frac{\mu_1 - \mu_0}{\sqrt{\frac{s_1^2 + s_0^2}{2}}} \tag{3}$$

where μ_0 and μ_1 represent the mean of the covariate in the experimental group and the control group, respectively. s_0^2 and s_1^2 represent the standard deviation of the covariate in the experimental group and the control group. To deal with the multidimensional data, the propensity score is used to represent the one-dimensional eigenvalues of all covariates, and check whether the matched covariates lack coincidence.

3.3 Propensity Score Matching Model

The purpose of this paper is to study the causal influence of the frequent use of mobile social APPs on mobile phone calls under the condition that other factors are the same. Since the data used in this paper is observational data related to users' online and call records, the research in this paper belongs to observational research. Observational research is different from experimental research that the assignment of treatment can not be controlled. Also, it is impossible to simultaneously observe the user's two different habits of mobile social APPs use.

The propensity score matching (PSM) means that the experimental group and the control group are screened by a certain statistical method, so that the selected research objects are comparable in the presence of confounding factors. The PSM method enables random assignment of assignment variable. At the same time, the method can control the confounding variables, so that the probability of frequent use of mobile social APP by the experimental group and the control group user is the same. So that the two groups are comparable, to achieve the purpose of simulation experiments. Therefore, the PSM [3] method is used to select users in the control group that are similar in all aspects to the experimental group.

We divided the samples into treatment and control groups according to the treatment assignment variable. Users in the experimental group have behaviors that frequently use a certain mobile social APP. Conversely, users of the control group do not use the mobile social APP very often. The propensity score is the probability that the user is assigned to the experimental group given the covariate, which is calculated as Eq. (4).

$$e(X) = Pr(Z = 1|X) = \frac{exp(\beta X)}{1 + exp(\beta X)} \tag{4}$$

After obtaining the estimated value by Eq. (4), the probability that the user frequently uses a certain mobile social APP that is, the PS (propensity score), can be obtained. In the case where the multidimensional covariate exists, the one-dimensional PS score will be used to find matching users between experimental group and control group. To satisfy the ignorable treatment assignment assumption, we first choose covariates that affect the frequent use of mobile social APPs by users and mobile phone calls. Then, the logistic regression model is used to estimate the probability that the user will frequently use the mobile social APP given the covariates. The machine learning method including neural network model, and XGBOOST model are also used for the estimation of propensity score, which has less assumptions. The neural network model can deal with high-dimensional data without considering the interactions or high-dimensional forms may exist in the covariate.

Common matching methods include 1:K nearest neighbor matching, radius matching. The nearest neighbor matching method includes replaceable and non-replaceable of the control sample. In the following empirical analysis, we will select the best matching method based on the balance effect of the covariates. After the matching, we analyze the causal effects of frequent use of mobile social APPs on mobile phone calls by comparing the values of the dependent variables in experimental and control group. This paper focuses on the effect of frequent use of mobile social APPs on mobile phone calls. That is, after frequent use of the mobile social APPs, how does the use of mobile phone calls change? In the sample of experimental group, we are unable to observe the behavior of users when they don't use mobile social APPs very often. So we use the propensity score matching method, under the assumption of ignorable treatment assignment, to select the sample in the control group instead. The formula that estimate the ATT (average treatment effect on the treated) of the experimental group is as shown in Eq. 5.

$$
\begin{aligned}
ATT &= E(Y^1 - Y^0|Z = 1) \\
&= E(Y^1|Z = 1) - E(Y^0|Z = 1) \\
&= E(Y^1|Z = 1, e(X) - E(Y^0|Z = 0, e(X))
\end{aligned}
\tag{5}
$$

where Y^1 represents the dependent variables of the experimental group, including the number, duration and user number of mobile phone calls. Y^0 represents the dependent variable of the control group.

An important issue in causal inference is that we choose the observed covariates that may affect users' habit using mobile social APPs and making mobile phone calls. However, in reality, there are often hidden variables in observing data. Sensitivity analysis is required when performing causal inferences based on propensity score matching model. Sensitivity analysis is to explore the impact of hidden bias on the ATT. That is, to what extent, the result of causal effects will change. In the sensitivity analysis, we assume that there are one or more hidden covariates that we can't control. If the large-scale changes in the effects of these uncontrolled variables on the outcome variables cannot change our conclusions, our conclusions are reliable. Assuming that the user and the user have the same covariates, Eq. (6) can be deducted by Logist regression.

$$
e(X) = \frac{1}{1 + e^{-(X\beta)}} \Rightarrow log(\frac{e(X)}{1 - e(X)}) = X\beta \Rightarrow \frac{e(X)}{1 - e(X)} = exp(X\beta)
\tag{6}
$$

For user j and user k, the odds ratio of frequent use of mobile social APP is $\frac{e_j(X)}{1-e_j(X)}$ divided by the $\frac{e_k(X)}{1-e_k(X)}$, which is between $\Gamma(\Gamma >= 1)$ and $\frac{1}{\Gamma}$. If there is no hidden deviation between the two users, $\Gamma = 1$. $\Gamma = 2$ indicates that even though j and k have the same observable covariates, the odds ratio of frequent use of mobile social APP by user j is twice that of user k. That is, j might be twice as likely as k to receive the treatment because they differ in ways that have not been measured or observed. There is a hidden deviation between users j and k. The sensitivity analysis displays how the casual effect changes with Γ. We uses the Wilcoxon signed rank test for sensitivity analysis [8]. The P-value for testing the null hypothesis of no treatment effect is considered.

4   Experimental Results and Analysis

4.1   Assessment of Covariate Overlap and Balance

The methods mentioned in reference [18] are used for calculating the propensity score, including traditional logistic regression model, neural network model, and

XGBOOST boosted model based on decision tree algorithm[21]. We first assess covariate overlap and balance. Rosenbaum and Rubin believe that the absolute value of the standard deviation of the matched variables is significantly less than 20%, indicating that the matching method is appropriate. Figure 1 reports, for each model, the boxplots of the SMD in covariates between the experimental and control group. Specifically, Fig. 1a shows the matching results when studying the influence of frequent use of WeChat on the mobile phone calls. It can be seen that in the experiment, the matching effect using the XGBOOST model is the best. Compared with the other two models, the SMD of the covariates between the experimental and control group are closer to zero. While studying the impact of QQ, as shown in Fig. 1b, the matching effect is best when using traditional logistic regression model. Regardless of which model is used, the SMD is reduced to less than 20% in each experiment. We also use the t-test to assess the balance of the covariates in the two groups, and found that the mean difference between the experimental and the control group was not statistically significant. In the subsequent empirical analysis, we will use different models to estimate the propensity score to test the robustness of the results.

Meanwhile, we used different matching methods to find individuals in the control group that were similar to the individuals in the experimental group, including repeatable 1:1 nearest neighbor matching, non-repeatable 1:1 nearest neighbor matching and radius matching method. From the Fig. 1b, the non-repeatable 1:1 nearest neighbor matching method works best. The SMD after matching of all covariates in the experimental group and the control group was below 0.1, which effectively reduced the difference in the covariates between the two groups. In particular, when the control sample is repeatable, that is, after applying the repeatable 1:1 nearest neighbor matching method, the deviation between the experimental group and the control group is even increased. Therefore, in order to obtain a more accurate and convincing conclusion of the causal influence, in the following all experiments, we use the results of the non-repeatable nearest neighbor matching for analysis. We use the bar graph to assess the overlap of the covariate. In order to better display the sample distribution in various propensity score areas, we indicate the specific sample size in various areas. As shown in the Fig. 2a and b, the propensity scores of the experimental and the control group were not similar before the matching. After matching, there shows a satisfactory overlap in the support of the propensity score. The matched samples satisfy the requirements of the balance and overlap of the covariates, and the subsequent causal influence analysis can be performed.

4.2 Estimation Results of ATT

In this article, our focus is on those who use mobile social APPs frequently. That is, changes in the use of mobile phone calls after the experimental group samples frequently use mobile social APP. The variables used to estimate the causal effects include the total number of calls, the number of calling times and the total duration of mobile phone calls, the number of calling user and called user. In order to test the robustness of the experimental results, we use the

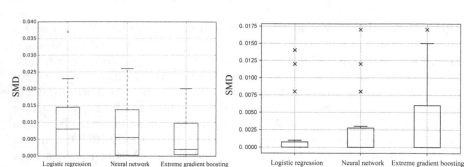

(a) The SMD of the covariates after matching in different models

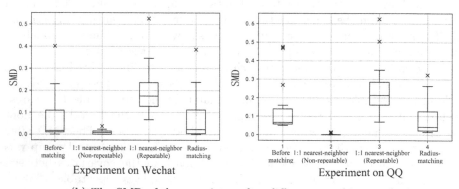

(b) The SMD of the covariates after different matching method

Fig. 1. The SMD of the covariates after matching

traditional logistic regression model, neural network model, Xgboost boosted model to estimate the propensity scores separately, and then estimate the ATT of experimental group based on the sample matching. Tables 2 and 3 show the causal effect of frequent use of Wechat and QQ on voice calls after eliminating the difference in covariates between the experimental and the control group by matching. $M0$ represents the mean of the experimental group and $M1$ represents the mean of the control group.

Note: (1) Figures in brackets are the standard error of ATT, which was calculated by using Bootstrap sampling for 500 times.

(2): *Control group is significantly different from the experimental group at the 0.10 level, paired samples T test.

**Control group is significantly different from the experimental group at the 0.05 level, paired samples T test.

***Control group is significantly different from the experimental group at the 0.01 level, paired samples T test.

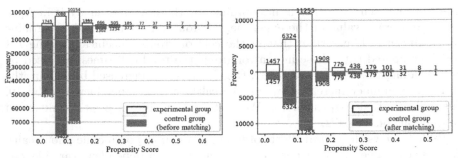

(a) Distribution of PS in experimental group that frequent use Wechat and control group

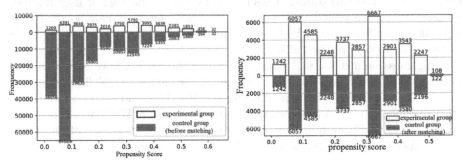

(b) Distribution of PS in experimental group that frequent use QQ and control group

Fig. 2. Distribution of PS (propensity score)

Table 2. ATT of frequent use of WeChat on mobile phone calls (April)

Dependent variable	M0	LR model		NN model		XGBOOST model	
		ATT	M1	ATT	M1	ATT	M1
Call times	174	60***(2.38)	114	59***(2.28)	115	58***(2.35)	116
Calling times	91	31***(0.89)	60	30***(0.91)	61	30***(0.89)	61
Call duration	235	72***(4.52)	163	71***(4.24)	164	70***(2.35)	116
Calling user number	64	20***(0.53)	44	19***(0.54)	44	20***(0.19)	44
Called user number	57	19***(0.20)	38	18***(0.19)	39	18***(0.52)	39

Table 3. ATT of frequent use of QQ on mobile phone calls (April)

Dependent variable	M0	LR model		NN model		XGBOOST model	
		ATT	M1	ATT	M1	ATT	M1
Call times	82	−9***(0.93)	91	−9***(1.77)	91	−10***(1.17)	92
Calling times	44	−3***(0.35)	47	−3***(0.61)	47	−4***(0.37)	48
Call duration	121	−7***(2.52)	128	−7***(2.86)	128	−8***(2.75)	129
Calling user number	32	−2***(0.07)	34	−2***(0.24)	34	20***(0.08)	34
Called user number	27	−4***(0.20)	31	−4***(0.59)	31	−4***(0.27)	31

As can be seen from the results obtained by the user data analysis in April 2018, the average value of the experimental group on each dependent variable was significantly larger than that of the control group. Specifically, using LR Model, compared with those in control group, the total call times increased by 60, the calling times increased by 31, the call duration increased by 72 min, the calling user number increased by 20, the called user number increased by 19. This indicates that frequent use of WeChat has a significant positive impact on using mobile phone calls.

Table 3 shows the causal effects of frequent use of QQ on mobile phone calls. The average value of the experimental group on each dependent variable was significantly less than that of the control group. Using LR Model, compared with those in control group, the total call times decreased by 9, the calling times decreased by 3, the call duration decreased by 7 min, the calling user number decreased by 2, the called user number decreased by 4. It can be seen that unlike the causal influence of WeChat, frequent use of QQ reduces the frequency of users using mobile phone calls.

Using the same method and steps, we analyze the data in May 2018 of mobile phone users. Tables 4 and 5 show the results. There is not much difference from the data analysis results in April. Combined with the results of two months of empirical analysis, we can conclude that the frequent use of WeChat will promote the use of traditional mobile phone call function, the frequent use of QQ has a negative effect on mobile phone call.

Table 4. ATT of frequent use of WeChat on mobile phone calls (May)

Dependent variable	M0	LR model		NN model		XGBOOST model	
		ATT	M1	ATT	M1	ATT	M1
Call times	172	$56^{***}(2.91)$	116	$56^{***}(2.15)$	116	$56^{***}(2.46)$	117
Calling times	89	$29^{***}(1.59)$	61	$28^{***}(1.52)$	61	$28^{***}(1.71)$	62
Call duration	235	$71^{***}(4.79)$	164	$70^{***}(4.53)$	165	$70^{***}(3.70)$	116
Calling user number	62	$18^{***}(0.34)$	44	$18^{***}(0.29)$	44	$18^{***}(0.54)$	44
Called user number	57	$19^{***}(0.34)$	38	$18^{***}(0.28)$	39	$17^{***}(0.56)$	40

Table 5. ATT of frequent use of QQ on mobile phone calls (May)

Dependent variable	M0	LR model		NN model		XGBOOST model	
		ATT	M1	ATT	M1	ATT	M1
Call times	77	$-14^{***}(1.35)$	91	$-14^{***}(1.66)$	91	$-14^{***}(1.08)$	91
Calling times	41	$-6^{***}(0.35)$	47	$-6^{***}(0.91)$	47	$-4^{***}(0.89)$	47
Call duration	115	$-12^{***}(2.52)$	127	$-12^{***}(4.24)$	128	$-12^{***}(2.35)$	127
Calling user number	29	$-4^{***}(0.20)$	33	$-4^{**}(0.19)$	33	$-4^{***}(0.52)$	33
Called user number	25	$-6^{***}(0.07)$	31	$-6^{***}(0.47)$	31	$-6^{***}(0.19)$	31

Table 6. Sensitivity analysis of the causal effects of frequent use of WeChat on mobile phone calls

Γ		1	2	4	4.8	5.2
Y_0	sig^+	<0.0001	<0.0001	<0.0001	<0.0001	0.0694
	sig^-	<0.0001	<0.0001	<0.0001	<0.0001	<0.0001
Y_1	sig^+	<0.0001	<0.0001	<0.0001	0.00681	>0.05
	sig^-	<0.0001	<0.0001	<0.0001	<0.0001	<0.0001
Y_2	sig^+	<0.0001	<0.0001	<0.0001	0.0001	>0.05
	sig^-	<0.0001	<0.0001	<0.0001	<0.0001	<0.0001
Y_3	sig^+	<0.0001	<0.0001	<0.0001	<0.0001	>0.05
	sig^-	<0.0001	<0.0001	<0.0001	<0.0001	<0.0001
Y_4	sig^+	<0.0001	<0.0001	<0.0001	<0.0526	>0.05
	sig^-	<0.0001	<0.0001	<0.0001	<0.0001	<0.0001

Table 7. Sensitivity analysis of the causal effects of frequent use of QQ on mobile phone calls

Γ		1	2	2.6	2.8
Y_0	sig^+	<0.0001	<0.0001	<0.0001	<0.0001
	sig^-	<0.0001	<0.0001	0.1841	>0.05
Y_1	sig^+	<0.0001	<0.0001	<0.0001	<0.0001
	sig	<0.0001	<0.0001	<0.0001	0.0526
Y_2	sig^+	<0.0001	<0.0001	<0.0001	<0.0001
	sig	<0.0001	<0.0001	<0.0001	0.3015
Y_3	sig^+	<0.0001	<0.0001	<0.0001	<0.0001
	sig^-	<0.0001	<0.0001	<0.0001	0.0721
Y_4	sig^+	<0.0001	<0.0001	<0.0001	<0.0001
	sig^-	<0.0001	<0.0001	0.0029	>0.05

4.3 Sensitivity Analysis

The sensitivity analysis results are shown in Tables 6 and 7. $Y_i(i = 0, 1, 2, 3, 4)$ represent the total call times, calling times, call duration, calling user number, called user number respectively. Rosenbaum [13] pointed out that the sensitivity is considered low as long as $\Gamma > 2$. It can be seen from Table VI, if $\Gamma > 4.8$, the P-value of the Wilcoxon signed rank test of the calling times in the month will be greater than 0.05. that is, if mobile users may differ by a factor of $\Gamma = 4.8$ in their odds of visit WeChat frequently, then the original conclusion that frequent use of WeChat will increase the number of voice calling times is simply mistaken. Also, if Γ increased to 5.2, the P-value of all dependent variables are checked to be > 0.05, the conclusion will be overturned. It indicates that the research has low sensitivity to the influence of hidden bias and the conclusion is reliable. Similarly, the Table 7 shows the sensitivity analysis results of the casual effect of QQ on mobile phone calls.

5   Conclusion and Discussion

In this paper, the frequent use behavior of mobile scoial APP is regarded as the assignment variable, based on the potential outcome model and ignorable treatment assignment assumption, the propensity matching method is used to calculate the causal effects of WeChat and QQ on mobile phone calls. The study found that the frequent use of WeChat has a significant positive influence on users mobile phone calls. As another major mobile social APP, QQ has a different effect on the use of mobile phone calls by users. The results show that the frequent use of QQ has a significant negative impact on mobile phone calls. The causal analysis results sheds new light for business package recommendation. For WeChat users who use WeChat frequently, they are more inclined to provide business package containing high call duration. At the same time, based on the analysis results, we provide advice on the cooperation between operators and APP software developers. When operators choose to promote their own activities on WeChat platform, due to the high demand for voice calls of users who often use WeChat, operators should focus on promoting "high traffic + high voice" plan for consumers who use WeChat frequently on the platform of WeChat. On the QQ platform, they should focus on promoting the "high traffic + low voice" plan for consumers who use QQ frequently.

References

1. Althoff, T., Jindal, P., Leskovec, J.: Online actions with offline impact: how online social networks influence online and offline user behavior (2016)
2. Atzmueller, M.: Analyzing and grounding social interaction in online and offline networks. In: Calders, T., Esposito, F., Hüllermeier, E., Meo, R. (eds.) ECML PKDD 2014. LNCS (LNAI), vol. 8726, pp. 485–488. Springer, Heidelberg (2014). https://doi.org/10.1007/978-3-662-44845-8_41
3. Austin, P.C.: An introduction to propensity score methods for reducing the effects of confounding in observational studies. Multivariate Behav. Res. **46**(3), 399–424 (2011)
4. Burke, M., Kraut, R.E.: The relationship between facebook use and well-being depends on communication type and tie strength: Facebook and well-being. J. Comput.-Mediat. Commun. **21**(4), 265–281 (2016)
5. Dunbar, R.I.: Do online social media cut through the constraints that limit the size of offline social networks? R. Soc. Open Sci. **3**(1), 150292 (2016)
6. Dunbar, R.I.M., Arnaboldi, V., Conti, M., Passarella, A.: The structure of online social networks mirrors those in the offline world. Soc. Netw. **43**, 39–47 (2015)
7. Gwenn Schurgin, O., Kathleen, C.P.: The impact of social media on children, adolescents, and families. Pediatrics **127**(4), 800 (2011)
8. Hsu, J.Y., Small, D.S., Rosenbaum, P.R.: Effect modification and design sensitivity in observational studies. J. Am. Stat. Assoc. **108**(501), 135–148 (2013)

9. Laranjo, L., et al.: The influence of social networking sites on health behavior change: a systematic review and meta-analysis. J. Am. Med. Inform. Assoc. **22**(1), 243–256 (2014)

10. Meng, J.: Your health buddies matter: preferential selection and social influence on weight management in an online health social network. Health Commun. **31**(12), 1 (2016)

11. Oh, H.J., Ozkaya, E., Larose, R.: How does online social networking enhance life satisfaction? The relationships among online supportive interaction, affect, perceived social support, sense of community, and life satisfaction. Comput. Hum. Behav. **30**(1), 69–78 (2014)

12. Reich, S.M., Subrahmanyam, K., Espinoza, G.: Friending, iming, and hanging out face-to-face: Overlap in adolescents' online and offline social networks. Dev. Psychol. **48**(2), 356 (2012)

13. Rosenbaum, P.R.: Design of Observational Studies (2010)

14. Sabatini, F., Sarracino, F.: Online social networks and trust. Soc. Indicat. Res. **2**, 1–32 (2015)

15. Shi, J., Salmon, C.T.: Identifying opinion leaders to promote organ donation on social media: network study. J. Med. Internet Res. **20**(1), e7 (2018)

16. Song, H., et al.: Does facebook make you lonely?: A meta analysis. Comput. Hum. Behav. **36**(36), 446–452 (2014)

17. Utz, S.: The function of self-disclosure on social network sites: not only intimate, but also positive and entertaining self-disclosures increase the feeling of connection. Comput. Hum. Behav. **45**, 1–10 (2015)

18. Westreich, D., Lessler, J., Funk, M.J.: Propensity score estimation: neural networks, support vector machines, decision trees (CART), and meta-classifiers as alternatives to logistic regression. J. Clin. Epidemiol. **63**(8), 826–833 (2010)

19. Yadav, M., Joshi, Y., Rahman, Z.: Mobile social media: the new hybrid element of digital marketing communications. Proc. - Soc. Behav. Sci. **189**, 335–343 (2015)

20. Yang, S., Wang, B., Lu, Y.: Exploring the dual outcomes of mobile social networking service enjoyment: the roles of social self-efficacy and habit. Comput. Hum. Behav. **64**, 486–496 (2016)

Cognitive Hierarchy Based Coexistence and Resource Allocation for URLLC and eMBB

Kexin Yang, Yuanyuan Zeng, Hao Jiang[✉], and Qimei Chen

School of Electronic Information, Wuhan University, Wuhan, China
{yiren,zengyy,jh,chenqimei}@whu.edu.cn

Abstract. 5G networks will serve both enhanced mobile broadband (eMBB) and ultra-reliable low-latency communications (URLLC) traffics, indicating the heterogeneity of future communication systems. The coexistence of eMBB and URLLC and the resource allocation problem may be pretty challenging due to various quality of service (QoS) requirements. Inspired by 802.11e standard, we study a novel coexistence scheme for eMBB and URLLC devices with their vastly different demands considered, i.e., throughput for eMBB devices and error probability for URLLC. Furthermore, a realistic cognitive hierarchy (CH) theory is utilized to solve the distributed resource allocation problem. The applicability of our proposed scheme is evaluated by the simulation results.

Keywords: Cognitive hierarchy · Resource allocation · 5G

1 Introduction

In the past few years, there has been a consensus in the industry that the future 5G communication systems can serve different types of devices: enhanced mobile broadband (eMBB), ultra-reliable low-latency communications (URLLC) and massive machine-type communications (mMTC). eMBB may require a pretty high data transmission rate. URLLC devices are required to meet ultra lower latency with high reliability, and mMTC supports massive devices which sporadically send small packets [1]. Topics such as edge computing and Internet of things have been extensively studied [2–4], which may provide solutions for 5G new scenarios. Besides, due to the limited available spectrum and different quality of service (QoS) requirements, the coexistence of URLLC and eMBB has been a hot topic in both industry and academia. The variable 5G frame structure has provided a feasible way for researchers to satisfy the URLLC latency [5,6], where slots are further divided into mini-slots and a puncturing mechanism is applied. And [7] proposed a novel resource allocation scheme based on flexible numerology of 5G. In addition, network slicing schemes for different services have also been studied [8].

© Springer Nature Switzerland AG 2019
M. Qiu (Ed.): SmartCom 2019, LNCS 11910, pp. 150–160, 2019.
https://doi.org/10.1007/978-3-030-34139-8_15

However, they haven't paid much attention to the heterogeneity of devices resulted by their computation capacity and QoS requirements. Inspired by the enhanced distributed channel access (EDCA) and HCF controlled channel access (HCCA) mechanisms defined in 802.11e standard [9], which respectively guarantee QoS requirements of users belonging to different access categories (AC) and achieve real-time data transmission, we consider to utilize the characteristics of EDCA and HCCA in our work to achieve access of eMBB and URLLC users in the shared frequency band. Furthermore, game theory have been widely used to solve distributed resource allocation problems. Since the assumptions of Nash equilibrium that all devices have the same computation capacity and are completely rational are not practical, we turn to a more realistic model, i.e., cognitive hierarchy (CH) theory which is based on the concept of bounded rationality. Our main contributions of this paper are as follows:

- We develop a novel coexistence scheme based on the features of EDCA and HCCA for eMBB and URLLC users with the heterogeneity considered.
- A realistic and low-complexity CH theory is utilized to solve the distributed resource allocation problem based on the various QoS requirements of users.

The rest of this paper is organized as follows. A description of the our system model is discussed in Sect. 2. Section 3 introduces our proposed resource allocation algorithm, and Sect. 4 evaluates the performance of our model. Finally, the paper is concluded in Sect. 5.

2 System Model and Problem Formulation

2.1 System Model

In this paper, we consider a scenario where URLLC and eMBB users coexist. According to the strict delay requirements, packets of URLLC users should be transmitted first, so we control them to access with the HCCA mechanism which is free of contention. Different from the original HCCA mechanism, we assume URLLC packets can be transmitted as soon as they arrive by interrupting existing transmission of eMBB users, which is based on the feature of EDCA that packets can be sent during several transmission opportunities (TXOPs). eMBB users requiring huge throughput are assumed to have data to transmit all the time and they will adopt EDCA mechanism to access, which is based on the CSMA/CA protocol. Note that we think eMBB users just access the channel based on the EDCA mechanism while still transmitting in a general manner to satisfy their demands.

For simplicity, all transmission information is assumed to be contained in the beacon, and HC will spontaneously arrange users to transmit data based on packet arrival time and user priority. It should be emphasized that we think the traffic of URLLC users can be predicted with the earlier information, but this is not discussed in our paper. Owing to the ability of HC to start the controlled access phrase (CAP) at any time throughout the interval, we can ignore the

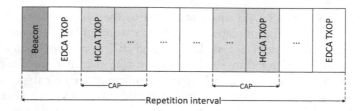

Fig. 1. The structure of frame.

boundary between CP and CFP, as shown in Fig. 1. In addition, the backoff time is so short that will not cause effect if ignored. So we will only discuss how to allocate the transmission time fractions in the following paragraphs.

We assume that there are M URLLC users and N eMBB users, which are denoted as $\mathscr{M} = \{0, ..., M - 1\}$ and $\mathscr{N} = \{0, ..., N - 1\}$, respectively. The total length of the repetition interval is set as L. Our system model can be seen in Fig. 2.

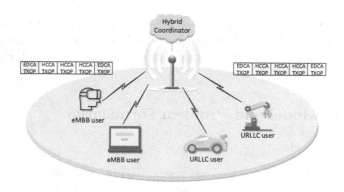

Fig. 2. System model.

Considering the heterogeneity of users, the requirement of each user is determined by its type, and we should derive the time fraction for each user. Details of the requirements of both URLLC and eMBB users are shown below.

(1) **URLLC Users Requirements**

URLLC users, such as autonomous vehicles and industrial sensors, have strong needs for real-time performance, i.e., they have to deliver packets as soon as they arrive. Since most of these bursty packets are short packets, traditional Shannon formula may not apply. According to [10], for a given packet error rate ϵ_m, for each user $m \in \mathscr{M}$, the achievable data rate can be expressed as

$$q_m \approx \log\left(1 + \frac{|h_m|^2 P_m}{\sigma^2}\right) - \sqrt{\frac{V_m}{B\tau_m}}Q^{-1}(\epsilon_m)\log e, \qquad (1)$$

where B is the bandwidth. h_m denotes the channel gain, and P_m denotes the fixed transmission power of user m. The variance σ^2 of the Additive Gaussian white noise is considered to be constant for all users. And τ_m is the time fraction of each user. In addition,

$$Q(x) = \int_x^\infty \frac{1}{\sqrt{2\pi}} \exp(-\frac{t^2}{2})dt, \tag{2}$$

and V_m is the channel dispersion

$$V_m = 1 - \frac{1}{(1 + \frac{|h_m|^2 P_m}{\sigma^2})^2} \approx 1 \tag{3}$$

Let

$$b_m = B\tau_m q_m$$
$$= B\tau_m \left[\log\left(1 + \frac{|h_m|^2 P_m}{\sigma^2}\right) - \sqrt{\frac{V_m}{B\tau_m}} Q^{-1}(\epsilon_m) \log e \right], \tag{4}$$

where b_m denotes the packet size. We can get the error probability

$$\epsilon_m = Q(\frac{\sqrt{B\tau_m} \log(1 + \frac{|h_m|^2 P_m}{\sigma^2})}{\log e} - \frac{b_m}{\sqrt{B\tau_m} \log e}), \tag{5}$$

Since it is obvious that $Q(x)$ decreases with x, our objective to minimize the error probability of each URLLC user can be converted to maximizing the content in parentheses on the right side of (5).
The optimization problem of each URLLC user is therefore

$$\max_{\tau_m} \frac{\sqrt{B\tau_m} \log(1 + \frac{|h_m|^2 P_m}{\sigma^2})}{\log e} - \frac{b_m}{\sqrt{B\tau_m} \log e}, \tag{6}$$

subject to

$$\tau_m \leq L - \sum_{m' \in \mathcal{M}} \tau_{m'} - \sum_{n \in \mathcal{N}} l_n, \tag{7}$$

$$0 \leq \tau_m \leq L, \tag{8}$$

$$P_m \cdot \tau_m \leq P_m^T, \tag{9}$$

$$\frac{\sqrt{B\tau_m} \log(1 + \frac{|h_m|^2 P_m}{\sigma^2})}{\log e} - \frac{b_m}{\sqrt{B\tau_m} \log e} \geq Q^{-1}(\epsilon_m^T), \tag{10}$$

where ϵ_m^T is the maximum error rate that can be tolerated. And P_m^T denotes the set energy threshold during the repetition interval with the purpose of energy saving.

(2) **eMBB Users Requirements**
Different from URLLC users, eMBB users access spectrum through the EDCA mechanism, which means that users must contend with each other.

Since users may have different QoS requirements, the ACs of different priorities may be helpful. We assume that those users are of I ACs, which are endowed with different parameters, such as contention window (CW) and arbitration interframe space (AIFS) to enable high-priority users to preferentially access channels.

Thus the data rate of an eMBB user n belonging to AC_i can be expressed as

$$r_n(i) = P_{s,i} \cdot B \log \left(1 + \frac{|h_n|^2 P_n}{\sigma^2} \right), \tag{11}$$

where $P_{s,i}$ denotes the successful transmission probability for each user of AC_i. And the detailed derivation is shown in [11].

In view of the strong demand for data rate, each eMBB user should solve the optimization problem

$$\max_{l_n} \; r_n \cdot l_n, \tag{12}$$

subject to

$$l_n \leq L - \sum_{n' \in \mathcal{N}} l_{n'} - \sum_{m \in \mathcal{M}} \tau_m, \tag{13}$$

$$0 \leq l_n \leq L, \tag{14}$$

$$P_n \cdot l_n \leq P_n^T, \tag{15}$$

$$r_n \cdot l_n \geq R_n^T, \tag{16}$$

The constraints show that both minimum data rate requirement and maximum energy limit should be satisfied.

2.2   Problem Formulation

The main objective of this paper is to find an optimal resource allocation solution for our proposed coexistence mechanism, i.e., τ_m and l_n of (6) and (12). Besides, in the light of that there may be a large amount of users in the system and the heterogeneity of users, it is not practical to solve the problem directly because of the probability of causing a great deal of computation. Thus, a distributed resource allocation scheme is required in our paper. We can see that the optimal time fraction of user m and user n is relevant with the time fractions of the remaining users, which motivates us to adopt a method of game theory.

3   Resource Allocation Algorithm

3.1   CH-Based Game

According to (6)–(16), we can define a noncooperative game $\left(\mathcal{I}, (\mathcal{S}_i)_{i \in \mathcal{I}}, (U_i)_{i \in \mathcal{I}} \right)$. $(\mathcal{S}_i)_{i \in \mathcal{I}}$ is the strategy space for players in $\mathcal{I}$, i.e., URLLC and eMBB users. And

$(U_i)_{i \in \mathcal{I}}$ represents their utility functions. The utility function of each URLLC user can be expressed as

$$U_m (\tau_m) = \frac{\sqrt{B\tau_m} \log(1 + \frac{|h_m|^2 P_m}{\sigma^2})}{\log e} - \frac{b_m}{\sqrt{B\tau_m} \log e}, \tag{17}$$

Likewise, the utility function of each eMBB user

$$U_n (l_n) = r_n \cdot l_n, \tag{18}$$

It is obvious that the utility functions in (17) and (18) are separately increasing with τ_m and l_n.

We denote the upper bound of τ_m and l_n as ub_m and ub_n. It's easy to find that the generalized nash equilibrium (GNE) solution is unique and exactly the upper bound of users when $\sum_{m \in \mathcal{M}} ub_m + \sum_{n \in \mathcal{N}} ub_n \leq L$ because they has no incentive to change their strategies. Otherwise GNE is not unique. However, traditional game theory based on nash equilibrium which holds that all players are completely rational and always needs information exchange is undoubtedly unrealistic. In view of the heterogeneity of users in our system, that is, they may have different requirements and computation capabilities, as well as the confidentiality of user information, bounded rationality will be a more suitable assumption. So we will think about a game of cognitive hierarchy (CH) theory [12,13], which is based on the concept of bounded rationality.

In a CH-based game, players are divided into different levels of rationality. The original cognitive hierarchy theory assumes that player at level k will select its strategy based on the strategies of players belonging to lower levels, and players at level 0 will choose strategies randomly according to a uniform distribution. However, it's not fit for our model since there may be a lot of users having similar computation capacity, i.e., in the same level. So we extend the original model by considering that player at level k will regard the levels of the rest users as $0 \sim k$. Details are shown below:

(1) The number of users of each level is considered to yield to the Poisson distribution f with mean value τ. And in our system model, eMBB users are endowed with higher levels (over q) than URLLC users $(0 \sim q)$ due to their greater computation capacities.

(2) Users of level k know exactly the proportions of users belonging to levels $0 \sim k$, i.e., $f(0), ..., f(k)$. After normalization, we will get the relative frequency $g_k(h)$ of players at a level h $(0 \leq h \leq k)$ as $g_k(h) = f(h)/\sum_{i=0}^{k} f(i)$, and $g_k(h) = 0$ for $h > k$.

(3) Level 0 users are assumed to choose strategies within $[lb_m, ub_m]$ in case of wasting too much resource. lb_m denotes the lower bound of user m.

(4) The cognitive hierarchy equilibrium (CHE) is defined to be composed of strategies s_i^* if and only if $s_i^*(k) = arg \max U_i(s_i^*)$.

We can note that the strategy of a level-k user depends on decisions of users of level $0 \sim k$, i.e., the strategy space of each user is based on its beliefs g_k about other users. Thus for a level-k user, constraints (7) and (13) can be converted to

$$\sum_{h=0}^{k} g_k(h) \sum_{m \in \mathcal{U}} \tau_m^*(h) \leq L, k \leq q \tag{19}$$

$$\sum_{h=0}^{q} g_k(h) \sum_{m \in \mathcal{U}} \tau_m^*(h) + \sum_{h=q+1}^{k} g_k(h) \sum_{n \in \mathcal{U}} l_n^*(h) \leq L, k > q \tag{20}$$

where $\mathcal{U} = \mathcal{M} \cup \mathcal{N}$, so $U = M + N$ is the total number of users. $\tau_m^*(h)$ and $l_n^*(h)$ represent the CHE strategy of URLLC and eMBB users in level h, respectively. (19) can be further converted to

$$g_k(k) \cdot \tau_m^*(k) \leq L - g_k(k) \sum_{m' \in \mathcal{U}} \tau_{m'}^*(k) - \sum_{h=0}^{k-1} g_k(h) \sum_{m \in \mathcal{U}} \tau_m^*(h), k \leq q \tag{21}$$

However, while considering the behavior of peer players, each solving step is like an equilibrium problem, resulting in large computational complexity. According to the characteristic that players of the same type may have similar demands and capabilities, we assume that k-level players believe that players of the same level will choose the same action ($\tau_m^*(k) = \tau_{m'}^*(k)$). Then (21) can be further expressed as

$$\tau_m^*(k) \leq \frac{1}{g_k(k) \cdot U} \left(L - \sum_{h=0}^{k-1} g_k(h) \sum_{m \in \mathcal{U}} \tau_m^*(h) \right), k \leq q \tag{22}$$

While solving the optimization problems of URLLC and eMBB users, each user will find its CHE strategy based on its own beliefs instead of iterated process, and has no trend to change its action, indicating the stability of CHE. We can express the CHE solutions of URLLC user m at k level as

$$\tau_m^*(k) = min \left\{ \frac{1}{g_k(k) \cdot U} \left(L - \sum_{h=0}^{k-1} g_k(h) \sum_{m \in \mathcal{U}} \tau_m^*(h) \right), ub_m \right\}, \tag{23}$$

Likewise, for eMBB user n

$$l_n^*(k) = min \left\{ \frac{1}{g_k(k) \cdot U} \left(L - \sum_{h=0}^{q} g_k(h) \sum_{m \in \mathcal{U}} \tau_m^*(h) - \sum_{h=q+1}^{k-1} g_k(h) \sum_{n \in \mathcal{U}} l_n^*(h) \right), ub_n \right\}, \tag{24}$$

However, the sum of CHE time fractions may exceeds the total duration due to their bounded rationality, i.e., $\sum_{m \in \mathcal{M}} \tau_m^*(h_m) + \sum_{n \in \mathcal{N}} l_n^*(h_n) > L$. Then the allocated time fractions should be further normalized.

We should note that apart from lower computational complexity of the CH-based game, the communication overhead will be greatly reduced because there is no need to exchange strategies of users among them when they are making decisions.

4   Simulation Results

In this section, simulation results are shown to evaluate the performance of our proposed URLLC and eMBB coexistence scheme. We set URLLC users to level 0 and 1 and eMBB users to level 2 and 3 according to their computation capacity and QoS requirements. Besides, higher level eMBB users are thought to have higher priority in the EDCA mechanism, which is achieved by the parameters in [11]. And we consider the bandwidth of 20 MHz and interval of 100 ms. The noise power is $-174\,\mathrm{dBm/Hz}$. Transmission powers of each level are set to 0.2, 0.5, 1 and 1.5 W, respectively. The mean value τ of the Possion distribution is 1.2. And each user knows the parameters of each type of devices before the time interval.

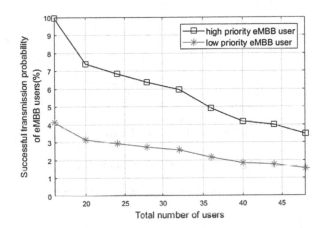

Fig. 3. Successful transmission probability of each eMBB user in level 2 and level 3.

Figure 3 shows successful transmission probability of each eMBB user in level 2 and level 3, which correspond to lower and higher priority ACs, respectively. It is obvious that the successful transmission probability of higher-level users is much larger than that of the lower-level users. And with the increase of total user numbers in the system, the probabilities decrease significantly, which may result in the degradation of the transmission rate of eMBB users expressed in (11). Besides, the lower bound of each user from (10) and (16) will increase along with the number of users, as depicted in Fig. 4(b) and (c).

Figure 4 shows the average CHE solutions of users in level 1, 2 and 3 and the sum of CHE solutions versus the total number of users. It's obvious that when there are a few users in the system (less than 40), the CHE solution is just the upper bound ub_i of each user, which is consistent with the only GNE solution when $\sum_{i\in\mathcal{U}} ub_i \leq L$. When users continue to increase (over 40), from the red curve we can see the sum of CHE time fractions exceeds the total duration and then the CHE solutions of users will decrease because of the normalization. Besides, the bottom curve in Fig. 4(b), i.e., the lower bound of eMBB users

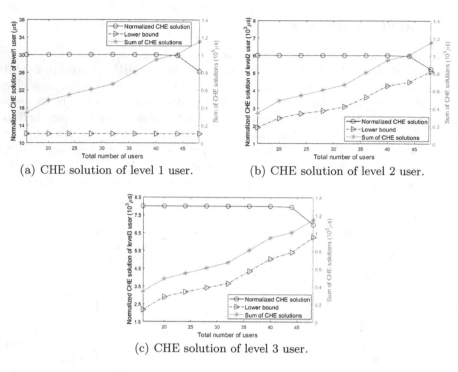

(a) CHE solution of level 1 user.   (b) CHE solution of level 2 user.

(c) CHE solution of level 3 user.

Fig. 4. Normalized CHE solution.

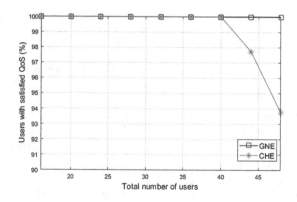

Fig. 5. Percentage of users with satisfied QoS requirements.

almost exceeds the upper bound due to the continuous reduction of successful transmission probability, which means that requirements of users will not be satisfied when there are more users in the system. And Fig. 5 shows that compared to GNE the performance of CHE will not drop much with only several users failing to meet their requirements due to the normalization.

Thus we can conclude that CH theory performs well when the number of users is proper in the system with significantly reduced computational complexity and communication overhead, while excessive users may cause degradation of system performance. For the propose of guaranteeing performance of both URLLC and eMBB users, we should control the number of total users within an appropriate range.

5   Conclusion

In this paper, we have proposed a coexistence scheme of URLLC and eMBB users. Firstly, the access mechanisms defined in EDCA and HCCA are utilized to achieve the access of URLLC and eMBB users, aiming to satisfy different QoS requirements of users. And a more realistic CII-based game is utilized to solve the distributed resource allocation problem. The simulation results demonstrate that the CH-based coexistence and distributed resource allocation scheme can achieve good performance with low computational complexity and communication overhead when there are not too much users in the system.

References

1. 3GPP TSG RAN WG1 95, Technical report, November 2018
2. Gai, K., Qiu, M., Zhao, H., Tao, L., Zong, Z.: Dynamic energy-aware cloudlet-based mobile cloud computing model for green computing. J. Netw. Comput. Appl. **59**, 46–54 (2016)
3. Qiu, H., Noura, H., Qiu, M., Ming, Z., Memmi, G.: A user-centric data protection method for cloud storage based on invertible DWT. IEEE Trans. Cloud Comput. (2019)
4. Gai, K., Qiu, M., Zhao, H.: Cost-aware multimedia data allocation for heterogeneous memory using genetic algorithm in cloud computing. IEEE Trans. Cloud Comput. (2016)
5. Pedersen, K.I., Pocovi, G., Steiner, J., Khosravirad, S.R.: Punctured scheduling for critical low latency data on a shared channel with mobile broadband. In: 2017 IEEE 86th Vehicular Technology Conference (VTC-Fall), pp. 1–6. IEEE (2017)
6. Anand, A., De Veciana, G., Shakkottai, S.: Joint scheduling of URLLC and eMBB traffic in 5G wireless networks. In: IEEE INFOCOM 2018-IEEE Conference on Computer Communications, pp. 1970–1978. IEEE (2018)
7. You, L., Liao, Q., Pappas, N., Yuan, D.: Resource optimization with flexible numerology and frame structure for heterogeneous services. IEEE Commun. Lett. **22**(12), 2579–2582 (2018)
8. Popovski, P., Trillingsgaard, K.F., Simeone, O., Durisi, G.: 5G wireless network slicing for eMBB, URLLC, and mMTC: a communication-theoretic view. IEEE Access **6**, 55765–55779 (2018)
9. IEEE802.11e: 802.11e-2005 IEEE standard for information technology telecommunications and information exchange between systems local and metropolitan area networks specific requirements part 11: wireless LAN medium access control (MAC) and physical layer (PHY) specifications: Amendment 8: Medium access control (MAC) Quality of Service enhancements (2005)

10. Yang, W., Durisi, G., Koch, T., Polyanskiy, Y.: Quasi-static multiple-antenna fading channels at finite blocklength. IEEE Trans. Inf. Theory **60**(7), 4232–4265 (2014)
11. Chen, Q., Yu, G., Ding, Z.: Enhanced LAA for unlicensed LTE deployment based on TXOP contention. IEEE Trans. Commun. **67**(1), 417–429 (2018)
12. Camerer, C.F., Ho, T.H., Chong, J.K.: A cognitive hierarchy model of games. Q. J. Econ. **119**(3), 861–898 (2004)
13. Abuzainab, N., Saad, W., Hong, C.S., Poor, H.V.: Cognitive hierarchy theory for distributed resource allocation in the internet of things. IEEE Trans. Wirel. Commun. **16**(12), 7687–7702 (2017)

Smart Custom Package Decision for Mobile Internet Services

Zhian Yang[1], Cong Zheng[2], Hao Jiang[2(✉)], Yuanyuan Zeng[2(✉)],
Zhiyi Hu[2], and Wen Du[3]

[1] National Center for Science and Technology Evaluation, Beijing, China
yangzhian@ncste.org
[2] School of Electronic Information, Wuhan University, Wuhan, China
{jh, zengyy}@whu.edu.cn
[3] DS Information Technology Co., Ltd., Shanghai, China
duwen@dscomm.com.cn

Abstract. With the rapid development of the mobile Internet services, the existing package decision of telecom operators has become the bottleneck of the mobile Internet services due to the high price. Mobile Internet application companies have begun cooperating with telecom operators to promote free-flow packages. Based on the users' online data provided by the telecom operator, we propose a smart custom packet decision scheme based on user behavior analysis. A two-side market model is proposed to formulate the package decision. Experimental results show that our scheme is with good efficiency of profit and social welfare.

Keywords: Custom package decision · Online sequential behavior · Two-sided market model

1 Introduction

Mobile Internet services are developing fast in recent years. According to research statistics, the global total mobile business traffic will reach 292 EB in 2019, of which intelligent traffic accounts for about 97%. About 70% of traffic will be applied to bandwidth-sensitive services such as video services. With the rapid development of Mobile Edge Computation (MEC) and Cloud Computation, more and more traffic will be used by mobile terminals [1–3]. With the increase of the mobile Internet market, many Internet companies have launched their own APP services. The number of APPs in Google Play and APP Store has reached 5.0 million in 2019. Under this circumstances, traditional traffic packages provided by telecom operators can't meet the needs of users and Internet companies.

Chinese telecom operators propose unlimited traffic packages for certain types of APPs by cooperating with Internet companies. This kind of custom package is benefit to both mobile users and Internet companies by reducing the burden of telecom operator. The King Card issued by Tencent is a typical example.

© Springer Nature Switzerland AG 2019
M. Qiu (Ed.): SmartCom 2019, LNCS 11910, pp. 161–170, 2019.
https://doi.org/10.1007/978-3-030-34139-8_16

We propose smart custom package decision scheme for Mobile Internet services based on online user behavior pattern. Two-side market model is used to formulate the problem, in order to achieve maximum profit with good social welfare in the same time.

The rest of this paper is organized as follows. Section 2 reviews the main solutions related to users' online behavior pattern. Section 3 formalize the problem and propose the result mathematically. Section 4 describes the custom package decision scheme. Section 5 evaluates the performance of the method proposed in Sect. 4. Section 6 conclude the contributions of this paper.

2 Related Work

User Persona technology is used to extract the user's Internet characteristics. User Persona is proposed by Alab Copper, whose basic function is to describe one user or a class of users with some characteristics. Holden et al. describe users with photos and user interests [4].

Researchers choose different description objects in different scenarios. Kumar, Chikhaoui and others build User Portrait models for individual users and extract features for tasks such as user behavior prediction or content recommendation [5, 6]. User Portraits for single user can be used for personalized customization. When User Portrait technology is used for group users, all users is broken down into groups which are described with multiple tags. Lerouge analyzed the characteristics of the elderly population in China using group User Portrait [7]. Rossi determine whether the airport is congested using real-time data of population on airport [8]. Group User Portrait technology is mainly used for population characteristic analysis.

Timing characteristics are another important feature of the user behavior. Many effective methods have been proposed to depict users' Internet habits, such as collaborative filtering, factor model [9] and Markov model. However, those methods ignored other information such as time and location. Many context-based analysis methods that used time information, spatial information and social relationships have been proposed [10, 11].

Users should be segmented while designing different plans for different users. K-means algorithm can solve the problem. However, there is no solution to the pricing of each type of user's package. Among many economic theories, the two-sided market can describe the relationship between operators, users and Internet manufacturers reasonably.

Armstrong proposed the two-sided market model firstly and put forward the basic model of the two-sided market [12], which is mainly used to describe the intermediary market. Armstrong, Wright, Rochet and others research the pricing strategy of the platform in different ways [13, 14]. However, the two-sided market is still one of the developing economic models.

3 Problem Formulation

First of all, the symbols used in the following equations is shown in Table 1.

Table 1. Common symbol table

Symbols	Meanings
$S(t)$	State transfer list of users
q_{rs}	Transfer intensity from state r to state s
p_{rs}	Transfer probability from state r to state s
Q	Transfer intensity matrix
P	Transfer probability matrix
π	Telecom operator utility function
f	The static cost of telecom operator
C	The cost of telecom operator for providing traffic
F	Traffic flow
W	Utility function of social welfare

The notations in Table 1 with a subscript m indicate the values corresponding to a particular package m.

Fig. 1. A diagram of user's online behavior

A discrete sequence of user accessed content is used to describe the user's Internet behavior. The user's online behavior pattern in Fig. 1 can be described by the sequence "WeChat-PayPal-WeChat-QQ-Alipay". It is assumed that the user will still access the last accessed content before the user accesses the next content.

To build a user state transfer matrix, define a discrete transfer tendency as:

$$q_{rs}(t, z(t)) = \lim_{\Delta t \to 0} \frac{P(S(t + \Delta t) = s | S(t) = r)}{\Delta t} \tag{1}$$

Formula (1) is used to calculate the content state transfer intensity matrix Q, and fit the state transfer probability matrix P. The fit method is:

$$\begin{cases} p_{rs} = 0, r = s \\ p_{rs} = \frac{q_{rs}}{q_{rr}}, r \neq s \end{cases} \tag{2}$$

State transfer probability matrix P will provide the basic input.

Two different groups in a market are connected through the platform, and the interests of one group on one side of the platform depend on the size of the other, which is the two-sided market. In the package pricing problem, telecom operator provides the platform. The demander and the platform form one edge, and the manufacturer and the platform form the other. As a representative of two-sided market, the structure of mobile operators is shown in Fig. 2.

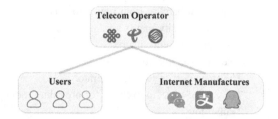

Fig. 2. Two-sided market model architecture diagram

Utility refers to the benefit of a participant. Logarithmic function is used to describe the utility function of users and Internet companies.

$$u_1 = \alpha_1 \times \ln(1 + F \times n_2) - P_{s1} \tag{3}$$

$$u_2 = \alpha_2 \times \ln(1 + F \times n_2) - P_{s2} \tag{4}$$

The operator utility function is shown in Eq. (5):

$$\pi = (P_{s1} - C \times F - f) \times n_1 + P_{s1} \times n_2 \tag{5}$$

4   Custom Package Decision Scheme

Factor model is used to analyze the user's Internet characteristics and design the contents of the traffic plan. The model is generally expressed as:

$$R \cong PQ^T \tag{6}$$

$P \in R^{M \times K}$ and $Q \in R^{N \times K}$ are the factor matrix for the user and the accessing content consisting. M represents the number of users. N represents the number of accessed contents. K is the number of factors.

It is found that users' online behavior is similar, which is referred as the user's behavior pattern. It is assumed that each user has several independent Internet timing characteristics. Each pattern affects the user's behavior with different weight ω_P.

The timing characteristics and the current accessing content A_t jointly determine the upcoming access to the content A_{t+1}.

$$P(A_t, A_{t+1}) = \sum_k \omega(P_k) * f(P_k, A_t, A_{t+1}) \tag{7}$$

When all users are taken into consideration, the formula is converted into a volume, as shown in the Eqs. (7) and (8).

$$(U, A_t, A_{t+1}) = F(P, A_t, A_{t+1}) \times W(P, U) \tag{8}$$

The problem is transformed into a tensor decomposition problem. The data is processed with the Non-negative Tensor Factorization method (NTF) and the High Order Singular Value Decomposition Method (HOSVD).

$$\mathbb{R} = \chi \times A \times B \times C \tag{9}$$

$$W(P, U) = A \tag{10}$$

$$F(P, A_t, A_{t+1}) = \chi \times B \times C \tag{11}$$

Finally, according to the weight matrix, the online behavior mode with the highest weight for each user is found, which is regarded as the main online behavior pattern of the user. The proportion of different online behavior patterns is analyzed to find the top K pattern with the largest proportion, which is the main patterns of all users.

It's found user number n is related to utility function u, which is described as φ.

$$n_1 = \varphi_1(u_1) = \frac{1}{1 + e^{\omega_1 u_1}} \tag{12}$$

$$n_2 = \varphi_2(u_2) = \frac{1}{1 + e^{\omega_2 u_2}} \tag{13}$$

While maximizing social welfare, the overall welfare of users, Internet companies and telecom operator is required to be the greatest.

$$v_1(u_1) = \varphi_1'(u_1) \tag{14}$$

$$v_2(u_2) = \varphi_2'(u_2) \tag{15}$$

$$\begin{aligned} W &= \pi(u_1, u_2) + v_1(u_1) + v_2(u_2) \\ &= (\alpha_1 \times \ln(1 + F \times n_2) - u_1 - C \times F - f) \times \varphi(u_1) \\ &\quad + (\alpha_2 \times \ln(1 + F \times n_1) - u_2) \times \varphi(u_2) + \varphi_1'(u_1) + \varphi_2'(u_2) \end{aligned} \tag{16}$$

Solve the optimal conditions:

$$\begin{cases} \frac{dW}{du_1} = 0 \\ \frac{dW}{du_2} = 0 \end{cases} \tag{17}$$

$$u_1 = \alpha_1 \times \ln(1 + F \times n_2) - C \times F - f + \alpha_2 \times n_2 \times \frac{F}{1 + F \times n_1} \tag{18}$$

$$u_2 = \alpha_2 \times \ln(1 + F \times n_2) - C \times F - f + \alpha_1 \times n_1 \times \frac{F}{1 + F \times n_2} \tag{19}$$

$$P_{s1} = C \times F + f - \alpha_2 \times n_2 \times \frac{F}{1 + F \times n_1} \tag{20}$$

$$P_{s2} = -\alpha_1 \times n_1 \times \frac{F}{1 + F \times n_2} \tag{21}$$

Formula (21) shows that under the optimal conditions of social welfare, the platform should subsidize Internet manufacturers. At the same time, it should charge the user at a price below the cost price $(C \times F + f)$.

Platform profit optimization requires the most profit of telecom operators.

$$W = \pi(u_1, u_2) \tag{22}$$

Solve the optimal conditions:

$$u_1 = \alpha_1 \times \ln(1 + F \times n_2) - C \times F + f + \alpha_2 \times n_2 \times \frac{F}{1 + F \times n_1} - \frac{\varphi_1(u_1)}{\varphi_1'(u_1)} \tag{23}$$

$$u_2 = \alpha_2 \times \ln(1 + F \times n_1) + \alpha_1 \times n_1 \times \frac{F}{1 + F \times n_2} - \frac{\varphi_2(u_2)}{\varphi_2'(u_2)} \tag{24}$$

$$\begin{aligned} P_{s1} &= C \times F - \alpha_2 \times n_2 \times \frac{F}{1 + F \times n_1} + \frac{\varphi_1(u_1)}{\varphi_1'(u_1)} \\ &= C \times F - \alpha_2 \times n_2 \times \frac{F}{1 + F \times n_1} + \frac{1}{(1 - n_1) \times \omega_1} \end{aligned} \tag{25}$$

$$\begin{aligned} P_{s2} &= -\alpha_1 \times n_1 \times \frac{F}{1 + F \times n_2} + \frac{\varphi_2(u_2)}{\varphi_2'(u_2)} = \\ &- \alpha_1 \times n_1 \times \frac{F}{1 + F \times n_2} + \frac{1}{(1 - n_2) \times \omega_2} \end{aligned} \tag{26}$$

While maximizing the profit of the platform, it charges the user and the Internet manufacturer an additional fee, which is related to parameters ω.

Under the competition condition, this paper analyzes the pricing strategy under the optimal condition of social welfare and optimal condition of platform profit.

The calculation process of optimal condition of social welfare is shown below.

$$W = \pi(u_1, u_2) + v_1(u_1) + v_2(u_2) \tag{27}$$

$$u_{1m} = \alpha_1 \times \ln(1 + F_m \times n_2) - C \times F_m - f + \alpha_2 \times n_2 \times \frac{F_m}{1 + F_m \times n_{1m}} \tag{28}$$

$$u_{2m} = \alpha_2 \times \ln(1 + F_m \times n_{1m}) + \alpha_1 \times n_{1m} \times \frac{F_m}{1 + F_m \times n_{2m}} \tag{29}$$

$$P_{s1m} = C \times F_m + f - \alpha_2 \times n_2 \times \frac{F_m}{1 + F_m \times n_1} \tag{30}$$

$$P_{s2m} = -\alpha_1 \times n_{1m} \times \frac{F_m}{1 + F_m \times n_{2m}} \tag{31}$$

The calculation process of optimal condition of platform profit is shown below.

$$W = \pi(u_1, u_2) \tag{32}$$

$$u_{1m} = \alpha_1 \times \ln(1 + F_m \times n_2) - C \times F_m - f + \\ \alpha_2 \times n_2 \times \frac{F_m}{1 + F_m \times n_{1m}} + \frac{\varphi_1(u_{1m})}{\varphi'_1(u_{1m})} \tag{33}$$

$$u_{2m} = \alpha_2 \times \ln(1 + F_m \times n_{1m}) + \alpha_1 \times n_{1m} \times \frac{F_m}{1 + F_m \times n_{2m}} + \frac{\varphi_2(u_2)}{\varphi'_2(u_2)} \tag{34}$$

$$P_{s1m} = C \times F_m + f - \alpha_2 \times n_2 \times \frac{F_m}{1 + F_m \times n_{1m}} + \frac{1}{\sum_{i=1}^{M}(\omega_{1mm} + \omega_{1mj})n_j} \tag{35}$$

$$P_{s2m} = -\alpha_1 \times n_{1m} \times \frac{F_m}{1 + F_m \times n_{2m}} + \frac{1}{(1 - n_{2m}) \times \omega_{2m}} \tag{36}$$

Formulas (31) and (36) shows the result under competition condition.

5 Performance Evaluations

The dataset is provided by China Unicom, which including a record of all information about the user's online behavior within a natural month. Users are classified according to behavior pattern weight, as is shown in Table 2.

Table 2. Package design results for telecom operators

Class	Content		Rate
Class I	Tao Bao	Tencent	46.9%
	Xi Gua Video	UC Browser	
Class II	Tencent	Baidu	23.1%
Class III	Tencent	Ku Gou	30.0%
	Sou Gou	Kuai Shou	

Figure 3(a) and (b) describes the fees charged to each user for different packages under the condition of maximizing social welfare or the platform's profit. It's founded that package I has the largest pricing cost and package II has the lowest pricing fee.

The number of users is equivalent to the probability that users will participate in this package. When there are many users ($n_1 > 0.8$), the platform can charge a higher fee from the users.

Figure 4(a) and (b) describes how the platform charges Internet manufacturers under the condition of maximizing social welfare or platform benefits.

It is found that the total cost of Internet companies in different packages is basically the same. Formula (34) shows that the charges do not reduce the flow consumption. As a result, more Internet companies involved in the package means less fees for each

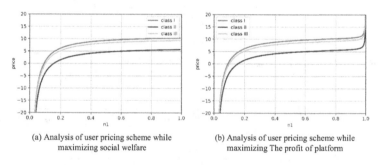

(a) Analysis of user pricing scheme while maximizing social welfare

(b) Analysis of user pricing scheme while maximizing The profit of platform

Fig. 3. User-side pricing strategy in monopoly scenarios

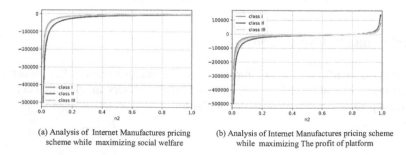

(a) Analysis of Internet Manufactures pricing scheme while maximizing social welfare

(b) Analysis of Internet Manufactures pricing scheme while maximizing The profit of platform

Fig. 4. Internet manufactures pricing strategy in monopoly scenario

internet companies. When Internet companies aren't willing to join the packages ($n2 <$ 0.2), the platform needs to subsidize Internet companies. When Internet companies tend to join this package ($0.2 < n2 < 1$), the platform should adopt a free strategy. However, under the condition that the platform profit is optimized, the Internet companies should be charged.

Figures 5 and 6 shows the experimental results. Traffic doesn't determine the cost of Internet manufacturers. It is the willingness of Internet companies to join packages and the number of Internet companies involved in the package that determines the cost of Internet manufacturers.

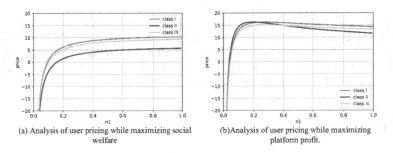

(a) Analysis of user pricing while maximizing social welfare

(b)Analysis of user pricing while maximizing platform profit.

Fig. 5. User pricing strategy in competitive scenarios

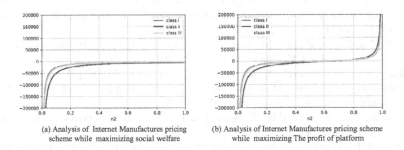

(a) Analysis of Internet Manufactures pricing scheme while maximizing social welfare

(b) Analysis of Internet Manufactures pricing scheme while maximizing The profit of platform

Fig. 6. Internet manufacture pricing strategy in competitive scenario

Table 3 shows the quantitative calculation results.

Table 3. Package pricing result

Class	Proportion	Monopoly scenario		Competitive scenario	
		Maximizing social welfare	Maximizing platform profit	Maximizing social welfare	Maximizing platform profit
Class I	46.9%	9.15	9.26	9.15	9.86
Class II	23.1%	2.52	2.56	2.52	3.55
Class III	30.0%	7.02	7.07	7.02	7.77

6 Conclusion

Based on the UDR data provided by mobile operators, this paper designs a free-flow package mechanism based on users' online behavior. Firstly, a factor model based on tensor decomposition was proposed to analyze the user's online behavior. For two different scenarios, this paper designs the utility functions of users, internet manufacturers and mobile operators. While maximizing social welfare and maximizing platform profit, They are analyzed respectively, and the package pricing formula under different conditions is obtained. Finally, this paper makes a quantitative analysis of the model through empirical data, and completes the pricing design of the free-flow package.

Acknowledgement. This work was supported in part by the National Natural Science Foundation of China under Grant 11571383, the Natural Science Foundation of Hubei Province of China under Grant 2017CFB302, the Science and Technology Program of Guangzhou, China under Grant 201804020053, and Shanghai Special Fund Project for Artificial Intelligence Innovation and Development under Grant 2018-RGZN-01013.

References

1. Gai, K., Qiu, M., Hui, Z., Tao, L., Zong, Z.: Dynamic energy-aware cloudlet-based mobile cloud computing model for green computing. J. Netw. Comput. Appl. **59**(C), 46–54 (2016)
2. Gai, K., Qiu, M., Hui, Z.: Energy-aware task assignment for mobile cyber-enabled applications in heterogeneous cloud computing. J. Parallel Distrib. Comput. **111**, S0743731 517302319 (2017)
3. Gai, K., Xu, K., Lu, Z., Qiu, M., Zhu, L.: Fusion of cognitive wireless networks and edge computing. IEEE Wirel. Commun. **26**(3), 69–75 (2019)
4. Holden, R.J., Kulanthaivel, A., Purkayastha, S., Goggins, K., Kripalani, S.: Know thy eHealth user: development of biopsychosocial personas from a study of older adults with heart failure. Int. J. Med. Inform. **108**, 158–167 (2017)
5. Kumar, H., Lee, S., Kim, H.G.: Exploiting social bookmarking services to build clustered user interest profile for personalized search. Inf. Sci. (Ny) **281**, 399–417 (2014)
6. Chikhaoui, B., Wang, S., Xiong, T., Pigot, H.: Pattern-based causal relationships discovery from event sequences for modeling behavioral user profile in ubiquitous environments. Inf. Sci. An Int. J. **285**(C), 204–222 (2014)
7. LeRouge, C., Ma, J., Sneha, S., Tolle, K.: User profiles and personas in the design and development of consumer health technologies. Int. J. Med. Inform. **82**(11), E251–E268 (2013)
8. Rossi, R., Gastaldi, M., Orsini, F.: How to drive passenger airport experience: a decision support system based on user profile. IET Intell. Transp. Syst. **12**(4), 301–308 (2018)
9. Deerwester, S., Dumais, S.T., Furnas, G.W., Landauer, T.K., Harshman, R.: Indexing by latent semantic analysis. J. Assoc. Inf. Sci. Technol. **41**(6), 391–407 (2010)
10. Kawazu, H., Toriumi, F., Takano, M., Wada, K., Fukuda, I.: Analytical method of web user behavior using Hidden Markov Model. In: IEEE International Conference on Big Data (2017)
11. Park, J., Lee, D.S., González, M.C.: The eigenmode analysis of human motion. J. Stat. Mech: Theory Exp. **2010**(11), P11021 (2016)
12. Armstrong, M.: Competition in two-sided markets. RAND J. Econ. **37**(3), 668–691 (2006)
13. Armstrong, M., Wright, J.: Two-sided markets, competitive bottlenecks and exclusive contracts. Econ. Theory **32**(2), 353–380 (2007)
14. Rochet, J., Tirole, J.: Two-sided markets: a progress report. RAND J. Econ. **37**(3), 645–667 (2006)

A Space Dynamic Discovery Scheme for Crowd Flow of Urban City

Zhaojun Wang[2], Hao Jiang, Xiaoyue Zhao[1], Yuanyuan Zeng[1(✉)], Yi Zhang[1], and Wen Du[1]

[1] Wuhan University, Wuhan, China
zengyy@whu.edu.cn
[2] Springer Heidelberg, Tiergartenstr. 17, 69121 Heidelberg, Germany

Abstract. Crowd flow analysis is a important part of urban computing, which is playing an vital role in urban plan and management. This paper addresses the challenges in current population flow analysis. We propose a user space dynamic discovery method based on graph signal model. Taking the base station as a spatial node, the spatial dependence relationship between the nodes is modeled as a spatial network map. The spectral wavelet operator is applied to the spatial map signal to generate wavelet coefficients on different wavelet scales. The simulation results, show that our scheme can be used for valuable information such as the origin, spread and span of population mobility.

Keywords: Crowd flow · Urban computing · Graph signal model · Spectral wavelet operator · Wavelet coefficients

1 Introduction

Urban crowd flow analysis plays an important role in urban planning, management and development. Such as, reduce the blindness of commercial location based on regional crowd flow. Combining regional crowd flow and crowd consumption attributes such as purchasing power and consumption level can provide multi-dimensional digital support for the location of the business circle, in order to achieve the overall selection of layout and maximize overall benefits. Also traffic planning based on regional flow data makes urban governance more forward-looking. Consider the regional crowd flow attributes of various time periods or holidays, including data such as changes in crowd flow, population density, and effective flow of population. In order to plan new roads, public transportation, peak control measures, and large-scale transportation hubs in urban traffic. Make regional governance more subtle by analysis crowd flow. Real-time dynamic analysis of crowd flow through interaction data between mobile phones and base stations, analysis of regional population characteristics, and data support for urban managers.

Most of the existing crowd traffic analysis methods only consider the crowd itself, ignoring the spatial connection between the locations, and not being able to perceive the spatial flow of the crowd. This paper focuses on the problem to obtain location data and the dynamic analysis of population flow data. We propose to use Crowd Flow Analysis based on Graph Signal Processing to discover the characteristics of user mobile behavior in cities.

© Springer Nature Switzerland AG 2019
M. Qiu (Ed.): SmartCom 2019, LNCS 11910, pp. 171–179, 2019.
https://doi.org/10.1007/978-3-030-34139-8_17

2 Related Work

Research on user space movement dynamics is an important part of crowd flow research. Most of the existing research focuses on various methods based on user location time series. Yang [1] proposed a coupled Bayesian robust principal component analysis method. Senaratne et al. [2] modeled the user's access location sequence, projected the location trajectory into the position matrix, and designed the similarity indicator of the position matrix to identify the user movement pattern. Rawassizadeh et al. [3] extended the user trajectory into multiple events and mined the frequent item association rules for the user's time combination to discover the typical behavior of the user. Landesberger et al. [4] proposed a graph-based visual analysis method that reveals the occluded motion patterns in the flow chart by combining the user's temporal and spatial information.

Graph signal processing is an emerging field of signal processing, and it has important applications in image processing and other aspects. Spectral wavelet transform is an emerging multi-scale geometric analysis theory. It combines wavelet transform and spectral graph theory with good scale invariance and local adaptability. Mallat et al. [5] proposed wavelet transform with good time-frequency locality and multi-resolution. Shuman et al. [6] used a graphical model to represent irregularly sampled data sets, and processed signal signals through harmonic analysis and spectral theory. David K, Pierre et al. [7] systematically studied the spectral wavelet transform theory and analyzed the application of spectral wavelet transform in various fields. Narang and Ortega [8] proposed the construction of a two-channel spectral wavelet filter bank, analyzing the functions of defining arbitrary finite-weighted undirected graph vertices, and extending the classical signal processing domain, such as Fourier decomposition, signal filtering and downsampling. In the graphics field, create a graph signal framework.

3 System Model

Using a connected undirected weighted graph $G = (V, E, W)$ as an abstraction of base station spatial dependence. The set of vertices $V = \{v_1, v_2, \ldots, v_N\}, |V| = N < \infty$ on the spatial dependence graph represents all base stations in the area, and the edge sets E describe the relationship between the nodes, weight function is $w : E \rightarrow R^+$. And for an adjacency matrix A of a weighted graph composed of N base stations, the elements $a_{mn} = w(e)$. For the weight function $w(e)$, this paper separates the time-series node pairs $Z_{pair} = \left[[Z_{t1}, Z_{t2}], [Z_{t2}, Z_{t3}], \cdots, [Z_{t(k-1)}, Z_{tk}]\right]$ from the user's position time series $Z = [Z_{t1}, Z_{t2}, \cdots, Z_{tk}]$. The time interval between the nodes is determined by the time interval of the node pair, and then the weight function $w(e)$ is determined according to the relationship of reachability, as shown in the Eq. (1).

$$a_{mn} = w(e) = \begin{cases} 1, arr(m, n) = True \\ 0, otherwise \end{cases} \tag{1}$$

In which, $arr(m, n)$ indicates that the nodes are reachable, the reachable is true, and the unreachable is false.

We use the idea of Crowd-Sensing to perceive user movement behavior and determine base station dependencies according to the user's movement trajectory.

4 Space Dynamic Discovery Based on Crowd Flow

For the massive user mobile information in large-scale mobile data, the node dependency discovery method used in this paper can restore the spatial connectivity of the base station more reliably. In terms of spatial structure, the spatial network map based on the user's natural mobility replaces it. The graph topology construction method based on the traditional spatial distance comprehensively considers the human mobile situation and the base station spatial distance in the real world, so that the base station can be used as a spatial mobile checkpoint, which is better as an observation entry point for human mobile behavior. In terms of application, it is obvious that the base station relationship discovery method used in this paper is derived from the data itself, and does not require any external auxiliary tools, which saves a lot of resources compared to the method based on Geographic Information Systems (GIS).

The specific base station dependency discovery algorithm is shown in Algorithm 1.

Algorithm 1. : Node Dependency Discovery Algorithm

---

1. Input. : records : Position time series ; Δt : time interval, V : Number of base stations
2. Output. : G : Spatial network diagram topology
3. function Node_dependency (records, Δt, V)
4. //Topology initialization
5. $G = zeros(N, N)$

6. for record in records do
7.   //Calculate whether the nodes are reachable
8. $Q = [record, record\_next]$
9. $t_Q = \left[t_{record}, t_{record\_next}\right]$
10.   if $\Delta t > t_{record\_next} - t_{record}$ and $record\_next \neq record$ do
11. $G_{V.index(record), V.index(record\_next)} = 1$
12.   end if
13.   end for
14.   return G
15. end function

On the spatial network diagram, the graph signal is defined as a set of finite samples, each of which is defined on the nodes of the graph, expressed as $f : V \rightarrow R^N$. Where the nth component of the signal represents the number of users at the nth node in V. In the urban space network diagram signal model, the definition of the number of users depends on the duration of the user's Internet access. If the user has an online behavior within the time window of Δt, the user is recorded to have effective access to the node in Δt, one The user's effective access record exists only once at most in the time window, and the graph signal is the sum of the valid access records recorded under the time window.

Assume that the proposed spatial network graph topology is $G = (V_G, E_G)$, and the time series structure of the signal is $H = (V_H, E_H)$. V_H is each time point divided by Δt. E_H in turn connect each V_H. τ_i and l_j are nodes in V_G and V_H. In the Cartesian product graph $G \times H$ obtained by G and H, If the node τ_i at the i position in G is adjacent to the node τ_k at position k, and the node l_j at the j time in H is adjacent to the node l_l at time l, nodes (τ_i, l_j) and (τ_k, l_l) in $G \times H$ will have a side. In the figure, assuming that the topology of the spatial network graph G is time-invariant, the Cartesian product graph $G \times H$ can be regarded as a copy of the spatial network graph G stacked by the nodes in the time series H. Such a network structure comprehensively considers the spatiotemporal dependence of nodes. Since the time slice nodes in H are connected by spatial nodes in G, the wavelet function can be applied to analyze the signal function defined on the nodes in G, thereby detecting the temporal and spatial changes of user movement. The Cartesian product graph construction process is shown in Fig. 1.

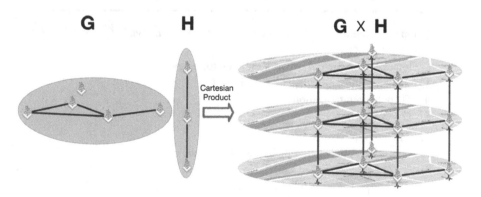

Fig. 1. Graph signal model topology based on Cartesian product graph

In order to dig deep and fine-grained user-moving features, we use the Spectral Graph Wavelets Transform (SGWT) method to obtain wavelet coefficients of different scales on the nodes by wavelet decomposition of the graph signal model. The coefficients represent the low to high frequency characteristics of the network. Specifically, the low-frequency wavelet coefficients exhibit low-frequency sensitivity, that is, when the node signal v_i connected to a node is close to the v_i signal amplitude, the low-frequency wavelet coefficients exhibit a large dimensionless value. On the contrary, when the wavelet filter filters the graph signal model, the high-frequency wavelet coefficients exhibit a small value for the above case.

In the graph signal model, $G \times H$ is used as the topology of the graph signal model, and node V as a set of finite number of base stations in each period divided by Δt, as well as the symmetric adjacency matrix $A, \forall a_{mn} = R^+$, the real-valued signal $f(v_i)$ defined on the vertex v_i on the graph is a column vector representing the number of users of the node at a certain time period. The denormalized Tulaplas operator is defined as shown in Eq. (2).

$$L = D - A \in R^{N \times N} \tag{2}$$

Where D is the diagonal matrix of the graph adjacency matrix, and satisfies $d_{mm} = \sum_n a_{mn}$, and d_{mm} represents the degree of the vertex m. Due to the real symmetry of L, the Laplacian matrix $G \times H$ is diagonalizable, and its eigenvector is defined as $\{\chi_0, \chi_1, \cdots, \chi_{N-1}\}$. According to the corresponding feature value $0 = \lambda_0 < \lambda_1 \leq \lambda_2 \leq \cdots \leq \lambda_{N-1}$, a set of orthogonal bases of the graph is generated. Therefore, the rearranged single-column feature vectors are as shown in the Eq. (3).

$$\chi = [\chi_0, \chi_1, \cdots, \chi_{N-1}] \tag{3}$$

At the same time, for the diagonal array $\Lambda = diag([\lambda_0, \lambda_1, \cdots, \lambda_{N-1}])$, L can be converted into the form of the Eq. (4).

$$L = \chi \Lambda \chi^H \tag{4}$$

The superscript H represents the Hermitian transposition operation of the matrix. The characteristic of the Hermitian matrix is that the elements of each row and column in the matrix are equal to the conjugate of the corresponding positional elements of the transposition. Therefore, the Fourier Transform (GFT) of the signal on $G \times H$ is the inner product of the graph signal and the eigenvector sequence [9], as shown in Eq. (5).

$$\hat{f}(l) = \langle f, \chi_l \rangle = \sum_{n=1}^{N} f(n) \chi_l^*(n), l = 0, 1, \cdots, N - 1 \tag{5}$$

f can be recovered by the graph signal reconstruction formula, as shown in Eq. (6).

$$f(n) = \left\langle \hat{f}, \chi_l^* \right\rangle = \sum_{l=0}^{N-1} \hat{f}(l) \chi_l(n), n = 1, 2, \cdots, N \tag{6}$$

Using vector and matrix notation, Eqs. (5) and (6) can be converted into the following form.

$$\hat{f}_\theta = \left[\hat{f}_\theta(0), \hat{f}_\theta(1), \cdots, \hat{f}_\theta(N - 1)\right]^T = \chi^H f \tag{7}$$

$$f = [f(1), f(2), \cdots, f(N)]^T = \varphi \hat{f} \tag{8}$$

GFT follows the Parseval theorem, that is, for any signal sum defined on the graph, the relationship is as in Eq. (9).

$$\langle f, h \rangle = \left\langle \hat{f}, \hat{h} \right\rangle \tag{9}$$

The spectral wavelet transform is an extension of GFT. For the user number signal $G \times H$ on f, the spectrum wavelet transform defined by g is as shown in Eq. (10).

$$W_f(s, n) = \left(T_g^s f \right)(n) = \sum_{l=0}^{N-1} g(s\lambda_l) \hat{f}(l) \chi_l(n), n = 1, 2, \cdots, N \tag{10}$$

T_g^s is a wavelet operator on the s scale and satisfies $T_g^s = g(tL)$. The wavelet kernel g is a continuous function defined in the positive real space and satisfies Eq. (11):

$$g(0) = \lim_{x \to +\infty} g(x) = 0; \int_0^{+\infty} \frac{g(x)}{x^2} dx = C_g \in R^+ \tag{11}$$

Therefore, combined with Eq. (5), by inner product of a single graphics wavelet, the spectral wavelet transform formula is converted to:

$$W_f(s, n) = \left(T_g^s f \right)(n) = \sum_{m=1}^{N} f(m) \psi_{s,n}^* m = \langle f, \psi_{s,n} \rangle, n = 1, 2, \cdots, N \tag{12}$$

$W_f(s, n)$ represents the wavelet coefficient of the signal and exists:

$$\psi_{s,n}(m) = \sum_{l=0}^{N-1} g(s\lambda_l) \chi_l(m) \chi_l^*(n), m = 1, 2, \cdots, N \tag{13}$$

5   Performance Evaluations

This paper uses data from one major operator in Beijing for one day as a data source for analysis and experimentation. The main information is shown in Table 1.

Table 1. Data table format

User ID	Start time	End time	Base station information	URL
460023585748125	2014-11-21 20:45:23	2014-11-21 20:46:00	5791_4F1F	https://jingyan. baidu.com/
460026354178206	2014-11-21 20:00:01	2014-11-21 20:00:08	6893_379A	http://m.sohu. com/
460006815738450	2014-11-21 20:43:34	2014-11-21 20:43:44	5890_2B07	https://pao.qq. com/main.shtml

We used Mexican Hat Wavelets (MHW) as the bandpass filter for the graph signal. Extracting wavelet coefficients in the graph signal model by defining such a set of filters. We set the number of wavelet filters M of different scales in filter bank $F=[F_1, F_2, \ldots, F_M]$ to 6, which in turn represent the MHW of high frequency to low frequency. For the graph signal model topology considered in this paper, the frequency domain wavelet kernel response in the finite support interval is shown in Fig. 2.

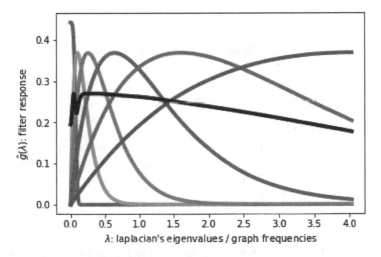

Fig. 2. MHW frequency domain response

Considering the sparsity of the signal and facilitating the visualization of the method, high frequency wavelet is selected as the basis of wavelet analysis in wavelet analysis. Under the high-frequency wavelet filter, the wavelet coefficients are sensitive to sudden changes in adjacent nodes. Specifically, when the node signal is close to the adjacent node signal value, the wavelet coefficient approaches 0, the node signal is larger than the adjacent node signal, and the wavelet coefficient is larger. In order to discover the relationship between the signal on the graph and the wavelet coefficients, and the performance of the wavelet coefficients, we randomly selected a node #902 on the graph and studied it. The wavelet coefficient is determined by the signal relationship between the node signal and the adjacent node, and the adjacent relationship is found by the time and space correlation of the node. Therefore, this paper constructs a 1-hop self-centered network, randomly taking #902 nodes and a total of five 1-hop nodes connected to it as the research target, and the connection relationship is shown in Fig. 3a and Fig. 3b left shows the signal changes for each node throughout the day in. Figure 3b right shows the variation of the high-frequency wavelet coefficients for the #902 node throughout the day.

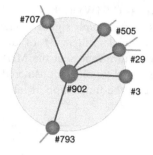

a #902 node's 1-hop egocentric network

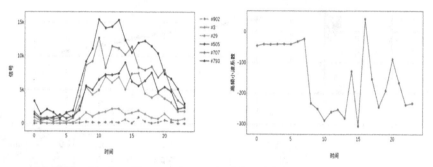

b left: Signal in the self-centered network, right: High frequency wavelet coefficient in self-centered network

Fig. 3. Comparison of #902 node signal and high frequency wavelet coefficient (Color figure online)

The blue dotted line in Fig. 3b left shows the full-day signal amplitude of #902, and the solid line indicates the signal amplitude of the spatial neighboring nodes. Comparing the two figures, it is obvious that:

- The signal amplitude of #902 in e is significantly lower than that of other nodes in e. Compared with Fig. 3b right #902 all day wavelet coefficients are mostly less than zero.
- At 0:00–6:00, the signal of #902 and spatial adjacent nodes changes stably, and the time dimension has no significant fluctuation. The absolute value of #902 high frequency wavelet coefficient is low and stable, and the low frequency characteristic is significant.
- At 8:00, the signal amplitude of adjacent nodes in #902 space increased significantly, and the corresponding #902 high-frequency wavelet coefficient decreased significantly. At 14:00 and 16:00, #902 showed a relatively high mutation in the time dimension, corresponding to a significant increase in the #902 high frequency wavelet.

6   Conclusion and Future Work

Using the idea of Crowd-Sensing, this paper uses the user's mobile behavior between base stations to determine the dependencies between base stations, and then constructs the spatial network map topology. We models the number of users of the base station as the signal on the graph and use the theory of spectral wavelet decomposition to find the spatial behavior characteristics of the graph signal model. Through the high-dimensional behavioral characteristics, it is found that wavelet coefficients of different scales can finely represent the high-frequency features and low-frequency features of the user moving in space. It provides a new understanding of urban population movement characteristics from the perspective of spectrum map, and the obtained results can also be applied to important aspects such as abnormal behavior monitoring and urban infrastructure construction in urban supervision.

References

1. Yang, S., Kalpakis, K., Biem, A.: Spatio-temporal coupled bayesian robust principal component analysis for road traffic event detection. In: 16th International IEEE Conference on Intelligent Transportation Systems (ITSC 2013), pp. 392–398. IEEE (2013)
2. Senaratne, H., Mueller, M., Behrisch, M., et al.: Urban mobility analysis with mobile network data: a visual analytics approach. IEEE Trans. Intell. Transp. Syst. 19(5), 1537–1546 (2018)
3. Rawassizadeh, R., Momeni, E., Dobbins, C., et al.: Scalable daily human behavioral pattern mining from multivariate temporal data. IEEE Trans. Knowl. Data Eng. 28(11), 3098–3112 (2016)
4. Von Landesberger, T., Brodkorb, F., Roskosch, P., et al.: MobilityGraphs: visual analysis of mass mobility dynamics via spatio-temporal graphs and clustering. IEEE Trans. Vis. Comput. Graph. 22(1), 11–20 (2016)
5. Mallat, S.G.: A theory for multiresolution signal decomposition: the wavelet representation. IEEE Trans. Pattern Anal. Mach. Intell. 11(7), 674–693 (1989)
6. Shuman, D.I., Narang, S.K., Frossard, P., et al.: The emerging field of signal processing on graphs: extending high-dimensional data analysis to networks and other irregular domains. IEEE Signal Process. Mag. 30(3), 83–98 (2012)
7. Hammond, D.K., Vandergheynst, P., Gribonval, R.: Wavelets on graphs via spectral graph theory. Appl. Comput. Harmon. Anal. 30(2), 129–150 (2011)
8. Narang, S.K., Ortega, A.: Perfect reconstruction two-channel wavelet filter banks for graph structured data. IEEE Trans. Signal Process. 60(6), 2786–2799 (2012)
9. Shuman, D.I., Narang, S.K., Frossard, P., et al.: The emerging field of signal processing on graphs: extending high-dimensional data analysis to networks and other irregular domains. arXiv preprint arXiv:1211.0053 (2012)

Automated Classification of Attacker Privileges Based on Deep Neural Network

Hailong Liu[⊠] and Bo Li

Beijing Advanced Innovation Center for Big Data and Brain Computing,
Beihang University, Beijing 100191, China
{liuhl,libo}@act.buaa.edu.cn

Abstract. Attack graphs generated from the detected vulnerabilities in a network depict all possible attack paths that an intruder can take. Conventional approaches to generating attack graphs require well-categorized data of prerequisites and postconditions for the identified vulnerabilities. However, generating them in an automated way is an open issue. Hence automatic classification methods are desirable to effectively generate attacker privilege fields as prerequisites and postconditions, improve the generation of the attack graph, and reduce the security risks of the system. In this paper, we propose a new automatic attacker privilege model (IG-DNN). The information gain (IG) is used for obtaining an optimal set of feature words from vulnerability description, and the deep neural network model is served as an automatic attacker privilege classifier. We use the National Vulnerability Database (NVD) to validate the effectiveness of the IG-DNN model. We observe that prerequisite and postcondition privileges can be generated with overall average F-measure of 99.53% and 98.90% with the IG-DNN models, respectively. Moreover, compared with Naïve Bayes, KNN, and SVM, the IG-DNN model has achieved the best performance in precision, recall, and F-measure.

Keywords: Deep neural network · Information gain · Vulnerability · Software security · Attacker privilege

1 Introduction

With the rapid development of the digitalization level of various industries, today's computer networks are facing increased numbers of cyberattacks, providing safety and security for such systems is more urgent than ever [16]. In order to evaluate potential threats, attack graphs are widely used for modelling attack scenarios that exploit vulnerabilities in computer systems and networked infrastructures. So risk assessments generated from probabilistic attack graphs assist further security decisions [2,21].

Supported by National Key R&D Program of China (2018YFB0803500), the 2018 joint Research Foundation of Ministry of Education, China Mobile (5–7) and State Key Laboratory of Software Development Environment (SKLSDE-2018ZX).

M. Qiu (Ed.): SmartCom 2019, LNCS 11910, pp. 180–189, 2019.
https://doi.org/10.1007/978-3-030-34139-8_18

Most of the proposed attack graph generation techniques are based on Prerequisite/Postcondition Models. *Prerequisites* stand for the necessary conditions of exploiting the vulnerabilities. *Postconditions* are the effects and capabilities obtained by the attackers as a result of the vulnerability exploitations. Topological Vulnerability Analysis (TVA) [8] is one of the famous attack graph generation tools, which utilizes a knowledge database of prerequisites and postconditions that relate to vulnerability exploitation steps. But the prerequisites and postconditions need manually generated from the vulnerability descriptions. Network Security Planning Architecture (NETSPA) [7] generates prerequisites and postconditions via a logistic regression model trained with a sample manual data. However, their privilege classification schemes seem to be limited, such that not cover application level privileges. The other attack graph generation methods proposed in [12,17,19] all rely on manually determining the attacker privileges corresponding to all vulnerabilities, which seems time-consuming.

A direct solution is to extract the prerequisites and postconditions from publicly accessible vulnerability databases automatically. However, the vulnerability descriptions in the databases are usually not entirely machine-readable, impeding the easy parsing of the vulnerabilities [9]. Fortunately, deep learning has a significant impact on the field of text processing [10,18]. Conneau et al. [4] propose a very deep convolutional network which using up to 29 convolutional layers for natural language processing. Hassan et al. [6] describe a joint CNN and RNN framework for sentence classification to overcome the locality of the convolutional and pooling layers.

Therefore, in order to generate the prerequisites and postconditions of vulnerabilities in an automated way, we propose an automatic attacker privilege classification model IG-DNN. In this model, we first use the information gain (IG) algorithm to extract the feature words of the vulnerability descriptions, then construct a DNN neural network model based on deep learning. The IG-DNN model was trained and tested using vulnerability data derived from the National Vulnerability Database (NVD). The experimental results show that the proposed model effectively improves the performance of attacker privilege classification.

The remainder of this paper is arranged as follows: Sect. 2 introduces the definition of relevant concept and algorithm. Section 3 describes the implementation details of our model. Experiment dataset and results are discussed in Sect. 4 with comparative analysis. And in Sect. 5, the conclusions are outlined.

2   Related Definition

The automatic classification model of attacker privilege (IG-DNN) is constructed in this paper. The relevant definitions are as follows.

2.1   Attacker Privilege

We use a general categorization of attacker privileges based on the privilege categories proposed in [1]. As illustrated in Table 1, five attacker privilege levels are depicted in descending order from OS ($Admin$) level to the $None$. OS/APP level privileges indicate privilege requirements or gains for specific operating systems/applications. And $Admin$ level privileges are more capable than privileges at $User$ levels. The $None$ level implies the attacker does not need/gain any of the four privileges listed at the operating system or application level.

Table 1. Categorization of attacker privilege levels.

Privilege	OS (Admin)	OS (User)	APP (Admin)	APP (User)	None
Level	5	4	3	2	1

2.2 Information Gain

Information gain measures on how mixed up the features are [5]. In text classification domain, information gain is used to measure the importance of feature A to class C. The expected value of the information gain is the mutual information $I(C, A)$ between classes C and feature A.

$$I(C,\ A) = H(C) - H(C \mid A) \tag{1}$$

$H(C)$ is the entropy of the class, and $H(C|A)$ is the conditional entropy of class given feature, their calculation formula are as follows.

$$H(C) = -\sum_{i=1}^{k} p(C_i)\, log_2\, p(C_i) \tag{2}$$

$$H(C \mid A) = -\sum_{i=1}^{k} p(C_i \mid A)\, log_2\, p(C_i \mid A) \tag{3}$$

Based on the feature selection method of the information gain criterion, the information gain of each feature is calculated, and usually, a feature with larger information gain value should be preferred to other features.

3 Description of the Proposed IG-DNN Model

The attacker privilege automatic classification model IG-DNN is mainly composed of IG and DNN. The original vulnerability data is preprocessed first, then IG is used to extract the feature words of the vulnerability descriptions, and then the DNN is constructed to realize the automatic training and classification of the attacker privilege. The workflow of the IG-DNN model is shown in Fig. 1.

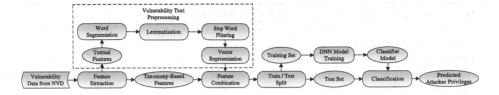

Fig. 1. Framework of the proposed method.

3.1 Feature Selection

The NVD provides comprehensive information about the vulnerability, such as vulnerability description, CVSS score, and the Common Vulnerability Enumeration (CVE) identifiers. For prerequisites and postconditions generation, we select the following data fields derived from NVD as taxonomy-based features. Their detailed definitions can be found at CVSS 2.0 [15] and CVSS 3.0 [20] specifications.

Access Vector indicates the context by which the vulnerability is exploited. It takes the value of *Network, Adjacent Network, Local* and *Physical*.

Privileges Required denotes the level of privileges an attacker must possess before successfully exploiting the vulnerability, but we can not distinguish it as the operating system or application level.

Authentication metric measures the number of times an attacker must authenticate to a target. It takes the values of *None, Single* and *Multiple*.

Common Platform Enumeration (CPE) [3] describes a set of vulnerable platforms with regard to each identified vulnerabilities. The vulnerable platforms are split into three classes, operating systems, firmwares and applications.

The *Impacts* metrics capture the loss of Confidentiality, Integrity, and Availability induced at the victim. These fields are especially helpful in determining the privilege gained of a successfully exploited vulnerability.

In addition to the above taxonomy-based features, vulnerability descriptions are also selected as textual features since they are proved to be useful in determining attacker privileges [1]. We use IG to extract feature word set from the textual features. The steps are shown in Algorithm 1.

3.2 Privileges Classification Using IG-DNN

As illustrated in Fig. 2, the IG-DNN model contains two input layers, the *main_input* layer and *aux_input* layer. As input to the *main_input* layer, we use a set of vulnerability descriptions represented in vectorized form. And the input of *aux_input* is a set of selected taxonomy-based features.

An embedding layer is connected behind the *main_input* layer to encode the input sequence into a sequence of dense vectors for dimension reduction. Then the output of the embedding layer is provided to a convolution layer as input. The convolution layer is used for detecting the special pattern of words in the vulnerability texts [10].

Algorithm 1. Feature Words Extraction Algorithm

Input: $total\_words$(array of unique word A and its class C), N(the number of extracted feature words)
Output: $feature\_words$(feature word set)

calculate $H(C)$
for each word in $total\_words$ **do**
    calculate $H(C|A)$
    $I(C, A) \leftarrow H(C)$ - $H(C|A)$
end for
sort $total\_words$ in descending by $I(C, A)$
$feature\_words \leftarrow$ { select the first N words in $total\_words$ }
return $feature\_words$

Next, we max-pool the result of the convolutional layer into a long feature vector and concatenate the vector of taxonomy-based features with it. Then the combined vectors are fed to a deep densely-connected network that consists of a dropout layer and three fully-connected layers. The dropout layer stacked behind the first fully-connected layer is used to avoid overfitting, thus increasing the generalizing power.

In addition, the forward propagation of the convolution layer and fully-connected layers uses ReLU as the activation function. The cross-entropy is selected as the loss function to measure the loss between the predicted output and the actual output. Moreover, the extended stochastic gradient descent algorithm Adam [11] is used as the optimization algorithm to minimize the loss function.

Finally, the output layer uses softmax as activation function to assign probabilities to different objects for the final output. As the output, the attacker privilege categories are determined.

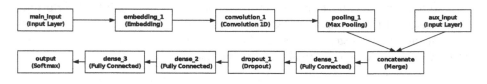

Fig. 2. The architecture of IG-DNN.

4   Performance Evaluation

In this section, we evaluate the performance of the proposed model for attacker privilege classification and compare our results with the other models.

4.1   Dataset

In order to verify the proposed model, we collect the vulnerability information from NVD as experimental data. By the end of 2018, NVD hosts more than 109,000 vulnerability entries which recorded in a series of JSON files. We extract the required vulnerability information from the JSON files using Python and label the vulnerability entries manually by carefully analyzing their description texts and other base fields. Finally, we get two datasets, a prerequisite labelled dataset that contains 45,958 vulnerabilities, and a postcondition labelled dataset consists of 88,730 vulnerabilities. The distribution of privilege classes on the experimental datasets is depicted in Table 2.

Table 2. Distribution of privilege classes on the experimental dataset.

	OS (Admin)	OS (User)	APP (Admin)	APP (User)	None	Total
Prerequisite	419	11,695	1,068	8,425	24,351	45,958
Postcondition	15,586	20,242	2,158	495	50,249	88,730

4.2   Experimental Procedure

Given the original dataset at Table 2, 75% of the data is used for training, and 25% is used for testing in all 5 cases. As we mentioned in Sect. 3.1, the extracted features are split into two parts, taxonomy-based features and textual features. For taxonomy-based features, their original metric values are directly mapped into proper float values based on the CVSS 2.0 and CVSS 3.0 specifications. For textual features, TextBlob [14] is used for word segmentation, and the Word-NetLemmatizer of Natural Language Toolkit (NLTK) [13] is used for lemmatization. We use the English stop word list of NLTK, and extend it by adding the professional stop words (e.g., "vulnerability") which frequently appear in vulnerability texts for stop word filtering.

Next, the information gain value of each unique word in the filtered words list is calculated, and the results are arranged in descending order. The top 5,000 words are extracted as feature words to build a vocabulary. Based on the vocabulary, each vulnerability description is expressed as an m-dimensional vector $vec = < d_1, d_2, d_3, \cdots, d_m >$ (m is the max number of words in the filtered words list), where d_i ($i \in \{1, 2, \cdots, m\}$) representing the index of the i-th word of the current filtered words in the vocabulary.

After the vectorization representation of vulnerability description, we use the deep learning framework Keras to construct the DNN model as shown in Fig. 2. Various configuration parameters of the DNN model were tested, and the final parameters are set as follows.

The convolution layer with a stride of 1 contains 256 kernels of size 1×3. And the number of neurons in the three fully connected layers are all set to 256. An Adam optimizer is used to optimize the DNN model with a batch size set to 128, and an initial learning rate set to 0.001. The number of epochs of DNN model training is 20.

4.3   Evaluation Metrics

We calculate the standard classification metrics of Precision, Recall, and F-Measure as the evaluation metrics, which defined in Eqs. (4), (5) and (6) where TP, TN, FP, and FN stand for true positive, true negative, false positive and false negative, respectively.

$$Precision = \frac{TP}{TP + FP} \tag{4}$$

$$Recall = \frac{TP}{TP + FN} \tag{5}$$

$$F - Measure = 2 \cdot \frac{Precision * Recall}{Precision + Recall} \tag{6}$$

4.4   Comparisons Between IG and TF-IDF

In order to evaluate the effect of IG for feature words selection, we compare it with the method of TF-IDF based on the same configured DNN model. The evaluation results for privilege prerequisites and postconditions are shown in Figs. 3 and 4, respectively.

The DNN model based on IG achieves better performance than the TF-IDF's in precision, recall and F-measure. Because TF-IDF is not comprehensive that only considers the word frequency for importance measuring. IG takes into account the importance of words to the category of attacker privilege, which may enhance the performance in privilege classification.

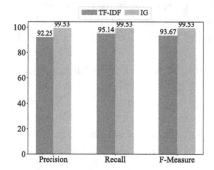

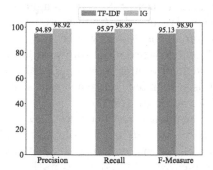

Fig. 3. Comparison for privilege prerequisites.

Fig. 4. Comparison for privilege postconditions.

4.5   Comparison of the Models

To verify the performance of IG-DNN in attacker privilege classification, we compare and evaluate it with the traditional machine learning algorithms, including Naïve Bayes(NB), KNN, and SVM. The experimental results are shown in

Table 3. The corresponding confusion matrix of IG-DNN for privilege prerequisites is provided in Fig. 5 and for privilege postconditions in Fig. 6.

For the IG-DNN model, we get the F-measure of 99.53% and 98.90% for privilege prerequisites and postconditions, respectively. Comparing the results of these four models, the IG-DNN model achieves significantly better results for both the privilege prerequisites and postconditions. This promising result has validated the effectiveness of the IG-DNN model in the automatic classification of attacker privileges.

Table 3. Results of different models for prerequisite/postcondition classification.

Model	Precision	Recall	F-measure
NB	84.69/88.63	84.72/88.94	84.68/88.63
KNN	89.92/89.44	90.17/89.57	90.00/89.48
SVM	90.54/89.49	90.53/89.46	90.12/89.21
IG-DNN	99.53/98.92	99.53/98.89	99.53/98.90

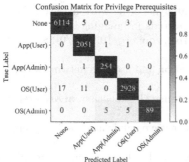

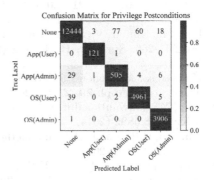

Fig. 5. Confusion matrix of IG-DNN for privilege prerequisites.

Fig. 6. Confusion matrix of IG-DNN for privilege postconditions.

5   Conclusion

In this work, we applied a deep neural network for generating attacker privileges as prerequisites and postconditions from the vulnerabilities in the NVD. The proposed IG-DNN model achieved an F-measure of 99.53% and 98.90% for privilege prerequisites and postconditions, respectively. And compared to the traditional machine learning algorithms, the IG-DNN model outperforms others in precision, recall and F-measure. This promising result demonstrates the effectiveness of IG-DNN in attacker privilege classification. Moreover, it also indicates that deep learning can be used successfully for privilege determination in order to generate attack graphs in an automated way.

References

1. Aksu, M.U., Bicakci, K., Dilek, M.H., Ozbayoglu, A.M., et al.: Automated generation of attack graphs using NVD. In: Proceedings of the Eighth ACM Conference on Data and Application Security and Privacy, pp. 135–142. ACM (2018)
2. Aksu, M.U., Dilek, M.H., Tatlı, E.İ., Bicakci, K., Dirik, H.I., Demirezen, M.U., Aykır, T.: A quantitative CVSS-based cyber security risk assessment methodology for it systems. In: 2017 International Carnahan Conference on Security Technology (ICCST), pp. 1–8. IEEE (2017)
3. Cheikes, B.A., Cheikes, B.A., Kent, K.A., Waltermire, D.: Common platform enumeration: naming specification version 2.3. US Department of Commerce, National Institute of Standards and Technology (2011)
4. Conneau, A., Schwenk, H., Barrault, L., Lecun, Y.: Very deep convolutional networks for text classification. arXiv preprint arXiv:1606.01781 (2016)
5. Gray, R.M.: Entropy and Information Theory. Springer, Heidelberg (2011). https://doi.org/10.1007/978-1-4419-7970-4
6. Hassan, A., Mahmood, A.: Convolutional recurrent deep learning model for sentence classification. IEEE Access **6**, 13949–13957 (2018)
7. Ingols, K., Lippmann, R., Piwowarski, K.: Practical attack graph generation for network defense. In: 2006 22nd Annual Computer Security Applications Conference (ACSAC 2006), pp. 121–130. IEEE (2006)
8. Jajodia, S., Noel, S., Oberry, B.: Topological analysis of network attack vulnerability. In: Kumar, V., Srivastava, J., Lazarevic, A. (eds.) Managing Cyber Threats, pp. 247–266. Springer, Heidelberg (2005). https://doi.org/10.1007/0-387-24230-9_9
9. Kaynar, K.: A taxonomy for attack graph generation and usage in network security. J. Inf. Secur. Appl. **29**, 27–56 (2016)
10. Kim, Y.: Convolutional neural networks for sentence classification. arXiv preprint arXiv:1408.5882 (2014)
11. Kingma, D.P., Ba, J.: Adam: a method for stochastic optimization. arXiv preprint arXiv:1412.6980 (2014)
12. Lippmann, R.P., Ingols, K.W., Piwowarski, K.J.: Generating a multiple-prerequisite attack graph, 17 May 2016. US Patent 9,344,444
13. Loper, E., Bird, S.: NLTK: the natural language toolkit. arXiv preprint cs/0205028 (2002)
14. Loria, S., Keen, P., Honnibal, M., Yankovsky, R., Karesh, D., Dempsey, E., et al.: Textblob: simplified text processing. Simplified Text Processing, Secondary TextBlob (2014)
15. Mell, P., Scarfone, K., Romanosky, S.: A complete guide to the common vulnerability scoring system version 2.0. In: Published by FIRST-Forum of Incident Response and Security Teams, vol. 1, p. 23 (2007)
16. Qiu, H., Kapusta, K., Lu, Z., Qiu, M., Memmi, G.: All-or-nothing data protection for ubiquitous communication: Challenges and perspectives. Information Sciences (2019)
17. Salahi, A., Ansarinia, M.: Predicting network attacks using ontology-driven inference. arXiv preprint arXiv:1304.0913 (2013)
18. Silver, D., et al.: Mastering the game of go with deep neural networks and tree search. Nature **529**(7587), 484 (2016)

19. Singhal, A., Ou, X.: Security risk analysis of enterprise networks using probabilistic attack graphs. Network Security Metrics, pp. 53–73. Springer, Cham (2017). https://doi.org/10.1007/978-3-319-66505-4_3
20. Team C: Common vulnerability scoring system V3. 0: specification document. First.org (2015)
21. Wang, H., Chen, Z., Zhao, J., Di, X., Liu, D.: A vulnerability assessment method in industrial internet of things based on attack graph and maximum flow. IEEE Access **6**, 8599–8609 (2018)

NnD: Shallow Neural Network Based Collision Decoding in IoT Communications

Zhe Wang[1], Linghe Kong[1(✉)], Guihai Chen[1], and Ming Ni[2]

[1] Shanghai Jiao Tong University, Shanghai, China
{wang-zhe,linghe.kong,chen-gh}@sjtu.edu.cn
[2] China Electronics Technology Group Corporation, Beijing, China
13801626070@139.com

Abstract. Internet of Things (IoT) has been widely used in intelligent warehouse, environment monitoring and smart buildings. In these application scenarios, concurrent transmissions frequently occur in which multiple transmitters send packets to one receiver simultaneously, causing severe collisions and low throughput. The state-of-the-art methods are able to decompose collided packets from different transmitters. However, they rely heavily on random time offsets and has poor performance under inferior channel conditions. In this paper, we present a new physical layer mechanism *Shallow Neural Network based Collision Decoding* (nnD) to resolve multi-packet collisions. We first collect collision-free symbols or history single packets as the training set. In order to improve the decoding accuracy, we model the mapping relationship between overlapped symbols and their symbol values by neural networks. Since overlapping combinations of symbols are limited which are decided by corresponding chips' value, we can predict values of unknown symbols by classifying different kinds of overlapping combinations. By introducing neural networks, nnD can not only achieve a high decoding precision but also can dynamically choose neural network architecture to adapt to different collision scenarios. To evaluate the performance of nnD, extensive trace-driven simulations are conducted. The results demonstrate that nnD outperforms existing methods in terms of bit error rate and the number of concurrent transmissions.

1 Introduction

IoT has been widely used in a variety of application scenarios, e.g., intelligent warehouse [4], environment monitoring [5] and smart buildings [6]. With the prosperity of IoT [10,11], concurrent transmissions become frequently, resulting in severe collisions and low throughputs.

In this paper, we focus on a typical wireless technology ZigBee [1], which is a low-power wireless protocol elaborated for IoT applications based on IEEE 802.15.4 standard. Adopting star, tree, or mesh topology in ZigBee based network, concurrent transmissions appear frequently in which a receiver (RX)

© Springer Nature Switzerland AG 2019
M. Qiu (Ed.): SmartCom 2019, LNCS 11910, pp. 190–199, 2019.
https://doi.org/10.1007/978-3-030-34139-8_19

receives multiple packets from several transmitters (TXs) simultaneously. However, conventional ZigBee cannot directly decode these collided packets, resulting in retransmissions and low throughput. To resolve such packet collision problem, standard ZigBee implements Carrier Sense Multiple Access with Collision Avoidance (CSMA/CA) in its Media Access Control (MAC) layer to avoid collisions [7]. But there are several inherent limitations of CSMA/CA, it introduce additional time delay and energy overhead.

Instead of collision avoidance, the state-of-the-art strategy attempts to resolve collision directly exploiting collision itself. While ZigZag [2] can depart packets from different transmitters, it can only achieve limited throughput due to the multiple retransmissions. mZig [8] makes use of ZigBee's waveform and amplitude to decompose collided chips. However, mZig falls into high accumulative error and has poor performance under inferior channel conditions.

Decoding the collided packets precisely has two main challenges: First, the collided packets are entangled together. Second, not only the collided packets but also the status of channel increase the difficulty of decoding.

To tackle these challenges, we propose a new mechanism *Shallow Neural Network based Collision Decoding* (nnD) in IoT communications. Utilizing powerful classification ability of neural network (NN), the main idea of our design is to distinguish different kinds of overlapping status in a collided packet. On the one hand, we can manually overlay known chips, e.g., collision-free chips or history single packets, from different TXs to generate training set. On the other hand, the known overlapped chips from current collided packets can be used for fine tuning the NN to model the dynamic channel status. As a result, collided packets can be decoded chip-by-chip according to the corresponding classification result of NN.

Considering a concurrent transmission, two TXs named Alice (A) and Bob (B) send packets to a RX simultaneously. As a result, two packets from different TXs overlay with each other and a collision happens in the RX. Since precise synchronization is not ensured in concurrent transmissions, time offsets exist between packets from multiple TXs. Time offsets can be depicted by two parameters which are chip cycles and sample intervals respectively, i.e., time offsets are composed of several chip cycles and sample intervals.

Without losing generality, we give an example of time offset which consists of only several sample intervals as presented in Fig. 1. The overlapped chips can be labeled with a two-bit sequences, i.e., 00, 01, 10, and 11 as shown in Fig. 1. Labels of the overlapped chips is determined by the chip values of two overlapped chips from A and B. Chips from the same TX has the same half-sin waveform and amplitude while the amplitudes of chips from different TXs are distinguished. Based on the identity of waveforms and amplitudes divergence, overlapped chips which have different labels can be distinguished from each other. Besides, overlapped chips of the same labels is almost identical. Thus, known overlapped chips with labels can be regarded as a training set for classification. History data received in short terms can also be utilized to train the NN since channel is relatively stable in short terms. As a result, there are adequate training samples to achieve high accuracy and the whole collided packets can be accurately decoded chip-by-chip according to their labels.

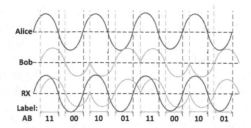

Fig. 1. Labels of two overlapped packets.

The main contribution of this paper can be concluded as follows:

- We present a new mechanism based on shallow neural network which can resolve multi-packet collisions directly. The origin multi-packet decomposition problem is translated into a classification process and collided packets can be decoded by a trained NN in a relatively low computing cost.
- We implement extensive trace-driven simulations to estimate the performance of nnD. The results demonstrate that nnD significantly outperforms existing methods in terms of bit error rate and the number of concurrent transmissions.

2   Background

ZigBee is a low-power wireless protocol based on IEEE 802.15.4 standard. The IEEE 802.15.4 PHY layer supports three ISM bands: 868.3 MHz in Europe, 902–928 MHz in America, and 2.4 GHz all over the world. ZigBee of 2.4 GHz ISM band is the most widely used and its associated bandwidth is 2 MHz. A standard PHY Protocol Data Unit (PPDU) of ZigBee physical layer consists of three parts, Synchronization Header (SHR), PHY Header (PHR) containing frame length information and Protocol Service Data Unit (PSDU), a variable length payload. The 32-bit preamble is a part of SHR and consists of 32 zeros.

The PPDU in TX goes through several processes before sending to a RX and the RX decodes data by an inverse procedure. We concentrate on the (de)modulation related to our design. First, binary data from PPDU is divided into symbols which consists of 4-bit. After that, each 4-bit symbol is spread to a 32-bit chip sequence which is known as Direct Sequence Spread Spectrum (DSSS). Next, chip sequence is modulated into I and Q phase according to Offset Quadrature Phase Shift Keying (OQPSK). Thus, amplitude of chips from the same packet is uniform. Then pulse shaping is performed based on chips' value and chips in one packet are shaped as half-sine waveform of the same amplitude.

3   The Core Design of NnD

3.1   Overview of NnD

nnD is designed to decode collided packets directly taking advantage of known collision-free or overlapped chips. It has three main components: (i) collecting

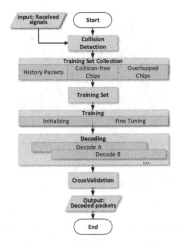

Fig. 2. Working diagram of nnD.

training set from history packets and current collided packet; (ii) training strategy to initializing and fine tuning the NN; (iii) decoding or predicting unknown overlapped chips' values. The working diagram of nnD is shown in Fig. 2.

Training Set Collection. First, we collect abundant training set making fully use of known chips. We observe that overlapping status of chips from different packets are limited because time offset between packets from different TXs is determined. Time offsets between packets can be detected and calculated by correlation with preamble's chip sequence [8]. After time offset is obtained, the original overlapped packets can be partitioned into basic segments as shown in Figs. 1 and 5. As a result, each segment is the overlapping result of single chip from different packets, while samples of a single chip are from the same chip cycle in a packet. Thus, each segment can be labeled with a definite bit sequence according to the values of chips belong to this segment as shown in Figs. 1 and 5. It can be seen that for a 2 or 3 packets' collision there are 4 or 8 kinds of labels respectively. Generally, there are 2^n kinds of labels for an n-packet collision.

Chips with the same label are nearly identical since chips of the same value from one packet have the same waveform and amplitude. Considering a specific chip from a single packet, multiple samples forming a half-sine pulse shaping can be indicated as:

$$X[i] = c \cdot \alpha \cdot sin(\pi f t). \tag{1}$$

where $X[i]$ is the value of i-th sample, c is the sign indicator (positive for chip '1' and negative for chip '0'), α is the amplitude which depends on TX power and distance. Besides, history packets recently received are also available and effective when the transmission power of TXs is fixed and channel is considered to be relatively stable in short terms [3]. To collect adequate training set, for one thing, we take the collision-free chips from both current packet and history packets into consideration. We manually overlay these chips under various time

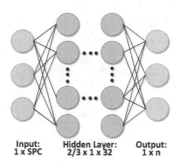

Fig. 3. Structure of shallow NN.

offsets to generate overlapped chips. For another, known overlapped chips in preamble from current packet can be used to fine tune the trained NN.

The samples for training in overlapped chips are related to time offsets between collided packets. We define the number of complete chip cycles and sample intervals in the time offset as chip offset and sample offset respectively. We choose segments of overlapped chips which have the maximum length, e.g., labeled part in Figs. 1 and 5, for training. As the NN needs inputs of fixed-length vectors, we normalize all segments to the length of complete chips by complementing zeros.

How to Structure and Train the NN. Second, the shallow fully connected neural network is implemented for classification. The whole training set is composed of current and history overlapped chips. We utilize history packets to initialize the NN and known chips from current packet to fine tune the NN. The training set is divided into 80% training set and 20% validating set randomly. In each hidden layer, we adopt a fully connected layer with sigmoid function as activation. Considering a specific hidden layer, we can represent its output as:

$$h_l = \frac{1}{1 + e^{-(\omega h_{l-1} + b)}}. \tag{2}$$

where ω and b is the weight and bias of current layer, h_{l-1} is the output of previous layer. The output from the last hidden layer is connected to the output layer. We use cross entropy as loss function for classification which can be formulated as follows:

$$\mathcal{L}(X, Y) = -\frac{1}{N} \sum_{i=1}^{N} (y_i \log \hat{y}_i + (1 - y_i) \log(1 - \hat{y}_i)). \tag{3}$$

where X and Y are collections of N training samples and labels, y_i and $\hat{y}_i$ is the ground truth and predicted result which are 1 **x** n vectors as shown in Fig. 3. Performance of the neural network is measured by bit error ratio (BER) and packets reception ratio (PRR) rather than conventional classification accuracy.

In order to maintain high classification precision and low computing cost, we introduce adaptive NN structure based on the number of collided packet and signal to noise ratio (SNR). In two and three collision scenarios, we train neural

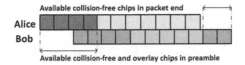

Fig. 4. Available training data of two collided packets when $t = 4$.

networks with two and three hidden layers of 32 neurons each layer. The NN architecture is shown in Fig. 3. The input vector length equals to the number of samples per chip (SPC) after complementing zeros. The output depends on the number of collided chips.

To ensure the sufficiency of training set at the same time of avoiding overfitting, sliding window strategy for training set updating is employed. We retain known labeled data from 64 history packets and updating training set when RX receives a new collided packet. Whenever a packet arrives, the neural network will be retrained using current and history data. As a result, high classification accuracy can be achieved. Besides, because the number of weights and bias is limited as the neural network architecture is very simple, time and computing overhead of training and decoding procedure is tolerative. In general, the design of nnD is practicable and is able to decode collided packets accurately.

Packet Decoding. Last, the trained NN is used to predict labels of unknown overlapped chips. We maintain a NN for each received packet in collisions. The decoding result of multi-packet can be used for cross-validation for high accuracy.

3.2   Two and Three Collided Packets Decoding Examples

Two-Packet Collision Decoding. In Fig. 1, we give an example of two packets collision. The number of samples in a chip is denoted as SPC. Time offset of packet from B compared with packet of A can be represented as T_b. Chip offset and sample offset can be indicated as C_b and S_b similarly. According to relationship between total time offset and chip offset and sample offset, it can be concluded that C_b is equal to $\frac{T_b}{SPC}$ while S_b is equal to $T_b\%SPC$.

Denoting chip values of A and B as A_i and B_j respectively, we can express segments of collided packets received in RX as $R_{(i,j)}$ which means the segment $R_{(i,j)}$ is the superimposed result of the partial i-th chip and j-th chip of A and Bob, e.g., $R_{(1,1)}$ is the overlay result of the partial samples in first chip of A and B. And the corresponding true label of $R_{(i,j)}$ is A_iB_j. The number of samples in a segment is determined by time offset as the whole overlapped packets is partitioned by beginning or ending positions of chips from multi-packet. In this example, segments with labels have more available samples the number of which is $(SPC - S_b)$ as indicated in Fig. 1.

Considering two packets from A and B of the same length L, the preamble length is denoted by t. There existing known chips in preamble or collision-free chips represented as $A_i(1 \leq i \leq t)$ and $B_i(1 \leq i \leq t, L - C_b + 1 \leq i \leq L)$, we want to estimate chip values of the rest chips, which can be achieved by predicting labels of $R_{(i,i-C_b)}(t + 1 \leq i \leq L)$.

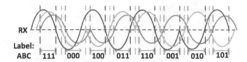

Fig. 5. Labels of three overlapped packets.

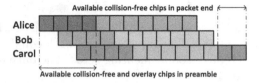

Fig. 6. Available training data of three collided packets when $t = 4$.

When $t \leq C_b$, there is no available known overlapped segments for training. Overlapped chips for training can be generated by overlaying collision-free chips of A and B with a specific sample offset of S_b. When $t > C_b$, there existing known overlapped chips so that segments with different labels for training can be obtained. Besides, history packets can also be used for training. As shown in Fig. 4, training set can be generated from overlapped chips or combination of collision-free chips.

Three-Packet Collision Decoding. In this subsection, we present how to decode a three-packet collision in details. Adopting similar terminology with two-packet collision example, time offset of B and Carol (C) is denoted as T_b and T_c; Chip offset and sample offset of B and C is represented as C_b,S_b and C_c,S_c respectively. A_i, B_j and C_k is the corresponding values of the i-th, j-th and k-th chip of packets from A, B and C.

As shown in Fig. 5, the whole collided packet is partitioned into basic segments according to the beginning and ending position of chips. Each segment is the overlapped result of three single chips from A, B and C. As a result, each segment can be labeled by the corresponding chips' bit sequence as depicted in Fig. 5. After that, segments with labels in Fig. 5 which have maximum length $SPC - S_c$ will be used for training. Each segment can be represented as $R_{(i,j,k)}$ with label $A_i B_j C_k$.

Assuming that packets from A, B, C are of the same length L and t is the preamble length in one packet, we need to predicting labels of $R_{(i,i-C_b,i-C_c)}(t + 1 \leq i \leq L)$ based on known data. When $t \leq C_c$, known three overlapped chips is absent in the collided packet. Known overlapped segments can be generated by overlaying known collision free and two-overlapped chips. When $t > C_c$, there existing available three-overlapped chips which can be directly used for training. As indicated in Fig. 6, two kinds of data source can be utilized to generate data set. Besides, we can also seek to history collided packets in short terms for more available training data.

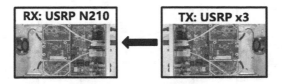

Fig. 7. Data collection platform.

Extend NnD to Multi-packet Collision Decoding. In a multi-packet collision scenario, n packets from different TXs overlay with each other in the RX. The collided packet is partitioned into basic overlapped segments in which there only existing partial samples of a single chip from a TX. By predicting the labels of all unknown segments, the whole superimposed packet can be decoded chip-by-chip.

4   Simulation

To estimate performance of nnD, we conduct extensive trace-driven simulations of two- and three-packet collision decoding.

We first collect vast collided packets in two- and three-packet collisions. Our data collection platform is based on several USRP N210 devices with SBX daughterboard as shown in Fig. 7. Our trace-driven simulation is based on Matlab platform. We implement the state-of-the-art mZig [8] for comparison since conventional ZigBee cannot decode packets in a collision. The objective of our simulation is to validate the capability of nnD from different perspectives. While nnD is a PHY layer design, bit error rate (BER), chip error rate (CER) and packet reception ratio (PRR) of PHY layer are used to evaluate the performance of nnD, mZig and traditional ZigBee under different signal to noise ratio (SNR) level. We set a threshold of BER below which a packet is considered decoding correctly, and the value of threshold is 10^{-3} in our simulation.

In our simulation, we set the sampling frequency in the RX as 32M/s, i.e., 32 sampling points in a chip cycle. We collect known labeled segments of the maximum length as training set. The labeled segments are normalized to the length of 32 by complementing zeros.

In Fig. 8(a), (c) and (e), we exhibit CER, BER and PRR of two-packet collision under different SNR. nnD can achieve a low CER and BER, i.e., less than 10^{-2}, even under low SNR. The PRR of nnD under different SNR retain relative stable whose value is more than 90% while mZig is more susceptible to noise.

We also extend nnD to three-packet collision decoding. In three-packet collision scenarios, we implement NN with three layers of the same number of neurons as two-packet situation. As shown in Fig. 8, nnD can also achieve lower BER and higher PRR under different SNR compared with mZig, which demonstrate that nnD has a preferable scalability and superior performance.

We perform plenty of repeated experiments in each case, e.g., two hundred repetitions under each SNR. The simulation results show that nnD significantly outperforms existing methods in terms of BER, PRR and the number of concurrent transmissions.

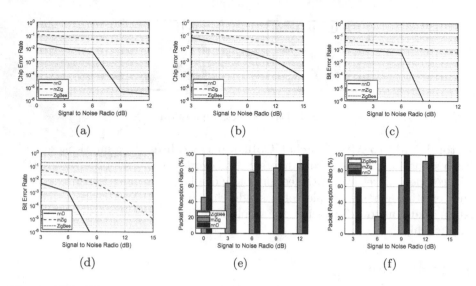

Fig. 8. CER, BER and PRR of two- (left) and three- (right) packet collision under different SNR

5   Related Works

In wireless transmission like ZigBee, collision happens frequently in which multi-transmitter send packets simultaneously. In order to avoid collision, conventional ZigBee implement CSMA/CA [7] in its MAC layer. However, CSMA causes delay of packet and performance of wireless network adopting CSMA is difficult to predict [9,14]. Besides, CSMA is invalid when hidden terminal exists. CSMA combined with RTS/CTS can resolve hidden terminal problem [13]. However, the handshake procedure of RTS/CTS will introduce extra cost resulting in low throughput [12].

Instead of collision avoidance, the state-of-the-art strategy attempts to resolve collision directly exploiting collision itself. Utilizing time offsets divergence between multiple collided packets, ZigZag [2] can depart packets from different transmitters. ZigZag has to retransmit collided packets several times according to the number of collide packets, resulting in limited throughput. mZig [8] make use of ZigBee's waveform and amplitude to decompose collision chip-by-chip. However, mZig falls into high accumulative error and has poor performance under inferior channel conditions.

In this paper, we propose a new design to decode the collided packet directly. The original collision decomposition problem is translated into a classification problem. As a result, we can decode the whole packet by a trained neural network accurately.

6 Conclusion

We present a new design based on shallow neural network which can resolve multi-packet collision directly. The origin multi-packet decomposition problem is translated into a classification procedure and collided packets can be decoded by a trained network. We implement extensive simulations to estimate the performance of nnD. The results demonstrate that nnD significantly outperforms existing methods in terms of bit error rate and the number of concurrent transmissions.

Acknowledgements. This work was supported in part by the National Key R&D Program of China 2018YFB1004703, NSFC grant 61972253, 61672349, 61672353.

References

1. Alliance, Z.: Introduction to Zigbee (2018). http://www.zigbee.org
2. Gollakota, S., Katabi, D.: Zigzag decoding: combating hidden terminals in wireless networks. In: ACM SIGCOMM (2008)
3. Halperin, D., Hu, W., Sheth, A., Wetherall, D.: Predictable 802.11 packet delivery from wireless channel measurements. In: ACM SIGCOMM (2010)
4. Jabbar, S., Khan, M., Silva, B.N., Han, K.: A REST-based industrial web of things' framework for smart warehousing. J. Supercomput. **74**, 4419–4433 (2018)
5. Justino, C., Duarte, A., Rocha-Santos, T.: Recent progress in biosensors for environmental monitoring: a review. Sensors **17**, 2918 (2017)
6. Kelly, S.D.T., Suryadevara, N.K., Mukhopadhyay, S.C.: Towards the implementation of IoT for environmental condition monitoring in homes. IEEE Sens. J. **13**, 3846–3853 (2013)
7. Kleinrock, L., Tobagi, F.: Packet switching in radio channels: part i - carrier sense multiple-access modes and their throughput-delay characteristics. IEEE Trans. Commun. **23**, 1400–1416 (1975)
8. Kong, L., Liu, X.: mZig: enabling multi-packet reception in ZigBee. In: ACM MOBICOM (2015)
9. Laufer, R., Kleinrock, L.: The capacity of wireless CSMA/CA networks. IEEE/ACM Trans. Netw. **24**, 1518–1532 (2016)
10. Liu, Y., Yang, C., Jiang, L., Xie, S., Zhang, Y.: Intelligent edge computing for IoT-based energy management in smart cities. IEEE Netw. **33**, 111–117 (2019)
11. Ronen, E., Shamir, A., Weingarten, A.O., Flynn, C.O.: IoT goes nuclear: creating a ZigBee chain reaction. In: IEEE S&P (2017)
12. Sobrinho, J.L., de Haan, R., Brazio, J.M.: Why RTS-CTS is not your ideal wireless LAN multiple access protocol. In: IEEE WCNC (2005)
13. Tobagi, F., Kleinrock, L.: Packet switching in radio channels: Part II - the hidden terminal problem in carrier sense multiple-access and the busy-tone solution. IEEE Trans. Commun. **23**, 1417–1433 (1975)
14. Ziouva, E., Antonakopoulos, T.: CSMA/CA performance under high traffic conditions: throughput and delay analysis. Computer Communications (2002)

Subordinate Relationship Discovery Method Based on Directed Link Prediction

He Nai[1], Min Lin[2], Hao Jiang[1(✉)], Huifang Liu[2], and Haining Ye[2]

[1] School of Electronic Information, Wuhan University, Wuhan, China
{naihe, jh}@whu.edu.cn
[2] China Unicom Group Co., Ltd., Guangdong Branch, Guangzhou, China
{linmin23, liuhf67, yehnl}@chinaunicom.cn

Abstract. The subordinate relationship is the important relationship of the users in an enterprise. However, traditional knowledge discovery method cannot found this relationship. The directed link prediction can get the direction information of the nodes, and this direction information also reflect some subordinate relationship. In this paper, we propose a directed link prediction method to get the potential direction relationship in a network and judging the relationship between users in the network through a directed connection. Because the subordinate relationship cannot get directly, so we use the relationship recurrence rate to verify the effectiveness. The experiment proves that the prosed directed link prediction method can discover the relationship of users, and there is a stable relationship between users.

Keywords: Subordinate relationship · Knowledge discovery · Link prediction · Directed

1 Introduction

Subordinate relationship is shared between the superior and the subordinate. It exists in the enterprise, the subordinate and its immediate supervisor have certain interests or benefits of both parties. The well leader-member relationship in an enterprise can enhance the organizational loyalty of lower-level employees, thereby improving the organizational commitment of subordinates and reducing the turnover intention of subordinates. In mobile data mining, using call record and online log of employees to build complex networks and discover the leader-member relationship has the great significance for perceiving the manager and management model within an enterprise.

In the relationship discovery method for mobile data, community discovery has always been a common method. These methods have algorithms based on network topology and algorithms based on semantic clustering. The algorithm based on network topology only divides the community structure from the external link form, and ignores the user's online behavior and attribute characteristics. The algorithm based on semantic clustering has combined the strength of uses' relationship with the attribute information to discover the semantic community. The advantage is that the community mining results are more accurate and more cohesive, and more suitable for discovering overlapping community structures.

M. Qiu (Ed.): SmartCom 2019, LNCS 11910, pp. 200–211, 2019.
https://doi.org/10.1007/978-3-030-34139-8_20

However, the above method based on community discovery only judges whether the user is in a community by the similarity of the users' attribute and the online behavior. It can only judge whether the user has a certain association, and cannot find the level of the users. However, the directed link prediction for the network can get the relationship of the nodes and this direction can express the subordinate relationship.

Link prediction methods are mainly divided into two categories: content-based and graph-based. In both categories, a higher metric means that vertex pairs will be connected with a high probability and vice versa. In content-based measures, attributes of vertices and links are employed. In graph-based measures, the topological features of complex networks are used to measure and perform link prediction. Graph-based link prediction can be divided into three categories: neighbor-based, path-based and pattern-based. The neighbor-based link prediction method calculates the characteristics of the common neighbors of the vertex pairs. If the characteristics of the common neighbors are more, the more likely the vertex pairs are connected. Method proposed by Adamic and Adar [1], Salton Index [2] and Hup Promoted Index [3] are belong to neighbor-based measures. In path-based measures, consider the transition possibilities of the path through the edge between the vertices and the random walk from the vertices to its neighbors. Some pattern-based measures studies are described in [2, 3]. Due to the difficulty of content-based information acquisition, most link prediction methods focus on graph-based measurements.

Systematic analysis of traditional graph-based link prediction measures in unsupervised link prediction model [4]. In the unsupervised link prediction models, the scores of all unlinked vertex pairs are calculated from predetermined link prediction metrics. After that, the node with the highest score is predicted to be connected. The above methods have inherent drawbacks of unsupervised learning methods. In order to overcome these drawbacks, supervised learning models were proposed to predict links. Most content-based and graph-based link prediction methods are supervised. Since the supervised learning method uses a large amount of data to train the model and is more in line with real-life situations, the link prediction method for supervised learning is more accurate than the unsupervised learning link prediction method. In link prediction, the most commonly used supervised learning models are classification, probabilistic, matrix factorization and graph kernel based models [5]. Hasan et al. [3] proposed a classification-based link prediction method, which uses content-based and graph-based features, such as keyword matching count of vertices, shortest distance between vertex pairs, and clustering index of vertices. It uses very few computing resources, efficiently uses the classification method for link prediction, and achieves good results. Backstrom and Leskovec uses a transition probability on vertices to develop a supervised link prediction algorithm based on random walk model. The proposed algorithm learns edge strengths by effectively combining structural information of vertex and edge attributes. The key idea of this study is that a random walker is most probably to visit the vertices to which links will be formed. Dai et al. [10] proposed a nonnegative matrix factorization based link prediction algorithm to predict links in multi-relational networks. They used similarity and influence among distinct types of links. Brouard et al. [7] formulated the link prediction problem as an output kernel learning problem and presented a semi-supervised link prediction approach based on output kernel regression.

Many of the link prediction methods described in the literature are applied to undirected networks. Neighbor-based link prediction measures don't use direction of edges in directed social networks. Path based measures cannot effectively cover local topological structures when it is not possible to reach from a source vertex to target vertex in directed networks. A small number of studies described in the literature have considered direction of links for effective link prediction. For instance, Schall [4] presented an unsupervised link prediction method using directional graph patterns. He introduced a pattern-based measure named as Triadic Closeness (TC). TC is based on ratio of the count of closed triads, which are matched to pattern of a given vertex pairs, versus possible closed triads. Lichtenwalter and Chawla [2] defined a new concept named as vertex collocation profile (VCP) for link prediction and analysis. VCP is a vector of all possible sub-graphs containing vertex pairs, which are to be predicted, with total n vertices over r edges. VCP can present rich graph-based structures such as directed and multi-relational edges and also additional information like weight and temporal information of edges. Behfar et al. [5] analyzed link formation mechanisms on inlinks and outlinks. They put forward the idea that inlinks and outlinks have distinct link formation mechanisms, because they have different degree distributions in directed networks. They concluded that power-law distribution is followed on inlink formation, while heavy-tailed degree distribution isn't followed on outlink formation. Shang et al. [5] introduced a new directional link prediction measure to reveal the difference roles of one-directional links and bi-directional links on link formation mechanism. They concluded that vertex pairs linked by a bi-directional edge are more likely to be linked to common neighbors than vertex pairs linked by a onedirectional edge. Aghabozorgi and Khayyambashi [2] proposed a new link prediction measure based triad network patterns having distinct collocations of directed edges. The proposed measure was employed in classification models to predict links in social networks. Zhao et al. [8] developed a new link prediction method for ranking potential links by using topological structures of network and edge covariates information for both directed and undirected networks. It is assumed that if endpoints of vertex pairs are similar, they are more likely to be linked in directed networks. Ding and Li [2] proposed a probabilistic based method for reconstructing the topological structure of directed weighted network to predict trade actions in world trade networks. Wang et al. [8] extended the study of Zhou et al. [7] as directed to predict link direction in directed networks. They added extra ground vertex to the original network to take advantage of topological structures as much possible. Guo et al. [13] developed a new link prediction method based on ranking of vertices to predict link directions in directed networks. They assumed that links are mostly established from lower ranked vertices to higher ranked vertices. They proposed a recursive subgraph based ranking algorithm by combining local and global structures to rank vertices. In this paper, we have extended neighbor-based measures into pattern-based measures based directed edge structures to improve accuracy of link prediction in directed networks. This work generalizes our previous [9] work for extension of all traditional undirected neighbor-based similarity measures into directional pattern-based measures. The proposed method also takes into account weight and temporal information of edges. The works described in [12] suggested that weighted and temporal based link prediction measures could improve the accuracy of link prediction. So, we extend traditional neighbor-based measures and the proposed method as temporal and weighted by combining an existing weighted method [11] and the proposed temporal method. The proposed measure has been compared to traditional neighbor-based measures in supervised link prediction algorithms. The reported results demonstrate its effectiveness and applicability.

2 Related Work

The traditional method of the link prediction is based on the neighbor nodes. A number of neighbor-based link prediction measures are described in the literature. Adamic-Adar Coefficient (AA) was firstly proposed to determine whether two given web pages are strongly related or similar. This measure was also adopted to predict links in social networks. In terms of link prediction, the vertex pairs having fewer common vertices are weighted more heavily by AA measure. So, vertex pairs sharing fewer relations have higher probability to be connected. Common Neighbors (CN) is also one of the basic link prediction measures because of the simplicity of its calculation. Vertex pairs sharing more common neighbors are more likely to be linked with respect to the CN measure. Newman's study shows that there is a correlation between number of common neighbors and future collaborations among scientists in collaboration networks. Jaccard's Coefficient (JC) is assumed that two vertices are more likely to be linked when they share more common neighbors in proportion to their total number of neighbors. Sørensen Index was proposed to establish equal amplitude groups in plant sociology based on the similarity of species. It is also used to calculate similarities of vertices in complex networks. It is determined by common neighbors of vertex pairs relative to their sum of individual degrees. *Hup Promoted Index (HP) assigned* vertex pairs adjacent to hub vertices as higher score. Hub vertices play a role that directs vertices having low degree to central vertices having high degree. *Hup Depressed Index (HD)* is similar to HP measure but it is affected by higher degree. Any vertex which has high degree is penalized by this measure. *Leicht–Holme–Newman Index (LHN)* gives higher score for vertex pairs having more common neighbors in proportion to their expected number of neighbors. *Resource Allocation Index (RA)* is similar to AA measure. However, it produces lower score value than AA measure for vertex pairs whose common neighbors have high vertex degree. *Salton Index (SA)* proposed by Salton and McGill is based on cosine similarity which is most widely used in similarity measurement.

3 Directed Link Prediction Method

In this section, we will introduce the traditional method of link prediction, build a general model of link prediction, and then propose our weighted directional link prediction method. The link prediction method based on topological similarity has been deeply studied by scholars for a long time. Among these methods, the link prediction method based on the local prediction indices, quasi-local prediction indices, global prediction indices are the most typical. Due to its high accuracy and low complexity, quasi-local indices-based link prediction method is the most widely used. In the next subsection, we will present our directional weighted link prediction method based on this method.

We first establish a general model of link prediction. The link prediction method in this paper are implemented in directed graph $G(V, E)$, where V and E indicate set of vertices and edges respectively. $\Gamma(v_x)$ indicate the set of neighbors of a vertex $x \in V$, connected x with in or out edges. The $w(v_x, v_z)$ indicate the weight of the edge from v_x to v_z. k_{v_x} indicate the degree of vertex v_x, it shows the number of neighbors of vertex v_x.

3.1   Quasi-Local Indices in Weighted Directional Graph

The CN measure for unweighted networks is defined as the number of nodes with a direct relationship with both evaluated nodes v_x and v_y.

$$CN(x, y) = \left| \Gamma(v_x) \cap \Gamma(v_y) \right| \tag{1}$$

The CN measure is one of the most widely adopted metrics in link prediction, mainly for its simplicity. Also, it is intuitive because it is expected that a high number of common neighbors make easier future contacts between two nodes. Now to estimate weight based on CN measure, the WCN measure is defined as:

$$WCN(v_x, v_y) = \frac{\sum_{z \in |\Gamma(v_x) \cap \Gamma(v_y)|} w(v_x, v_z) + w(v_y, v_z)}{||\Gamma(v_x) \cap \Gamma(v_y)||} \tag{2}$$

The JC measure is well explored in Data Mining. It assumes higher values for pairs of nodes that share a higher proportion of common neighbors relative to the total number of neighbors they have. For unweighted networks, the JC measure is defined as Jaccard:

$$JC(v_x, v_y) = \frac{||\Gamma(v_x) \cap \Gamma(v_y)||}{||\Gamma(v_x) \cup \Gamma(v_y)||} \tag{3}$$

To calculate weight from this similarity metric, the JC coefficient can be expressed as:

$$WJC(v_x, v_y) = \frac{\sum_{z \in |\Gamma(v_x) \cap \Gamma(v_y)|} w(v_x, v_z) + w(v_y, v_z)}{\sum_{v_z' \in |\Gamma(v_x)|} w(v_x, v_z') + \sum_{v_z'' \in |\Gamma(v_y)|} w(v_y, v_z')} \tag{4}$$

The PA measure assumes that the probability that a new link is created from a node x is proportional to the node degree k_{v_x} (which means the nodes that currently have a high number of relationships tend to create more links in the future). And someone have proposed that the probability of a future link between a pair of nodes could be expressed by the product of their number of collaborators. For unweighted networks, the PA measure is given by:

$$PA = k_{v_x} * k_{v_y} \tag{5}$$

For weighted networks, the PA measure can be extended as:

$$WPA = \sum_{a \in \Gamma(v_x)} w(a, x) * \sum_{b \in \Gamma(v_y)} w(b, y) \tag{6}$$

The AA measure for unweighted networks is defined as:

$$AA(v_x, v_y) = \sum_{z \in |\Gamma(v_x) \cap \Gamma(v_y)|} \frac{1}{\log(\Gamma(v_z))} \tag{7}$$

Adamic and Adar formulated this metric related to Jaccard's coefficient. It defines a higher importance to the common neighbors which have fewer neighbors. Hence, it measures the relationship be- tween a common neighbor and the evaluated pair of nodes. The AA measure is extended for weighted networks as:

$$WAA(v_x, v_y) = \sum_{z \in |\Gamma(v_x) \cap \Gamma(v_y)|} \frac{w(v_x, v_y) + w(v_y, v_z)}{\log\left(1 + \sum_{c \in \Gamma(v_z)} w(v_z, v_c)\right)} \tag{8}$$

Whereas each link prediction method is calculated based on common neighbors, there are some different characteristics in the measures such as AA measure ranks higher vertex pairs sharing fewer relations, HP measure assigns higher score value to vertex pairs adjacent to hub vertices, etc. This indicates that a measure might not always be best in different domains. This fact is also shown in the study described. From this point of view, it is a worthwhile task to propose a general approach by extending all Link prediction into pattern-based measures containing directional links to achieve higher link prediction accuracy.

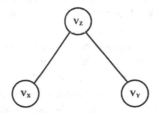

Fig. 1. Open triad pattern (OPT)

3.2 Directed Link Prediction Method in Weighted Directed Graph

In this paper, we perform link prediction on the general substructure of the graph, we call it open triad pattern (OTP). The substructure of OPT is shown in Fig. 1, it has three vertices v_x, v_y, v_z, and edges between only vertex pairs (v_x, v_z) and (v_y, v_z). In an

$OTP(v_x, v_y, v_z)$, vertex v_x and v_y does not connect and the vertex v_z is the common neighbor of vertex v_x and v_y. We use the substructure of $OTP(v_x, v_y, v_z)$ to predict whether there is an edge between vertex v_x and v_y.

As can be seen from the above model, for each vertex v_z, it can be described in the equations as $v_z \in \Gamma(x) \cap \Gamma(y)$, forms an OTP with vertices v_x and v_y. In undirected networks, only one OTP type, shown in Fig. 1. We only need to judge whether there is the connection between any vertex pairs v_x and v_y. But different types of OTP are possible in directed networks. Directional OTP structures have been also used in the other works for directed networks, e.g., In this study, we use directed OTP structures in supervised learning algorithms to improve accuracy of link prediction in weighted, directed networks. The next part provides all forms of OTP types with distinct directional edges for two vertices and our directional link prediction measure.

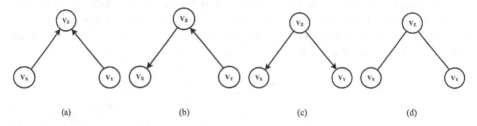

Fig. 2. (a), (b) and (c) are several forms of $OTP(v_x, v_y, v_z)$ with directional edges, (d) the only possible form of $OTP(v_x, v_y, v_z)$ with undirected edges.

Distinct OTPs for a given pair of vertices (v_x, v_y) in directed networks are not differently taken into account by Link prediction reported. For example, Link prediction can use only one OTP (v_x, v_y, v_z), shown in Fig. 2(d), and compute same scores for different OTP (v_x, v_y, v_z) in Fig. 2(a–c). However, there are different attentions in Fig. 2 (a–c). The vertex v_z has attracted attention of vertices v_x and v_y in Fig. 2(a), whereas it is vice versa in Fig. 2(c). In Fig. 2(b), the vertex v_x has directly attracted attention of the vertex v_z and indirectly interested the vertex v_y. These various situations have different effects on forming links. Traditional undirected neighbor-based link prediction measures might be adopted to directed networks by taking into account only out edges or only in edges. However, this proposal has a disadvantage that it cannot use both in and out edges at same local structures. Other probable proposal, already adopted to Link prediction in Table 1, is that using both in and out edges in calculation of Link prediction. Nevertheless, link prediction cannot effectively figure out link formation mechanisms in directional OTPs. To address this issue, we extend Link prediction as pattern-based by taking advantage of edges directions. All of the possible OTP types in directed networks are showed in Fig. 3. General definition of the proposed extended Link prediction named as Link prediction is expressed as follow:

$$DLP(v_x, v_y) = \{score_{OPT1}, score_{OPT2}, score_{OPT3}, \ldots, score_{OPT4}\} \tag{9}$$

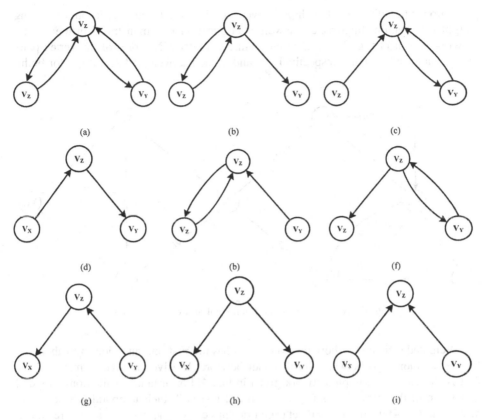

Fig. 3. Open triad pattern types.

Where directed link prediction (DLP) is a set of OTP scores corresponding to undirected link prediction. Firstly, for each $v_z \in \Gamma(v_x) \cap \Gamma(v_y)$, we first identify OTP type including v_x, v_y and v_z nodes. Then, we calculate all NLPM in Table 1 for nodes v_x, v_y and v_z; and save type information and score value of them. Score of the triple vertices, including v_x, v_y and one of their common neighbors and having identical OTP type are summed. The given training graph might be split to sub-graphs with time frames. However, this proposal represents a drawback that it is not possible to identify OTP types which have edges in distinct sub-graphs. Therefore, the whole training graph data are employed.

We depict a sample network in Fig. 4; directed link prediction scores for vertex pairs (v_x, v_{y1}) and (v_x, v_{y2}) are given in Table 1. Edge attributes show, respectively, weight and time values in the sample network. While vertex pairs (v_x, v_{y1}) and (v_x, v_{y2}) have different OTPs, Link prediction generate only one score value for each vertex pair. But the proposed directed link prediction generates OTP8 and OTP9 score values for the vertex pair (v_x, v_{y1}), and the OTP4 and OTP5 score values for the vertex pair (v_x, v_{y2}). This way, we get better topological features in complex networks. Weight and temporal information are used as edge attributes in Link prediction and directed link prediction. Strength of relationships between vertices are taken into account by using weight information. Importance of weight information is demonstrated in the sample network shown in Fig. 4. For example, while weighted CN scores of the vertex pairs (v_x, v_{y1}) and (v_x, v_{y2}) are, respectively, 6 and 9, their unweighted score is 2 for both.

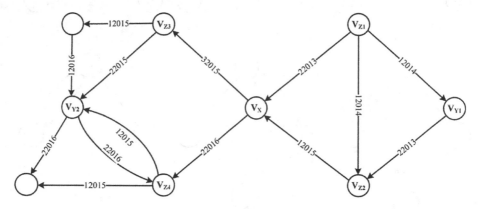

Fig. 4. A sample weighted, temporal and directed network

Weighted CN scores show that vertex v_{y2} has more strong attention to vx than vy_1. Recent relationships between vertices can be more decisive on edge formation. This fact is shown in the sample network given in Fig. 4. For instance, while non-temporal CN score of the vertex pairs (v_x, v_{y1}) and (v_x, v_{y2}) is 2, their temporal CN score are 5.193 and 6.804; v_{y2} has more recent relationships close to v_x than v_{y1}, so it is rewarded with high score.

Table 1. Undirected Link prediction (ULP) and directed Link prediction (DLP) scores for vertex pairs (v_x, v_y1) and (vx, v_y2) in the sample network in Fig. 4.

Indicator	ULP scores for $(v_x, vy1)$	DLP scores for (v_x, v_y1)	ULP scores for (v_x, v_y2)	DLP scores for (v_x, v_y2)
WCN	7.38	(0, 0, 0, 0, 0, 0, 3.8, 3.58)	16.81	(0, 0, 0, 8.77, 8.04, 0, 0, 0, 0)
WJC	0.46	(0, 0, 0, 0, 0, 0, 0, 0.24, 0.22)	0.63	(0, 0, 0, 0.33, 0.3, 0, 0, 0, 0)
WPA	2.06	(0, 0, 0, 0, 0, 0, 1.06, 1)	1.36	(0, 0, 0, 0.71, 0.65, 0, 0, 0, 0)
WAA	4.08	(0, 0, 0, 0, 0, 0, 2.08, 2)	7	(0, 0, 0, 3.6, 3.4, 0, 0, 0, 0)

4 Experiments

We have China Unicom's mobile call list for a city in southern China. The data were recorded for 30 days from August 1, 2018 to August 31, 2018. We use the record from August 1, 2018 to August 15, 2018 as the train set and use the record from August 16, 2018 to August 31, 2018 as the test set to build the weighted directed graph.

According to the behavior of using the APP, we have made a user portrait for the user and selected the user who found it to be an office worker. And using these users' call list to build a weighted directed graph. In this graph, the direction of the edge is represented as the caller and called in the call list, the direction of the edge is from the caller to the called. The weight of the edge is expressed as the total duration of the call between the two users in half a month. Because in the enterprise, people usually use other social software to communicate, the call is usually considered as a social way in an emergency, and it has a strong relationship attribute, so the call network in the enterprise can also reflect the level relationship of the user in an enterprise. In an emergency, the boss will call the subordinates to complete some of the corresponding tasks, but the number of subordinates' emergency is less than the number of the boss, so there will be less time for the boss to call. It is with this attribute that we can judge the level of users in the enterprise by the directionality of the call. We use the directed link prediction to determine the hidden relationship of the user in the graph, and find all the subordinate relationship attributes of the entire user in the graph.

Because in terms of data acquisition, we can't get the user's hierarchical relationship in the enterprise, this information belongs to the user's privacy, so we can only judge the effectiveness of our method by capturing the stability of this relationship. Through link prediction, we observe whether this relationship is consistent in the first half of the month and the second half of the month. In the graph, that is, after the prediction, whether the direction of the edge between the common vertex pair is same.

Table 2. The result of the SVM and KNN

Indicator	SVM	KNN
WCN	0.748985749	0.783627566
WJC	0.789043234	0.798756432
WPA	0.773456245	0.804567432
WAA	0.807847323	0.813456743

We use SVM and K-NN for supervised learning, and regard directed link prediction as a multi-classification problem with connected edges. There are four types of edge relationships: no edge, vertex v_x points to vertex v_y, vertex v_y points to vertex v_x, and vertex v_x and vertex v_y are pointed at the same time. If there is only one direction for the edge, the user being pointed to is a subordinate, and if there are two directions in the same edge, then the two users are considered in a same level. The level judgment result of the user in the graph is shown in Table 2. The accuracy rate in the table indicates the probability of determining the stability of the user relationship in the first half of the month and the second half of the month. As can be seen from the figure, the judgment of the user relationship is stable, and the accuracy rate exceeds 75%.

5 Result

This paper proposes a directed link prediction method to get the potential direction relationship in a network and judging the relationship between users in the network through a directed connection. We use the direction of the edge in the call list graph to determine the relationship between the upper and lower levels of the enterprise user. If the user is pointed, the user is in the lower level for this two user. If users are pointed at the same time, the two users are in the samelevel. Because the subordinate relationship cannot get directly, so we use the relationship recurrence rate to verify the effectiveness. The experiment proves that the prosed directed link prediction method can discover the relationship of users, and there is a stable relationship between users.

References

1. Dafre, S.F., de Rijke, M.: Discovering missing links in Wikipedia. In: Proceedings of the 3rd International Workshop on Link Discovery, pp. 90–97 (2005)
2. De Sá, H.R., Prudêncio, R.B.C.: Supervised link prediction in weighted networks. In: The 2011 International Joint Conference on Neural Networks, IJCNN, pp. 2281–2288 (2011)
3. Huang, Z.: Link prediction based on graph topology: the predictive value of generalized clustering coefficient, Available SSRN 1634014 (2010)
4. Li, X., Chen, H.: Recommendation as link prediction: a graph kernel-based machine learning approach. In: Proceedings of the 9th ACM/IEEE-CS Joint Conference on Digital Libraries, pp. 213–216 (2009)
5. Lü, L., Zhou, T.: Role of weak ties in link prediction of complex networks. In: Proceedings of the 1st ACM International Workshop on Complex Networks Meet Information & Knowledge Management, pp. 55–58 (2009)
6. Murata, T., Moriyasu, S.: Link prediction of social networks based on weighted proximity measures. In: IEEE/WIC/ACM International Conference on Web Intelligence, pp. 85–88 (2007)
7. Rossetti, G., Guidotti, R., Pennacchioli, D.: Interaction prediction in dynamic networks exploiting community discovery. In: Proceedings of the 2015 IEEE/ACM International Conference on Advances in Social Networks Analysis, pp. 553–558 (2015)
8. Xiang, R., Neville, J., Rogati, M.: Modeling relationship strength in online social networks. In: Proceedings of the 19th International Conference on World Wide Web, pp. 981–990 (2010)
9. Zhu, J., Hong, J., Hughes, J.G.: Using Markov models for web site link prediction. In: Proceedings of the Thirteenth ACM Conference on Hypertext and Hypermedia, pp. 169–170 (2002)
10. Wind, D.K., Morup, M.: Link prediction in weighted networks. In: 2012 IEEE International Workshop on Machine Learning for Signal Processing, pp. 1–6 (2012)

11. Brouard, C., d'Alché-Buc, F., Szafranski, M.: Semi-supervised penalized output kernel regression for link prediction. In: Proceedings of the 28th International Conference on Machine Learning (ICML 2011) (2011)
12. Brzozowski, M.-J., Romero, D.M.: Who Should I Follow? Recommending People in Directed Social Networks (2011)
13. Al Hasan, M., Chaoji, V., Salem, S., Zaki, M.: Link prediction using supervised learning. In: SDM 2006: Workshop on Link Analysis, Counter-Terrorism and Security (2006)

An Elephant Flow Detection Method Based on Machine Learning

Kaihao Lou[1], Yongjian Yang[1], and Chuncai Wang[2(✉)]

[1] Department of Computer Science and Technology, Jilin University,
Changchun, China
[2] Changchun Polytechnic University, Changchun, China
whyeccw@126.com

Abstract. Software-Defined Networking (SDN) is regarded as the next generation network. Current network is difficult to be configured and managed, and SDN is proposed to change this situation, which makes it attract a lot of attention of the academia and industry. The detection of Elephant Flow is an important service of SDN, based on which we can achieve the management of the network traffic and implement services such as the load balancing of traffic, congestion avoidance and so on. This paper focuses on the iterative method to detect Elephant Flow. We propose a method which uses the random forest to learn the arguments produced in the iterative detection and to improve the accuracy and speed of the detection. The experiments show that our method can efficiently improve the accuracy and speed of the detection compared to other methods.

Keywords: Software-Defined Networking · Elephant flow detection · Machine learning · Random forest

1 Introduction

Accurate measurement of network traffic is the key to the implementation of a range of network applications, including traffic engineering, abnormal flow detection, security analysis and so on [1,2,4–7]. A large number of network management decisions, such as blocking abnormal network traffic, load balancing network traffic, etc., require real-time acquisition and analysis of network traffic status. Elephant flow detection [3] is an important branch in network traffic detection. An elephant flow usually refers to traffic that exceeds a certain threshold (such as 1 Mbytes/s) per unit time. Because of the high proportion of elephant flows in network traffic, The control of elephant flows can effectively complete most of the control tasks of network traffic, such as congestion avoidance, traffic load balancing, etc. [8–12].

In order to achieve the detection of traffic in the network, the simplest method is to count all the flows in the network. But because the network traffic in the current network is huge and the arrival rate is high, this method has

© Springer Nature Switzerland AG 2019
M. Qiu (Ed.): SmartCom 2019, LNCS 11910, pp. 212–220, 2019.
https://doi.org/10.1007/978-3-030-34139-8_21

high requirements for storage and is not suitable for real-time statistics on network flows. The improvement method is sampling method [13], which faces the problem of low precision. In addition there are some sketch methods, such as Count-Min [14], which requires additional hardware support to be implemented in a software-defined network. This paper focuses on the elephant flow detection based on iterative method, which has the advantages of low consumption of detection resources and easy deployment in software-defined networks.

Although the iterative detection method has many related researches [3,10, 15], it still faces problems in detection accuracy and detection speed. The reason why these methods have these problems is because the flow characteristics of the elephant flow are not considered in the detection, so the elephant flow cannot be detected accurately. In this paper, the characteristics of the elephant flow are learned by the machine learning method to improve the detection speed and accuracy during detection. The main ideas of our method are as follows: first, we use the iterative method to detect the elephant flow and collect the parameters generated during the detection process (such as the flow of an address range, etc.), and then process and classify these parameters through the off-line data processing to determine whether these parameters belongs to an elephant flow. Then we can use machine learning to learn the relationship between these parameters and the types of their corresponding flows, so that we can distinguish whether a flow is an elephant flow. Next, these flows are reasonably operated in an iterative method to increase the accuracy and speed of flow detection.

The main contributions of this paper are summarized as follows:

- We formulate a problem for network traffic monitoring to detect elephant flows.
- We propose an improved algorithm for iterative elephant flow detection in networks, based on machine learning, in order to realize network monitoring.
- We conduct extensive simulations to verify the effectiveness of the proposed algorithm, and the results show the proposed algorithm is effective compared with the previous methods.

The remainder of this paper is organized as follows. We review the iterative elephant flow detection method in Sect. 2. The elephant flow detection algorithm is proposed in Sect. 3. In Sect. 4, we conduct simulations to determine the performance of our proposed algorithm. We conclude this paper in Sect. 5.

2 Iterative Elephant Flow Detection Method and Current Problems

The iterative elephant flow detection method is similar to the binary search method of data. Specify an address interval A, assuming that we need to find an elephant flow in this address interval. Then the process of the iterative detection method is as follows, which can be referred to the literature [3]:

We can find that the idea of the iterative detection method is very simple by Algorithm 1, but it faces the problem of insufficient detection accuracy, where

Algorithm 1

Input: : Address range A, Elephant flow threshold β, Number of divisions n
Output: : Elephant flow set H

1: put A into Set W
2: Assign a flow entry to the address in W
3: After a detection cycle, update the traffic corresponding to the address in W
4: $\forall w \in W$
5: **if** the flow of w ¿ β **then**
6:     remove w from W, divide w into n segments and put them into W, put w into H
7: **else**
8:     remove w from W
9: report H and return to step 2

---

the specific problem description can be referred to the literature [6]. In a real network environment, traffic is constantly fluctuating, even an elephant flow is in a state of constant fluctuation. When a certain granularity address of an elephant flow is detected, the Algorithm 1 may be lost the detection due to fluctuations in the elephant flow. Hence, we may not detect the corresponding elephant flow due to the fluctuations of the elephant flow. The following Fig. 1 is an example of the detection when we use the iterative method. The vertical axis in the figure shows the number of addresses of the detected flow (or the depth in the address prefix tree [6]). The larger the number, the higher the accuracy of our detection. For example, when we detect the address (source address and destination address) of a flow, the exact address of the flow we get should be 64 bits (depth is 64). When we only know an elephant flow at the source address within the interval 10.0.0.1/24, the number of addresses we get for this flow is 24 (the detected depth is 24). The horizontal axis represents the number of cycles of the iteration. As we can see from Fig. 1, our method can only obtain a thicker address range of an elephant flow due to fluctuations in traffic, and the detection accuracy is poor. Similarly, due to the loss of elephant flow detection, the iterative method needs to detect the flow again, which results in a long time to detect an elephant flow or no elephant flow can be detected at all.

In [10], researchers propose a method called DM to improve the detection accuracy, but through experiments we find that it is still difficult to effectively improve the accuracy of detection. The main reason is that the method uses a comprehensive history of a flow, which can be released after a period of observation to obtain more reliable detection results. But this also causes a large number of flow entries to be released in a short period of time, which make all available table items be consumed quickly. After the table item is exhausted, the method tends to release a large number of detection items. At the same time, the items that are detected together with the elephant flows are also released, so the detection accuracy is not high.

By analysing of the shortcomings of the DM method, we can find that the key to improving the accuracy and speed of detection is to correctly distinguish

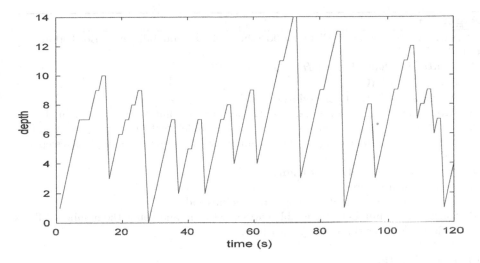

Fig. 1. Example of the impact of flow fluctuations on detection

whether a flow is an elephant flow to reasonably allocate the entries of these data flows: for a real elephant flow, we need to slice it in order to detect whether there is an elephant flow in its sub-flows. For other flows, we should release their detection flow entries as soon as possible, so that resources can be used to detect the elephant flows. Therefore, we need to distinguish whether a flow is an elephant flow according to the parameters generated in the iterative process. Hence, it is easy to associate machine learning with the detection of elephant flows.

Based on the DM method, we propose the following elephant flow detection method as shown in Algorithm 2. The meanings and usages of the related symbols like: *momentum*, *pForce*, *static*, *depth*, in the algorithm are the same as those in the literature [10]. *momentum* represents the impulse of the flow, and *static* is the number of cycles in which a flow is continuously less than the threshold of an elephant flow. *depth* indicates the current depth of a flow, and *pForce* is used to comprehensively measure the size of the flow. The meanings of other symbols are as follows: $w.f$ represents the traffic of a flow w (or address), and we make some changes to the calculation of *pForce*, where the calculation method is $w.pForce = \frac{w.momentum}{e^{w.static/w.depth}}$. The parameter a indicates that we will use the predicted result when the accuracy of the random forest prediction is greater than a. The key of this algorithm is in step 5, if a random forest method is used to determine that a flow is not an elephant flow, then $w.momentum = w.f$. In this way, the added value of *momentum* is eliminated, so that the flow can be released quickly. We will describe the process of training parameters using a random forest model in the next section.

Algorithm 2

Input: : Address range A, Elephant flow threshold β, Probability a, Ratio of additional impulse δ

Output: : Elephant flow set H

1: put A into Set W
2: Assign a flow entry to the address in W
3: After a detection cycle, update the traffic corresponding to the address in W
4: $\forall w \in W$, apply the trained random forest model (w.f, w.momentum, w.static, w.pForce) to predict whether the stream w corresponding to the tuple is a elephant flow
5: **if** the Probability of $w > a$ **then**
6:     w.momentum=w.f
7: $\forall w \in W$, merging small streams using the method of [15].
8: Calculate the number of available entries, set to n, and count the number of flows with flow greater than β in W, set to m
9: $\forall w \in W$
10: **if** $w, f \geq \beta$ **then**
11:     remove w from W, divide w into n/m segments and put them into W, put w into H. For each segment w', set $w.static = 0, w'.momentum = w.f$
12: **else if** $w.pForce \geq \beta$ **then**
13:     w.static=w.static+1
14: **else if** $w.pForce \leq \beta$ **then**
15:     w.static=0
16: set w.momentum=δ w.momentum+w.f
17: report H and return to step 2

3   Use Random Forest to Determine the Type of Data Flow

In each iteration of the detection process, we can obtain a tuple T for each flow w, where $T = (wf, w.momentum, w.static, w.pForce)$. In the DM method, only the judgment of $pForce$ value is used to decide whether to abandon the detection of a flow or not. The $pForce$ value takes into account the historical traffic of a flow and the number of currently available flow entries. However, as mentioned earlier, the DM method cannot correctly determine whether a flow is a small flow. The other methods in the previous literatures considered simpler, using only the current traffic of a flow, i.e. $w.f$, to determine whether a flow is an elephant flow, which would lead to more serious detection accuracy problems. In this paper, we propose to use machine learning to determine whether a flow w is an elephant flow by learning its corresponding tuple T. And then we can apply reasonable operations for different flows to control their detection process (as shown in the algorithm above).

In order to collect the relationship between the tuple T and flow types, we need to make some changes to Algorithm 2. Because we have not acquired a trained random forest model. Hence, we need to remove step 4 of Algorithm 2 and then execute the algorithm. Each detected flow will correspond to a tuple

T in each iteration, but we don't know if this flow is an elephant flow. For each flow, we need to record its traffic in the next t iterations, and calculate the mean value of the traffic, so that we know whether the flow is an elephant flow and construct the training data. Our training data has five fields, namely (f, $momentum$, $static$, $pForce$, $isElephantFlow$), where f represents the traffic of a flow, $momentum$ represents the impulse of the flow, and $static$ is the number of iterations in which the flow is continuously smaller than the threshold of the elephant flow, $pForce$ is used to measure the size of the flow comprehensively. $isElephantFlow$ indicates whether the flow is an elephant flow. If a flow is an elephant flow, the value of $isElephantFlow$ is 1, if not, the value is 0.

After the training data is acquired, the data needs to be preprocessed first. Since the random forest has few requirements on data, we only remove some extreme values from the training data to reduce the impact on the training results. The extreme values of the data we removed are mainly generated at the beginning of the iteration. At this time, since the detection address interval of the detection entry is usually coarser, the detected traffic is large. The $momentum$ value of most flow is very large, where most of these flows are actually small flows. In the actual detection, this kind of situation rarely occurs, therefore we do not need to consider these data.

In order to avoid over-fitting in actual training, we set the ratio of the number of samples in the random forest leaf node to the training data to 0.001, and then we use the grid search method to find the most suitable parameters. We will show the results of the training in the next section.

4   Experiments

In order to verify the performances of the proposed algorithms, we use Java to implement a simulation platform to simulate the iterative detection method. In the simulation platform, real network traffic can be injected and the elephant flows can be detected. The data flow we inject into the simulation network comes from CAIDA's packet capture data [16]. Its average traffic is 2 Gbps. In addition, we also insert a certain number of elephant flows into the simulation network. The average traffic of each elephant flow is 1 MB/s, and there is a maximum of 50% random fluctuations above and below its mean value. An example of the elephant flow we inject into the network is shown in Fig. 2, where the red line represents the mean value of the flow. In this paper, the ratio of the depth detected by an elephant flow to its true depth is used to measure the accuracy of the detection. Equation 1 is the calculation method of precision, where H represents the elephant flow set and $w.depth'$ represents the detected depth of elephant flow w, $w.depth$ represents the true depth of the elephant flow.

$$score = \frac{\sum_{w \in H} \frac{w.depth'}{w.depth}}{|H|} \tag{1}$$

We use the random forest classification algorithm in the scikit learn library to train the data, where we select 80% of the training data as the training

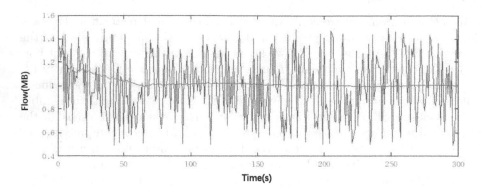

Fig. 2. An example of a elephant flow inserted into a network (Color figure online)

set, and the rest data as the test set. During the process of finding the most suitable parameters, the candidate parameters we set are shown in Table 1. The number of shards for cross validation is set to 5. After Grid Search, the optimal parameters are $n\_estimators = 10$, $max\_features = 3$. At this time, the root mean square error of the classifier on the training set is 0.112., and the root mean square error of the test set is 0.113. It is not difficult for us to find that the classifier performs almost identically on the training set and the test set.

Table 1. Candidate parameters of Grid Search

Parameter	Candidate parameter
n_estimators	1, 10, 30
max_features	2, 3, 4
min_weight_fraction_leaf	0.001

After the random forest classifier is trained, in order to directly use this model for prediction, we use Python to build a simple server, where we can run the prediction model. The simulation platform contacts the server through the network to send it Tuple T and obtain prediction results. The parameters a and δ of Algorithm 2 are set to 0.9 and 0.5, respectively.

We conduct two set of experiments to verify the performances of the proposed algorithm, where both sets of experiments are compared to the DM method. In the first set of experiments, we set up different numbers of flow entries and insert 100 elephant flows into the simulation network to test the detection accuracy (score) of our algorithm and DM method. As shown in Fig. 3, the $OUR500$ indicates the average precision of our algorithm when the total number of available entries is 500, the $DM500$ indicates the average precision of the DM method and so on. we calculate the average accuracy by only consider the inserted elephant flows for the convenience of calculations. The horizontal axis in Fig. 3 represents the detection period, and the vertical axis represents the detection accuracy. In the second set of experiments, we set the total number of available flow entries

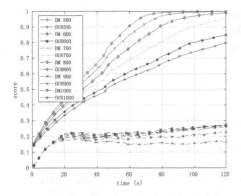

Fig. 3. Detection results when the detection resources are different and the number of elephant flows is the same

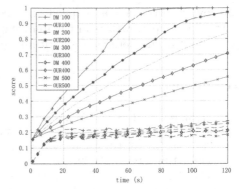

Fig. 4. Detection results when the detection resources are the same and the number of elephant flows is different

to 1000, and insert a different number of elephant flows to test the detection accuracy of the two algorithms. As shown in Fig. 4, the $OUR100$ indicates the average precision of our algorithm when inserting 100 elephant flows, $DM100$ represents the average precision of the DM method. The meanings of the vertical axis and the horizontal axis are the same as those in Fig. 3. It is obvious that our proposed algorithm is superior to the DM method in both detection speed and detection accuracy. In other words, our algorithm can obtain higher precision in a shorter time than the DM method.

By observing Figs. 3 and 4, we can find that the DM method cannot detect elephant flows stably. We believe that the reasons are as follows: because the small flows are given a large impulse, thus these small flows are difficult to be released, which will lead to the exhaustion of available entries in a relatively short time. After available entries are exhausted, the value of *pull* will become large. At this time, the DM method tends to release a large amount of flow during this detection iteration, whose traffic value is less than the threshold of elephant flows. As a result, some elephant flows that fluctuate to the trough are also released. Hence these elephant flows cannot be effectively detected, and the detection accuracy of the DM method is poor. We also test the effect of the DM+ER method through experiments. The results are similar to those of the DM method, where the elephant flow cannot be effectively detected. Hence we don't show these results in this paper.

5   Conclusion

The elephant flow detection method is an important service in a software-defined network. Based on the random forest method, we propose an improved algorithm for iterative elephant flow detection in this paper. By implementing the simulation platform and conducting experiments, it is verified that the proposed algorithm is effective compared with the previous methods. And it can effectively improve the accuracy and speed of detection. In the future work, we will try to extract more parameters in the iterative detection process, so that the accuracy and speed of the detection algorithm can be further improved.

References

1. Akyildiz, I.F., Lee, A., Wang, P., et al.: A roadmap for traffic engineering in SDN-OpenFlow networks. Comput. Netw. **71**, 1–30 (2014)
2. Thottan, M., Ji, C.: Anomaly detection in IP networks. IEEE Trans. Signal Process. **51**(8), 2191–2204 (2003)
3. Jose, L., Yu, M., Rexford, J.: Online measurement of large traffic aggregates on commodity switches. In: Hot Topics in Management of Internet, Cloud, and Enterprise Networks and Services. USENIX Association (2011)
4. Qiu, H., Noura, H., Qiu, M., et al.: A user-centric data protection method for cloud storage based on invertible DWT. IEEE Trans. Cloud Comput. 1 (2019)
5. Gai, K., Qiu, M., Zhao, H., et al.: Dynamic energy-aware cloudlet-based mobile cloud computing model for green computing. J. Netw. Comput. Appl. **59**(C), 46–54 (2016)
6. Gai, K., Qiu, M., Zhao, H.: Energy-aware task assignment for mobile cyber-enabled applications in heterogeneous cloud computing. J. Parallel Distrib. Comput. S0743731517302319 (2017)
7. Gai, K., Xu, K., Lu, Z., et al.: Fusion of cognitive wireless networks and edge computing. IEEE Wirel. Commun. **26**(3), 69–75 (2019)
8. Alizadeh, M., Edsall, T., Dharmapurikar, S., et al.: CONGA: distributed congestion-aware load balancing for datacenters. ACM SIGCOMM Comput. Commun. Rev. **44**(4), 503–514 (2014)
9. Alizadeh, M., Yang, S., Sharif, M., et al.: pFabric: minimal near-optimal datacenter transport. ACM SIGCOMM Comput. Commun. Rev. **43**(4), 435–446 (2013)
10. Benson, T., Anand, A., Akella, A., et al.: MicroTE: fine grained traffic engineering for data centers. In: Proceedings of the Seventh COnference on Emerging Networking EXperiments and Technologies, p. 8. ACM (2011)
11. García-Teodoro, P., Díaz-Verdejo, J., Maciá-Fernández, G., et al.: Anomaly-based network intrusion detection: techniques, systems and challenges. Comput. Secur. **28**(1–2), 18–28 (2009)
12. Kabbani, A., Alizadeh, M., Yasuda, M., et al.: AF-QCN: approximate fairness with quantized congestion notification for multi-tenanted data centers. In: 2010 18th IEEE Symposium on High Performance Interconnects, pp. 58–65, 2191–2204. IEEE (2010)
13. Duffield, N.: Sampling for passive internet measurement: a review. Stat. Sci. **19**(3), 472–498, 2191–2204 (2004)
14. Cormode, G., Muthukrishnan, S.: An improved data stream summary: the count-min sketch and its applications. J. Algorithms **55**(1), 58–75 (2005)
15. Moshref, M., Yu, M., Govindan, R., et al.: DREAM: dynamic resource allocation for software-defined measurement. ACM SIGCOMM Comput. Commun. Rev. **44**(4), 419–430 (2015)
16. The caida ucsd anonymized internet traces 2015[EB/OL], 06 April 2019. http://www.caida.org/data/passive/passive_2015_dataset.xml

AI Enhanced Automatic Response System for Resisting Network Threats

Song Xia[1], Meikang Qiu[2,3(✉)], Meiqin Liu[4], Ming Zhong[2], and Hui Zhao[5]

[1] College of Electronic and Information, Wuhan University, Wuhan, Hubei, China
songxia@whu.edu.cn
[2] College of Computer Science, Shenzhen University, Shenzhen, Guangdong, China
{mqiu,mingz}@szu.edu.cn,
[3] Department of Computer Science,
Harrisburg University of Science and Technology, Harrisburg, USA
mqiu@HarrisburgU.edu
[4] College of Electrical Engineering, Zhejiang University, Zhejiang, China
liumeiqin@zju.edu.cn
[5] School of Software, Henan University, Kaifeng, China
zhh@henu.edu.cn

Abstract. Network threats are malicious attacks that endanger network security. With terabits of information stored in the network and much of this information being confidential, cyber security turns to be very important. Most network protection mechanisms are based on firewall and Intrusion Detection System (IDS). However, with the diversification of cyber-attacks, traditional defense mechanisms cannot fully guarantee the security of the network. In this paper, we propose an automatic network threat response system based on machine learning and deep learning. It comprises three sub-modules: threat detection module, threat identification module and threat mitigation module. The experimental results show that the proposed system can handle 22 types of network threats in the KDD99 dataset and the rate of successful response is over 97%, which is much better than the traditional ways.

Keywords: Cyber security · Artificial intelligence · Automatic response system · Threat detection · Threat identification · Threat mitigation

1 Introduction

With terabits of information stored in the network and much of this information being confidential, its protection work turn to be very important. Cyber-security is a measure protecting computer systems, networks, and information from disruption [1]. The data leakage caused by network threats every year brings tens of thousands of losses to society. It is therefore important to have a system that monitors activity of users with intent of detecting malicious activities.

Nowadays, there are two ubiquitous network security products to protect cyber from those threats: firewall and Intrusion Detection System (IDS) [2].

© Springer Nature Switzerland AG 2019
M. Qiu (Ed.): SmartCom 2019, LNCS 11910, pp. 221–230, 2019.
https://doi.org/10.1007/978-3-030-34139-8_22

Many scholars such as Gai et al. [17–19] and Qiu et al. [20] have done numerous valuable work in the Cyber-security field. However, with the diversification of cyberattacks, traditional defense products cannot fully guarantee the security of the network. AlFayyad et al. evaluated the performance of personal firewall systems but it indicated that personal firewalls were poorly used which leaded to vulnerabilities in security [3]. Intrusion detection systems are similar to burglar alarms which could look for suspicious activity and alert the system and network administrators [4], but traditional *IDS* might miss some unknown threats [12].

The threat detection systems based on machine learning, such as *SVM* [5], *KNN* [6,7] and deep learning such as *CNN* [8], *RNN* [9] have achieved the high detection accuracy rate, but most current systems are only suitable for a specific type of threat and lack a complete defense mechanism for threats. Since many users of the network lack basic knowledge about the defense against cyber threats, they cannot choose a system for a specific threat detection, and it is difficult for them to find a corresponding solution after the detection is completed [3]. In order to make the network threat response mechanism more efficient and practical, we propose an automatic system which combines machine learning with deep learning, for threat detection, identification and mitigation. It is a brand new system which can automatically complete the entire process of threat response. The main advantages of our system is elaborated below:

(1) It not only can detect but also identify and mitigate the threat automatically.
(2) It is capable to handle many types of threats.
(3) It has a relatively low false positive rate.

The rest of the paper is organized as follows: Sect. 2 describes the related work about the network threat response system; Sect. 3 introduces the framework of our system; Sect. 4 presents the experiment and analysis of the results; Sect. 5 concludes our work and gives a prospect.

2   Related Work

The Intrusion Detection System (*IDS*), first proposed by Denning in 1987, is widely used in threat detection [10]. People researched on intrusion detection approaches mainly from two views: anomaly detection and misuse detection [11]. Mena et al. [12], proposed an intrusion detection system based on misuse intrusion. The advantage of misuse detection system is its ability to detect all known threats with a high accuracy rate. Garcia [13] gave a review of the intrusion detection system based on anomaly detection. The advantage of this system is the potential to detect previously unseen threats. However the misuse methods are not capable of detecting new, unfamiliar intrusions and the anomaly methods have a relatively high false positive rate. Recently, artificial intelligence has developed rapidly and achieved good results in many fields [14,15]. Elike Hodo et al. [16], established a neural network based threat detection system to protect the Internet of things network and achieved relatively high accuracy. However in their experiment, the system just worked for *DOS* threat. Vinayakumar et al.

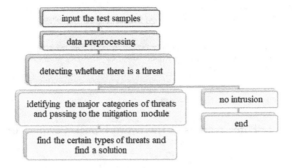

Fig. 1. The flow chart of the model.

[8] analyzed the effectiveness of convolution neural network for intrusion detection by modeling the network traffic events as time series of TCP/IP packets. The result showed CNN could reach a good performance in the intrusion detection. Kevin Ross [5] used multiple machine learning methods in SQL injection detection, which included decision Tree, rule-based, support vector machine and random forest algorithm.

Those methods above show the machine learning and deep learning ways can be more efficient in network threat response when compared to the IDS and firewall. However the systems mentioned above have the following deficiencies: only response for a certain type of threat and lack of a complete handling process for threats. In this paper, we combined the merits of machine learning and deep learning, and built a hierarchical threat response system. This system overcame the shortcomings of the above methods.

3 System Model

As shown in Fig. 1, the overall framework of our proposed system consists of four important phases: data preprocessing, threat detection, threat identification and threat mitigation. We collect a large number of network connection samples with different types of threats from the internet. Those samples are preprocessed by vectorization and normalization.

The detection module judges whether there is a malicious information in the input samples. If not, next modules will ignore those samples. Otherwise those malicious samples will be pushed into the identification module to get their labels, which indicate the major categories of them. In the last step, the mitigation module can find a certain type of the threat and give a solution. The details of those modules will be elaborated below.

3.1 Threat Model

In our system, we will detect the threats through characteristics of network packet sequences, such as TCP packet sequence. Every packet sequence is labeled

2, tcp, smtp, SF, 1684, 363, 0, 0, 0, 0, 0, 1, 0, 0, 0, 0, 0, 0, 0, 0, 0, 0, 0, 1, 1, 0.00, 0.00, 0.00,
0.00, 1.00, 0.00, 0.00, 104, 66, 0.63, 0.03, 0.01, 0.00, 0.00, 0.00, 0.00, 0.00, normal.

0, tcp, private, REJ, 0, 0, 0, 0, 0, 0, 0, 0, 0, 0, 0, 0, 0, 0, 0, 0, 0, 0, 38, 1, 0.00, 0.00, 1.00,
1.00, 0.03, 0.55, 0.00, 208, 1, 0.00, 0.11, 0.18, 0.00, 0.01, 0.00, 0.42, 1.00, portsweep.

0, tcp, smtp, SF, 787, 329, 0, 0, 0, 0, 0, 1, 0, 0, 0, 0, 0, 0, 0, 0, 0, 0, 0, 1, 1, 0.00, 0.00, 0.00,
0.00, 1.00, 0.00, 0.00, 76, 117, 0.49, 0.08, 0.01, 0.02, 0.00, 0.00, 0.00, 0.00, normal.

Fig. 2. Three records of the network packet sequences.

to be a normal connection or an attack. The attack is divided into four major kinds of threats: denial-of-service (DOS), unauthorized access from a remote machine to a local machine ($R2L$), unauthorized access to local super user privileges by a local unprivileged user ($U2R$), and surveillance and probing. In Fig. 2, some samples including the normal and threatening network packet sequences are given to explain the threat model.

In the above figure, each record contains 42 different parameters, separated by the comma. The first 41 parameters are expressed as the features to describe the network connection. Those features can be divided into four categories: basic features of TCP connection (1–9), content features of TCP connections (10–22), time-based network traffic statistical features (23–31), and host-based network traffic statistical features (32–41). The last parameter indicates the type of connection. Excepting the normal records, others are different kinds of malicious connection, the threats coming from the internet.

3.2 Threat Detection

In the detection module, we will introduce a machine learning method, logistic regression algorithm, to detect whether there is an attack from the network. The logistic regression algorithm is a tool that uses input parameters to predict the status of the sample. The main idea of logistic regression is to classify the input samples into two category: 0 representing normal connection and 1 representing malicious connection. When the probability of prediction is between 0–1, we get 1 if the probability is greater than 0.5, and 0 if the probability is less than 0.5. The decision process is implemented by the sigmoid function. The calculation process is shown in the Eqs. 1 and 2.

x is the feature value vector of the input samples and w^T is regression coefficient vector. The optimal regression coefficient vector is obtained by the gradient descent algorithm. After that, we multiply the feature values of each preprocessed sample by regression coefficients and add the results up as z, the input of the sigmoid function σ.

$$z = w_0 \cdot x_0 + w_1 \cdot x_1 + w_2 \cdot x_2 + w_3 \cdot x_3 + ... + w_n \cdot x_n = w^T \cdot x \qquad (1)$$

$$\sigma(z) = \frac{1}{1 + e^{-z}} \qquad (2)$$

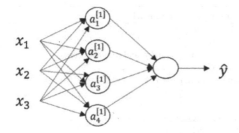

Fig. 3. The computing process of neural network.

3.3   Threat Identification

In the identification module, we identify the intent of the attack by analyzing the incoming data flows in *CNN*. The main idea of the algorithm is to update the coefficients of each layer by comparing the difference between the output value and the expected value. The convolution layer convolves the input with a preset convolution kernel. The aviation layer will performs a nonlinear mapping on the output of the convolutional layer by the aviation function. The aviation function $f(x)$ is generally a ReLu function in the Eq. 3.

$$f(x) = \max\{x, 0\} \tag{3}$$

The function of the pooling layer is to reduce the dimension of the data and avoid overfitting. We choose the maximum pooling method to select the maximum value in the feature map. The last layer is the full connection layer, through which we can get the result of the classifying. Figure 3 shows the calculation process of the full-connected layer. The output of the layer will be calculated from the expression in Eq. 4. $W^{[1]}$ and $W^{[2]}$ are the optimal coefficients we get from the training process and σ represents the sigmoid function. $b^{[1]}$ and $b^{[2]}$ are the offsets of the function. Given the input x, the result of classification will be $a^{[2]}$.

$$\begin{aligned} z^{[1]} &= W^{[1]}x + b^{[1]} \\ a^{[1]} &= \sigma(z^{[1]}) \\ z^{[2]} &= W^{[2]}a^{[1]} + b^{[2]} \\ a^{[2]} &= \sigma(z^{[2]}) \end{aligned} \tag{4}$$

We will compare the output with the expected value. When the error is greater than our Expectation, the error is transmitted back to the network to update the parameters in each layer. When the error is equal to or less than our expected value, the training is ended.

Algorithm 1. System scheduling algorithm
Input: network packet sequences *x*.
Output: solution *y*.
1: preprocess the input *x* by ***vectorization*** and ***normalization*** .
2: assign the output as *x'*.
3: call the detection module (input *x'*).
4: ***if*** the output = 0 .
5:   ***end if***.
6:   ***else*** label this sample as malicious sample.
7:   sort the coefficient values of *x'*.
8:   delete the smallest 23 coefficient values .
9:   assign the output as *x''*.
10:   call the identification module (input *x''*).
11:   assign the major threat categories to the sample.
12:     ***case*** category = 1 call the Probe mitigation module (input *x''*).
13:     ***case*** category = 2 call the DOS mitigation module (input *x''*).
14:     ***case*** category = 3 call the U2R mitigation module (input *x''*).
15:     ***case*** category = 3 call the R2L mitigation module (input *x''*).
16:   return the output *y* .
18:   ***end if***.
19: ***end*** .

3.4   Threat Mitigation

In the mitigation module, we will use machine learning methods, *KNN* algorithm and decision tree, to find a solution for threat mitigation. The input of the k-nearest neighbor algorithm is the feature vectors of different samples, corresponding to the points in the feature space; the output is the type of the each sample. The new type of sample is predicted by majority vote according to the type of its k nearest neighbors. The value of k is usually no more than 20. We choose the Euclidean Distance to calculate the distance between two samples. Equation 5 gives the expression of calculating the distance between 2 samples. *x* are the feature values of input samples and x' are the feature values of training samples.

$$d = \sqrt{(x_1 - x_1')^2 + (x_2 - x_2')^2 + (x_3 - x_3')^2 + ... + (x_n - x_n')^2} \tag{5}$$

The output of the *KNN* is used as the input of the decision tree to find a solution. The principle of dividing the decision tree is to minimize the information entropy of the dataset. The calculation expression of information entropy is shown in Eq. 6. p_i means the probability of each type of threats appearing in the samples space. The working scheduling of this system are shown in Algorithm 1.

$$H(U) = E[-\log(p_i)] = -\sum_{i=1}^{n} p_i \log p_i \tag{6}$$

4   Dataset and Experiment Result

4.1   Dataset

The dataset used in the system is called *KDD99*, which is the benchmark in the network threat detection realm. In this dataset, it contains 39 types of threat, including 22 types in the training samples and 17 types in the test samples. Table 1 gives the number of each category of the threats (10% of this dataset).

Table 1. the number of each category.

Label	Category	Number of training set	Number of testing set
0	*Normal*	97278	60593
1	*PROBE*	4017	4166
2	*DOS*	391458	229853
3	*U2R*	52	228
4	*R2L*	1126	16189

In our experiment, we only take 10% of this dataset to verify our threat response model. 22 types of threat are extracted from the dataset and handled by our system.

4.2   Experiment Result

The above dataset is used in our experiment. We test the efficiency of each module sequentially. The features are divided into two types: real-time features and statistic features. The result shows that the rate of successfully respond to threats in our system is over 97%. The detail of the results are elaborated below.

Figure 4 shows the results of logistic regression for threat detection. We randomly select 8000 samples from the training dataset and 2000 samples from the testing dataset. Because there are two types of feature, we have tried two detection methods; one is to use the real-time features of data for detection, and the other is to combine the statistical features and real-time features for detection. Under 10 iterations, the accuracy of the detection module using real-time features is 97.3%, and the accuracy of the detection module based-on real-time and statistical feature is 98.9%. The results show that the threat detection with statistical features will have a better accuracy rate, but the statistical module will generally have a delay. Therefore, in practical application, those two modules can be used in different scenarios.

After the system gives an alert of the threat, the threat identification module based-on *CNN* neural network will try to classify the current threat. We used 50,000 traffic data with different tags, including *DOS, U2R, R2L, PROBING*, to train the neural network, and used 10000 unknown traffic data to perform the

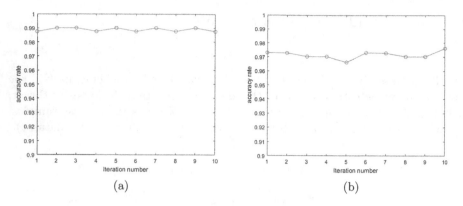

(a)   (b)

Fig. 4. The result of the threat detection: (a) the accuracy of statistical detection module (b) the accuracy of real-time detection module.

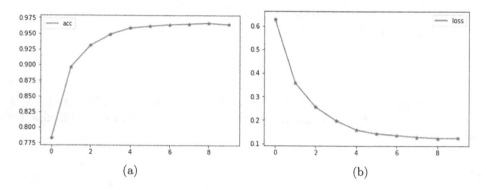

(a)   (b)

Fig. 5. The result of the identification module: (a) the accuracy rate (b) the value of loss function.

identification test. Figure 5 shows the accuracy rate of the test is 97.33% with 0.098 loss. The results show that our model can classify those four categories of threats precisely.

In mitigation module, we will subdivide the four major categories of threat into more specific types by *KNN* algorithm and then use decision tree make a quick response for each threat type. We extracted 50,000 samples from the DOS category for training and 20,000 samples for testing. We subdivided DOS into eight more specific categories: Apache2, Teardrop, Land, Mail-bomb, Neptune, Pod, Processtable, and Smurf. The accuracy of assigning the right type of each samples is 99.82%. Then we will represent those eight types of threat by a three dimensions vector and use the decision tree to find a solution. The structure of the tree is in Fig. 6.

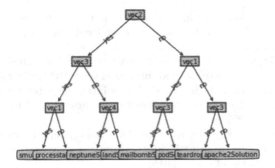

Fig. 6. The structure of the decision tree.

5 Conclusion

This paper has proposed an *AI* enhanced automatic network threat response system, which combined the advantages of machine learning and deep learning. It overcomes the deficiencies of traditional threat response system and can handle those unforeseen threats with a much lower false positive rate. In addition, it remedies the drawbacks that many current systems have high usage threshold (having to choose a proper system for a specific threat) and are hard to realize popularization (lack of a complete automatic threat response mechanism). It can handle 22 types of threats in the *KDD99* dataset and the accuracy of each model is above 97%.

The future work includes collection of additional samples from internet traffic flow and testing our system by the new samples. Additionally, we will comprehensively compare more learning algorithms to improve the efficiency of our system.

Acknowledgment. This work is supported by the National Natural Science Foundation of China (No.61728303) and the Open Research Project of the State Key Laboratory of Industrial Control Technology, Zhejiang University, China (No. ICT1800417); this work is also supported by China NSFC 61836005 and 61672358.

References

1. Thakur, K., Qiu, M., Gai, K., Ali, M.: An investigation on cyber security threats and security models. In: 2015 IEEE 2nd International Conference on Cyber Security and Cloud Computing, pp. 307–311. IEEE, New York, November 2015
2. Tidwell, K., Saurabh, K., Dash, D., Njemanze, H.S., Kothari, P.S.: Threat detection in a network security system. U.S. Patent 7,260,844. Washington, DC, August 2007
3. Alfayyadh, B., Ponting, J., Alzomai, M., Jøsang, A.: Vulnerabilities in personal firewalls caused by poor security usability. In: 2010 IEEE International Conference on Information Theory and Information Security, pp. 682–688, Beijing, January 2011

4. Rietta, F.: Application layer intrusion detection for SQL injection. In: ACM-SE 44 Proceedings of the 44th Annual Southeast Regional Conference, pp. 531–536, Florida, March 2016

5. Ross, K.: SQL injection detection using machine learning techniques and multiple data sources. Master's Projects. 650. https://doi.org/10.31979/etd.zknb-4z36

6. Li, W., Yi, P., Wu, Y., Pan, L., Li, J.: A new intrusion detection system based on KNN classification algorithm in wireless sensor network. J. Electr. Comput. Eng. **2014**(240217), 1–9 (2014)

7. Punithavathani, D.S., Sujatha, K., Jain, J.M.: Surveillance of anomaly and misuse in critical networks to counter insider threats using computational intelligence. Clust. Comput. **18**(1), 435–451 (2015)

8. Vinayakumar, R., Soman, K., Poornachandran, P.: Applying convolutional neural network for network intrusion detection. In: IEEE International Conference on Advances in Computing, Communications and Informatics (ICACCI), p. 2017. Udupi, September 2017

9. Hamed, H., Ali, D., Raouf, K., Kim-Kwang, R.: A deep Recurrent Neural Network based approach for Internet of Things malware threat hunting. Future Gener. Comput. Syst. **85**, 88–96 (2018)

10. Denning, D.E.: An intrusion-detection model. IEEE Trans. Softw. Eng. **SE-13**(2), 222–232 (1987)

11. Liao, H., Lin, C., Lin, Y., Tung, K.: Intrusion detection system: a comprehensive review. J. Netw. Comput. Appl. **36**(1), 16–24 (2013)

12. Mena, J.: Investigative Data Mining for Security and Criminal Detection. Butterworth Heinemann (2003)

13. Teodoro, P.G., Verdejo, J.D., Fernández, G.M., Vázquez, E.: Anomaly-based network intrusion detection: techniques, systems and challenges. Comput. Secur. **28**(1–2), 18–28 (2009)

14. Ma, Z., Xue, J., Leijon, A., Tan, Z., Yang, Z., Guo, J.: Decorrelation of neutral vector variables: theory and applications. IEEE Trans. Neural Netw. Learn. Syst. **29**(1), 129–143 (2016)

15. Ma, Z., Lai, Y., Kleijn, W.B., Wang, L.K., Guo, J.: Variational Bayesian learning for Dirichlet process mixture of inverted Dirichlet distributions in non-Gaussian image feature modeling. IEEE Trans. Neural Netw. Learn. Syst. **30**(2), 449–463 (2016)

16. Hodo, E., et al.: Threat analysis of IoT networks using artificial neural network intrusion detection system. In: 2016 International Symposium on Networks. Computers and Communications (ISNCC), pp. 1–6, Yasmine, May 2016

17. Gai, K., Qiu, M., Zhao, H., Tao, L., Zong, Z.: Dynamic energy-aware cloudlet-based mobile cloud computing model for green computing. J. Netw. Comput. Appl. **59**, 46–54 (2016)

18. Gai, K., Qiu, M., Zhao, H.: Energy-aware task assignment for mobile cyber-enabled applications in heterogeneous cloud computing. J. Parallel Distrib. Comput. **111**, 126–135 (2018)

19. Gai, K., Xu, K., Lu, Z., Qiu, M., Zhu, L.: Fusion of cognitive wireless networks and edge computing. IEEE Wirel. Commun. **26**(3), 69–75 (2019)

20. Qiu, H., Noura, H., Qiu, M., Ming, Z., Memmi, G.: A user-centric data protection method for cloud storage based on invertible DWT. IEEE Trans. Cloud Comput. https://doi.org/10.1109/TCC.2019.2911679

A Cross-Plane Cooperative DDoS Detection and Defense Mechanism in Software-Defined Networking

Yongyi Cao[1] ⓘ, Jing Wu[1], Bo Zhu[1], Hao Jiang[1(✉)], Yuchuan Deng[1], and Wei Luo[2]

[1] Wuhan University, Wuhan 430072, Hubei, China
jh@whu.edu.cn
[2] China Ship Development and Design Center, Wuhan 430064, Hubei, China

Abstract. Distributed Denial of Service (DDoS) has been one of the biggest threats in the field of network security and a big problem to many researchers and large enterprises for years. In SDN, traditional DDoS attack detection mechanisms are mostly based on intermediate plug-ins or SDN controllers, most of which have problems of large southbound communication overhead, detection delay or lacking network-wide monitoring information. In this paper, we propose a cross-plane cooperative DDoS defense system (CPCS) under the architecture of SDN, which filters abnormal traffic through coarse-grained detection on the data plane and fine-grained detection on the control plane. On the data plane, a preliminary screening is performed to reduce the detection range of the control plane, and the K-means clustering algorithm is used to perform fine-grained analysis of traffic on the control plane. In addition, an anti-false positive module is added ingeniously. The proposed method captures the key characteristics of DDoS attack traffic by polling the value of counters in OpenFlow switches which leverages the computational power of OpenFlow switches that currently not fully utilized. We conducted experiments on a campus network center including OpenFlow switches and RYU controllers. The results show that the framework and traffic monitoring algorithms proposed in this paper can greatly improve detection efficiency and accuracy, and reduce detection delay and southbound communication overhead.

Keywords: DDoS · Software-defined networking · Cross-plane · K-means

1 Introduction

Distributed Denial of Service (DDoS), as a cyber-attack, is easy-to-initiate and highly destructive. An attacker initiates an access attack by forging massive virtual IP addresses through multiple distributed attack sources. Servers under attack cannot respond to requests from normal users due to resource exhaustion [1]. This kind of cybersecurity threat existed since the early days of the Internet is still one of the most popular and efficient attacks on the Internet.

Most of the existing DDoS detection mechanisms under SDN architecture use the control plane to perform feature inspection [2, 3], or determine whether a flow is DDoS

© Springer Nature Switzerland AG 2019
M. Qiu (Ed.): SmartCom 2019, LNCS 11910, pp. 231–243, 2019.
https://doi.org/10.1007/978-3-030-34139-8_23

attack traffic by calculating the entropy value on the control plane [4]. The existing methods have some shortcomings: (1) Most of the methods only consider the detection process but ignore the defense strategy, that is, these methods do not involve dealing with the detected DDoS attack traffic. A few methods directly DROP these packets which might accidentally injure normal traffic. (2) If all the work is done by the controller, the load of southbound interface will be very high, and continuous polling increases the overhead of the detection system.

In this paper, we extract the features of DDoS attack traffic that suitable for data plane computing, offload some lightweight DDoS detection mechanisms to the data plane, and design a cross-plane collaborative system with verification and defense functions. This system includes not only DDoS detection but also defense strategies and long-term effective black and white list mechanism to ensure high detection rate and low false positive rate. Firstly, a coarse-grained screening is performed on the data plane. If the data plane generates an alarm, then a fine-grained test which based on machine learning will be performed on the control plane to determine whether the traffic is DDoS attack traffic. This method greatly reduces system overhead and southbound communication overhead.

When the verification module determines that a flow is DDoS attack traffic, we add a flow table through the controller to set the source IP address of the flow to blacklist. After that, the packet which contains this source IP address will be dropped directly when it passes through the switch, which greatly reduce the system overhead consumed caused by duplicate inspections. Similarly, we have also established a whitelisting mechanism. We add a flow table for the source IP of a packet that determined to be normal traffic by the verification and anti-false positive module. Packets from this source IP will be forwarded directly without verification.

The main contributions of this paper can be summarized as follows:

- We designed a lightweight algorithm for detecting DDoS attacks on the data plane, using the switch CPU for coarse-grained detection and sending alarm information to the control plane.
- We propose a DDoS attack detection framework for cross-plane collaboration, performing two levels of detection on the data plane and the control plane. If the data plane coarse-grained detection generates an alarm, a KNN-based fine-grained detection is performed on the control plane.
- We conducted a verification experiment at the campus network center. The experimental results show that our method has a low southbound communication overhead and detection delay, which greatly improves the detection efficiency and accuracy.

The rest of this paper is organized as follows. Section 2 covers the related works. Section 3 presents an overview of our framework. Experimental verification is presented in Sect. 4. This paper is concluded in Sect. 5.

2 Related Work

Nowadays, the main solution to the security defense of DDoS attack is real-time network monitoring. When a DDoS attack occurs, the attack traffic cleaning device is started to shield the DDoS attack source, thereby preventing the network from being attacked by the DDoS attack and achieving the purpose of security defense [5]. The implementation of the process mentioned above mainly includes the following methods: (1) Confirm the legality of the source IP address in a network forwarding device such as a switch or a router, and then establish a blacklist/whitelist; (2) Real-time monitoring of network traffic from changes in network flow density based on statistical methods; (3) Establish an inbound port mapping table corresponding to the source addresses and the forwarding devices in the routing and forwarding devices.

Most DDoS attack detection under SDN is performed on the control plane [6]. A classic method is to calculate the entropy value at the control plane to determine the dispersion degree of the source IP in the traffic. This method detects abnormal traffic by using the characteristics of high diversity of forged source IPs. The accuracy of the detection system depends on the threshold of entropy. However, the selection of the threshold is obtained by adjusting the size of the parameter, so the method is one-sided. Another method is to use the scalable computing power of the control plane to extract the key features of DDoS attack traffic from the header of packets, and use machine learning algorithms for detection [3, 7, 8]. These machine learning methods for detecting DDoS attacks at the control plane have lower false-positive rate, but have higher controller system consumption and southbound communication load.

Most of the current DDoS attack detection mechanisms only have detection parts but don't have specific defense strategies. Each time attack traffic reaches the controller, it causes high southbound communication load and control plane system overhead, furthermore, there are many other problems such as prolonged detection, low detection accuracy, high false-positive rate and weak detection capability for new DDoS attacks.

Based on the characteristics of the components such as OpenFlow switch counter, we assign some lightweight DDoS detection tasks on the data plane to cooperate with the fine-grained detection method of the control plane [9]. This method greatly improves the efficiency of the detection system and the flexibility of the scheme. The cross-plane mechanism reduces the system overhead and the communication load of the southbound interface, the detection speed and accuracy are improved too.

3 Cross-Plane Cooperative DDoS Detection Mechanism

3.1 System Description

In SDN, packets are forwarded at the data plane before being captured by the control plane, in order to improve the performance of DDoS attack detection and reduce the detection delay, it is considered to deploy a filtering function on the data plane. However, the typical SDN-based DDoS attack detection mechanism requires switch to continuously provide polling statistics to maintain the overall view of the network at the controller [10], which greatly increases the communication overhead of the southbound interface and reduces the delay of detection.

Our system architecture is shown in Fig. 1. We assign pre-detection function to the data plane to perform coarse-grained detection. In fact, most OpenFlow switches or hybrid switches that support the OpenFlow protocol consist of one or more CPUs with rich computing resources that are usually far from being fully utilized [11]. We use the switch CPU to perform lightweight traffic detection operations and perform a coarse-grained attack detection on the data plane. In addition, since the data plane has undergone a coarse-grained screening, the control plane detection method should have higher accuracy and detection efficiency. We choose k-means algorithm to perform finer-grained detection on DDoS. The detection speed of this method is fast and the accuracy is high.

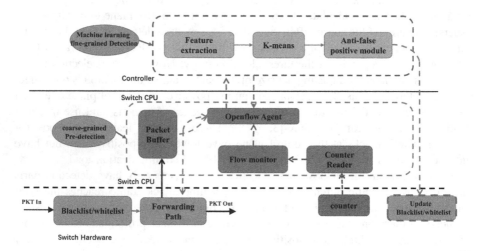

Fig. 1. Cross-plane collaborative DDoS defense system architecture

Our solution also adds blacklist and whitelist mechanisms and incorporates anti-false positives modules after control plane detection. Our method greatly reduces the communication load and system overhead of the southbound interface due to the use of event trigger instead of polling mechanism when detecting. Next, we will discuss the main modules of the system and how the coarse-grained and fine-grained detections are performed in detail.

3.2   Data Plane

Usually, the counters of OpenFlow switches calculate the number of packets and bytes passed by. Since OpenFlow Protocol 1.0 [12], the OpenFlow protocol defines a set of counters for each ingress, each flow table and each switch port, respectively. As shown in Fig. 2, the counter readers poll the counter values in turn and set these values as inputs to the flow monitor module. Then, these values are processed by the flow monitoring algorithm in the flow monitor module to filter abnormal traffic.

In this part, we propose a lightweight flow monitoring algorithm, which is used by the flow monitoring module of the data plane, to detect abnormal traffics caused by DDoS attacks. Unlike many other flow monitoring algorithms, the purpose of this lightweight algorithm is to extract key features of DDoS attack traffic by polling counter values of OpenFlow switches.

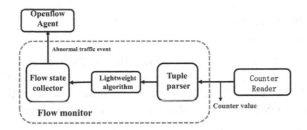

Fig. 2. Flow monitor workflow in data plane

Feature Extraction for Lightweight Detection Algorithms. Next, we will briefly introduce the volume and asymmetry characteristics of DDoS attacks and the methods of extracting two features of DDoS attack traffic using counters in OpenFlow switches.

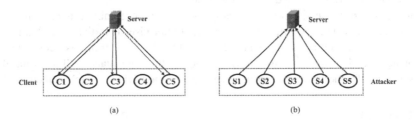

Fig. 3. Asymmetric characteristics of DDoS attack traffic

As we discussed in the first section, the differences between DDoS attack traffic and normal traffic are: (1) The arrival of large-scale traffic in a short time. The amount of arrived packets and bytes per unit time under DDoS attacks are much higher than normal traffic. (2) There is usually a large difference between the rates of flows when entering and flowing out of the victim server during the attack. As shown in Fig. 3, DDoS attacks are often initiated in the form of IP forging, fake IP addresses are used to send packets. So, when a DDoS attack occurs, the single-flow growth rate increases rapidly while the proportion of pair-flow is small. (3) When a DDoS flood attack occurs, the flow duration of different source IP addresses is short, so the average flow duration is also an important feature. (4) The same as the IP forging caused by DDoS attacks, the attacker can also perform a scanning attack by randomly generating ports, so the growth rate of different ports in the DDoS attack traffic is much higher than normal traffic [13].

Fortunately, these four features can be determined directly by polling the counter values of OpenFlow switches. These four characteristics of DDoS attack traffic described above can be represented as follows:

- Average packets per second.
- Average bytes per second.
- Percentage of pair-flow.
- Growth rate of single-flow.
- Average durations per flow.
- Growth rate of different port.

Among the six indicators represented above, 1th and 2th indicators come from the volume characteristics of the traffic, 3th and 4th indicators come from the asymmetric characteristics of DDoS attack traffic, 5th and 6th indicators respectively show the characteristics of DDoS attack traffic short-time multi-flow and forged ports.

Lightweight Detection Algorithm of Data Plane. In this section, we present a lightweight algorithm that can be used to capture changes in the six indicators represented above. The algorithm uses the previous n values of the six indicators in a piece of traffic to estimate future values. If values of these indicators in the next cycle falls within the predicted range, it means that the current flow is normal. Otherwise, the deviation between the predicted value and the observed value represents a change in the behavior of the network. If all six indicators are out of acceptable range, we identify it as an abnormal traffic caused by a DDoS attack.

If one or more of the six ratio metrics fall within an acceptable range, then there is no DDoS attack in the specific flow currently. Otherwise, it indicates that this is an abnormal traffic caused by a DDoS attack. Once the abnormal traffic is detected by the monitoring thread in the flow monitoring module, the data plane will send an alarm message to notify the controller to perform fine-grained DDoS attack detection.

3.3   Control Plane

In the control plane, we propose a fine-grained detection method that uses clustering algorithms to combine related features. The flow of the method is shown in Fig. 4. The dotted line indicates the training process and the solid line indicates the detection process.

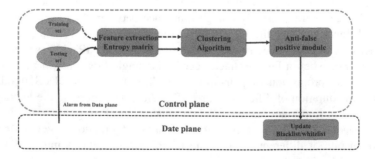

Fig. 4. Fine-grained detection of the control plane

Feature Extraction. We can extract various features from the header of packets sent from the data plane for the clustering algorithm. Since the most prominent feature of DDoS attack traffic is that it sends out a large number of packets by forging the source IP address and port, the quintuple contains most of the DDoS feature information, therefore, we extract the quintuple information of each packet. Because entropy is a good representation of uncertainty, based on the characteristics of the DDoS attack random forgery source IP and port, we calculate the entropy value as the input eigenvalue separately. The definition of entropy is:

$$H(X) = -\sum_{i=1}^{N} \left(\frac{n_i}{S}\right) \log\left(\frac{n_i}{S}\right) \tag{1}$$

Where S is the total number of packets, N is the number of different IP addresses or ports, and n_i is the number of times a particular indicator appears. We find that the DDoS attack has a strong influence on the entropy of the following quintuple (destination IP address, destination port, source IP address, packet size, duration of the flow).

In addition, since the normal burst large traffic will also change the entropy of the packet size, we have improved the packet size entropy to distinguish it from the DDoS attack. i_{max} is the packet size level, a total of five levels. The above characteristics represent the basic characteristics of DDoS. Therefore, we believe that although the experimental test set only contains a part of the DDoS category, our model can be used to detect various types of DDoS.

$$H^*(size) = -i_{max} \sum_{i=1}^{5} \left(\frac{n_i}{S}\right) \log\left(\frac{n_i}{S}\right) \tag{2}$$

Clustering Algorithm K-means Classification and Detection. In the training process, the clustering method is used to model the traffic and determine the detection threshold. It should be noted that all of our training data only contains normal traffic.

We use k-means to meet the requirements of real-time detection because it is much faster than other clustering algorithms [14]. The K-Means algorithm divides similar data by a preset K value and the initial centroid of each category. The optimal clustering result is obtained by the iterative optimization of the divided mean values. The Euclidean distance is used to quantify the similarity of two entropy vectors.

We use the feature matrix composed of the above features as the input of K-means, and the m nodes of the input represent the records with m features, for example, $X = \{x_1, x_2, \ldots, x_m\}$. After the clustering is completed, the clusters with points fewer than $0.05n$ are eliminated. For each cluster, we record the cluster center C and radius r of the training data. C is determined by the average of all points, r is determined by the maximum distance between C and any other point in the cluster [15–17].

The steps of fine-grained detection of DDoS attacks on the control plane are as follows:

- For the suspicious traffic detected in unit time, the entropy value is calculated to obtain the entropy vector X in the preprocessing module.

- Calculate the Euclidean distance from X to the center C_i of all clusters and record the result as d_i.
- Select the minimum distance $d_t = \min\{d_i\}$ and assign the sample X to the appropriate cluster.
- Compare d_i with the cluster radius r_t, if $d_t < r_t$, then the sample X is judged as normal data.

When the traffic is normal traffic, we save the source address of these flows, update the flow table to update the whitelist library of the data plane. Otherwise, the sample is judged to be abnormal data, and we believe this traffic is DDoS attack traffic. The source addresses are also saved. After the error prevention module is checked, if there is no misjudged traffic, the data plane blacklist is updated.

Anti-false Positive Module. After previous coarse filtering on the data plane and fine-grained detection on the control plane, the detection accuracy of the system is greatly improved and the total system overhead is reduced. However, since our fine-grained inspection methods are based on multiple, that is, it is difficult to pick it out when normal traffic is also mixed in DDoS attack traffic. The result only indicates whether the traffic within a period contains DDoS attacks. Therefore, after the detection by clustering algorithm, the anti-false positive module is added, in this way, the normal traffic flow mixed in the DDoS attack traffic can be distinguished and added to the list. It is worth mentioning that our anti-false positive module is based on probability statistics. The larger the traffic, the better the effect. The principle is described in detail below.

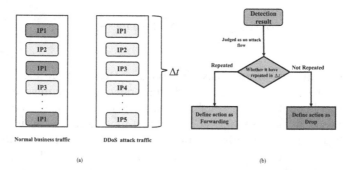

Fig. 5. Anti-false positive mechanism

As shown in Fig. 5, DDoS attack has the characteristics of forging source IP, and these forged source IPs are randomly generated, therefore, the flow of the same source IP will not appear twice in a short period of time, in other words, the probability of this situation is extremely small and negligible. However, when the traffic contains normal traffic, the flow of the same source IP occurs twice or more in short time and that is normal. In this case, we believe that the flow of this source IP is normal traffic rather than DDoS attack traffic. We save the source IP and add it to the whitelist to prevent misjudgment. We use this feature of DDoS attack traffic to develop an anti-false positive module. It's noted that the same IP flow here refers to two flows with intervals, rather than consecutive packets.

4   Experiments

4.1   Experimental Environment and Settings

The network test bed of this experiment consists of three OpenFlow switches in the campus network center. As shown in Fig. 6, the client and attack host are connected to switch S1, and the server is connected to S3. Three switches are connected to the controller, and the collection module is connected to the source switch S1. The compute server is equipped with an Intel e5-2620v3 CPU, 64 GB of RAM and GeForce GTX titan x. The operating system is ubuntu16.04, we chose onos1.13 as the SDN controller.

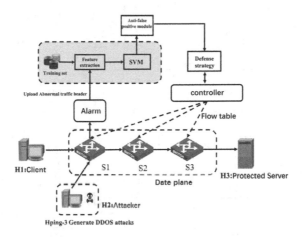

Fig. 6. Diagram of our testbed network

The experimental data was collected before the experiment and divided into normal traffic and DDoS attack traffic. DDoS attack traffic is generated using the attack tool Hping3. Our training set only includes normal traffic, excluding DDoS attack traffic, and the purpose of training phase is to determine the threshold of cluster radius.

4.2   Algorithm Efficiency Evaluation of the Data Plane

In order to evaluate the effectiveness of the lightweight algorithm deployed on the data plane, we perform the following steps: We use hping3 to send DDoS attack traffic from H2 to H3 within 20 s, while H1 send normal background flow to H3. Figure 7 describes the changes of the six metrics in the algorithm we proposed when the DDoS attack occurred. Figure 7 shows that after the DDoS attack, the six metrics in our algorithm can capture the variation characteristics of the abnormal traffic, which proves the effectiveness of the algorithm we propose.

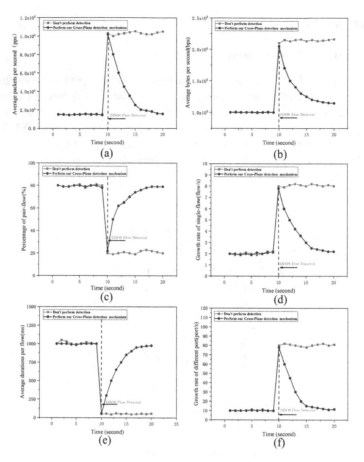

Fig. 7. Changes of data plane feature indicators before and after DDoS attack.

4.3 Comparison of System Evaluation Indicators

In order to verify that our cross-plane collaboration method is superior to the existing methods in DDoS detection evaluation indicators, controller CPU consumption and southbound interface load, etc., we use the most commonly used entropy-based detection method and SVM-based machine learning detection algorithm as a comparison group and perform the following experiments.

The results of three methods are shown in Table 1. It can be seen that the accuracy of our method is better than that of the comparison group. It's because the cross-plane detection method has been tested twice by coarse- and fine-grain respectively. We find that the precision and recall rate are greatly improved compared to traditional methods. This is because we added an anti-false positive module to prevent normal packets from being misidentified as DDoS attack traffic, which greatly reduced the probability of false positives.

Table 1. Evaluation results under different methods

Detection method	Accuracy	Precision	Recall	F-measure
Cross-plane	98.04%	98.56%	98.06%	97.80%
SVM	95.78%	95.11%	94.68%	94.68%
Entropy-based	93.10%	93.79%	92.80%	93.29%

Southbound Interface Communication Load. The change of the southbound interface communication load during the period of an attack is shown in Fig. 8. Before the attack occurs, the SVM method starts polling and sends packets to the control plane, so the load of southbound interface is higher. However, our method only sends a warning message to the controller and starts control plane detection when the data plane detects an abnormal traffic, so the southbound interface overload is close to zero. When the data plane detection coarse-grained method detects a DDoS attack, the fine-grained detection of the control plane starts. At this time, the southbound interface overload of both methods increases sharply and continues for a while. When the detection is completed, the southbound interface overload under our method is back to zero. This is because our method is pushed by the event trigger mechanism. When there is no abnormal traffic in the network, no flow is sent to the control plane.

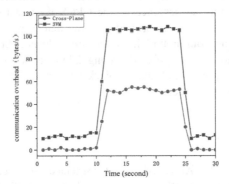

Fig. 8. Southbound interface communication overhead of different methods

Controller CPU Consumption. We evaluate the computational resource overhead by the CPU utilization of the control plane, where CPCS is the method we used and SVM method represents the control group. Figure 9 shows that in an attack cycle, the CPU consumed by this method is at a low level (about 10%) before the attack, which is lower than the CPU consumption of the comparison group. Obviously, it's an advantage brought by offloading the coarse-grained flow monitoring mechanism to the data plane. In this case, the controller only performs conventional operations. The other two methods need to use OpenFlow polling or SFlow to sample, so the consumption of CPU is maintained at about 40%. When the attack flow comes, the packets that need to be processed increase instantaneously, in the controller-based SVM algorithm, the CPU runs at full capacity, and our Cross-Plane method also achieves 80% CPU utilization.

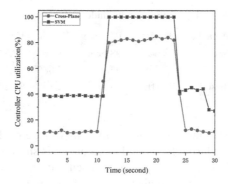

Fig. 9. Controller CPU utilization of different methods

5 Conclusion

This paper introduces an inter-plane cooperative DDoS attack detection framework (CPCS) based on SDN. The method we propose filters the abnormal traffic through coarse-grained detection of the data plane and fine-grained detection of the control plane, which improves the detection performance and overcomes the challenges of controller system overhead and southbound interface communication load. In experiments, it is found that the performance of the CPCS relative to the original control plane detection method is greatly improved, and the detection delay and the communication overhead of the southbound interface are reduced. At the same time, our system is an end-to-end system. After detecting DDoS attack traffic, it immediately implements the defense policy and adds a black and white list mechanism, which is meaningful for large network scenarios.

References

1. Wang, R., Jia, Z., Ju, L.: An entropy-based distributed DDoS detection mechanism in software-defined network. In: 2015 IEEE Trustcom/BigDataSE/ISPA, vol. 1, pp. 310–317. IEEE (2015)
2. Dou, W., Chen, Q., Chen, J.: A confidence-based filtering method for DDoS attack defense in cloud environment. Future Gener. Comput. Syst. **29**(7), 1838–1850 (2013)
3. Ye, J., Cheng, X., Zhu, J., et al.: A DDoS attack detection method based on SVM in software defined network. Secur. Commun. Netw. **2018** (2018)
4. Qin X., Xu T., Wang C.: DDoS attack detection using flow entropy and clustering technique. In: 2015 11th International Conference on Computational Intelligence and Security (CIS), pp. 412–415. IEEE (2015)
5. Gil, T.M., Poletto, M.: MULTOPS: a data-structure for bandwidth attack detection. In: USENIX Security Symposium, pp. 23–38 (2001)
6. Mousavi, S.M., St-Hilaire, M.: Early detection of DDoS attacks against SDN controllers. In: 2015 International Conference on Computing, Networking and Communications (ICNC). IEEE, pp. 77–81 (2015)

7. Barki, L., Shidling, A., Meti, N., et al.: Detection of distributed denial of service attacks in software defined networks. In: 2016 International Conference on Advances in Computing, Communications and Informatics (ICACCI). IEEE, pp. 2576–2581 (2016)

8. Niyaz, Q., Sun, W., Javaid, A.Y.: A deep learning based DDoS detection system in software-defined networking (SDN). arXiv preprint arXiv:1611.07400 (2016)

9. Braga, R., de Souza Mota, E., Passito, A.: Lightweight DDoS flooding attack detection using NOX/OpenFlow. In: LCN, vol. 10, pp. 408–415 (2010)

10. D'Cruze, H., Wang, P., Sbeit, R.O., Ray, A.: A software-defined networking (SDN) approach to mitigating DDoS attacks. In: Latifi, S. (ed.) Information Technology - New Generations. AISC, vol. 558, pp. 141–145. Springer, Cham (2018). https://doi.org/10.1007/978-3-319-54978-1_19

11. Yang, X., Han, B., Sun, Z., et al.: SDN-based DDoS attack detection with cross-plane collaboration and lightweight flow monitoring. In: GLOBECOM 2017-2017 IEEE Global Communications Conference. IEEE, pp. 1-6 (2017)

12. Zhao, T., Li, T., Han, B., et al.: Design and implementation of software defined hardware counters for SDN. Comput. Netw. **102**, 129–144 (2016)

13. Yan, Q., Yu, F.R., Gong, Q., et al.: Software-defined networking (SDN) and distributed denial of service (DDoS) attacks in cloud computing environments: a survey, some research issues, and challenges. IEEE Commun. Surv. Tutor. **18**(1), 602–622 (2015)

14. Qin, X., Xu, T., Wang, C.: DDoS attack detection using flow entropy and clustering technique. In: 2015 11th International Conference on Computational Intelligence and Security (CIS). IEEE, pp. 412–415 (2015)

15. Qiu, H., Noura, H., Qiu, M., et al.: A user-centric data protection method for cloud storage based on invertible DWT. IEEE Trans. Cloud Comput. (2019)

16. Qiu, H., Memmi, G.: Fast selective encryption method for bitmaps based on GPU acceleration. In: 2014 IEEE International Symposium on Multimedia, pp. 155–158. IEEE (2014)

17. Qiu, H., Kapusta, K., Lu, Z., et al.: All-or-nothing data protection for ubiquitous communication: challenges and perspectives. Inf. Sci. (2019)

A Hardware Trojan Detection Method Design Based on TensorFlow

Wenzhi Wu[1,3(✉)], Ying Wei[2], and Ruizhe Ye[1]

[1] Network Information Center, Xiamen University of Technology, Xiamen, China
wuwenzhi@xmut.edu.cn
[2] Xiamen University Tan Kah Kee College, Xiamen, China
[3] Engineering Research Center for Software Testing and Evaluation of Fujian Province, Xiamen, China

Abstract. As an extra circuit inserted into chip design, Hardware Trojan can achieve malicious functional changes, reliability reduction or secret information disclosure. Meanwhile, the design of the hardware Trojan circuit is concealed, triggered only under rare conditions, and is in a waiting state for most of the life cycle. It is quite small compared to the host design and has little influence on circuit parameters. Therefore, it is difficult to detect hardware Trojans. Fast and accurate detection technology is provided by Google's open source machine learning framework TensorFlow. The hardware Trojan circuit adopts the standard circuit provided by Trust-Hub. It is realized through FPGA programming. ISE is used for compiling and simulation to obtain the characteristic value of the circuit; Finally, a hardware Trojan detection platform based on machine learning is established by simulating the data via TensorFlow machine learning. The experimental test results verify the correctness of the design and provide a simple hardware Trojan detection for IC.

Keywords: Hardware trojan · Detection · TensorFlow · Machine learning · FPGA

1 Introduction

Informatization, as an important achievement in the continuous progress of human beings, is an important trend in the development of contemporary world economy and human society [1]. Research on hardware Trojans, Internet of Things, and IPv6 is very popular [2–4]. Human beings are highly dependent on integrated circuits and chips. However, due to the globalization of chip design and manufacturing, integrated circuits and chips are vulnerable to malicious changes and attacks. Hardware Trojan (HT) is an extra circuit inserted into chip design, and it can achieve malicious functional changes, reliability reduction and secret information disclosure [5]. Meanwhile, the design of the hardware Trojan circuit is quite concealed, which is only triggered in rare conditions. The most life cycle of hardware Trojan circuit is in a waiting state. Hardware Trojan circuit design is small compared to the host design, and has little influence on circuit parameters. Consequently, hardware Trojan can hardly be detected [6]. The hardware

© Springer Nature Switzerland AG 2019
M. Qiu (Ed.): SmartCom 2019, LNCS 11910, pp. 244–252, 2019.
https://doi.org/10.1007/978-3-030-34139-8_24

Trojan circuit is composed of a trigger and a useful load to activate and execute expected objectives [7]. According to the Trojan design, when the trigger signal reaches a rare expected value, the hardware Trojan activation signal is triggered and the useful load is enabled, which will influence the stability of the system and lead to system function loss or information leakage [8].

Since hardware Trojan activation is rare, the system cannot detect hardware Trojan by exhaustive method [9]. To this end, this paper designs a hardware Trojan detection system based on TensorFlow. A feature matrix is formed by acquiring extrinsic features of the hardware circuit. Meanwhile, a machine learning model is designed and trained. Finally, a machine learning model which can correctly detect hardware Trojan is designed.

2   Overall Design of Hardware Trojan Detection Plan

The United States holds the information security month every year since 2007. Most American universities, such as Yale University, New York University and Carnegie Mellon University, have carried out in-depth research on hardware Trojans. Great progresses have been achieved in hardware Trojan design and detection technology. The research method evolved from the initial software simulation to FPGA experiment. The detection based on bypass signal has developed rapidly, and the effect is continuously improved. The chips of various types of hardware Trojans can be detected. The structural diagram is shown in Fig. 1 [10]. The hardware Trojan circuit is composed of trigger logic and function logic. When the system is running under certain conditions, the trigger signal of the hardware Trojan circuit is triggered. The system operates according to the Trojan design, thus influencing the system function. Meanwhile, the hardware Trojan circuit can detect the temperature and the electromagnetism surrounding the system. The hardware Trojan circuit will be activated at a certain temperature of the system.

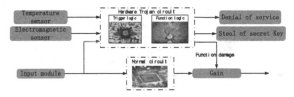

Fig. 1. Structure of hardware Trojan circuit

In the design, a feature matrix is formed based on the circuit characteristics of the system. By comparing with the golden template without Trojan, a Trojan feature matrix is generated. A machine learning model is established and trained to obtain the correct hardware Trojan detection model. The structure diagram is shown in Fig. 2. The machine learning model learns the existing Trojan matrix information, and adjusts the parameters, so that the model outputs a more appropriate value. Finally, the logic formed by the arithmetic formula is the final model obtained by the system. Afterwards, the trained model is saved. By extracting a specific feature matrix and inputting a machine learning model, the hardware Trojan is detected.

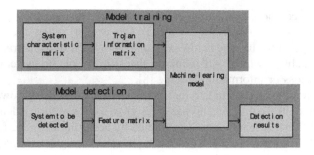

Fig. 2. Machine learning test model structure

3   Extraction of Hardware Trojan Circuit Characteristic Value

In hardware Trojan circuit detection, the IP core is detected by describing the hardware description language. The key is to build a comprehensive hardware Trojan database. The hardware Trojan characteristics are extracted based on the hardware circuit in the Trust-Hub benchmark [11, 12]. Firstly, the hardware circuit is realized by hardware description language. The characteristic matrix of the hardware circuit is obtained through integrated wiring and system simulation for extraction analysis. The characteristic matrix of the hardware Trojan is obtained by comparing with the Gold template.

Figure 3 shows the FPGA RTL schematic diagrams of RS232-T100 in the Trust-Hub benchmark. As shown in Fig. 3, the RS232-T100 system is composed of three modules, the RS232 module, the Trojan_Trigger module and the Trojan module. When the system reaches a specific state (i.e., State is a specific value), the Trojan module is triggered, which influences the normal operation of RS232.

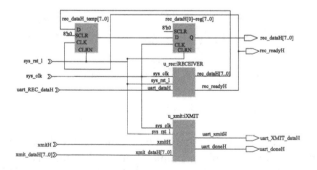

Fig. 3. Schematic diagram of RS232-T100 FPGA RTL

Figure 4 shows the output of the simulated hardware circuit using Cyclone V 5CEFA9F31C7 of Altera. After the hardware Trojan is inserted to the system, the Logic Utlization number, register number and IO power consumption of the system change obviously, but there is no obvious change in static power consumption.

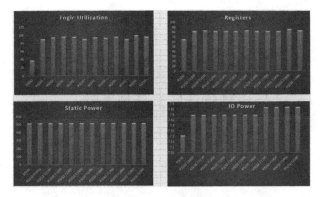

Fig. 4. Output feature of Quartus simulation circuit

This paper uses Xq7vx330t chip of Xilinx Company to obtain the register number, Look-Up Table number, Flip-Flop number and power consumption information of the system by simulation in the ISE software. The power consumption information is collected by carrying out XPower software analysis [13]. Table 1 list the output feature values of 12 circuits of RS232, RS232-T1000 ～ RS232-T2000 in the Trust-Hub benchmark platform simulated by Xilinx ISE software, including registers, LUT, Slices and FF. The hardware Trojan realizes the hardware Trojan function circuit by occupying LUT and Flip-Flop of the system. There are 52 LUTs and 64 Flip-Flops without hardware Trojan. In the circuit inserted with hardware Trojan, the two values will increase significantly and show significant correlation. The RS232 hardware Trojan simulation output values are shown in Fig. 5.

Table 1. Trust-Hub RS232 Trojan circuit simulation output value

Name	Slice registers	Slice LUTs	Occupied slices	Flip-Flop pairs
RS232	50	52	27	64
RS232-T1000	58	107	73	110
RS232-T1100	59	87	65	95
RS232-T1200	59	102	71	111
RS232-T1300	58	95	48	101
RS232-T1400	59	105	74	113
RS232-T1500	59	107	69	116
RS232-T1600	59	112	69	118
RS232-T1700	58	115	80	121
RS232-T1800	59	105	73	114
RS232-T1900	62	115	76	124
RS232-T2000	59	115	69	122

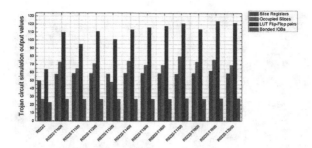

Fig. 5. RS232 Trojan circuit simulation output values

The power consumption of Trust-Hub benchmark RS232 hardware Trojan circuit at the clock frequency of 25 MHz is shown in Table 2. The static power consumption is between 177.32 and 177.33 mW, which is the same as the simulation results by Altera. The clock, logic, signal and IO power consumption change obviously. The static power consumption and the total power consumption are described in Fig. 6.

Table 2. RS232 hardware Trojan circuit power consumption (mW)

Name	Clocks	Logic	Signals	IOs	Static Power	Total Power
RS232	0.51	0.04	0.06	0.37	177.32	178.30
RS232-T1000	1.09	0.12	0.22	0.59	177.33	179.34
RS232-T1100	0.71	0.09	0.15	0.59	177.32	178.86
RS232-T1200	1.08	0.10	0.26	0.60	177.33	179.37
RS232-T1300	0.60	0.09	0.13	0.59	177.32	178.74
RS232-T1400	1.16	0.12	0.23	0.60	177.33	179.44
RS232-T1500	0.74	0.12	0.18	0.60	177.33	178.96
RS232-T1600	0.75	0.12	0.17	0.59	177.33	178.95
RS232-T1700	0.82	0.13	0.21	0.61	177.33	179.10
RS232-T1800	0.93	0.12	0.22	0.59	177.33	179.18
RS232-T1900	0.93	0.14	0.20	0.62	177.33	179.21
RS232-T2000	0.69	0.13	0.16	0.61	177.33	178.91

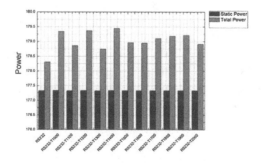

Fig. 6. RS232 hardware Trojan circuit power output

From the above analysis, it can be concluded that the register number, flip-flop number and power consumption information in the hardware Trojan infection circuit change significantly, while the static power consumption information and the IO number change slightly. Therefore, the register number, flip-flop number and power consumption information are taken as the input information of the system, and the LUT number as the output information. A two-dimensional matrix is established and compared with the gold template, thus forming the final Trojan information matrix.

4　Design of Machine Learning Prediction Model

TensorFlow is Google's second-generation software library used for digital computation. It is a deep learning framework with complete data flow and processing mechanism. Meanwhile, a large number of efficient algorithms and functions built by neural network are integrated [14]. Since the system is a nonlinear system, the design is completed using a multi-layer neural network [15].

Figure 7 shows the hardware Trojan prediction network model. In the three-layer neural network model, the known data is input to the system by the input layer, and preprocessed by the hidden layer. Finally, the prediction result is output by the output layer.

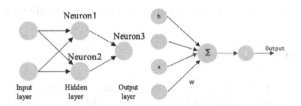

Fig. 7. Hardware Trojan prediction network model

The network model of a single neuron is shown in Fig. 7, and its calculation formula is Eq. 1.

$$z = \sum_{i=1}^{n} w_i \times x_i + b \tag{1}$$

Where z is the output result, x is the input, w is the weight, and b is the offset value. The values of w and b are constantly adjusted to suitable values in model learning. The logic formed by the value and the formula is the neural network model [16–22].

Commonly used activation functions are Sigmoid, Tanh, Relu and Softplus. Their mathematical forms are as shown in Eqs. 2–5.

$$\text{Sigmoid}(x) = 1/(1 + e^x) \tag{2}$$

$$\text{Tanh}(x) = 2\text{Sigmoid}(2x) - 1 \tag{3}$$

$$\text{Relu}(x) = \max(0, \ x) \tag{4}$$

$$\text{Softplus}(x) = \ln(1 + e^x) \tag{5}$$

The Relu function is taken as the activation function of the system, while the output of the intermediate layer is a 1 * 2 matrix. Its calculation formula is Eq. 2. There are two nodes in the hidden layer, and the model is designed at the learning rate of 0.0001. The design steps are as follows:

Firstly, the learning parameters are designed. The weight w and the offset value b are defined in the form of a dictionary. h1 represents the hidden layer, and h2 represents the final output layer. The forward structure entry of the design model is x, which is multiplied by w of the first layer and plus b. The result is activated and transformed by the Relu function, and y_pred_layer_1 is generated. y_pred_layer_1 is substituted into the second layer, and the Relu function generates the final output of y_pred.

Secondly, the back propagation structure of the model uses the mean squared difference reduce_mean() to calculate the loss function, which is optimized by AdamOptimizer.

Thirdly, the simulated dataset is manually generated, and the simulated data are obtained from the dataset in Table 1, which are fed into the x of the model to obtain the final output y. The system iterates 50,000 times. The model is trained and saved.

Finally, the data set x to be predicted is input in to generate the final result. The accuracy of the system is obtained by comparing the predicted value and the true value.

5   Experimental Verification

In hardware Trojan detection platform design, the data set is first simulated and acquired. The FPGA experimental platform is connected to the PC through the JTAG interface, and the output interface is connected to the oscilloscope. After the system is powered on, the Verilog file on the Trust-Hub benchmark platform is input into ISE and compiled for comprehensive wiring. The comprehensive wiring and the data in the XPower system are read, and the results are shown in Tables 1 and 2.

Through the test platform simulation design, the prediction results are obtained, as shown in Table 3. The accuracy rate is above 93%, which has good robustness.

Table 3. Experimental results

Circuit name	SVM	Tensorflow
RS232-T1000	53%	93.95%
RS232-T1100	58%	99.87%
RS232-T1200	80%	96.74%
RS232-T1300	89%	99.08%
RS232-T1400	83%	98.73%
RS232-T1500	83%	96.64%
RS232-T1600	89%	98.22%

Meanwhile, the accuracy rate using the SVM method is approximately 83% [9]. The prediction accuracy percentage of the experiment platform is presented in Fig. 8. The system has a high accuracy and can better predict the hardware Trojan.

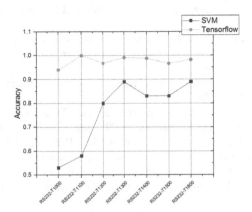

Fig. 8. Experimental results

6 Conclusions

This paper proposes a hardware Trojan detection method design based on Tensorflow. This method is designed based on machine learning to prevent the integrated circuit and chip from being attacked by hardware Trojan. This technique can improve hardware Trojan detection success rate. However, further studies are still needed. (1) This paper concentrates on RS232 series circuit, more series circuit have not been tested. (2) The RS232 series circuit has been tested, but no classification discussion has been explored to explore possible results. As hardware Trojans and machine learning are widely investigated by research scholars or industry participants, its application will be improved and the problems at this stage will be solved. Proposed detection technique can be applied to chip inspection, such as chip design and testing.

This research was support by Key Construction Discipline under project number 6081700310; Key Laboratory and Scientific Research Platform under project number 6161700206 and 6161700202; Fujian Provincial Education Department Science and Technology Project under project number JAT170435; CERNET Innovation Project (NGII20180510).

References

1. Lei, Z., Mengxi, Y., Chaoen, X., Youheng, D.: Hardware trojan detection based on optimized SVM algorithm. Appl. Electron. Tech. **44**(11), 17–20 (2018)
2. Liang, W., et al.: A security situation prediction algorithm based on HMM in mobile network. WCMC **2018**(4), 1–11 (2018)

3. Liang, W., et al.: Efficient data packet transmission algorithm for IPV6 mobile vehicle network based on fast switching model with time difference. FGCS **100**, 132–143 (2019)
4. Liang, W., Long, J., Weng, T.H., Chen, X., Li, K.C., Zomaya, A.Y.: TBRS: a trust based recommendation scheme for vehicular CPS. FGCS **92**, 383–398 (2019)
5. Cakir, B., Malik, S.: Hardware Trojan detection for gate-level ICs using signal correlation based clustering. In: Proceedings Design, Automation and Test in Europe (DATE), p. 47147 (2015)
6. Xue, M., Bian, R., Liu, W., et al.: Defeating untrustworthy testing parties: a novel hybrid clustering ensemble based golden models-free hardware Trojan detection method. IEEE Access **7**, 5124–5140 (2018)
7. Dong, C., He, G., Liu, X., et al.: A multi-layer hardware trojan protection framework for IoT chips. IEEE Access **7**, 23628–23639 (2019)
8. Hasegawa, K., Yanagisawa, M., Togawa, N.: Hardware Trojans classification for gate-level netlists using multi-layer neural networks. In: 2017 IEEE 23rd International Symposium on On-Line Testing and Robust System Design (IOLTS). IEEE, pp. 227–232 (2017)
9. Hasegawa, K., Yanagisawa, M.: A hardware-Trojan classification classification method using machine learning at gate-level netlists based on Trojan features. IEEE (2017)
10. Lin, N., Lei, S., Kun, H., Shaoqing, L.: Hardware Trojan detection of IP soft cores based on feature matching. Comput. Eng. **43**(03), 176–180 (2017)
11. Salmani, H., Tehranipoor, M., Karri, R.: On design vulnerability analysis and trust benchmarks development. In: 2013 IEEE 31st International Conference on Computer Design (ICCD). IEEE, pp. 471–474 (2013)
12. Shakya, B., He, T., Salmani, H., Forte, D., Bhunia, S., Tehranipoor, M.: Benchmarking of hardware Trojans and maliciously affected circuits. J. Hardw. Syst. Secur. (HaSS) **1**, 85–102 (2017)
13. FIFO Generator v13.2 LogiCORE IP Product Guide. Xilinx (2017). www.xilinx.com
14. Chang Zhanguo, P., Baoming, L.X., Shuai, W., Shuo, Y.: Automatic detection of myocardial infarction via machine learning. Comput. Syst. Appl. **04**, 218–224 (2019)
15. Fangyu, R., Yang, X., Siyuan, Z., Renyuan, H.: Research on remote sensing image feature recognition based on TensorFlow. Sci. Technol. Innov. Her. **15**(11), 53–54 (2018)
16. Huang Rui, L., Yilin, X.W.: Handwritten digital recognition and application based on TensorFlow deep learning. Appl. Electron. Tech. **44**(10), 6–10 (2018)
17. Gavai, N.R., Jakhade, Y.A., Tribhuvan, S.A., et al.: MobileNets for flower classification using TensorFlow. In: 2017 International Conference on Big Data, IoT and Data Science (BID), pp. 154–158. IEEE (2017)
18. Saxena, A.: Convolutional neural networks: an illustration in TensorFlow. XRDS: Crossroads ACM Mag. Stud. **22**(4), 56–58 (2016)
19. Thakur, K., Qiu, M., Gai, K., et al.: An investigation on cyber security threats and security models. In: 2015 IEEE 2nd International Conference on Cyber Security and Cloud Computing. IEEE, pp. 307–311 (2015)
20. Gai, K., Qiu, M., Elnagdy, S.A.: Security-aware information classifications using supervised learning for cloud-based cyber risk management in financial big data. In: 2016 IEEE 2nd International Conference on Big Data Security on Cloud (BigDataSecurity), IEEE International Conference on High Performance and Smart Computing (HPSC), and IEEE International Conference on Intelligent Data and Security (IDS), pp. 197–202. IEEE (2016)
21. Qiu, H., Qiu, M., LU, Z., et al.: An efficient key distribution system for data fusion in V2X heterogeneous networks. Inf. Fusion **50**, 212–220 (2019)
22. Qiu, H., Kapusta, K., Lu, Z., et al.: All-Or-Nothing data protection for ubiquitous communication: challenges and perspectives. Inf. Sci. (2019)

Resolving the Loop in High-Level SDN Program for Multi-table Pipeline Compilation

Xin Wang[1]([✉]) [iD], Linghe Kong[2]([✉]), and Changjun Jiang[1]

[1] Tongji University, Shanghai, China
{13xinwang,cjjiang}@tongji.edu.cn
[2] Shanghai Jiao Tong University, Shanghai, China
linghe.kong@sjtu.edu.cn

Abstract. Software-Defined Networking (SDN) is one of the key technologies to support smart computing and communication in the network domain. Though recent developments in high-level SDN programming have improved programming flexibility, loops (*e.g.*, while) in an SDN program cannot yet be deployed in a datapath due to existing hardware constraints. In this paper, we conduct a novel study of loops in SDN programs for pipeline design, and propose the repeated software pipeline (RSP) transformation as a solution to compiling loops in a program. The proposed approach supports dynamic loop conditions and proves efficient at scale, even when the number of loops is very large. Evaluations found that the efficiency of RSP is 10x faster than the unrolling approach in some cases.

Keywords: SDN · High-level programming · Loop

1 Introduction

Software-Defined Networking (SDN) is one of the key technologies to support smart computing and communication [12,17] in the network domain. Recent developments in high-level SDN programming reduce the latency of packet processing while maintaining the flexibility of the programming model to make SDN applications smarter. The proactive approach that compiles the program to the datapath achieves this by removing the control message transfer between switches and the controller for the arriving packets. Keeping the high-level programming model for SDN programs reduces the risk of program bugs by increasing the readability of the program. Moreover, the high flexibility of the programming model allows programmers to describe complex logics with simple syntax such as if, else, while.

However, due to the hardware constraints, it is difficult to deploy complex logics into datapath; especially loops, which are very useful in high-level programming, but cannot be supported in the current datapath architecture (*i.e.*,

© Springer Nature Switzerland AG 2019
M. Qiu (Ed.): SmartCom 2019, LNCS 11910, pp. 253–265, 2019.
https://doi.org/10.1007/978-3-030-34139-8_25

multi-table pipeline). Therefore, to deploy loops in the datapath, they must be transformed while maintaining the logic.

A simple transformation is to apply a black-box model that views the whole loop as a single statement with multiple inputs and outputs. However, the single statement structure of the black-box approach cannot leverage the multi-table pipeline in the datapath. Potential flow table explosions due to the cross-product of match fields can substantially increase the number of flow rules.

Another transformation is the unrolling approach from the compiler domain that transforms the loop into sequential statements. Specifically, the unrolling approach in the compiler considers each iteration with a fixed, explicit iteration index, *e.g.*, i for most loops, and unfolds the loop into blocks of statements for each iteration based on the value of i. The blocks are then connected together. However, the unrolling approach is limited as it can only support loops with explicit numbers of iterations such as `while i in range(10)` (*i.e.*, *static loop condition*). More general loops such as `while pkt.vlan is None` and `while i <` `len(pkt.segmentList)` only determine the number of iterations during execution (*i.e.*, *dynamic loop condition*).

In this paper, we propose the RSP (Repeated Software Pipeline) transformation for the compilation of loops that can leverage the underlying multi-table pipeline structure (*i.e.*, the target of the transformation of the loop is a pipeline) and support dynamic loop conditions. The proposed approach shows improved efficiency when computing the *optimal* pipeline for a loop. Specifically, we demonstrate that for a class of n iteration loops to be deployed into multi-table pipelines with a limited number of tables (*i.e.*, the maximum number of tables is k), the pipeline design only takes into account the first k iterations of the loop (we assume that $n > k$). This property can be very useful when handling loops of no fixed number of iterations `while pkt.vlan is None`.

To summarize, this paper contributes the following:

- The first study of resolving dynamic loops in high-level SDN programs when compiling a program to multi-table pipelines.
- The RSP transformation, a new loop transformation which demonstrates that for a class of n iteration loops to be deployed to a multi-table pipeline with a limited number of tables (*i.e.*, the maximum number of tables is k), the pipeline design only needs to handle the first k iterations of the loop.

The rest of this paper is organized as follows. Section 2 gives the background of pipeline design and motivation for resolving loops in the pipeline design. Section 3 introduces the RSP transformation with definitions of basic concepts. Section 4 gives an analysis of the RSP transformation. Section 5 evaluates the RSP transformation. Section 6 surveys related work, and Sect. 7 concludes.

2   Pipeline Design and Motivation

In this section, we will first give a brief description of pipeline design in high-level SDN programs. Then, we will give the motivation for handling loops in these pipeline designs.

Fig. 1. The three flow tables for the simple routing program with the structure of each table $a \rightarrow b$ representing the matches of table a being written to table b.

2.1 Pipeline Design

High-level SDN programs specify what happens to every packet entering the network in a high-level language (compared to OpenFlow flow rules). In this paper, to ensure generality, we consider the "onPacket" programming model from SNAP [4] and the packet transaction [15] where conceptually each statement can be viewed as a flow table in the datapath pipeline [4,15]. For example, consider the following simple routing program:

```
L1: def onPacket(pkt):
L2:     policy = policy(pkt.srcIP)
L3:     dstSW = switch(pkt.dstIP)
L4:     route = route(policy, dstSW)
L5:     return route
```

This simple routing program routes packets based on policies specified by the source ip address of each packet. As each statement can be viewed as a flow table, the program can be converted to a pipeline with three flow tables as shown in the Fig. 1 (*i.e.*, the proactive program compilation to datapath). Note that the `return` statement does not require conversion. However, to satisfy the hardware conditions of openflow switches (*e.g.*, limited number of flow tables), some tables should be merged in the pipeline. For example, if the number of tables is limited to 2, then *sTable* and *rTable* can be merged into a single table whose matches are *dstIP* and *policy*. We denote this process as the *pipeline design* (*i.e.*, deciding which tables should be merged). Specifically, we denote the initial pipeline as the *software pipeline* and the new pipeline as *hardware pipeline* as it satisfies the hardware constraints.

Given the many pipeline design strategies with differing objectives and constraints, in this paper, we choose to focus on minimizing the total number of flow rules with limited numbers of flow tables in pipeline design. For example, in the simple routing software pipeline with 2 flow tables allowed, if the number of flow rules of both *pTable* and *sTable* are 1000 each, and the number of flow rules of *rTable* is 900, then merging *sTable* and *rTable* (where the total number of flow rules is 1000 + 1000 * 900) is preferable to merging *pTable* and *sTable* (where the total number of flow rules is 1000 * 1000 + 900). We further show that the second design is optimal. Note that in this paper, we do not consider table merging algorithms or corresponding flow rule compression as they have been well studied [9,11].

2.2 Motivation of Resolving Loops in Pipeline Design

To support high flexibility of programming which can realize smarter SDN applications, we should minimize constraints in the programming model. However, existing related works [4, 15] cannot support loops in their languages. The simple loop program demonstrates the utility of loops:

```
L1: def onPacket(pkt):
L2:     p = None; u = Max; ports = allPorts(pkt.dstIP)
L3:     for tp, tu in ports:
L4:         if u > tu:
L5:             u = tu
L6:             p = tp
```

The simple loop program first initiates a port (p) and its utilization (u), and selects a set of potential ports (line 2). Then it iterates all the potential ports (line 3 to line 6) and compares their port utilization to select the least utilized port. Though this can be achieved by defining the libraries for port selection without using a loop, the libraries would add constraints to the selection policies. Programmers should have enough flexibility to specify their own policies with high-level language (*i.e.*, line 4 to line 6).

As existing SDN datapaths (*e.g.*, [1]) do not support loops, transformation is required to generate loops in the hardware pipeline. There are two potential methods for the transformation:

The first method is the black-box approach that considers the whole loop as a single statement. The loop in the simple loop program can be viewed as a single flow table where the matches include p, u, and *dstIP*. The issues for this approach are: (1) It cannot leverage the multi-table pipeline structure in the datapath; (2) The table merging in the pipeline design used to compute the flow table rules is difficult to implement due to loop dependencies.

The second method is to leverage the unrolling technique in the compiler domain. The unrolling unfolds the loop by iterating the index of the loop (*i.e.*, the value of i). For example, the loop in the simple loop program may be transformed to:

(We first convert `for tp, tu in ports` to `for i in len(ports)`.)

```
L1: def onPacket(pkt):
L2:     ...
L3:     i = 0
L4:     ... #the loop body
L5:     i = 1
L6:     ... #the loop body
L7:     ... #i from 2 to len(ports) - 1
```

The benefits of the unrolling approach is that the transformed program can be applied by the pipeline design. But the limitations are: (1) The unrolling approach can only handle static loop conditions (*e.g.*, explicit numbers of iterations (*i.e.*, i)) which is limiting as the loop condition can be dynamic (*e.g.*, `while pkt.vlan is None`); (2) Even though the loop can be transformed into sequential statements, the long sequence of statements may degrade the pipeline design performance.

In this paper, we aim to resolve the loops in SDN programs by proposing efficient, repeated software pipeline (RSP) transformations which support the dynamic loop condition.

3   Repeated Software Pipeline (RSP) Transformation

In this section, we will first clarify some key concepts behind the introduction of loops to pipeline design before introducing the RSP transformation as motivated by these concepts.

3.1   Key Concepts

Pipeline: A pipeline pl consists of a sequence of tables, $t_1, t_2, ...t_m$. Each table t_i specifies a set of variables $t_i.inputV$ as the input variables and another set of variables $t_i.outputV$ as the output variables. (*i.e.*, packets in t_i can match $t_i.inputV$ and write values to $t_i.outputV$). The terminal actions, such as DROP or PORT(i), are instances of special output variables. After a packet pkt passes through t_i without any terminal action, pkt can jump to table t_j where $i < j$ to guarantee that there is no loop in pl. We denote a set of variables $pl.inputV$ as the input variables of pl that $pl.inputV = (\cup_{i=1,2,...,m} t_i.inputV - \cup_{i=1,2,...,m} t_i.outputV)$, and a set of variables $pl.outputV$ as the output variables of pl that $pl.outputV = (\cup_{i=1,2,...,m} t_i.outputV - \cup_{i=1,2,...,m} t_i.inputV)$. Specifically, the input/output variables of a pipeline refer to the variables that are accessed externally to the pipeline (*i.e.*, they can be set before the pipeline and read after the pipeline). If a table t has v_a as the input variable, the variable v_a is a hidden output variable of t. This is because if a rule in t matches a value of v_a, it means that the rule also outputs the same value of v_a.

Static Single Assignment: Given a pipeline pl, a static single assignment (SSA) form of pl means that each variable in pl can only be assigned once. An example of SSA can be found in the Fig. 2. From now on, we assume that every pipeline is of the SSA form.

Loop Condition and Loop Body: Given a loop in an SDN program, the loop condition is the control statement to check whether packets enter the loop or not. The loop body is the repeated process applied to the packets. In this paper, for simplicity, we consider the *while-loop* that has a boolean condition as the loop condition and a repeated code block as the loop body. We denote a loop condition is dynamic if it specifies the number of iterations during the execution.

3.2   Repeated Software Pipeline (RSP) Transformation

Given a loop in an SDN program, the RSP transformation does the following: (1) Extracts the loop condition and loop body, and links them together to generate a new set of statements; (2) Computes the software pipeline of the new set of statements (each statement can be viewed as a flow table); (3) Links multiple copies of the software pipelines to generate the RSP. As an example, if the loop condition is `while i < len(pkt.segmentList)` and the loop body is `test = True if check(pkt.srcAddr, pkt.segmentList[i++]) else False`, then the software pipeline is $(i, segmentList) \rightarrow None$, $(srcAddr, segmentList, i) \rightarrow (i, test)$. The first table is used to check whether to move to the next iteration or to break the loop. The RSP is multiple copies of the software pipeline connected together. Here is the formal definition of the RSP:

Repeated Software Pipeline (RSP): Given n pipelines (denoted as pl_1, pl_2, ... pl_n) that have the **same** layout and flow rules, we denote pl^n as the n RSP constructed as sequentially connecting pl_1, pl_2, ... pl_n. When a packet pkt passes through pl_i without any terminal action, such as DROP or PORT(i), pkt will arrive at pl_{i+1} for $1 \leq i < n$. An example of RSP and its SSA form are shown in Fig. 2.

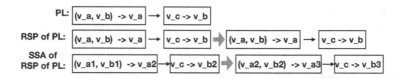

Fig. 2. Examples of a pipeline (PL), 2 RSP of PL and their SSA forms.

We observe that for a given a loop and its corresponding RSP, if a packet pkt enters the loop by repeating n times and then produces an output, pkt would have the same output as if pkt were to enter the n RSP. The intuition is that (considering the loop iterates $i = 0, 1, ..., n$) though for each software pipeline in the repeated pipeline, it has no difference from its peers, each pipeline would increment i by one each time. Therefore, a packet arriving at different pipeline may apply different rules and by passing through the n repeated pipeline, it can have the same output as the n iteration of the loop.

Having introduced the RSP, we apply it to pipeline design. In the next section, we give an analysis of the pipeline design based on RSP to show that it can be done efficiently and supports dynamic loop conditions (*i.e.*, effectiveness of RSP).

4   Analysis

In this section, we first give an analysis of the optimal pipeline design. We then give an analysis of the RSP to demonstrate its efficiency and efficacy.

4.1   Optimal Pipeline Design

We model the pipeline design as a partition problem based on the dataflow graph of the pipeline.

Dataflow Graph (DFG): Given a pipeline pl, we denote $DFG(pl)$ as the dataflow graph of pl which is a directed acyclic graph (V, E) in which a vertex $v \in V$ specifies a variable in pl and if there is a table t_i with $t_i.inputV = \{v_{i1}^i, v_{i2}^i, ... v_{i|t_i.inputV|}^i\}$ and $t_i.outputV = \{v_{i1}^o, v_{i2}^o, ... v_{i|t_i.outputV|}^o\}$ in pl, there are

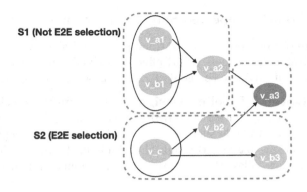

Fig. 3. The DFG of a pipeline and the source vertices selection. (Color figure online)

$|t_i.inputV| * |t_i.outputV|$ directed edges, $v_{i1}^i \rightarrow v_{i1}^o$, $v_{i2}^i \rightarrow v_{i1}^o$, ..., $v_{i|t_i.inputV|}^i \rightarrow v_{i|t_i.outputV|}^o$, in E. The DFG of the SSA formed pipeline in Fig. 2 is shown in Fig. 3.

Source Vertices Selection: Select a subset of source vertices in the DFG into a set S and if a vertex v in the DFG has all of its parent vertices in S, then v can be added to S. One selection can have multiple iterations of the adding process. After the selection, remove S (i.e., S is partitioned) from the original DFG and then S can be viewed as a flow table t such that a vertex without any parent in S is added to $t.inputV$ and a vertex without any child in S is added to $t.outputV$. The example of source vertices selection is shown in Fig. 3 where v_{a2} can be added to $S1$ but v_{a3} cannot (even after adding v_{a2} to $S1$) as some of its parents are not in $S1$. And by adding v_{b2} and v_{b3} to $S2$, the current selection can have three tables (as shown in the red dot line in Fig. 3): $(v_{a1}, v_{b1}) \rightarrow v_{a2}$, $v_c \rightarrow (v_{b2}, v_{b3})$, and $(v_{a2}, v_{b2}) \rightarrow v_{b3}$.

We model the pipeline design as several steps of the selections on the DFG of the pipeline. If the pipeline design has limited k tables, then there will be, at most, $k-1$ iterations of the selection process.

Greedy Property of the Optimal Pipeline Design: If a pipeline design is optimal, then it means the generated pipeline has the minimum number of flow rules. In this case, each step of the selection should be "greedy". That is, if v can be added to S, it is added. We denote this property as the *greedy* selection property. For example, in Fig. 3, to achieve the optimal pipeline, v_{b3} should be added to $S2$ otherwise there is another table: $v_c \rightarrow v_{b3}$. Given the limited number of pages, we omit an exhaustive proof but provide intuition in that, if there are two flow tables t_1 and t_2, and $t_2.inputV \subseteq (t_1.inputV \cup t_1.outputV)$, then merging t_2 into t_1 will not add extra flow rules. This means t_2 should be merged into t_1 in the optimal pipeline design to reduce the number of processing steps a given packet encounters, improving the per-packet processing latency.

4.2   Analysis on the Repeated Software Pipeline

Based on the *greedy* property of the optimal pipeline design, we start to demonstrate (by analysis) the efficiency and effectiveness of applying pipeline design on the RSP. We initially give the goal of the optimal pipeline design.

Goal of the Optimal Pipeline Design: To compute the pipeline with the minimum number of flow rules for the RSP pl^n with the hardware constraint that at most k tables are available such that $k < n$. As the pipeline depth influences the latency of packets passing through the pipeline, if two pipelines have the same number of flow rules, the pipeline with the smaller number of tables is preferred.

Complexity: As the complexity of the pipeline design depends on the number of vertices in the DFG, the pipeline design of pl^n where n is very large is a complex process. However, we show that the complexity is dependent on k, not n.

We first outline three concepts: single-output pipeline, end-to-end selection, and full-output table.

Single-Output Pipeline: A pipeline pl for which the output variables of pl only appear in the last table of pl. We denote such a pipeline as a single-output pipeline (SO-PL).

End-to-End (E2E) Selection: We denote source vertices selection (proper subset of all source vertices) on the DFG in which there is at least one sink vertex v in the DFG is selected (*i.e.*, v becomes the output variable in the flow table generated by the selection) as the E2E selection. An example of E2E selection is shown in Fig. 3. $S1$ is not E2E as v_{a3} also depends on v_{b2}. However, $S2$ is E2E as v_{b3} only depends on v_c.

From the definition of E2E selection, we find that there is no E2E selection in SO-PL as for any selection that has at least one sink vertex v selected, the ancestor of v should be all the source vertices (not a proper subset).

Full-Output Table: Given pl^n, if a table t_x whose output variables include all the input variables of a pipeline pl_i, then t_x is a full-output table of pl^n. By the *greedy* property, all the remaining tables should be merged to t_x if it is the optimal pipeline design. If there are multiple pipelines whose input variables are included in the output variables of t_x, we define the minimum index of these pipelines as $MinIndexPL(t_x)$. An example of a full-output table in the SSA pipeline is found in Fig. 2. This figure is a table (denoted by t_y) that matches v_{a2}, v_{b2}, v_c which are the input variables of the second pipeline. If the second pipeline has been merged into t_y, then the third pipeline (not shown in the figure) can be merged into t_y. In this case, $MinIndexPL(t_y)$ is still 2 which is the index of the second pipeline.

We provide the following proposition on the existence of the full-output table in the pipeline design.

Proposition 1. *Existence: If there is no E2E selection in the $DFG(pl_i)$ $\forall i \in 1, 2, ...n$, then by the pipeline design of pl^n into k tables $(k < n)$, there must exist at least one full-output table t_x in the merged k tables such that the output variables (including hidden output variables) of t_x include the input variables of a pipeline pl_i.*

Proof: We will give a proof by contradiction by assuming that there is no t_x in merged k tables.

Based on this assumption, we give a pipeline design that merges pl^n into the *minimum* number of tables as shown in Fig. 4. For the first pipeline pl_1, we select a proper subset of input variables of pl_1 to get a table t_1. (We avoid the whole input variables as this will get a t_x). As there is no E2E selection, the output variables of t_1 cannot include any of the output variables of pl_1. We consider a second table t_2 where the input variables are all the source vertices in the remaining DFG (which is different with the original source vertices as a set of vertices have already been partitioned). We find the output variables of t_2 cannot be the whole input variables of pl_2 as there is no t_x. Recursively, the output variables of t_3 cannot include the whole input variables of pl_3.

We find that this pipeline design gives the minimum number of tables which is $n + 1$. However, we have $n + 1 > k$ (which overfills the limited number of flow tables), the assumption that there is no t_x is therefore false.

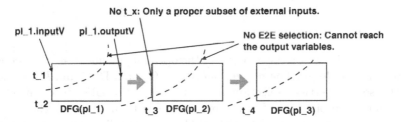

No t_x: Only a proper subset of external inputs.

pl_1.inputV   pl_1.outputV

No E2E selection: Cannot reach the output variables.

t_1

t_2   DFG(pl_1)   t_3   DFG(pl_2)   t_4   DFG(pl_3)

Fig. 4. The proof of existence proposition that three pipelines (pl_1, pl_2, pl_3) can only be merged to four tables (t_1, t_2, t_3, t_4) at least with the assumption. Each block is a DFG of a pipeline.

The existence proposition says that if we want to merge pl^n into k tables where $k < n$, and if there is no E2E selection in the DFG of pl^n, then there must exist at least one full-output table in the merged tables. Multiple full-output tables are available as the optimality of pipeline design is not involved in the existence proposition.

Based on the existence of the full-output table proposition, we now give the position proposition of the full-output table where we consider the *optimal* pipeline design.

Proposition 2. *Position: If there is no E2E selection in the $DFG(pl_i)$ $\forall i \in 1, 2, ...n$, then by the optimal pipeline design of pl^n into at most k tables $(k < n)$, there must exist exactly one full-output table t_x in the merged at most k tables and $MinIndexPL(t_x) \leq k$.*

Proof: If a full-output table appears, for the requirement of optimal pipeline design (*i.e.*, the *greedy* property), all the following tables/pipelines should be merged into the full-output table. Therefore, there is exactly one full-output table t_x. If $MinIndexPL(t_x) > k$, then the first k pipelines must be merged into $k - 1$ tables at least, which is excluded by the existence proposition.

Summary: If each software pipeline is the SO-PL (*i.e.*, no E2E selection) in the pl^n, then for the optimal pipeline design of pl^n into at most k tables ($k < n$), the pipeline design should only consider the first k software pipelines instead of all n pipelines (as the result of pipeline design with the first k pipelines is the same as the n pipelines by the position proposition), which demonstrates the efficiency as the complexity of the pipeline design does not scale with n pipelines. Further, for the effectiveness, even though the number of iterations cannot be specified prior to execution, it only requires us to consider the first k pipelines which will have the optimal pipeline design for the merging to at most k tables.

5   Evaluation

In this section, we evaluate the proposed RSP design from two aspects: the execution time of pipeline design and the number of flow rules of the generated pipeline. All evaluations are run on a 3.5 GHz Intel i7 processor with 16 GB of RAM running Mac OSX 10.13.

5.1   Execution Time

Methodology: Based on the analysis of the optimal pipeline design, we consider the following simple pipeline design algorithm: Given a DFG and k, recursively apply the source vertices selection $k - 1$ times on the DFG to enumerate all possible hardware pipelines. For the evaluation of both RSP and the unrolling approach, we randomly generate the DFG with the following criteria: For the RSP, we change the number of software pipelines in the RSP (*i.e.*, the number of iterations of the loop, n) and the number of vertices in the DFG of each pipeline (given the number of vertices, randomly generate the dataflow graph); For the unrolling approach, for each generated software pipeline in the RSP, we remove several vertices randomly. Then, we compare the execution time of the RSP approach to the unrolling approach. Note that the complexity of enumerating all the possible pipelines is equivalent to finding the optimal pipeline as we do not consider the merging algorithm.

Result: The results are shown in Fig. 5. The horizontal axis specifies the number of iterations of the loop (n). The difference between Fig. 5a and Fig. 5b is the number of vertices (m) in the DFG of each software pipeline (for the unrolling approach, it means the number before removing vertices randomly) where $m = 10$ in Fig. 5a and $m = 20$ in Fig. 5b. All the pipeline designs have the same $k = 10$ as the limited number of flow tables. From the results, we see that the RSP approach has reduced execution time compared with the unrolling approach

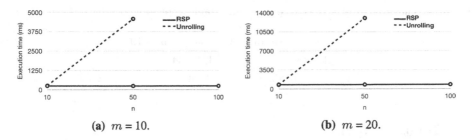

Fig. 5. The execution time of two approaches by changing the number of iterations (n) and the number of vertices (m).

when $k < n$ (around 10 times when $n = 50$ and $m = 10$). Note that when $n = 10$, both RSP and the unrolling approach consider 10 software pipelines in the pipeline design, therefore, the execution time of both approaches is the same. And when $n = 100$, the execution time of unrolling is too large compared with the RSP approach.

5.2   Number of Flow Rules

Methodology: To compute the number of flow rules, we assign each variable (*i.e.*, the vertex of DFG) the size of domain (*i.e.*, the number of available values for the variable) randomly. Specifically, for the source vertices in the DFG of each software pipeline, we set the value from 100 to 200. And for the internal vertices in the DFG, we set the value from 10 to 20. This is because for the source vertices, they may represent packet fields which should have a larger range of values compared with internal variables in the program. Also, given a flow table, the computation of number of flow rules equals to the product of the size of domain of all the input variables. The definitions of n and m remain the same as the evaluation of execution time. We compare the number of flow rules of RSP design with the black-box approach (*i.e.*, single table approach).

Result: The results are shown in Table. 1. As for the single table approach, the number of flow rules only depends on the first DFG of all software pipelines (which equals the product of the size of domains of all the source vertices of the first DFG), so the values are the same for different n. From the result, we find that the multi-table design can reduce the number of flow rules significantly compared with the single table approach. It is of note that the RSP approach, for each table, may have a lot of unused flow rules. For example, the `while i in range(100)` statement can be viewed as a flow table that matches i and writes to i with 100 flow rules (*i.e.*, i = 0, 2, ..., 99), which has 99 unused flow rules when the table is the first table. Therefore, the number of flow rules can be reduced further by existing work which will not be discussed in this paper.

Table 1. The number of flow rules of the single table approach and the RSP approach.

	n = 10, m = 10	n = 50, m = 10
Single	3898434	3898434
RSP	61856	224098

6   Related Work

High-Level SDN Programming Model: For the reactive high-level SDN programming models [8,14,16], packets are forwarded to the controller to compute actions. Maple [16] can support arbitrary processing on the packets including the loop. However, it processes the packets in the controller which increases latency. For the proactive programming models [4,15], though they can be compiled to the datapath by leveraging the multi-table pipeline, they do not support loops in their models.

SDN Control Platform: There are several SDN control platforms and architectures [2,3,6,7,10] that support loops for the upper layer applications by providing APIs to access packets in the controller. However, they are low-level programming models (OpenFlow [13] protocol) and also increase latency in packet handling.

Programming Datapath: P4 [5] provides the programming capability that the pipeline can be re-configured with the P4 language to the datapath. However, the P4 cannot support loops in its programming model.

7   Conclusions

In this paper, we have proposed RSP to resolve loops in SDN programs for the pipeline design. Specifically, for a class of n iteration loops to be deployed to a multi-table pipeline with a limited number of tables (i.e., the maximum number of tables is k), the pipeline design only needs to handle the first k iterations of the loop. It makes RSP very useful when there are dynamic loop conditions or the number of iterations of the loop is very large.

Acknowledgement. The authors would like to thank the anonymous reviewers for their insightful comments. This work is partly supported by National Key R&D Project 2018YFB2100800; NSFC 61972253, 61672349.

References

1. Broadcom: of-dpa. https://docs.broadcom.com/docs/12378911/
2. Floodlight openflow controller. http://floodlight.openflowhub.org/
3. The opendaylight project. https://www.opendaylight.org

4. Arashloo, M.T., Koral, Y., Greenberg, M., Rexford, J., Walker, D.: SNAP: stateful network-wide abstractions for packet processing. In: Proceedings of the 2016 Conference on ACM SIGCOMM 2016 Conference, pp. 29–43. ACM (2016)
5. Bosshart, P., et al.: P4: programming protocol-independent packet processors. SIGCOMM Comput. Commun. Rev. **44**(3), 87–95 (2014)
6. Chen, L., Qiu, M., Dai, W., Jiang, N.: Supporting high-quality video streaming with SDN-based CDNs. J. Supercomput. **73**(8), 3547–3561 (2017)
7. Erickson, D.: The beacon openflow controller. In: Proceedings of the Second ACM SIGCOMM Workshop on Hot Topics in Software Defined Networking, pp. 13–18. ACM (2013)
8. Foster, N., et al.: Frenetic: a network programming language. ACM Sigplan Not. **46**(9), 279–291 (2011)
9. Ge, J., Chen, Z., Wu, Y., E, Y.: H-SOFT: a heuristic storage space optimisation algorithm for flow table of openflow. Concurr. Comput. Pract. Exp. **27**(13), 3497–3509 (2015)
10. Gude, N., et al.: NOX: towards an operating system for networks. ACM SIGCOMM Comput. Commun. Rev. **38**(3), 105–110 (2008)
11. Gupta, P., McKeown, N.: Algorithms for packet classification. IEEE Netw. **15**(2), 24–32 (2001)
12. Han, Q., Meikang, Q., Zhihui, L., Memmi, G.: An efficient key distribution system for data fusion in V2X heterogeneous networks. Inf. Fusion **50**, 212–220 (2019)
13. McKeown, N., et al.: OpenFlow: enabling innovation in campus networks. ACM SIGCOMM Comput. Commun. Rev. **38**(2), 69–74 (2008)
14. Monsanto, C., Reich, J., Foster, N., Rexford, J., Walker, D.: Composing software defined networks. In: 10th USENIX Symposium on Networked Systems Design and Implementation (NSDI 2013), pp. 1–13 (2013)
15. Sivaraman, A., et al.: Packet transactions: high-level programming for line-rate switches. In: Proceedings of the 2016 ACM SIGCOMM Conference, pp. 15–28. ACM (2016)
16. Voellmy, A., Wang, J., Yang, Y.R., Ford, B., Hudak, P.: Maple: simplifying SDN programming using algorithmic policies. In: ACM SIGCOMM Computer Communication Review, vol. 43, pp. 87–98. ACM (2013)
17. Wang, X., Wang, C., Zhang, J., Zhou, M., Jiang, C.: Improved rule installation for real-time query service in software-defined internet of vehicles. IEEE Trans. Intell. Transp. Syst. **18**(2), 225–235 (2016)

DC Coefficients Recovery from AC Coefficients in the JPEG Compression Scenario

Han Qiu[1], Qinkai Zheng[1], Meikang Qiu[2(✉)], and Gerard Memmi[1]

[1] LTCI, Telecom Paris, 75013 Paris, France
{han.qiu,qinkai.zheng,gerard.memmi}@telecom-paris.fr
[2] Department of Computer Science, Texas A&M University-Commerce,
Commerce, TX, USA
meikang.qiu@tamuc.edu

Abstract. With the deployment of multimedia compression techniques, contents such as images or videos are transmitted through resource-constrained networks such as Internet of Things (IoT) scenarios. Traditional multimedia compression methods based on spatial-frequency transforms and coding techniques have been progressively improving and approaching the theoretical limit of Shannon. Therefore some new approaches are proposing to transmit only a part of the compressed data and recover the missing part at the receiver's end. In this paper, we propose to follow this idea to highly enhance the JPEG compression by transmitting all AC coefficients and only four DC coefficients of one image. On the receiver's end, we propose two methods to rebuild the missing DC coefficients based on the remaining DCT coefficient relationships. The first method considers the pixel relationship compared with the adjacent blocks on multiple directions. The second method considers not only the pixel relationship between adjacent blocks but also the existing relationship inside the adjacent blocks. As a result, our proposed method recovers the transmitted JPEG image with more than 25 dB considering PSNR while transmitting only 40–60% of the size of the JPEG images.

Keywords: DCT · Image compression · JPEG · Image transmission · Dc coefficients recovery

1 Introduction

Over the last few decades, big data generation and transmission have greatly evolved and expanded at a remarkably fast pace [2,9]. The most significant algorithms for multimedia transmission are compression algorithms which could compress large, raw multimedia data while preserving the content quality. For instance, lossy and lossless compression algorithms have allowed for the efficient and reliable transmission of multimedia data in images and/or videos [3].

© Springer Nature Switzerland AG 2019
M. Qiu (Ed.): SmartCom 2019, LNCS 11910, pp. 266–276, 2019.
https://doi.org/10.1007/978-3-030-34139-8_26

Most of today's multimedia data are compressed based on information theory. It generally can be seen as the combination of lossy transformation algorithms to generate frequency coefficients and lossless coding technology to compress the quantized frequency coefficients [13]. Discrete Cosine Transform (DCT), firstly introduced in [1], is the most widely used transform in multimedia coding supporting image and video coding standards such as JPEG, MPEG-1/2, MPEG-4, AVC/H.264 [10], and the more recent HEVC [14]. Such information-theory-based compression algorithms mainly requires two steps: quantization and coding. Quantization is commonly performed by dividing the frequency coefficients by a constant value (e.g. Q50 table in JPEG standard [6]) and then rounding these values into integers. The physical meaning of the DCT is to compress the energy of a highly-correlated discrete signal into a few coefficients which belong to the low frequency area; since human visual system (brain plus eyes) studies reveal that humans are more sensitive to low frequency coefficients than high frequency coefficients. Then, the quantization table is designed to reduce the values of the coefficients in the high frequency area. This typically leads to unrecoverable loss compared with initial pixel data in the spatial domain in standards such as JPEG with the Q50 table. This is then followed by the encoding for the quantized frequency coefficients (e.g. Huffman coding used in JPEG [6]).

However, with the wide deployment of big data technology, current compression algorithms for multimedia data are unable to meet modern requirements. As a standard that has been released for more than twenty years, the JPEG standard performs compression with using the quantization and rounding steps which introduces unrecoverable loss. As a result, former research has made an attempt to improve the compression standard. For instance, one approach is to improve the JPEG decompression by enhancing the image quality by rebuilding the details that are lost in the compression step. Another approach is to optimize the data compression ratios while preserving the same image quality.

In this paper, we explore another option which compresses the DCT coefficients by only keeping the AC coefficients at the sender's end while the DC coefficients are accurately recovered at the receiver's end. For the recovery and reconstruction process, previous research mostly aimed at recovering high frequency coefficients (they are the less significant ones) at the execution ends to improve the image/video quality. This could help provide better image/video quality which can improve the efficiency and accuracy of multimedia-based data mining [11]. However, recovering low frequency coefficients, especially DC coefficients, from the high-frequency ones are rarely addressed [7].

Our main contribution in this paper is that we update previous work in [8] by highly improving the accuracy of the DC coefficients recovery based on the AC coefficients. With this technique, the JPEG image can then be compressed with only AC coefficients and a very limited number of DC coefficients as references to rebuilding the remaining DC coefficients at the receiver's end.

The organization of this paper is as follows. We begin with a brief background on related research in Sect. 2. In Sect. 3, existing problems are introduced with our research motivation. Section 4 evaluates our recovery results based on visual and statistical analysis. We conclude in Sect. 5.

2   Research Background

2.1   Practical Definition of DC Coefficients

Since DCT has different types shown in [4], the most popular DCT algorithm is a two-dimensional symmetric variation of the transform that operates on 8×8 blocks (DCT 8×8) and its inverse (iDCT 8×8). This DCT 8×8 is used in JPEG compression routines [13] and has become an important standard in image and video compression steps.

According to the definition of the DCT transformation [4], the DC coefficient is the average value of the input elements. Thus, the DC coefficients of the DCT transform of image blocks represent the mean values of the pixel values in the corresponding image blocks. We illustrate this definition by an example of one 8×8 block shown in Fig. 1. In the Fig. 1(a), we list the pixel values on the z-axis for the original 8×8 block. Then, we add the DC coefficient in the DCT result and do the iDCT to get the pixel values with only the DC coefficient increased in Fig. 1(b). The pixel value distribution has not changed in Fig. 1(a) and (b) but only every pixel value is added with the same value.

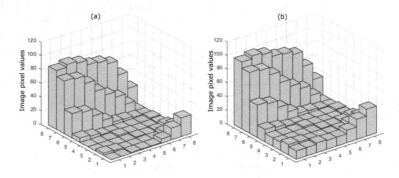

Fig. 1. An example of the definition of a DC coefficient in an 8×8 block: (a) original distribution of pixel values (b) distribution of pixel values when the DC coefficient is increased.

Thus, for one JPEG image, if all DC coefficients in every 8×8 block are replaced with zero, the relative difference of the pixel values still exist without any loss. We could consider that for the pixel value distribution on one JPEG image when all the DC coefficients are zero means that every 8×8 block still maintains the distribution inside the block, but the difference is the average value of the different blocks. Based on this practical explanation for the DC coefficients, the motivation of this research is to transmit only the AC coefficients in each block at the sender's end and to recover the corresponding DC coefficients at the receiver's end to achieve a higher compression ratio for JPEG images.

2.2   Previous Work on the DC Coefficient Recovery

The initial question of the DC coefficients recovery was proposed in [12] since the early stage of SE methods used to protect the DC coefficients of each 8×8 block to further protect the image content. Such image protection methods are deployed on the JPEG images or other images formats with DCT transformation. The implementation of such methods showed a hard visual deterioration for the images, but the authors in [12] showed that the DC coefficients of the 8×8 JPEG blocks can be estimated using the remaining AC coefficients.

The estimation method is based on the observed statistical distribution of the image property in [12]; in general, the distribution of differences at the pixel level and the DC coefficients have been modeled as a zero-mean Laplacian distributed variate. This distribution is generally narrow with a small value of variance. Therefore, we could assume the value of variance as zero to determine the difference of the DC coefficients of the adjacent 8×8 block. This method was tested in [12] for the DC coefficients recovery in JPEG images and further improved in [8]. However, one serious issue arises in that tiny errors occur if we use the DC coefficient in the 8×8 block $B_{(i,j)}$ to estimate the adjacent 8×8 block $B_{(i+1,j)}$ and this error will propagate. As shown in [8], although the recovery results have an acceptable PSNR value and the image contents can be observed, the error propagation will lead to multiple edges in the image contents.

The other approach is based on the optimization method shown in [5] as this issue can be solved by Linear Programming (LP) techniques for the basic DC recovery problem as well as the general DCT coefficients recovery problem. The authors in [5] were able to recover the image content even when more than 15 AC coefficients were missing. In a bitmap case, while more than half of the low frequency coefficients are missing, a rough recovery for the image content is still possible [7]. However, this approach does not suit our use case since the image format we want to support is JPEG. In JPEG images, after the quantization and rounding processing steps [6], most of the DCT coefficients are rounded to zeros (there could be more than 90% of the DCT coefficients in the JPEG images being zeros as pointed out in [8]). Although this LP approach can optimize the calculation and remove the edges due to the error propagation, the recovery results lost much detailed information. The summarized problem definition and the main motivation of our research is described in Sect. 3.1.

3   Design and Implementation

In this section, the motivation of our research is explained. The general design of the method is first presented and then followed by details of the experimentation. We also briefly point out how this method can be used in a practical image transmission scenario.

3.1   Research Motivation and Problem Definition

As discussed in Sect. 2.2, there are two main approaches to solve the DC coefficient recovery problems. In fact, in this special-use case where only DC coefficients are missing for JPEG images, all AC coefficients have remained which means that for each 8 × 8 block, the relative pixel value distribution accurately remains. If we use the method operated in the spatial domain or try to optimize the image content with the LP approach, even the recovered image is more smooth and most of the AC coefficients have changed. Therefore, we not only failed to recover the accurate DC coefficient but also incorporated the errors for the AC coefficients. Thus, we use the first approach that is focused on how to recover the image content by accurately recovering the DC coefficients without changing the AC coefficients.

We first indicate that the basic observed theory in [12] does not fit the practical scenario with an example shown in Fig. 2. These two 8 × 8 blocks are chosen from an image and the adjacent two vectors of the adjacent pixels are very different. In this case, the method in [8] which is always trying to find the DC value to achieve the minimum Mean Square Error (MSE) of two adjacent blocks will result in wrong predictions for the DC value since the real case is that the MSE is very large.

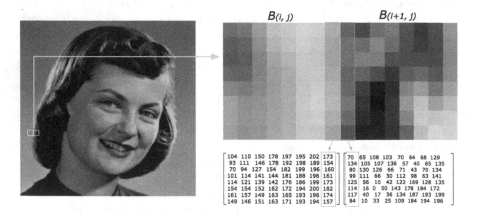

Fig. 2. An example of the real case of pixel value distribution that does not fit the zero-mean Laplacian distributed variance in adjacent two blocks.

In Fig. 2, if we know the DC value of the block $B_{(i,j)}$ is 80, based on the min MSE method in [8], the predicted DC value of the block $B_{(i+1,j)}$ is 82. The difference of the two adjacent vectors in Fig. 2 is $[7, -13, -15, 3, 9, -1, 2, 19]$ while the real DC value of the block $B_{(i+1,j)}$ is 49 and the difference of the adjacent 8 pixels is $[103, 20, 80, 62, 48, 68, 57, 73]$. Therefore, the problem to be solved is for cases shown in Fig. 2 which do not fit the observed statistical theory in [12], or how to accurately estimate the DC coefficients.

3.2   Proposed Method

In [8], the smallest MSE of the adjacent pixels between two adjacent blocks is considered to exist in three directions as shown in [12]. The Mean-Square

Error (MSE) [8] is used to test the variance between two adjacent blocks on the three directions respectively to pick out the smallest MSE as the estimation results. However, as pointed in Sect. 3.1, this smallest MSEs of the adjacent pixels between two adjacent blocks do not always exist. Therefore, we improve this method by further exploring the pixel relationships with two steps as shown in Fig. 4.

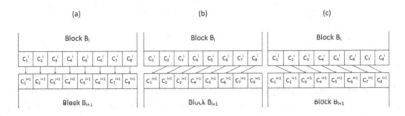

Fig. 3. Three directions to calculate the MSE of adjacent pixels of adjacent blocks [8].

The MSEs of the adjacent pixels of adjacent blocks for the three directions are calculated as shown in Fig. 3 and calculated as in the Eqs. (1)–(3):

$$MSE_a(B_i, B_{i+1}) = \frac{1}{8} \sum_{j=1}^{8} (c_j^i - c_j^{i+1})^2 \tag{1}$$

$$MSE_b(B_i, B_{i+1}) = \frac{1}{7} \sum_{j=1}^{7} (c_{j+1}^i - c_j^{i+1})^2 \tag{2}$$

$$MSE_c(B_i, B_{i+1}) = \frac{1}{7} \sum_{j=1}^{7} (c_j^i - c_{j+1}^{i+1})^2 \tag{3}$$

The method used in [8] is to estimate the DC coefficient of one block from its left adjacent block like a scan from left to right. This scan will move from up to down, from right to left, and from down to up respectively and then the DC coefficients of the blocks are calculated from the average value of the four scans. However, due to the error propagation, the calculation of the average cannot overcome the propagated errors of DCs and the results are in Fig. 5(c), (f), (j).

We improve this MSE-based calculation with two steps. The first is to calculate the three directions [8] of MSEs of the adjacent pixels for the vertical and horizontal adjacent blocks as shown in Fig. 4(a). The purpose is not to find the best estimation between two adjacent blocks in the vertical and horizontal adjacent blocks but to calculate the average value of these two predicted DC coefficients. Based on the observed results, some blocks are not smooth considering their left blocks but are smooth on pixel distribution comparing with their up blocks. This step can be used to make up the error due to the intensive pixel value change in the spatial domain.

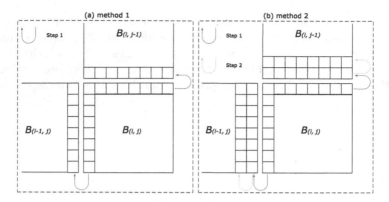

Fig. 4. An example of the proposed method: (a) calculate the average of the adjacent pixels' MSEs with the vertical and horizontal adjacent blocks; (b) calculate the pixels' MSEs most similar with the MSE of the pixels in the last two columns/rows of the adjacent blocks.

Then, the second step is to calculate the most similar MSE value considering the MSE values of the adjacent blocks' last two columns/rows as shown in Fig. 4(b). In other words, we do not calculate the DC value that can make the two adjacent blocks have the smoothest pixel distribution at its boundary. The predicted DC value we are looking for is the DC value that can make the pixel distribution of the boundary the most similar with the pixel distribution of the last two columns/rows of pixels in the adjacent blocks.

According to the JPEG standard [6], if the Q50 quantization table is deployed, the DC values in all 8×8 blocks are integers within the range: $DC \in [-64, +64]$. Thus, for the purposes of experimentation, we assume that the DC coefficients of the four corner 8 blocks are reserved and all other DC coefficients are stored as zeros for enhancing the JPEG compression. At the receiver's end, the DC recovery method is deployed to predict the DC values according to the only known DC coefficients of the four 8×8 blocks at the four corners of the image.

In other words, for Method 2, we try to consider the pixel distributions based on not only the adjacent blocks' relationship but also the pixel distributions of the last two columns/rows of the pixel distributions in the adjacent blocks. Since all AC values are preserved, the relative relationship of the pixel distribution inside one block still exists. This method is based on observations in [8] where the pixel distributions of the two columns/rows of pixels of the two adjacent blocks is similar to the pixel distributions of the last two columns/rows of pixels in the adjacent blocks. With a mathematical simulation, the calculation for one block $B_{(i,j)}$ is presented in Eq. (4) to find the smoothest pixel distributions with the last two columns/rows of the adjacent blocks.

$$\underset{DC \in (-64, +64)}{\arg\min} \left| MSE_a(B_{(i,j)}, B_{(i-1,j)}) - MSE_a(B_{(i-1,j)}[1:8,8], B_{(i-1,j)}[1:8,7]) \right| \quad (4)$$

After the DC prediction based on Eq. (4), which is the vertical direction, the DC prediction is also carried out horizontally which is to calculate the block $B_{(i,j)}$ and block $B_{(i,j-1)}$. Then, the two DC values are used to generate an average value to be the final predicted DC value.

As a result, this method does not change any of the AC values but only predicts the DC values based on the pixel distributions. Nor does it work at the boundary of the two adjacent blocks but also at the pixel distributions of the last two columns/rows inside the adjacent blocks.

4   Evaluation and Comparison

In this section, we evaluate the recovery results with the visual results and the statistical analysis. The statistical methods are also deployed to prove the effectiveness of the proposed methods.

4.1   Visual Effects Evaluation

Here, we take three images as examples to show the effectiveness of the recovery method. For the evaluation, we keep only four DC coefficients of the four 8 × 8 blocks at the four corners of the image. The recovery method is performed by recovering all DC coefficients from the four corners respectively and then calculating the average value as the predicted DC values. The visual results of recovered images and the comparison are listed in Fig. 5.

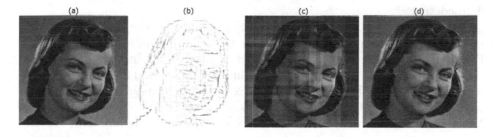

Fig. 5. The visual results: (a) original JPEG image; (b) visual results of the JPEG image when all DC coefficients are zeros; (c) Recovery result in [8]; (d) Recovery result based on the Method 2 in this paper.

We also compare the details of the recovered images by the two methods described in this paper. We pick two areas and the visual results are enlarged to show the difference of the block effects. The details of the comparison of Methods 1 and 2 are shown in Fig. 6. The observation is that the block effects are slightly reduced in these areas. Since the JPEG format is already losing the image details and block effects exist in the JPEG images, the results in Fig. 6(b) are very similar to the JPEG image.

Fig. 6. The comparison between method 1 and method 2 with details

4.2   Statistical Evaluation

We use the *Peak Signal to Noise Ratio (PSNR)* and *Structural SIMilarity (SSIM)* used in [9] to evaluate the recovered images compared with original images. Compared with the previous work, the statistical results of the PSNR and SSIM have clearly improved. One point must be made which is that the PSNR is used to measure the noise compared with the ground truth images and can also be used to measure the similarity between two images. However, the recovered images in Fig. 6 do not have noises according to the traditional definition [15] since the noise is defined as the errors mainly in the high frequency band. The recovered elements are only DC coefficients rather than the pixel values which means all the AC coefficients are exactly the same with the JPEG compression results. Thus, the block effects we observed in Fig. 6 are not caused by the traditional defined "noise".

We still use the PSNR to evaluate the results and the image in Fig. 5(a) is used as an example. Compared with the original image, we calculate the PSNR for the image without DC coefficients, the JPEG image, the recovered image with Method 1, and the recovered image with Method 2, respectively. The results are listed in Table 1 and Method 2 shows slight improvement compared with Method 1. For the SSIM results also listed in Table 1, the improvement of Method 2 compared with Method 1 is also shown. In fact, we also tested several images and there were always slight improvements using Method 2 on the image recovery compared to Method 1.

Table 1. PSNR between original JPEG images and recovered images.

Image	no DC	JPEG	Method 1	Method 2
PSNR	11.9 dB	30.1 dB	24.7 dB	25.3 dB
SSIM	66%	92%	85%	88%

4.3   Compression Ratio Evaluation

Since the practical use case in this paper is to transmit only four DC coefficients of the four corner blocks in one image, the compression ratio is obviously reduced since the DC coefficients are relatively larger than the AC coefficients. The calculation of the compression ratio is deployed with the practical coding process of the JPEG standard which is using the entropy coding (Huffman encoding and decoding) [6]. As there are always four DC coefficients kept, the compression ratio also relies on the image size since the block size is set to 8×8 and each block has one DC coefficient.

We test different sizes of images to calculate the compression ratio with the standard Huffman coding and the Q50 table. The evaluation results are that for small JPEG images such as 256×256, the compression ratio improved about 20%. However, for the large JPEG images such as 4000×3000, the compression improved about 200%. The compression ratio also depends on the image content. For instance, for one image with fewer details, there will be fewer high frequency coefficients so the DC coefficients take more storage space.

5   Conclusion

In this paper, we redesigned the DC coefficients recovery algorithm for the JPEG images to get an additional 40–60% compression ratio. Compared with existing solutions, our method can achieve the highest accuracy when recovering DC coefficients at the receiver's end. Based on only four DC coefficients at the corner blocks of the image, the remaining DC coefficients can be accurately recovered and the edge effects in the previous work are removed. This method can be used for enhancing the JPEG compression by only transmitting four DC coefficients at the four corners which highly improved the JPEG compression ratio.

References

1. Ahmed, N., Natarajan, T., Rao, K.R.: Discrete cosine transform. IEEE Trans. Comput. **100**(1), 90–93 (1974)
2. David, R., John, G., John, R.: Data age 2025: the digitization of the world, from edge to core. In: IDC White Paper. Seagate (2018)
3. Fisher, Y.: Fractal Image Compression: Theory and Application. Springer, Berlin (2012). https://doi.org/10.1007/978-1-4612-2472-3
4. Kresch, R., Merhav, N.: Fast DCT domain filtering using the DCT and the DST. IEEE Trans. Image Process. **8**(6), 821–833 (1999)
5. Li, S., Karrenbauer, A., Saupe, D., Kuo, C.C.J.: Recovering missing coefficients in DCT-transformed images. In: 2011 18th IEEE International Conference on Image Processing (ICIP), pp. 1537–1540. IEEE (2011)
6. Pennebaker, W.B., Mitchell, J.L.: JPEG: Still Image Data Compression Standard. Springer, Berlin (1992)
7. Qiu, H., Enfrin, N., Memmi, G.: A case study for practical issues of DCT based bitmap selective encryption methods. In: IEEE International Conference on Security of Smart Cities, Industrial Control System and Communications. IEEE (2018)

8. Qiu, H., Memmi, G., Chen, X., Xiong, J.: DC coefficient recovery for JPEG images in ubiquitous communication systems. Future Gener. Comput. Syst. **96**, 23–31 (2019)
9. Qiu, H., Noura, H., Qiu, M., Ming, Z., Memmi, G.: A user-centric data protection method for cloud storage based on invertible DWT. IEEE Trans. Cloud Comput. (2019)
10. Schwarz, H., Marpe, D., Wiegand, T.: Overview of the scalable video coding extension of the H. 264/AVC standard. IEEE Trans. Circuits Syst. Video Technol. **17**(9), 1103–1120 (2007)
11. Thuraisingham, B.: Data Mining: Technologies, Techniques, Tools, and Trends. CRC Press, Boca Raton (2014)
12. Uehara, T., Safavi-Naini, R., Ogunbona, P.: Recovering DC coefficients in block-based DCT. IEEE Trans. Image Process. **15**(11), 3592–3596 (2006)
13. Wallace, G.K.: The JPEG still picture compression standard. IEEE Trans. Consum. Electron. **38**(1), 18–34 (1992)
14. Zeng, J., Au, O.C., Dai, W., Kong, Y., Jia, L., Zhu, W.: A tutorial on image/video coding standards. In: 2013 Asia-Pacific Signal and Information Processing Association Annual Summit and Conference (APSIPA), pp. 1–7. IEEE (2013)
15. Zhang, J., Cox, I.J., Doerr, G.: Steganalysis for LSB matching in images with high-frequency noise. In: 2007 IEEE 9th Workshop on Multimedia Signal Processing. pp. 385–388. IEEE (2007)

A Performance Evaluation Method of Coal-Fired Boiler Based on Neural Network

Yingyue Chen[1]([⊠]), Lijun Xiao[2], and Osama Hosam[3]

[1] The School of Economic and Management, Xiamen University of Technology,
Xiamen 361024, Fujian, China
chenyingyue@xmut.edu.cn
[2] The Department of Accounting,
Guangzhou College of Technology and Business,
Guangzhou 5108501, Guangdong, China
[3] The College of Computer Science and Engineering College,
Saudi Arabia University, Riyadh, Saudi Arabia

Abstract. According to the evaluation and control of energy-saving and emission reduction performance of coal-fired boilers, the performance indexes of boiler combustion and emissions were studied, and a performance evaluation and control method based on neural network was proposed. Firstly, the influencing factors of boiler combustion emission are analyzed. A boiler combustion emission evaluation model based on AdaBoost-BP algorithm is designed. The model is trained and tested by coal-fired power plant data and national emission standards, and the principal component analysis method is adopted. The core parameters are adjusted to get the best control solution. Finally, experiments show that the model and method have better advantages in comparison with similar methods.

Keywords: Coal-fired boiler · Emission · Neural network · Performance evaluation · Control

1 Introduction

As people's demand for electric energy increases, NOX pollution emissions based on coal-fired power supply have become one of the largest sources of atmospheric pollution in China. At present, the average coal consumption of thermal power in China is 321 g/(kw h), and 90% of SO2 and 67% of NOX in the atmosphere comes from coal combustion. The air pollution caused by thermal power generation is very impressive. Therefore, China's coal industry energy conservation and emission reduction is imperative, which is related to the health of people and stability and harmony of society [1]. In recent years, there have been many researches on energy saving and emission reduction of coal-fired boilers at home and abroad, and many achievements have been made.

In terms of model construction, Zhao [2] used the data collected by power station boilers to perform multiple repeated simulation studies and emission processes; Chen [3] adopted fuzzy neural network modeling method to optimize model parameters by

© Springer Nature Switzerland AG 2019
M. Qiu (Ed.): SmartCom 2019, LNCS 11910, pp. 277–285, 2019.
https://doi.org/10.1007/978-3-030-34139-8_27

using an algorithm. And the better modeling effect is achieved; Safa and Spentzos [4, 5] used artificial neural network modeling, and combined genetic algorithm and fluid dynamics calculation to optimize the model parameters, and through experimental tests, satisfactory boiler combustion system mode was established.

In terms of model optimization, Xie [6] established a model of boiler combustion process by using neural network modeling. He also used genetic algorithm to optimize boiler thermal efficiency, and achieved good results. Wang [7] established the model of boiler combustion characteristics through genetics algorithm and neural network, optimized the oxygen content and the boiler combustion process. Gu [8] used the fuzzy correlation mining algorithm to optimize the model parameters and obtained a satisfactory model of boiler combustion characteristics.

The above studies have played a very beneficial role in improving the performance of coal-fired boilers. However, most studies have not given the causal relationship between the factors affecting the combustion of coal and the combustion effect. The specific control scheme is not given after the boiler performance evaluation. Because of the multi-factor, complexity and randomness of coal-fired boiler emissions, as well as its ambiguity, its precise evaluation and control methods still need to be further explored and revealed. In summary, in order to better evaluate and control the boiler combustion performance, this paper proposes a boiler performance parameter analysis method, establishes the boiler operating parameters and BP neural network analysis model based on boiler efficiency and emissions, and it verifies the feasibility and correctness of the method.

2 Performance Evaluation and Control Process of Coal-Fired Boilers

2.1 Traditional Performance Evaluation and Control Methods

The traditional coal-fired boiler combustion performance evaluation and control usually adopts the "single factor rotation method". That is, only one adjusted factor is changed, other factors remain unchanged, and then the influence of the change of the factor on the boiler operation is observed. Obviously, the traditional coal-fired boiler debugging method takes a long time, and the interaction between various factors were not considered, and the best working condition obtained is "not optimal". Therefore, it is necessary to design a mathematical model based on experimental data to describe the influence of operating parameters on NOX emission concentrations.

2.2 Performance Evaluation and Control Framework for Coal-Fired Boilers

In the case of correct information collection, the existing data indicators are used as network input parameters, and then the performance evaluation of coal-fired boiler equipment is carried out. Through scientific analysis of the evaluation results, under the premise of meeting national emission standards, combined with the evaluation results and with the boiler being artificially controlled. The specific process is shown in Fig. 1.

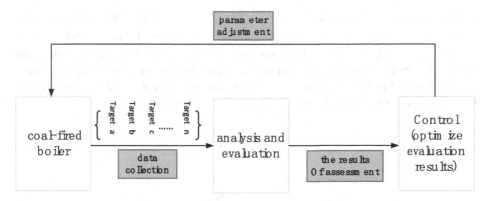

Fig. 1. Evaluation and control framework

3 Boiler Performance Evaluation Model Based on Neural Network

3.1 BP Neural Network

BP neural network is a simulation of biological neural network by artificial means. Its structure and working mechanism are basically based on the organizational structure and activity law of human brain, which reflects some basic characteristics of human brain. BP neural network expresses the function mapping relationship from an independent variable n to a dependent variable m. [9] According to Kolmogorov theorem [10], the reference formula for the number of nodes in the hidden layer is as follows:

$$\begin{cases} l < n - 1 \\ l < \sqrt{m+n} + a \\ l < \log_2^n \end{cases} \tag{1}$$

In formula (1), "n" represents the number of nodes in the input layer; "l" represents the number of nodes in the hidden layer; "m" represents the number of nodes in the output layer; "a" represents a constant between 0 and 10. The number of neurons in the hidden layer is not fixed. Firstly, the range of hidden layer nodes in the network analysis model is determined by the formula. Let the f(X) function be sigmoid function as follows:

$$f(x) = \frac{1}{1 + e^{-x}} \tag{2}$$

Input layer input vector $X = (x_1, x_2, \cdots, x_i, \cdots, x_n)^T$. Output layer output vector $O = (o_1, o_2, \cdots, o_k, \cdots, o_l)^T$. Output layer is expected to output vector $d = (d_1, d_2, \cdots, d_k, \cdots, d_l)^T$. When the network output and the expected output are not equal, there is an output error, and the weight of each layer is adjusted by error back propagation, that is, the adjustment amount of each layer weight should be proportional to the negative gradient of the error. Which is as follows:

$$\Delta w_{ij} = -\eta \frac{\partial E}{\partial w_{jk}} \tag{3}$$

$$\Delta w_{ij} = -\eta \frac{\partial E}{\partial w_{jk}} \tag{4}$$

According to formulas (3) and (4), the amount of change of each layer of weight can be obtained, thereby updating the ownership value of the entire network, and repeating until the requirement is met.

3.2   Control Method Based on Principal Component Analysis

The algorithm of principal component analysis (PCA) is to transform the sample data in the matrix into a completely new space, that is, to diagonalize the matrix and generate the feature root and feature vector, and the projection length of a feature vector direction is derived from the feature value.

From the perspective of decision theory, through the principal component analysis (PCA), the original performance indicators are simplified to find the indicators that affect the most performance. Secondly, it is necessary to compare the parameters of the factors and modify some of the assumptions and evaluate the results. Finally, compare the difference value between the implementation result and the intended goal.

The goal of principal component analysis is to determine which indicators are key indicators (the performance results of the group are dominant), which requires the completion of the screening of indicators (the implementation of control strategies based on evaluation results). In the experiment the dimension of the data of multiple indicators are reduced and the PCA method is usually used to screen out some indicators with a cumulative proportion of 85% or more.

4   Instance Verification

A 410T quadrangular pulverized coal boiler of a power plant was selected as the research object. Based on the above evaluation theory and analysis, the model uses a 3-layer BP network. Since there are 21 input neural nodes, the number of neurons in the middle layer is set to 11, thereby the BP network structure is as shown in Fig. 2.

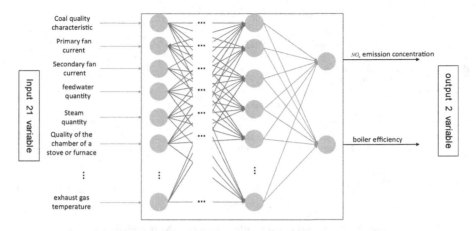

Fig. 2. BP neural network model of boiler combustion system

120 sets of working condition data were selected as training samples, and 100 sets of running data were selected as test samples. The operating data of the combustion test part of coal-fired boilers is shown in Table 1.

Table 1. Partial combustion data of a 410T coal-fired boiler in a thermal power plant

Working condition number	Coal quality			Primary fan current		Secondary fan current		Draft fan current		Boiler efficiency	Emission load
	Calorific value	Ash content %	Sulfur content %	(A)		(A)		(A)		(%)	(mg/m³)
				Left	Right	Left	Right	Left	Right		
1	5456	20.92	0.74	26.1	24.9	14.1	14.2	91.4	89	93.1066	44
2	5456	20.92	0.74	26.1	24.8	14.1	14.3	92.4	89	91.8803	47
3	5456	20.92	0.74	26.1	24.6	14.1	14.3	91.4	90	91.9308	46
4	5456	20.92	0.74	26	24.7	14.1	14.6		87	91.0616	54
......											
101	5627	13.39	0.42	24.5	24.7	15.5	15.8	95	94	95.0809	47
102	5627	13.39	0.42	14.9	15.3	14.9	15.3	95	93	95.7002	46
103	5627	13.39	0.42	14.9	15.4	14.9	15.4	95	93	98.6446	47
104	5627	13.39	0.42	14.9	15.1	14.6	15.2	95	94	95.8366	48
......											
237	5253	13.39	0.48	22.4	25.1	12.5	12.5	89	86	94.254	55
238	5253	13.39	0.48	22.5	25.1	12.4	12.4	88	84	98.254	46
239	5253	13.39	0.48	22.5	25.1	12.2	12.5	86	82	99.2087	50
240	5253	13.39	0.48	22.5	25.1	12.2	12.4	87	84	99.466	52

After the data is normalized, the accuracy and feasibility of the boiler combustion efficiency and emission prediction of the AdaBoost-BP algorithm are tested by using the selected 100 sets of operational data (case number 121–220). The actual value is shown in Fig. 3.

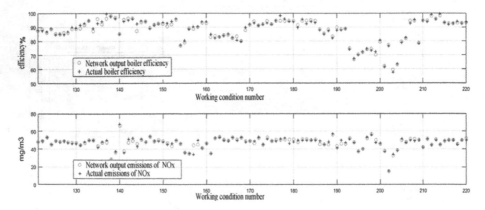

Fig. 3. BP network test results (efficiency, NOx emissions)

As can be seen from Fig. 3, the actual values of boiler combustion efficiency and emissions are generally consistent with the predicted values. Therefore, the established BP neural network model has a strong generalization ability, which can accurately reflect the true thermal efficiency and emissions of the boiler under working conditions, and lays a foundation for the subsequent adjustment of boiler operating parameters. The network model is used to evaluate the performance of the current combustion boiler operation data, as shown in Fig. 4.

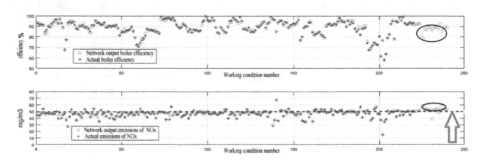

Fig. 4. Comparison of evaluation results (Color figure online)

The Black elliptical circle indicates the approximate distribution of the result. The combustion efficiency of the boiler is basically below 90%. The emission of nitrogen oxides is basically above 50. The red arrow indicates the national standard position. Therefore, the current overall performance of the coal-fired boiler is relatively poor. There is room for improvement.

5   Control Strategy Based on Performance Evaluation

5.1   Analysis of Core Indicators

The experiment carried out a comprehensive evaluation of the 21-dimensional coal-fired boiler data, but the completion of the forward control of the coal-fired boiler is ultimately required (even if the efficiency of the boiler is improved and the nitrogen oxide emissions are reduced). This paper uses the PCA benchmark Screening method, that is, the selection of important and reliable indicators, and the process of controlling all indicators is accomplished by controlling a small number of indicators.

Combined with the actual data collected by the factory, with the mainstream reduced dimension algorithm, the experiment is based on the main level analysis algorithm, and the screening of the core key indicators is completed. The screening results and the proportion values are shown in Table 2.

Table 2. The proportion of each indicator

Indicator	Proportion (%)	Ranking	Index	Proportion (%)	Ranking
Exhaust gas temperature (left)	31.35	1	Primary fan current (left)	5.46	6
Water supply	12.32	2	Exhaust gas temperature (right)	4 97	7
Secondary fan current (left)	10.72	3	Primary fan current (right)	4.28	8
Furnace oxygen	6.91	4	Furnace outlet temperature (left)	3.93	9
Steam volume	6.65	5	Other indicators	>13.39	>10

According to the principal component analysis theory, the index with the cumulative proportion of 85% is selected as the core index, that is, the first nine indicators are used as the core indicators. These indicators are: exhaust gas temperature (left), water supply, secondary fan current (left), Furnace oxygen, steam, primary fan current (left), exhaust temperature (right), primary fan current (right), furnace outlet temperature.

5.2   Parameter Control Based on Main Indicators

The working condition data used for evaluation and control is shown in Table 3. The indicator numbers 11, 2, 15, 19, 1, 13, 12, 14, 9 correspond to the indicator exhaust temperature (left), water supply, secondary fan current (left), furnace oxygen, steam volume, primary fan current. (Left), exhaust gas temperature (right), primary fan current (right), furnace outlet temperature, 9 core indicators in total.

Table 3. Raw data (before control adjustment)

Working condition number	Core indicator number								
	11	2	15	19	1	13	12	14	9
221	132	293	12.4	3.4	301	23.6	118	24.2	779
222	135	303	12	2.8	315	23.7	118	24.3	779
223	134	276	12.2	2.8	312	23.7	121	24.2	787
...	...	...	...	...	...	...	...	...	...
238	131	322	12.4	3.4	315	22.5	118	25.1	777
239	129	304	12.2	3.3	318	22.5	123	25.1	787
240	129	318	12.2	3.5	321	22.5	123	25.1	794

We randomly selected 20 sets of data in the data with better test results, that is, the data has higher coal-burning efficiency and NOx emission in accordance with the standard and the working conditions are selected to meet the requirement. The adjusted parameters are shown in Table 4.

Table 4. The adjusted parameters

Working condition number	Core indicator number								
	11	1	15	19	1	13	12	14	9
221	116	360	14	3.9	351	25	111	25	722
222	117	367	14	3.8	362	25	111	25	735
223	117	366	14	3.6	362	25	112	25	739
...	...	...	...	...	...	...	...	...	...
238	116	343	14.3	3.5	348	25.6	113	24.1	744
239	115	350	14.6	3.3	355	25.7	112	24.2	740
240	114	352	14.6	3.2	352	25.6	112	24	738

6   Conclusion

In this research, the combustion process of coal-fired boilers was studied. The boiler efficiency and combustion emission analysis model based on AdaBoost-BP algorithm was established. The principal component analysis method was introduced to analyze the combustion factors, and the internal relationship and regularity between coal combustion efficiency, emissions of NOX and various effects were studied. Through the evaluation and control process of the combustion emission of a 410T four-corner pulverized coal boiler in a power plant, it verified the effectiveness and feasibility of the method, and provided a guiding evaluation for the enterprise management personnel. The control method also provides a theoretical reference for energy saving and emission reduction of coal-fired boilers.

Acknowledgements. This work is supported by the Social Science Planning Project in Fujian Province Project (FJ2016C133), the Scientific Research Foundation for Young and Middle-aged Teachers of Fujian Province (JZ160163) and the Fujian Province Education Science "13th Five-Year Plan" Project (FJJKCG16-289).

References

1. Ministry of Environmental Protection: GB 13223-2011. Emission Standards for Air Pollutants in Thermal Power Plants. China Environmental Science Press, pp. 1–3 (2011)
2. Zhao, J., Pan, Q., Liu, T.: Analysis of application of intelligent control in boiler combustion system of thermal power station. Electron. Manuf. **368**(1), 142–148 (2019)
3. Chen, X., Gao, L., Zhou, J., Gao, H., Wang, L., et al.: Boiler combustion control model of large-scale coal-fired power plant with asymmetric artificial neural networks. In: 2017 IEEE 2nd Information Technology, Networking, Electronic and Automation Control Conference (ITNEC). IEEE (2017)
4. Safa, M., Samarasinghe, S., Nejat, M.: Prediction of wheat production using artificial neural networks and investigating indirect factors affecting it: case study in Canterbury Province, New Zealand. J. Agric. Sci. Technol. **17**(4), 791–803 (2018)
5. Spentzos, A., Barakos, G.N., Badcock, K.J., Richards, B.E., et al.: Computational fluid dynamics study of three-dimensional dynamic stall of various planform shapes. J. Aircr. **44**(4), 1118–1128 (2017)
6. Xie, C., Liu, J., Zhang, X., Xie, W., Sun, J., Chang, K., Kuo, J., et al.: Co-combustion thermal conversion characteristics of textile dyeing sludge and pomelo peel using TGA and artificial neural networks. Appl. Energy **212**, 786–795 (2018)
7. Wang, C., Liu, Y., Zheng, S., Jiang, A., et al.: Optimizing combustion of coal fired boilers for reducing NOx emission using Gaussian process. Energy **153**, 149–158 (2018)
8. Gu, Y., Zhao, W., Wu, Z.: Combustion optimization of power plant boilers using optimal MVs decision model. Proc. CSEE **32**(2), 39–44 (2012)
9. Yu, T., Liao, L., Liu, R.: Prediction of NOx emissions from coal-fired boilers based on support vector machines and BP neural networks. Nat. Environ. Pollut. Technol. **16**(4), 1043–1049 (2017)
10. Shi, Y., Han, L., Lian, X.: Neural Network Design Methods and Case Analysis, 2nd edn. Beijing University of Posts and Telecommunications Press, Beijing (2009)

Analysis and Prediction of Commercial Big Data Based on WIFI Probe

Xiao Zeng[1,2(✉)], Hong Guo[1,2], and Zhe Liu[1,2]

[1] College of Computer Science and Technology, Wuhan University of Science
and Technology, Wuhan, Hubei, China
zengxiao.alison@foxmail.com, guohong@wust.edu.cn,
624816113@qq.com
[2] Hubei Province Key Laboratory of Intelligent Information Processing
and Real-time Industrial System, Wuhan, China

Abstract. With the development of the Internet economy, offline physical
transactions are facing a huge test. The number of merchants in many shopping
malls has decreased, and the volume of physical transactions has fallen sharply.
As an important data of the operation status of the shopping mall, passenger
traffic can grasp the best operating time, arrange employees reasonably, and
judge the marketing volume of the shopping mall. Therefore, excellent mall
operators need to know the status of the passenger flow in the market in a timely
manner, and analyze the overall operation situation and make reasonable
operational decisions. Based on the above problems, this paper designs and
implements a commercial big data analysis and prediction system based on
WIFI probe, obtains basic data through WIFI probe hardware sensor, and provides relatively accurate passenger flow information for commercial field,
combined with big data analysis and machine learning prediction. The algorithm
analyzes a series of information about passenger flow, store quantity, bounce
rate, dwell time and other forecasting trend of passenger flow in the future,
providing reliable data support for the commercial field and becoming the reference for various decisions.

Keywords: WIFI probe · Big data · Data analysis · Data prediction

1 Introduction

In some countries, WIFI probes are widely used, such as the use of WIFI probes for
company sign-in, meeting sign-up and other occasions where inventory personnel need
to be counted; large-scale shopping malls generally have passenger flow detection and
statistical systems.

WIFI probe technology can count the number of consumers in the store according
to the wireless network card of the mobile phone, and can also track the trajectory
according to the MAC address of the mobile phone. WIFI probes have the advantage of
low cost, which has become a popular application. In the context of the booming big
data, the WIFI probe sensor collects the passenger flow information of the store,
combined with machine learning, it can provide the basic services of passenger flow

detection and passenger flow forecast for the commercial field, so as to accurately understand the passenger flow, arrange employee hours and warehouse storage for the commercial field. Management, scheduling of holiday promotions, etc. have helped.

Combined with big data, WIFI probes, analysis and prediction algorithms, it can bring low-cost customer analysis and forecasting to merchants, and make passenger flow analysis more accurate, thus helping to improve the overall operation of the store. At the same time, through the data feedback and prediction of the system, the merchant can timely understand the operation status of the store, adjust the operation strategy in time, provide powerful support operation capability, and promote the rapid economic development of the merchant [1].

2 Related Technology

2.1 WIFI Probe Detection Technology

In the WIFI probe-based commercial big data analysis and prediction system, WIFI probes shoulder the important work of data collection. The basic principle is to collect the radio signals transmitted by the smart phones in the nearby area, and analyze how many customers exist in the current area by collecting the number of signals; Through testing the strength of the collecting signal, the distance between the signal source and the probe can be analyzed. Therefore, we can get to know whether the customer enters the store [2].

2.2 Server Cluster

The system uses the Hadoop + Spark + HBase framework as the core for server cluster construction, the versions are Hadoop-2.8.4, Spark-2.2.0, HBase-1.3.0. Hadoop is an open source distributed computing platform under the Apache Software Foundation [3]. After more than ten years of development, the Hadoop community has become more and more perfect and has become the computing platform of choice in the era of big data. With HDFS (Hadoop Distributed File System) and MapReduce (Computational Algorithm), it has won more and more reputations.

Spark is an elastic distributed computing framework based on memory computing [4]. In addition to Spark SQL and Spark Streaming, Spark also provides MLib. MLib is a library of Spark machine learning that can implement many machine learning algorithms [5]. The HBase non-relational data warehouse stores unstructured raw data. HBase stores data on HDFS and is a high-performance distributed storage repository [6].

2.3 SSM (Spring + Spring MVC + Mybatis)

The visualization module adopts the SSM architecture. Among them, Spring MVC is the concrete implementation framework of the Spring family for the MVC pattern, which is used to process web requests and view forwarding. Spring is the core framework, which is equivalent to a container, manages all dependencies, and provides IoC (reverse control). The mechanism realizes the management of the life cycle of all objects, and integrates Mybatis according to the configuration; Mybatis acts as a persistence engine for data objects, which is convenient for quickly implementing data entity classes to data operations.

2.4   Data Prediction and Algorithm Optimization

In the machine learning algorithm, through a large number of data training models, the model with the best cost function is selected as the data prediction model to complete the forecast of the mall store in the future. This paper needs to use a scientific method to optimize the machine learning algorithm to get more accurate predictions.

First, the cross-validation set, referred to as CV, is adopted. The idea is to randomly confuse the original data so that the continuous data does not have regularity. The scrambled data is divided into a training set, a cross-validation set, and a test set according to a ratio of 6:2:2 [7]. To make predictions more accurate, you need to design many different models. All models were calculated for the CV error for the CV set, and the model with the smallest error was selected as the final model. Finally, the generalized error is calculated from the test set data using the model.

Secondly, the system draws a learning curve for two different errors: the definition learning curve is: the curve of the value obtained by the cost function of the model on the cross-validation set and the training set as the size of the training set increases [8]. The cost function defined on the training set is:

$$J_{train}(\theta) = \frac{1}{2m} \sum_{i=1}^{m} \left(h_\theta\left(x^{(i)}\right) - y^{(i)} \right)^2 \tag{1}$$

The cost function defined on the cross-validation set is:

$$J_{cv}(\theta) = \frac{1}{2m} \sum_{i=1}^{m_{cv}} \left(h_\theta\left(x_{cv}^{(i)}\right) - y_{cv}^{(i)} \right)^2 \tag{2}$$

3   System Design

3.1   The Architecture of the System

The system adopts modular development. The server is divided into three kinds of responsibilities: the server cluster is used for preprocessing and analyzing data, the data cache server is used for cache data and data persistent storage, and the web server is used to display the visualization platform (Fig. 1).

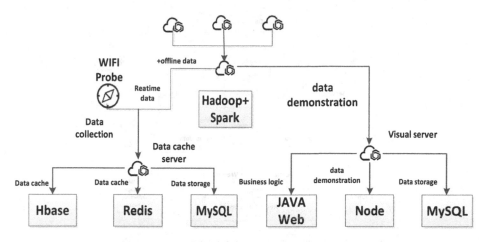

Fig. 1. System architecture

The left side of the figure is the data source - WIFI probe, which is responsible for collecting passenger flow data. The data is uploaded to the data cache server through the wireless network, and the data is preprocessed and then selected and stored to the HBase server. At this point, the data is passed to the server cluster through Kafka for calculation, and the calculation result is returned to the cache server for real-time display. The data persistence server architecture diagram is shown in Fig. 2.

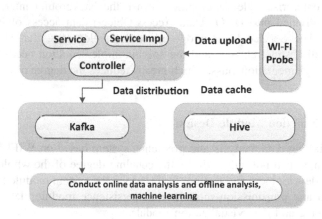

Fig. 2. Data persistence server architecture

After the data is received by the controller of the SSM framework, the prepro-cessing is performed, including deserializing the json data and then packaging it into an object. Once the pre-processing is complete, the data can be persisted for storage. At the same time, data is sent to the server cluster through the data distribution framework Kafka for subsequent data analysis, prediction and other operations. The visualization platform architecture diagram is shown in Fig. 3.

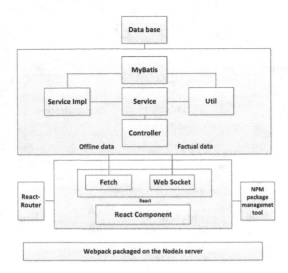

Fig. 3. Visual platform architecture

It can be seen from the figure that the technology used by the front end is implemented by the React framework and Nodejs. The front-end route mapping is fully controlled by React-Router, and the front-end operation is controlled by the NPM management tool. The background is built by the Spring MVC + Spring + Mybatis framework, which is routed through the controller and processes various requests. According to enterprise-style development, when the background interacts with the database, it is divided into DAO (Data Access Object) data access object layer and Service layer. The Service layer adopts abstract development, that is, the defined interfaces are all abstract classes, and the specific implementation needs to be reconstructed. The implementation class, which greatly reduces the degree of coupling of the system.

3.2   System Function Module Design

The commercial big data analysis and prediction system based on WIFI Probe adopts modular design, which not only reduces the coupling degree of the whole system, but also facilitates development and testing. In this paper, the system module is designed as data collection and transmission module, data persistence module, data analysis and prediction module and data visualization module.

Data Collection and Transmission Module
The function of this module: The WIFI probe is powered by the USB interface; the data is collected by the WIFI probe, and the data is automatically uploaded to the specified URL; when the WIFI probe receives the shutdown command, the WIFI probe stops collecting data and stops sending data.

The Algorithm flow: After the WIFI probe is in working state, it will always collect and send. When the stop command is encountered, the probe goes from the working state to the sleep state. The stop command can be controlled by the background management system that comes with the login probe. It can also be connected to a single computer or a single-chip computer to send a command to control a single-chip computer. After receiving the command, the single-chip computer will stop exploring. The needle is powered to complete the control of the working state of the probe.

Data Persistence Module

The function of this module: The data sent by the WIFI is received by the data persistence server; the data is preprocessed, deserialized, encapsulated into objects, and then the duplicate data is removed; the data is cached and persisted; the data is sent to the processing cluster.

The Algorithm flow: After the data is received by the data persistence server, the data is preprocessed. By deserializing and encapsulating json data into objects, object-oriented operations can be implemented to process the data. Then perform HBase storage and further analysis, and store the analyzed data in Redis.

Data Analysis and Prediction Module

The function of this module: According to the analysis algorithm, the data is started to calculate the basic data; the analysis result is sent to the persistent server to update the Redis operation; the online or offline task calls the prediction algorithm for prediction, and the regularized polynomial regression model is adopted, and the learning curve is used as an auxiliary tool., fit in the training set, and complete cross-validation, select the best model, and complete the hypothesis prediction.

There are six basic data calculation methods are as follows:

Regional overall passenger flows
The overall regional passenger flow refers to the number of customers passing through the area per unit time. Therefore, the calculation method is to obtain the number of addresses of the detected mobile phone wireless network card in the original data field;

Incoming amount
Assume that the overall passenger flow is N and the unit is human. Assume that the probe is placed 5 m away from the store door, and the signal strength of the actual store customer should be greater than -50, the unit is dbm. The data that satisfies the above requirements in N is counted as the amount of the store; otherwise it is only counted as the passenger flow. It is advisable to count the above-mentioned stores as N_{enter}.

Arrival rate
The store entry rate refers to the proportion of customers entering the store to the total passenger flow. The calculation formula is

$$R_{enter} = \frac{N_{enter}}{N} \tag{3}$$

New and old customers' visiting cycles
During the data analysis process, the user wireless network card information is extracted and HBase storage is performed. In this process, if there is already

corresponding user information, it is an old customer; if there is no corresponding user information, it is a new customer.

The visiting period refers to the statistics of the customers entering the store, and the difference between the last time they arrived and the calculated time. When the old customer visits again, the corresponding dwell time in HBase will be updated, and the latest appearance time will be refreshed, so that the customer visit cycle can be analyzed.

Resident duration and customer activity

The length of stay in the store is a measure of the time spent in a mall when a customer makes a purchase. The main algorithm is to record the customer's last visit time, if the time interval is short, it is recorded as continuous resident; if it is longer than the last visit time, only the last visit time is refreshed. The customer is divided into four different activity levels based on the visiting period and the dwell time: high activity, medium activity, low activity, and sleeping activity.

Quick visit rate, deep visit rate and bounce rate

The quick visit rate refers to the proportion of the number of customers who visit the store with a low depth to the total number of visits. It can be judged by the combination of the Rssi and Range fields, or the resident time can be used for the auxiliary judgment.

The deep visit rate refers to the proportion of customers who visit the store with a higher depth to the total number of visitors.

The bounce rate is the ratio of the number of customers who have left the store to a shorter time and will leave soon.

The Algorithm flow: The basic information of the shop passenger flow obtained by the data analysis is stored in the non-relational database Redis. For the data prediction module, the analyzed data is needed. After reading the data from Redis, the data is predicted using SparkML, and the prediction result is stored in Redis. If the presentation is needed at this time, the data is read from the Redis by the visualization platform, and the data is displayed to the visualization platform.

Data Visualization Module

The function of this module: The data is displayed on the homepage of the website in real time by WebSocket; the query method of different dimensions of year, month and day is provided; and various charts such as bar chart, pie chart and line chart are displayed.

The Algorithm flow: This article uses the query method of different latitudes of year, month and day. When the user selects a specific method, the visualization platform will request the corresponding server to notify the server of the selected query mode. The server selects data from the database according to the request, and then passes the data to the front-end interface. After receiving the data, the front-end React framework automatically renders and displays the data to implement responsive data display.

3.3 The Design of Database

The basic entities in this system: Probe entity: including probe mac address, bound shop id, latitude and longitude, address, sending rate; store entity, including store id, address, manager contact information, etc.; user entity, including user mac address, mobile phone brand, etc.; Store access record entity, including binding shop id, passenger flow, shallow, deep visit rate, recording time; task entity, including task name, creation time, start time, end time, task type, task status, task parameters, etc.; Entities, including probe mac address, store id, data collection period, data collection range, data signal strength, etc.

The system out of the structured data stored in the relational database, and the original data is stored in the HBase non-relational data warehouse. The pre-processed data is analyzed and the results are stored in a Redis non-relational database to improve data access speed.

The entity relationship designed by the relational database in this system is shown in Fig. 4:

Fig. 4. Entity relationship

4 System Implementation

4.1 System Operation Interface

After using the WebSocket protocol, the WIFI probe collects the data, uploads it to the persistent server, and then displays it in real time through the visualization platform server. The following figure is an example of the instore amount and deep visit rate in the store (Fig. 5).

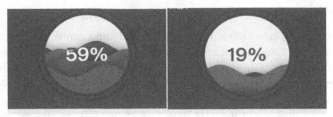

One day's instore rate   **One day's deep visit rate**

Show the overall traffic distribution of the store:

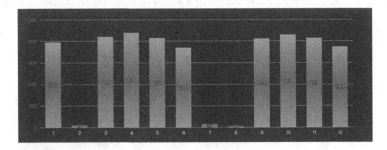

Fig. 5. The average rate of passenger flow in twelve months

Show the forecasting traffic for each time period in the coming day (The blue volume stands for the passenger flow and the red volume stands for the instore amount) (Fig. 6).

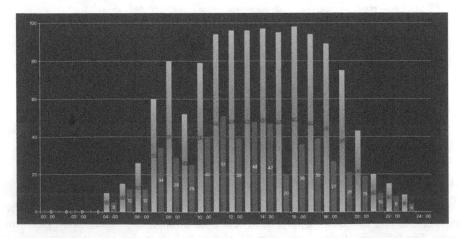

Fig. 6. The forecasting traffic for each time period in the coming day

5 Conclusion

This paper discusses commercial big data analysis and prediction based on WIFI Probe. The designed software and hardware combination system is built with distributed clusters. Different servers perform their duties, improve operational efficiency and achieve more powerful computing power. Storage capacity; using a variety of different databases to combine, the data with large query volume and small modification amount is stored in the relational database, and the large amount of modified and unformatted data is stored in the non-relational database, which improves the working efficiency of the database system. In the data prediction, a machine learning algorithm with regularized polynomial regression is adopted. In order to solve the problem that the selected model is in high deviation and high variance, the learning curve can be introduced to better understand the state of the current model. At the same time, the data visualization platform adopts The WebSocket protocol enables the server to push data in real time to the front page of the visualization platform. In addition, the visualization platform uses a variety of charts to show the data more clearly. The entire system of research and design can use scientific data to help mall managers better understand the current situation of the mall and make a series of scientific decisions to achieve better operational results.

References

1. Guozhi, Y.: Research on application of passenger flow detection based on Wi-Fi probe. Comput. Prod. Circ. 157–158 (2018)
2. Chang, X.: Design and Implementation of WiFi-Based Human Traffic Monitoring System, pp. 3–4. Beijing University of Posts and Telecommunications, Beijing (2017)
3. Mengmeng, L.: Research on Cluster Analysis Based on Hadoop, pp. 6–8 (2016)
4. Xuejun, J., Feng, W., Haixin, H.: Spark big data computing platform. Electron. World **549**(15), 82–84 (2018)
5. Wei, W., Rui, H., Yuxiang, J.: Distributed big data machine learning algorithm based on spark. Comput. Mod. **279**(11), 119–126 (2018)
6. Yun, Z., Liu, C.: HBase based storage system for the Internet of Things. In: 2016 4th International Conference on Machinery, Materials and Computing Technology, pp. 3–5 (2016)
7. Soekarno, I., Hadihardaja, I.K., et al.: A study of hold-out and k-fold cross validation for accuracy of groundwater modeling in tidal lowland reclamation using extreme learning machine. In: 2014 IEEE 2nd International Conference on Technology, Informatics, Management, Engineering & Environment (TIME-E), pp. 228–233. IEEE (2014)
8. Yajie, Z., Shengjun, L., Han, Y., Xiang, J., Robert, J.C., Li, H.: Robotic anatomical segmentectomy: an analysis of the learning curve. Ann. Thorac. Surg. **107**(5), 106–107 (2019)

Design and Optimization of Camera HAL Layer Based on Android

Yu Gan[1(✉)], Wei Hu[2], and Yonghao Wang[3]

[1] College of Computer Science and Technology,
Wuhan University of Science and Technology, Wuhan, China
Rorchach2k@gmail.com
[2] Hubei Province Key Laboratory of Intelligent Information Processing
and Real-Time Industria System, Wuhan, China
huwei@wust.edu.cn
[3] Digital Media Lab, Birmingham City University, Birmingham, UK
yonghao.wang@bcu.ac.uk

Abstract.. Nowadays, in the field of mobile and communication, with the rapid popularization and application of Internet and network, and the continuous expansion to the family field, the trend of integration of consumer electronics, computer and communication (3C) is becoming increasingly obvious, and embedded system naturally becomes a research hotspot. The embedded operating system Android has been widely used in mobile devices, such as smart phones, smart watches and so on. Our design is based on the Android platform to optimize and improve Camera HAL. This design is applied to the development of the Android system, the design of the Camera subsystem, the description of the Camera subsystem from the structure, function and data flow, and then proceed to structural optimization. This design uses TI AM335x as the hardware platform, based on Android system, designed and implemented the Android Camera hardware abstraction layer and Camera subsystem. At the end of the development, after the actual experimental test, the development of the system achieved the expected function and worked well.

Keywords: Android · Camera · HAL · Embedded system · System architecture

1 Introduction

The technology development in today's era is very rapid, especially the smart phone technology is rapidly emerging. Operating systems, including IOS and Android. They are attracting more and more attention from the market, and manufacturers around the world are beginning to enter the market. Due to the excellent interface and convenient environment of the Linux kernel-based operating system, more and more new players are investing in Android development in recent years. So in this article, we're gonna try to propose a method to optimize and improve Camera HAL based on the Android platform.

This paper first introduces the environment and background of this system design, explains the structure of the paper and introduces the key technologies used [1]. The

© Springer Nature Switzerland AG 2019
M. Qiu (Ed.): SmartCom 2019, LNCS 11910, pp. 296–303, 2019.
https://doi.org/10.1007/978-3-030-34139-8_29

article first introduces the Android system and some of the key technologies that need to be applied, and then introduces the overall design of the Camera subsystem, mainly for the improvement of the HAL architecture. Then, the specific process of Camera HAL development is described from the aspects of client, server and HAL layer. Finally, the entire process of design is summarized.

Android is the platform for this development. The core of its system is Linux, which is based on the mobile operating system of various services and UI. As former Android has a wide range of applications, Google has set up OHA (Open Handheld Alliance) to provide continuous updates. Its infrastructure is the Software Stack architecture, with the Linux kernel-based kernel layer as the lowest layer and the development language C [2]. The bottom layer provides a stable system interface to the upper layer. The middle layer is a system runtime layer, which uses C++-based function libraries and virtual machines. Further up is the Application layer. The basis for developing Android applications is the application framework layer.

HAL is proposed by the Android platform to protect the intellectual property of the manufacturer. It has the feature of bypassing the GPL development source of Linux, without having to publish all the code [3]. We can implement hardware control methods in the Android HAL, and only use the Linux driver to complete a simple data exchange, or directly map the hardware register space to the User Space. Android is based on the Aparch license, which means that the hardware vendor only needs to provide binary code or library files [4]. So we said that Android is extremely open as an operating system, but it is not open source. But Android does not comply with the GPL, and the contradiction between GPL and IC design vendors still exists.

Android layers use JNI and HAL middleware technologies [5]. As mentioned before, the system is highly open and provides an unlicensed fee service. Many advantages make Android the world's most used mobile operating system. Google has cooperated extensively with many parties, established a standardized and shared mobile communication platform, and built an open ecosystem chain to provide better services to users around the world.

2 Related Work

2.1 Android System Structure

Android divides the system architecture into four levels. The following describes the four layers in order from top to bottom.

Application layer (Application). The application layer contains a collection of applications [6]. The emails, calls, QQ, WeChat, maps, alarm clocks, etc. That we usually use are all listed, and the programs designed and written by the third-party developers downloaded from the app store using the Java language also run at this level [7].

Application Framework layer (Application Framework). This layer is the basic framework of Android application development, which contains a lot of interfaces and class objects, which are often applied in the upper layer application development. Designers can use the API framework provided by Google to provide a lot of convenience in designing the program architecture and logical structure, reducing a lot of tedious and repetitive projects.

System runtime library (Libraries). In order to implement the positioning function of Android, many components will need to be implemented by some C/C++ libraries, which are included in the system runtime layer.

Linux kernel layer (Linux Kernel). Android is developed on the basis of the Linux kernel and has many software stacks [8]. The Linux kernel is between the hardware device and the software stack, and is still the core of the system itself.

2.2 Camera Subsystem Design

Camera as a subsystem of Android of course also conforms to such a framework structure. So to implement the new architecture, we only need to modify the framework layer and HAL layer on the original basis. The application layer implements page layout in XML language, mainly completing interface and interaction design. The main code is stored in the Camera.java file, which is eventually compiled into Camera.apk. We implement most of the functions and interfaces here. When the application layer accesses the local library, it is often necessary to use the java virtual machine to run java in the virtual machine. The framework/base/core/jni/path is the corresponding code in this section. The key code provides a list of parameters for the application layer in the form of metadata for the data dictionary. The data will eventually be passed to the server. Camera belongs to the Android multimedia framework [9]. From the multimedia framework, the libui.so library is the interface library of the Android Binder mechanism in the Android multimedia framework, and the Camera as a subsystem also belongs to the multimedia framework. We use the libcameraservice.so shared library to implement the main features of Camera. But in addition to Camera, the video subsystem framework also calls libui.so, so Camera is not the only object.

3   Proposed Model

3.1   Android Development Kit

This design needs to be applied to some Android SDKs, which are available for free directly from the Android website. The SDKs of different versions of the device will be different. The platform has integrated the latest SDK into the tool. We can select and download it ourselves, or we can synchronize the SDK to an earlier version [10]. The SDK provides tools for developing on a variety of platforms including Windows, Linux, and Mac, and supports all platforms. Android originally supports C and C++, and the implementation of the SDK is encoded in Java, so to use the Android SDK you must use java to design. Google has announced that the Android virtual machine supports JNT technology, so all applications can call their own dynamic libraries through JNI. On the Android platform, it is possible to implement mixed programming of C language, C ++ and Java. But at the same time [11] Google has shown that the technology is still flawed, sometimes the development process is very complicated, or sometimes the code is very complicated. So they also provide the NDK tool (Native

Development Kit), the local language development kit. This tool user uses C and C+ to implement certain features.

3.2 Android Binder Mechanism

Since Android is a completely open platform with a wide range of applications, security issues are a top priority [12]. For users, of course, all users do not want Android-based applications to steal their own private data, and the conventional process communication is not safe, and it is very easy to be hijacked and utilized by various Trojans. Trojans can easily push the program's recipient address to get a connection, which is almost impossible to block [13]. Binder is a new mechanism that emerged in this context. Since the communication structure adopts the C/S structure, the transmission process only needs one data copy, and the data sender can identify the ID of the user and the process, so the transmission efficiency and the security performance are all improved. The Binder mechanism uses the client/server communication mode. One of the processes provides some system services as a server [1]. Other processes act as clients, and send service requests to the server, and are uniformly scheduled by the service management unit to provide related system services. The Binder framework sets up four objects for Server, Client, Service Manager and Binder. The server, client, and server management are all running on the User Space, and the Binder driver is running on the Kernel Space [14]. The relationship between the four objects can be compared to the Internet. The Server is the server, the Client is the client terminal, the Service Manager is like the DNS, and the driver is the router.

3.3 Summary

In this section, we focus on the key technologies used in this development process [15]. The development is based on the Android platform and applied to some official free development kits. The most critical part is the Android hardware abstraction layer and Binder-based communication. The C/S communication mechanism architecture built by way. It is not complicated by itself. The key to implementing this architecture is to distinguish the communication structure layer and the business logic layer of the application.

4 Experiments

4.1 Install JDK

JDK is a software development kit developed by Sun Microsystems for Java developers. In April 2014, Oracle acquired Sun, so the JDK is now officially available for download by Oracle. The Java Development Kit is the most frequently used toolkit for developers from Java [16]. The toolkit includes basic components such as javac (compiler), java (interpreter), jar (packaging tool), javadoc (document generator), jdb (debug tool) and jre (Java runtime environment). Developers can use many convenient development interface interfaces through the toolkit. After the 8.0 version update, the operation efficiency is greatly improved.

The system version before 5.0 is compiled with JDK, and then compiled with open JDK7 or higher. The installation of the system version may be different. We use the 6.0 version as an example. Advanced Packaging Tools is a powerful package management mechanism, generally referred to as APT. We use APT for installation, which has the advantage of being simple and convenient and does not require manual configuration of the path. The tool will configure the environment variables at the time of installation [17]. The APT mechanism reduces the threshold for user operations, whether it is an installation upgrade or an uninstall, which greatly reduces the amount of user operations.

We first need to get the Android source code. First create a repository with repo init, initialize the android source code repository to download the latest code.

4.2   Compile Environment Build and Compile

(1) Environmental requirements:
Operating system: Officially recommended Linux Ubuntu10.04 (LTS, long term support version) 64bit; does not support compiling under Windows and Mac OS. Memory and hard disk space size: 4G memory (the reason is to avoid "JVM run out of memory", while the larger the memory can speed up the compilation).
Disk space size: at least 25G or more storage space.
(2) Dependency package installation:
Refer to the official Android documentation, the following packages need to be installed to compile Android code under 64-bit ubuntu system.
Finally, the compilation section. We need to select a platform in the top level directory of the Android source code, and then select the required platform to compile with make. After the compilation is completed, the required image will be generated in the directory of the selected platform. The image is finally packaged into multiple image files such as ramdisk.img, system.img, and userdata.img. In addition to the root file system ramdisk, the other two images are mounted to their system and data directories after decompression.

4.3   Detailed Implementation of System Functions

The application framework layer mainly provides an interface for the application layer. The application layer's call to the local library is implemented by JNI [18]. Here, you need to register the method you added and establish the connection through the function pointer. The camera in the application framework layer is equivalent to the client. The most basic architecture in Android is the C/S layer architecture. Most of the functions are provided in the form of system services. The client provides access to the server interface. The work is still done through the server, the camera is also used in this architecture: the camera client process does not have any substantial camera data, but the server provides a complete service interface, the camera client can be easily obtained the storage address of the camera data can then be processed quickly.

The application layer is on the top, written by Android application developers, mainly designed the UI design and interaction of the camera, writing logic code. Next is the application framework layer, which provides a stable API for the application layer to ensure the most basic camera functionality [19]. Next is the JNI middleware, which can add a new camera function interface. The upper layer accesses the localization library and also needs to apply JNI technology. The Java method and the Native method are used to establish contact here.

Finally, we need to implement the camera client. We link the server here to implement the sending and receiving process.

The implementation of the Camera Client side is mainly to call the interface and method, and does not really implement the function. We implement the interface function implementation in the server side [20]. As mentioned above, the server side implements the RPC mechanism through the Binder mechanism to complete the camera subsystem architecture we designed.

The Camera HAL design mainly implements two control threads.

The picture thread, when the user uses the take Picture function, the system calls the camera thread, the program monitors the frame data in the buffer queue, and takes out the frame data from the buffer queue after the data arrives. We pass the data obtained by the camera to the Java layer, and the original data can be compressed into JPEG format and sent to the upper layer.

The bottom of the HAL layer exists as a daemon. Here, the core service of the camera is provided, the underlying camera driver is packaged, and the camera-related software stack is constructed. The C/S structure of the camera does not affect the upper layer, and the data processing and distribution are directly performed here to reduce the coupling.

5   Conclusions

The goal of this design is to develop Android source code level in Ubuntu system, which can be realized and verified by modifying Camera HAL.

The core of the design is the design of hardware abstraction layer, which is realized by modifying the Android platform.

The emphasis of development programming is as follows:

(1) Improve and optimize the design of Android native HAL and put forward its own HAL model.
(2) Write the corresponding Camera HAL code for the design of HAL.
(3) Compile and debug the program.

Specific tasks can be divided into:

1. Research the existing Android HAL design and embedded device HAL design, arrange the main process of development and design.
2. Theory learning - learning Android system-level development tools and methods, familiar with the use of ubuntu.

3. In the Android development environment that has been built, the corresponding coding work is realized by combining the HAL model designed.
4. Testing Camera module in application layer, improving the design of HAL layer through testing.
5. Finally, after comprehensive adjustment, report and paper will be compiled according to the results of implementation.

There are five objectives: first, to accurately analyze the key technologies needed in the design of Android HAL. Secondly, to develop and code Android at the source level in Ubuntu system; secondly, to test Camera HAL module through application software at the application level. Finally, to get the analysis report and paper collation after getting the test results.

After three months' efforts, we have basically realized the preview and photography functions of Camera subsystem, and improved the hardware abstraction layer of Android. The driver uses a general V4L2 framework, which is universal and improves the running efficiency of Camera subsystem. In the aspect of HAL design, the realization of photo threads and preview threads is completed. An optimization scheme is proposed for HAL. Core Service is added to the lower layer of HAL to improve the efficiency of program and realize the integration of software and hardware. In the later stage, it is necessary to improve the functions and further optimize the structure of HAL in order to achieve efficiency and versatility. Find a balance between them.

There is no standard evaluation of efficiency and performance. In the process of further optimization of the framework, hot spot function analysis, time stamp, process analysis and other methods should be introduced to test the performance of the system, including photo delay, focusing delay and so on. Good test system and targeted optimization can make the designed Camera subsystem more robust and efficient.

References

1. Bradley, A.P.: The use of the area under the roc curve in the evaluation of machine learning algorithms. Pattern Recogn. **30**(7), 1145–1159 (1997)
2. Arora, A., Peddoju, S.K.: Minimizing network traffic features for android mobile malware detection. In: Proceedings of the 18th International Conference on Distributed Computing and Networking, ICDCN 2017, pp. 32:1–32:10. ACM (2017)
3. Cimpanu, C.: CopyCat Adware Infects Zygote Android Core Process. BleepingComputer
4. Grace, M., Zhou, Y., Zhang, Q., Zou, S., Jiang, X.: Riskranker. In: Proceedings of the 10th International Conference on Mobile Systems, Applications, and Services, MobiSys 2012, pp. 281–294 (2012)
5. Kapratwar, A., Troia, F.D., Stamp, M.: Static and dynamic analysis of android malware. In: Proceedings of the 3rd International Conference on Information Systems Security and Privacy, pp. 653–662 (2017)
6. Liu, B., Nath, S., Govindan, R., Liu, J.: DECAF: detecting and characterizing ad fraud in mobile apps. In: Proceedings of the 11th USENIX Conference on Networked Systems Design and Implementation, NSDI 2014, pp. 57–70. USENIX Association (2014)
7. Moonsamy, V., Rong, J., Liu, S.: Mining permission patterns for contrasting clean and malicious Android applications. Future Gener. Comput. Syst. **36**, 122–132 (2014)

8. Sharma, D.: Android malware detection using decision trees and network traffic. Int. J. Comput. Sci. Inf. Technol. **7**(4), 1970–1974 (2016)
9. Stamp, M.: Introduction to Machine Learning with Applications in Information Security. Chapman and Hall/CRC, Boca Raton (2017)
10. Yan, L.-K., Yin, H.: DroidScope: seamlessly reconstructing the OS and Dalvik semantic views for dynamic android malware analysis. In: USENIX Security Symposium, pp. 569–584 (2012)
11. Zhang, L., Guan, Y.: Detecting click fraud in pay-per-click streams of online advertising networks. In: The 28th International Conference on Distributed Computing Systems, ICDCS 2008, pp. 77–84. IEEE (2008)
12. Aafer, Y., Du, W., Yin, H.: DroidAPIMiner: mining API-level features for robust malware detection in android. In: Proceedings of International Conference on Security and Privacy in Communication Systems, pp. 86–103 (2013)
13. Arp, D., Spreitzenbarth, M., Hubner, M., Gascon, H., Rieck, K.: DREBIN: effective and explainable detection of android malware in your pocket. In: 21st Annual Network and Distributed System Security Symposium, NDSS 2014, vol. 14, pp. 23–26. The Internet Society (2014)
14. Crussell, J., Stevens, R., Chen, H.: MAdFraud: investigating ad fraud in Android applications. In: Proceedings of the 12th Annual International Conference on Mobile Systems, Applications, and Services, pp. 123–134. ACM (2014)
15. Daswani, N., Stoppelman, M.: The anatomy of Clickbot.A. In: Proceedings of the First Conference on Hot Topics in Understanding Botnets, HotBots 2007, pp. 11–31. USENIX Association, Berkeley (2007)
16. Enck, W., et al.: TaintDroid: an information-flow tracking system for realtime privacy monitoring on smartphones. ACM Trans. Comput. Syst. **32**(2), 5 (2014)
17. Miller, B., Pearce, P., Grier, C., Kreibich, C., Paxson, V.: What's clicking what? Techniques and innovations of today's clickbots. In: Holz, T., Bos, H. (eds.) DIMVA 2011. LNCS, vol. 6739, pp. 164–183. Springer, Heidelberg (2011). https://doi.org/10.1007/978-3-642-22424-9_10
18. Qiu, H., Noura, H., Qiu, M.: A user-centric data protection method for cloud storage based on invertible DWT. IEEE Trans. Cloud Comput. (Early Access), 1 (2017)
19. Qiu, H., Memmi, G.: Fast selective encryption method for bitmaps based on GPU acceleration. In: IEEE International Symposium on Multimedia, pp. 155–158. IEEE (2014)
20. Qiu, H., Memmi, G., Kapusta, K., Lu, Z., Qiu, M.: All-or-nothing data protection for ubiquitous communication: challenges and perspectives. Inf. Sci. **502**, 434–445 (2019)

Music Rhythm Customized Mobile Application Based on Information Extraction

Yining Li[1($\boxtimes$)], Wei Hu[2], and Yonghao Wang[3]

[1] College of Computer Science and Technology,
Wuhan University of Science and Technology, Wuhan, China
wustlyn@gmail.com
[2] Hubei Province Key Laboratory of Intelligent Information
Processing and Real-Time Industria System, Wuhan, China
huwei@wust.edu.cn
[3] Digital Media Lab, Birmingham City University, Birmingham, UK
Yonghao.wang@bcu.ac.uk

Abstract. Information extraction technology to be able to measure, store, collect all kinds of information, especially the direct access to important information, which is based on mobile applications and more convenient for the information gathering process, user and information feedback, greatly reduce the cost of information technology, makes the implementation of large-scale information extraction technology possible. As for this paper, first of all, mainly introduces the basic theory of music rhythm customization mobile application; Secondly, the development and implementation of this application are introduced; Finally, it summarizes and anticipates the future development trend of music rhythm customization technology. After implementation, users only need to import music or video that they want to modify, select the corresponding style or double speed, and then get relevant audio results through system software processing. And make music rhythm customization easy to operate, which remove a lot of irrelevant operations, so that users do not need to know the relevant professional knowledge can be processed.

Keywords: Rhythm tracking · Audio processing · Information extraction · A mobile application

1 Introduction

The rhythm tracking mainly uses information extraction technology. This technology was first used in surveying and mapping to extract useful information for users in remote sensing images [1]. The earliest possible application of this technology to the field of music was the feature extraction of phrase-based music information retrieval published by Japanese scholars in 1999.

In this paper, the audio data is converted into an audio stream, and the audio data is transformed into a data frame by the rhythm extraction algorithm by using the frame changeable characteristics of the audio data stream, and the audio is clipped by using the selected double speed time stretching algorithm, and then the template is used. Process audio frames, create/edit your own audio, save it in the sandbox or share it with

© Springer Nature Switzerland AG 2019
M. Qiu (Ed.): SmartCom 2019, LNCS 11910, pp. 304–309, 2019.
https://doi.org/10.1007/978-3-030-34139-8_30

your friends. Developers only need to add their own customized templates, users only need to import the audio they need to modify, adjust the paragraphs that need to be modified, and select the corresponding speed and template to get their own music. In the end, this paper designed a rhythm customization application centered on information extraction, which realized a simple and clear audio editing method.

Rhythm tracking technology is essentially a technique that converts the music data imported by the user into an array of rhythms and edits the audio array accordingly [2]. The music rhythm customization technology based on information extraction is used for mobile application development. With the rhythm tracking algorithm and time stretching algorithm of ffmpeg audio and video framework on audio, the effect of customized music is achieved: (1) It is easy to operate, removes a lot of unrelated operations, can be processed without the user knowing the relevant professional knowledge; (2) rich rhythm templates are available; (3) free time stretching, software supports the start and end time interception and speed editing of imported audio.

2 Related Work

2.1 Rhythm Tracking Algorithm

There is no doubt about the importance of data. With the growing popularity of big data, the importance of data information extraction, data analysis and processing is also becoming increasingly prominent. At present, in addition to theoretical research on big data, there are also ongoing technical research abroad, with the focus on data application and data engineering. In China, the development of big data is relatively young. In the 13th five-year plan released by the Chinese government on November 3, 2015, the term "big data strategy" was put forward for the first time [3]. At present, the research of big data in China mainly lies in distributed storage and cloud computing. Only a few enterprises can use the integrated process of data acquisition, data analysis and data processing.

According to the current situation, information extraction system and data control system have been closely combined and developed in two directions: one is distributed information extraction and data control system, and the other is distributed information extraction and data control system. Information extraction technology is the data source of big data technology, and big data technology is the support of the current hot artificial intelligence technology. Therefore, the information extraction technology in the future will still develop at a very fast speed and towards the direction of extracting massive data.

In this paper, an iOS platform mobile application named LickMixeR-N was designed, which realized the rhythm tracking algorithm and time stretching algorithm based on ffmpeg audio and video framework, and used it in audio to realize the effect of changing music and video imported by users and realizing customized music. In this application, users only need to import the music or video they want to modify, select the corresponding style or double speed, and then through the system software processing to get relevant audio results.

3   Proposed Model

3.1   Rhythm Tracking Algorithm

Subsequent paragraphs, however, are indented. The main rhythm tracking algorithm consists of three steps: intermediate input representation, general state, and contextual state. The middle input representation, also known as rhythm detection function, converts the input audio signal into an array of audio frames, serving as an intermediate signal between the input audio rhythm and the output audio rhythm. The tracking formula is shown in formula (1):

$$\Gamma(m) = \sum_{k=1}^{K} \left| S_k(m) - \hat{S}_k(m) \right|^2. \tag{1}$$

In general, the main task is to detect the rhythm periodicity and the rhythm alignment without knowing the audio input [4]. The main task of context-dependent state is to merge and extract context-dependent information (including rhythm, time signature and past rhythm location) from audio input into relevant parameters [5]. In order to achieve the effect of emphasizing significant rhythm and discarding insignificant rhythm, the adaptive moving average range of a frame is calculated as shown in formula (2):

$$\bar{\Gamma}_i(m) = \text{mean}\{\Gamma_i(q)\} \quad m - \frac{Q}{2} \le q \le m + \frac{Q}{2} \tag{2}$$

Rhythm tracks are cut into the frame, query beat alignment, contextual, cycle a few characteristics, and the general state of running in the form of no memory, extracted by repeating rhythms cycle and alignment, the disadvantages of this method lies in the context, makes the final results do not have continuity, and the strong consistency we hear music is a big difference [6]. Single use general state can generate many unnecessary mistakes, therefore, need to introduce the contextual state is used to solve and separately to solve the problem of continuous audio output.

3.2   Time Stretch and Audio Spectrum Display

Time stretch means to stretch the length of input audio [7]. The source audio is cropped by selecting the start time and end time. The audio spectrum display uses the fast Fourier transform algorithm to transform the input audio into the corresponding spectrum array [8], which is finally displayed on the interface.

Time stretch can call the function in rubber band Audio, input the Audio rhythm array and corresponding doubling speed, select the corresponding conversion mode, and then get the result rhythm array [9]; Then the result array is transformed into a spectrum image by fast Fourier transform and displayed on the interface in real time. You can use the time stretch function to complete the audio processing [10].

4 Experiment

4.1 Audio Production

First of all, since this app is a pure iOS platform audio mobile app, what needs to be considered is how to import local audio [11]. Apple has made the API of audio selection for developers in its own framework. Just import the relevant framework and you can easily use MPMediaItem to store audio files of iOS.

Second, this article describes an audio editing application, so the second step is to process the audio just obtained, including the intermediate input layer representation, general state processing, and context-dependent state mentioned above in rhythm tracking theory, this part is mainly the use of rhythm tracking algorithm to achieve;

Then through the user's input to the audio file time and double speed editing, this part mainly USES the time stretch technology to achieve;

Finally, after editing audio in local or share out, for users to upload audio data security, did not use the cloud database, but instead USES application sandbox to save the audio data for the user, the user can see myself in the historical view of all the audio data, and view or delete it [10]; If users want to export/share their results, they can upload audio files from the sandbox to DropBox, and then further share/export. The workflow of the whole application is shown in Fig. 1:

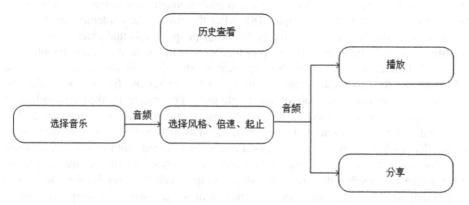

Fig. 1. A figure caption is always placed below the illustration. Short captions are centered, while long ones are justified. The macro button chooses the correct format automatically.

Can be seen from the diagram, the design of the audio file operations is the main process of the one-way, and users can at any time to back up one step operation, but not finished step, as long as the user will not be able to take the next step operation, so the application interface card operation, background using the album cover (the url of the picture in the MEMediaItem album Image attribute), will be applied to each function into one card [12]. Then according to the steps to use ScrollView paging was carried out on the card, and then set the card swiping to step on the unfinished disable mode [13].

4.2   Development of Implementation

In this paper, the development environment of music rhythm customized mobile application based on information extraction is taken as an example under the MacOS operating system [14]. It uses CocoaPods third-party library introduction tool to import DropBox library, directly introduces FFMPEG audio and video processing framework and Fourier transform for operation, and uses iOS development tool Xcode for development [15]. FFMPEG is a very powerful audio and video processing framework developed by iOS. Its main functions include recording, converting digital audio, video, and converting them into data stream, audio and video encoding/decoding, etc. [16].

The main design idea is to introduce FFMPEG framework from the outside, configure CocoaPods, import algorithm function and related files into the framework using ovocaine framework and other fast Fourier transform framework to play, and finally use Xib file based on Interface Builder tool to describe part of the view in a graphical way [17].

5   Conclusion

As a symbol of the inheritance of human civilization and a weathervane of times culture, music is the best mark of an era, and editing music only belongs to oneself has become the interest of many people [18]. After the rise of the contemporary Internet, music entertainment has become the just need of people's spiritual entertainment, and editing music only belongs to themselves has become the interest of many people. The music rhythm customization mobile application described in this article based on information extraction makes music editing no longer remote for non-professionals, and realizes the customization of music rhythm. The music rhythm customization mobile application described in this article based on information extraction makes music editing no longer remote for non-professionals, and realizes the customization of music rhythm [19]. This paper presents a music customized mobile application based on information extraction. By applying rhythm extraction and rhythm tracking algorithm to the audio submitted by users, users can turn their little inspirations into audio output that actually conforms to the definition of music template with simple operation. Due to the customization of uploaded audio, users can generate their own music [20]. In short, the music customized mobile application based on information extraction implemented in this paper does not require high design and development costs, and is of great practical value due to its simple operation, simple page and stable function.

References

1. Yu, Z.: The positioning, reasons and significance of the relationship between rites and music in early confucianism. Film Rev. Introduction **18**, 106–109 (2010)
2. Ravi, N.D., Bhalke, D.G.: Musical instrument information retrieval using neural network (2016)

3. Wang, Y.: Concept and practice of data journalism in the context of big data. Mod. Media **23** (6), 16–17 (2015)
4. Fu, H., Chen, C., Xiang, Y., et al.: Research and implementation of key technologies for distributed big data acquisition. Guangdong Commun. Technol. **35**(10), 7–10 (2015)
5. Davies, M.E.P., Plumbley, M.D.: Context-dependent beat tracking of musical audio. IEEE Trans. Audio Speech Lang. Process. **15**(3), 009–1020 (2007)
6. Chu, W., Champagne, B.F.: Further studies of a FFT-based auditory spectrum with application in audio classification. In: International Conference on Signal Processing, pp. 1–3 (2008)
7. Degara, N., Rua, E.A., Pena, A., et al.: Reliability-informed beat tracking of musical signals. IEEE Trans. Audio Speech Lang. Process. **20**(1), 290–301 (2012)
8. Mohapatra, B.N., Mohapatra, R.K.: FFT and sparse FFT techniques and applications. In: Fourteenth International Conference on Wireless & Optical Communications Networks, pp. 1–5. IEEE (2017)
9. Zhan, Y., Yuan, X.: Audio post-processing detection and identification based on audio features. In: International Conference on Wavelet Analysis & Pattern Recognition, pp. 3–7. IEEE (2017)
10. Greamo, C., Ghosh, A.: Sandboxing and virtualization: modern tools for combating malware. IEEE Secur. Priv. **9**(2), 79–82 (2011)
11. Pang, B.: Development trend of interface design from flat style. Decoration **4**, 127–128 (2014)
12. Roig, C., Tardón, L.J., Barbancho, I., et al.: Automatic melody composition based on a probabilistic model of music style and harmonic rules. Knowl.-Based Syst. **71**, 419–434 (2014)
13. Marchand, S.: Fourier-based methods for the spectral analysis of musical sounds. In: Signal Processing Conference, pp. 1–5. IEEE (2014)
14. Li, P., Zou, Z.: Loop of the scroll view class (UIScrollView) in apple iOS and algorithm of dynamic image loading. Comput. Telecom **10**, 54–55 (2011)
15. Liu, C., Zhou, B., Guo, S.: Load optimization of large quantity data based on UITableView in iOS. J. Hangzhou Univ. Electron. Sci. Technol. **4**, 46–49 (2013)
16. Ma, Z.: Digital rights management: model, technology and application. China Commun. **14** (6), 156–167 (2017)
17. Kim, B., Pardo, B.: Speeding learning of personalized audio equalization. In: International Conference on Machine Learning & Applications, 3–6 (2015)
18. Rong, F.: Audio classification method based on machine learning. In: International Conference on Intelligent Transportation, pp. 3–5. IEEE Computer Society (2016)
19. Liu, L., Bian, J., Zhang, L., et al.: Implementation of audio and video synchronization based on FFMPEG decoding. Comput. Eng. Des. **34**(6), 2087–2092 (2013)
20. Akram, F., Garcia, M.A., Puig, D.: Active contours driven by local and global fitted image models for image segmentation robust to intensity in homogeneity. PLoS ONE **12**(4), 1–32 (2017)

Computational Challenges and Opportunities in Financial Services

Art Sedighi$^{(\boxtimes)}$ and Doug Jacobson$^{(\boxtimes)}$

Department of Electrical and Computer Engineering, Iowa State University,
Ames, IA 50011, USA
{asedighi,dougj}@iastate.edu

Abstract. As one of the fastest growing areas of applied scientific computing, financial services uses high performance computing techniques to respond to both governmental regulatory bodies as well as to deal with a fast-paced business environment. Financial services industry is data driven and aims to resolve mathematical challenges to make sense out of data to solve complex problems in pricing, risk management, and portfolio optimization. These challenges are solved by financial institutions regularly, and the goal here is to provide a short survey of approaches and techniques used to solve these problems. Cloud is one of the areas of interest, since said challenges can benefit from the dynamicity and metered pricing of Cloud computing, plus being virtually limitless in scale. FPGA- and GPU-as-a-Service will also be explored as they are showing a great deal of benefit in solving such problems.

Keywords: Cloud · Financial services · Microsoft Azure · HPC · Machine learning · Risk calculation · Derivatives pricing · Portfolio optimization

1 Summary

Financial services is one of the fastest growing areas of applied scientific computing [1]. Computationally intensive problems solved by financial services require not only an extensive array of traditional x86 processors but have shown to benefit from other exotic and proprietary hardware such as GPU [2, 3], FPGA [4, 5] and even custom ASIC [6]. In addition to the heterogeneity of the infrastructure, different methods of computation have also been applied in financial services such machine learning, AI [7], various simulation methods [4, 5, 8–10], along with many different mathematical techniques from statistics, to numerical methods [11] to Stochastic Differential Equations [12]. This paper aims to provide a short survey of the top computationally intensive workloads in financial services, and the methods and techniques used to solve them. First, the top business questions that lead to computationally difficult problems will be outlined. This is followed by some methods used to solve these problems, albeit most use some form of heuristic method due to the difficulty entailed. We will then delve into the runtime aspect of these problems and what capabilities cloud, mainly Azure [13], provides vis-à-vis infrastructure capabilities to aide in solving said challenges.

© Springer Nature Switzerland AG 2019
M. Qiu (Ed.): SmartCom 2019, LNCS 11910, pp. 310–319, 2019.
https://doi.org/10.1007/978-3-030-34139-8_31

2   Overview of Challenges in Financial Services

The majority of the complex problems in finance stem from one of the following three areas: (a) pricing, valuing and hedging of securities, (b) risk management [14] and (c) portfolio optimization [15].

Pricing of securities involved complex mathematical methods, most of which can only be solved using numerical methods or heuristically using methods like Monte Carlo simulations [3, 16–18]. The complexity arises from the fact that stock prices follow Brownian Motion (BM) in that they move in an irregular, non-differentiable, and non-smooth fashion [19]. To model stock prices, and as a result, the rest of the financial markets, the non-differentiability aspect of Brownian Motion requires the use of Stochastic Differential Equations (SDEs) [12]. SDEs discretize stock prices into infinitesimal pieces, model or simulate each component, and collect the result set.

The primary goal of risk management is to estimate the loss with a certain level of confidence ($11.55–$11.57 million with a confidence level of 99%, for example). The potential loss translates to capital requirement from a regulatory perspective, and to trading decision from a portfolio optimization perspective [14]. Risk management encompasses a number of different risk calculations, some of which are regulatory enforced [20–23]. The majority of risk calculations require vast computational power due to the complexity of the problem [9, 10, 24–29].

Portfolio optimization is affected by the preferences set by the investor, the constraints set by the investor, governmental bodies, regulations, taxes and many other decisions made to optimize the portfolio based on the aforementioned preferences and constraints [1]. Taxes and tax implications have particularly shown to have a great implication on portfolio optimization [30].

The aforementioned complexities are caused by mathematical challenges. Solving these problems using the set of tools and techniques at our disposal has received a great deal of attention over the years, and that research is still ongoing. Some of the details behind the mathematical problems will further be explored in the next section.

The ability to efficiently use the available technologies such as cloud, multi-core processors, FPGA's, GPUs, and purpose-build hardware in order to adequately and cost effectively solve complex mathematical methods will be covered in the later section of this paper.

3   Computational Challenges in Pricing and Valuating Securities

Derivative securities have payoff functions that are dependent on other securities, known as the underlying [31]. The primary use of derivatives is to hedge own risk or transfer the risk to others [14]. Pricing and valuing European options, American options, Asian options, Mortgage Backed Securities (MBS), credit derivatives, credit default swaps, and collateral debt obligations [11, 16, 32–35] are examples of derivative securities which present a computational challenge in finance. They all depend on the value, price and performance of one or more underlying securities such as bonds or equities.

Monte Carlo (MC) method is used to simulate and determine options pricing. MC heavily depends of random numbers or pseudo-random numbers for pseudo-Monte Carlo [4] simulations. Generating truly random numbers at scale represents a computational challenge in financial services [36, 37]. The Computational complexity of the standard MC is O(n3) [38], with n representing the random number generated for the simulation. Reducing the computational complexity of MC to anything lower represents another challenge in financial services [39].

Pricing of exotic options [40] represent another computational challenge in finance [39]. Exotic options can be used in trading of different asset classes like commodities: coffee, corn, pork belly, and crude oil, along with equities, bonds and foreign exchange. All the aforementioned components need to be discretized individually. As different asset classes are added to the mix, discretizing will become a challenge, and prone to error [41]. As a result, the combinatorial of different choices of asset classes is explored, which itself introduces another computational challenge in financial services.

4   Computational Challenges in Risk Management

The core of risk management is to measure risk in the context of [42]:

- Market Risk as it relates to changes in prices of assets
- Value-at-Risk (VaR) as it relates to determining with a level of confidence the maximum loss over a period of time
- Credit Risk as it relates to the level of loss vis-à-vis probability of default of a payment of a loan or borrowing
- Operational Risk as it relates to the loss due to operational processes or an event, internal or externally caused
- Liquidity Risk as it relates to the inability of a financial institution to transform from one asset class to another

Monte Carlo (MC) or pseudo-Monte Carlo methods are generally used to calculate Value-at-Risk [9], and more generally speaking, to measure the risk posture in financial services. As mentioned in the prior section, the primary goal of risk management is to estimate the loss with a certain level of confidence. Calculating this loss function represents a challenge in financial services [39].

As is the case with heuristic approaches to solve complex problems, there is no single correct answer, so the simulations run many times with different parameters. Multi-level MC simulations are likely as the number of unknowns increase, and those unknowns need to be estimated as well, before final loss function estimation. Finding the balance between what is known as inner- and outer-Monte Carlo in terms of the number of unknowns and calculations represents another challenge in financial services. At the end, the results are collated and analyzed. This is a challenging problem by itself, although not computationally challenging but would fall under data challenges in financial services, as the correct result is not known, and further analysis is required to find the most likely result.

Computational challenges translate to longer running jobs. Even though tremendous amount of effort has gone into parallelizing these runs, there is still much more to be done. Risk calculations have normally been done overnight. Another computational challenge is to reduce the runtime of calculating risk, and moving towards what is known as intraday risk simulation and calculations [39, 43, 44].

5   Computational Challenges in Portfolio Optimization

Portfolio optimization involves a constraint-based allocation problem with an objective function that is based on the preferences set forth by the investor. As the number of investment options increase, so does the difficulty in the decision-making process. Computational finance has been used in portfolio optimization tasks [15], along with more advanced mathematical and optimization techniques [17]. Taxes and tax implication of portfolio optimization has added a level of difficulty to portfolio optimization as well [30]. The computational challenge with portfolio optimization is caused by the dynamicity aspect of the positions in a portfolio, and the quick response requirement that is elevated due to a vast pool of alternatives. Dynamic programming is used to model portfolio optimization [1, 15].

6   Data Challenges

Although the focus has been on computational challenges in finance, challenges in data are tied to the why and the how of the challenges presented.

Financial services has always been a data driven industry, but the conventional methods via which financial data has been managed have become a challenge for financial services. The telemetry generated by a financial transaction: seller information, buyer information, price, P&L, positions, along with industry-related telemetry such as interest rate, commodity prices, equity prices, bond rate, foreign exchange rate, have added to the level of interest coming from financial services. About 70% of US equity trades are machine-driven using High Frequency Trading (HFT) techniques. Due to advancement in technology, there is an exponential increase in data generated by recent HFT. This has translated to Ultrahigh Frequency Data (UHFD), and storing, accessing and making sense out of this data in a reasonable timeframe is a data challenge facing financial services [45]. The interest is shifting to UHFD as UHFD-based volatility models [46] have shown to have improved statistical efficiency, and be very useful in evaluation of daily volatility forecasts [47, 48]. With UHFD, financial services are now able to achieve accurate intraday volatility measures using machine learning techniques and statistical models [45, 49, 50].

However, computational challenges are now facing additional challenges brought upon by the increase in data volume.

7 Solutioning Options

Table 1 summarizes the different computational challenges outlined in this paper. These challenges are solved by financial institutions regularly, and the goal here is provide a survey of approaches to these challenges. This paper considers Microsoft Azure [13] as the cloud provider for this study. Azure offers a broad range of capabilities considered for this research including a range of Virtual machines [51], GPU's and FPGA's [52].

Table 1. Summary of challenges and solutioning options

Challenges	Bottleneck	Cloud	GPU	FPGA
Random number generation at scale	Computation and distribution	Yes [65]	Yes [2]	Yes [4, 39, 66]
Reducing $O(n^3)$ complexity of Monte Carlo	Computation and model creation	Yes [63]	Yes [63]	N/A
Discretization of [pricing] data that follows Brownian Motion	Model creation	Not needed or No Data Available	Yes [3]	Yes [39]
Multi-level Monte-Carlo (inner-loop vs. outer loop optimization)	Computation	Not needed or No Data Available	Yes [67, 68]	Yes [39, 67, 68]
Reducing VaR runtime to enable intraday risk calculation	Computation	Yes [69]	Yes [68]	Yes [39, 68]
Dynamic portfolio optimization that is tax efficient	Computation	Yes [1, 15, 17]	No Data Available	No Data Available
Portfolio optimization in highly dynamic portfolio positions	Computation and data distribution	Yes [1, 15, 17]	No Data Available	No Data Available
Ultra-high frequency data challenge	Data lifecycle management	Yes [60]	N/A	N/A

Properties of cloud [53–55] have shown to benefit the large-scale needs of financial services. General Purpose GPU (GPGPU) computation can aide in solving problems with high parallelization needs. Field Programmable Gate Arrays (FPGA) based computing has the capability to be customized to a specific problem, and as such to dramatically increase performance.

The overall goal for any option presented is to allow for intra-day risk calculation to occur. Intra-day risk calculation is hindered by strict time requirement. If calculation needs to occur to measure risk across the entire portfolio before the decision on the next transaction to take place, then the timing allotted to do such calculation is bound by the speed of business. In other words, there is no limit on the need to speed up these calculations. This requirement sets the basis for much of the large-scale deployments of compute in financial services.

7.1 Cloud

The properties of cloud such as metered usage, and dynamic provisioning is useful in most cases, specially more so in cases where quick response is needed that would require a dynamic buildout of a new environment [56]. The dynamic provisioning of resources can reduce computation time as it allows virtually unlimited scalability. The dynamicity of cloud to rapidly scale up to 1000's of VM's [57, 58] can reduce the need to spent time creating complex models and allow for rapid testing. This can potentially reduce the overall runtime of the calculations and allow for intra-day risk models [59] to run. Fast VMs coupled with the availability of high-speed networking and technology like Infiniband [57, 58] can reduce the interprocess communication delays, which in turn can assist with the task of random number distribution. To tackle the storage bottleneck introduced by UHFD on the cloud, a cloud-based high-speed storage environment would be desirable [60].

Machine learning and optimization techniques are often used for portfolio optimization [15, 61, 62]. A new approach that can potentially replace traditional Monte Carlo simulations with Neural Networks has shown to reduce calculation times exponentially [63].

In additions to the traditional VM-based machine learning deployments, machine learning and optimization models are now finding their way on both Cloud-based FPGAs [62], and GPUs [63, 64].

7.2 GPU

GPU-based infrastructure has been used to speed up risk and pricing calculation in financial services [2, 3, 70]. The many-core capability of GPU's have the ability to run potentially 1000's of tasks in parallel, thus reducing the overall runtime. Some cloud-based GPU's are capable of ~ 3 Teraflops of double-precision operation across ~ 5000 cores [71].

As mentioned before, one of the main challenges of financial services is options pricing, and more specifically, exotic options pricing. GPU's have been used to be able to do both very efficiently [72–74]. GPUs have been used develop a Neural Network-based approach to replace Monte Carlo simulations in pricing derivatives [63]. GPUs have the capability to provide raw computational power, with little to change to the method by which these models are solved. FPGA's, however, have the capability to introduce a new paradigm in solving computational challenges in financial services.

7.3   FPGA

FPGA's allow for an alternate method of solving computationally challenging problems. Random number generation is inherent in FPGA's and thus easier to compute as demonstrated in [66]. Quasi-random numbers have also been tested and proven to function at great speeds on FPGA's [4]. Putting an entire Monte Carlo simulation on an FPGA has also been demonstrated in [5, 75] with a good degree of success.

Azure has demonstrated the performance gain achievable with their FPGA-based SmartNIC [76] network cards. The authors demonstrate a <15 ms VM-VM TCP latencies and 40+ Gbps throughput. The reconfigurability of the FPGA-based network cards proved to be a valuable feature as changes and bugs could simply be deployed in real-time. FPGA's [and GPU's] are used as CPU offloads, in that tasks are off-loaded to the FPGA in order to reduce the load on the CPU cores. This does require code change, as the process needs to be FPGA aware to utilize its capabilities. Even though the development costs are higher, cloud providers are still providing FPGA computing -as-a-Service as part of their service portfolio.

8   Conclusion

Financial services need to respond to both governmental regulatory bodies as well as deal with fast paced business environments. The combination of the two has made the financial services sector a hotbed for challenging problems and innovation. Pricing, portfolio optimization, and risk management are the main three areas from which challenges are derived. Computation and data challenges outlined in this paper have received a great deal of attention from the research community. Computational challenges can benefit from the dynamicity and metered pricing of Cloud computing, plus being virtually limitless in scale. FPGA- and GPU-as-a-Service are also becoming available as they are showing a great deal of benefit in solving such problems. The next step for this research is to evaluate specific benefits that stems from using Cloud, FPGA and GPU in solving these challenges.

References

1. Haugh, M.B., Lo, A.W.: Computational challenges in portfolio management. Comput. Sci. Eng. 3(3), 54 (2001)
2. Grauer-Gray, S., et al.: Accelerating financial applications on the GPU. In: Proceedings of the 6th Workshop on General Purpose Processor Using Graphics Processing Units. ACM (2013)
3. Solomon, S., Thulasiram, R.K., Thulasiraman, P.: Option pricing on the GPU. In: 2010 IEEE 12th International Conference on High Performance Computing and Communications (HPCC). IEEE (2010)
4. Banks, S., Beadling, P., Ferencz, A.: FPGA implementation of pseudo random number generators for Monte Carlo methods in quantitative finance. In: 2008 International Conference on Reconfigurable Computing and FPGAs. IEEE (2008)

5. Woods, N.A., VanCourt, T.: FPGA acceleration of quasi-Monte Carlo in finance. In: 2008 International Conference on Field Programmable Logic and Applications. IEEE (2008)
6. Pottathuparambil, R., et al.: Low-latency FPGA based financial data feed handler. In: 2011 IEEE 19th Annual International Symposium on Field-Programmable Custom Computing Machines. IEEE (2011)
7. Krollner, B., Vanstone, B.J., Finnie, G.R.: Financial time series forecasting with machine learning techniques: a survey. In: ESANN (2010)
8. Eckhardt, R.: Stan Ulam, John von Neumann, and the Monte Carlo method. Los Alamos Sci. 15(131–136), 30 (1987)
9. Glasserman, P., Heidelberger, P., Shahabuddin, P.: Efficient Monte Carlo methods for value-at-risk (2010)
10. Tezuka, S., et al.: Monte Carlo grid for financial risk management. Future Gener. Comput. Syst. 21(5), 811–821 (2005)
11. Gobet, E.: Advanced Monte Carlo methods for barrier and related exotic options. In: Handbook of Numerical Analysis, pp. 497–528. Elsevier (2009)
12. Kloeden, P.E., Platen, E.: Numerical Solution of Stochastic Differential Equations, vol. 23. Springer, Berlin (2013). https://doi.org/10.1007/978-3-662-12616-5
13. Microsoft Azure (2018). http://azure.microsoft.com. Accessed 12 Feb 2018
14. Staum, J.: Monte Carlo computation in finance. In: L'Ecuyer, P., Owen, A. (eds.) Monte Carlo and Quasi-Monte Carlo Methods. Springer, Berlin (2009)
15. Joseph, T.: Computational financing techniques and fundamental challenges in portfolio optimization. IOSR J. Hum. Soc. Sci. 9(6), 51–58 (2013)
16. Black, F., Scholes, M.: The pricing of options and corporate liabilities. J. Polit. Econ. 81(3), 637–654 (1973)
17. Korn, R., Korn, E.: Option Pricing and Portfolio Optimization: Modern Methods of Financial Mathematics, vol. 31. American Mathematical Society (2001)
18. Korn, R., Müller, S.: Binomial Trees in Option Pricing—History, Practical Applications and Recent Developments. In: Devroye, L., Karasözen, B., Kohler, M., Korn, R. (eds.) Recent Developments in Applied Probability and Statistics, pp. 59–77. Springer, Berlin (2010). https://doi.org/10.1007/978-3-7908-2598-5_3
19. Karatzas, I., Shreve, S.E.: Brownian Motion and Stochastic Calculus. Springer, New York (1991)
20. Committee, B.: Basel III: a global regulatory framework for more resilient banks and banking systems. Basel Committee on Banking Supervision, Basel (2010)
21. Gleeson, S.: International Regulation of Banking: Basel II: Capital and Risk Requirements. OUP Catalogue (2010)
22. Hakenes, H., Schnabel, I.: Bank size and risk-taking under Basel II. J. Bank. Finance 35(6), 1436–1449 (2011)
23. Tarullo, D.K.: Banking on Basel: The Future of International Financial Regulation. Peterson Institute (2008)
24. Alexander, C.: Volatility and correlation: measurement, models and applications. Risk Manag. Anal. 1, 125–171 (1998)
25. Brummelhuis, R., et al.: Principal component value at risk. Math. Finance 12(1), 23–43 (2002)
26. Chong, J., Keutzer, K., Dixon, M.F.: Acceleration of Market Value-at-Risk Estimation. Available at SSRN 1576402 (2009)
27. Giot, P.: Market risk models for intraday data. Eur. J. Finance 11(4), 309–324 (2005)
28. Jorion, P.: Value at Risk. McGraw-Hill, New York (1997)
29. McNeil, A.J., Frey, R., Embrechts, P.: Quantitative Risk Management: Concepts, Techniques and Tools. Princeton University Press (2015)

30. Bertsimas, D., Lo, A.W.: Optimal control of execution costs. J. Financ. Mark. **1**(1), 1–50 (1998)
31. Bodie, Z., et al.: Investments. McGraw-Hill Education (2015)
32. Heston, S.L.: A closed-form solution for options with stochastic volatility with applications to bond and currency options. Rev. Financ. Stud. **6**(2), 327–343 (1993)
33. Giesecke, K.: An overview of credit derivatives. Available at SSRN 1307880 (2009)
34. Giesecke, K.: Portfolio credit risk: top-down versus bottom-up approaches. Front. Quant. Finance, 251 (2009)
35. Fabozzi, F.J.: The Handbook of Mortgage-Backed Securities. Oxford University Press (2016)
36. Gentle, J.E.: Random Number Generation and Monte Carlo Methods. Springer, Berlin (2006). https://doi.org/10.1007/b97336
37. Niederreiter, H.: Quasi-Monte Carlo methods and pseudo-random numbers. Bull. Am. Math. Soc. **84**(6), 957–1041 (1978)
38. Anderson, D.F., Higham, D.J., Sun, Y.: Computational complexity analysis for Monte Carlo approximations of classically scaled population processes. Multiscale Model. Simul. **16**(3), 1206–1226 (2018)
39. Desmettre, S., Korn, R.: 10 computational challenges in finance. In: De Schryver, C. (ed.) FPGA Based Accelerators for Financial Applications, pp. 1–31. Springer, Cham (2015). https://doi.org/10.1007/978-3-319-15407-7_1
40. Zhang, P.G.: Exotic options: a guide to second generation options. World Scientific (1998)
41. Dempster, M., Hutton, J.: Fast numerical valuation of American, exotic and complex options. Appl. Math. Finance **4**(1), 1–20 (1997)
42. Pan, S.-Q.: A survey of financial risk measurement. In: 6th International Conference on Management Science and Management Innovation (MSMI 2019). Atlantis Press (2019)
43. Sedighi, A., Deng, Y., Zhang, P.: Fariness of task scheduling in high performance computing environments. Scalable Comput.: Pract. Exp. **15**(3), 273–285 (2014)
44. Sedighi, A., Smith, M.: Fair Scheduling in High Performance Computing Environments. Springer, Cham (2019). https://doi.org/10.1007/978-3-030-14568-2
45. Seth, T., Chaudhary, V.: Big Data in Finance (2015)
46. Barndorff-Nielsen, O.E., Shephard, N.: Power and bipower variation with stochastic volatility and jumps. J. Financ. Econom. **2**(1), 1–37 (2004)
47. Bollerslev, T., Wright, J.H.: High-frequency data, frequency domain inference, and volatility forecasting. Rev. Econ. Stat. **83**(4), 596–602 (2001)
48. Grammig, J., Wellner, M.: Modeling the interdependence of volatility and inter-transaction duration processes. J. Econom. **106**(2), 369–400 (2002)
49. Comte, F., Renault, E.: Long memory in continuous-time stochastic volatility models. Math. Finance **8**(4), 291–323 (1998)
50. McAleer, M., Medeiros, M.C.: Realized volatility: a review. Econom. Rev. **27**(1–3), 10–45 (2008)
51. High performance compute VM sizes. Virtual Machine Documentation (2019). https://docs.microsoft.com/en-us/azure/virtual-machines/windows/sizes-hpc. Accessed 22 July 2019
52. What are field-programmable gate arrays (FPGA) (2019). https://docs.microsoft.com/en-us/azure/machine-learning/service/concept-accelerate-with-fpgas. Accessed 22 July 2019
53. Armbrust, M., et al.: Above the Clouds: A Berkeley View of Cloud Computing (2009)
54. Avram, M.-G.: Advantages and challenges of adopting cloud computing from an enterprise perspective. Procedia Technol. **12**, 529–534 (2014)
55. Armbrust, M., et al.: A view of cloud computing. Commun. ACM **53**(4), 50–58 (2010)
56. Smith, D.M.: Cloud computing primer for 2016. Gartner Inc., Stamford (2016)

57. Azure HC-series Virtual Machines cross 20,000 cores for HPC workloads (2019). https:// azure.microsoft.com/en-us/blog/azure-hc-series-virtual-machines-crosses-20000-cores-for-hpc-workloads/. Accessed 22 July 2019

58. Working with large virtual machine scale sets (2019). https://docs.microsoft.com/en-us/ azure/virtual-machine-scale-sets/virtual-machine-scale-sets-placement-groups. Accessed 22 July 2019

59. Enabling the financial services risk lifecycle with Azure and R. (2019). https://docs. microsoft.com/en-us/azure/industry/financial/fsi-risk-modeling. Accessed 22 July 2019

60. Cray in Azure (2019). https://azure.microsoft.com/en-us/solutions/high-performance-computing/cray/. Accessed 22 July 2019

61. What is axiomaBlue? (2019). https://www.axioma.com/products/axiomablue/. Accessed 22 July 2019

62. Deploy a model as a web service on an FPGA with Azure Machine Learning service (2019). https://docs.microsoft.com/en-us/azure/machine-learning/service/how-to-deploy-fpga-web-service. Accessed 22 July 2019

63. Ferguson, R., Green, A.D.: Deeply learning derivatives. Available at SSRN 3244821 (2018)

64. Deploy a deep learning model for inference with GPU (2019). https://docs.microsoft.com/ en-us/azure/machine-learning/service/how-to-deploy-inferencing-gpus. Accessed 22 July 2019

65. Kerrigan, B., Chen, Y.: A study of entropy sources in cloud computers: random number generation on cloud hosts. In: Kotenko, I., Skormin, V. (eds.) MMM-ACNS 2012. LNCS, vol. 7531, pp. 286–298. Springer, Heidelberg (2012). https://doi.org/10.1007/978-3-642-33704-8_24

66. Yap, A.Y.: Information Systems for Global Financial Markets: Emerging Developments and Effects: Emerging Developments and Effects. IGI Global (2011)

67. Tian, X., Benkrid, K.: High performance quasi-monte carlo financial simulation: FPGA vs. GPP vs. GPU. ACM Trans. Reconfigurable Technol. Syst. (TRETS) 3(4), 26 (2010)

68. Singla, N., et al.: Financial Monte Carlo simulation on architecturally diverse systems. In: 2008 Workshop on High Performance Computational Finance. IEEE (2008)

69. Kim, H., et al.: Online risk analytics on the cloud. In: Proceedings of the 2009 9th IEEE/ACM International Symposium on Cluster Computing and the Grid. IEEE Computer Society (2009)

70. Qiu, M., et al.: Data transfer minimization for financial derivative pricing using Monte Carlo simulation with GPU in 5G. Int. J. Commun Syst 29(16), 2364–2374 (2016)

71. Azure N-Series VMs and NVIDIA GPUs in the Cloud (2016). https://buildazure.com/azure-n-series-vms-and-nvidia-gpus-in-the-cloud/. Accessed 31 July 2019

72. Bernemann, A., Schreyer, R., Spanderen, K.: Accelerating exotic option pricing and model calibration using GPUs. Available at SSRN 1753596 (2011)

73. Gaikwad, A., Toke, I.M.: GPU based sparse grid technique for solving multidimensional options pricing PDEs. In: Proceedings of the 2nd Workshop on High Performance Computational Finance. ACM (2009)

74. Abbas-Turki, L.A., Lapeyre, B.: American options pricing on multi-core graphic cards. In: 2009 International Conference on Business Intelligence and Financial Engineering. IEEE (2009)

75. De Schryver, C. (ed.): FPGA Based Accelerators for Financial Applications. Springer, Cham (2015). https://doi.org/10.1007/978-3-319-15407-7

76. Firestone, D., et al.: Azure accelerated networking: SmartNICs in the public cloud. In: 15th USENIX Symposium on Networked Systems Design and Implementation (NSDI 2018) (2018)

A Shamir Threshold Model Based Recoverable IP Watermarking Scheme

Weidong Xiao[1], Weihong Huang[2(✉)], Wei Liang[3], Xia Lei[4],
Jiahong Cai[1], Yuanming Wang[1], and Yanting Li[1]

[1] The School of Software, Xiamen University of Technology,
Xiamen 361024, Fujian, China
[2] The College of Computer Science and Electronic Engineering,
Hunan University, Changsha 410082, Hunan, China
whhuang@hnu.edu.cn
[3] The School of Opto-Electronic and Communication Engineering,
Xiamen University of Technology, Xiamen 361024, Fujian, China
[4] The Department of Computer and Technology, University of Petroleum,
Beijing 102249, China

Abstract. In order to solve the problems of low IP capacity and low robustness in existing IP watermarking techniques, this paper proposed a novel recoverable IP watermarking algorithm based on Shamir threshold model. This method takes (t, n) the threshold secret sharing scheme with t as the recovery factor. By constructing a mapping relationship among n sub-keys and watermark information S, n sub-keys of watermark cross-inserted into the respective watermark information S, and finally the embedded watermark information S is reconstructed. Experiment result shows that this method greatly improves the robustness of the watermark while expanding watermark information capacity. Compared to others watermarking algorithms, this method has the advantages of large watermark embedding capacity and high watermark recovery ability.

Keywords: Threshold scheme · Recoverable IP watermark · Recovery factor · Robustness · Self-recoverability

1 Introduction

With the rapid development of semiconductor technology and the increasing integration on a single chip, SOC technology has become more and more possible to integrate more functional SoC (system on chip) technology on a single chip, and has gradually become the mainstream of IC design. IP multiplexing technology plays a key role in solving design hierarchy, reducing product cost, shortening design cycle and reducing market risk in SoC design, but the phenomenon of unauthorized IP reuse is becoming increasingly common. Therefore, how to effectively protect intellectual property rights of IP cores has attracted the attention of researchers [1, 2].

The usual IP watermarking technology mainly embeds specific watermark identification information into any abstraction level in the IP design process according to the FPGA design flow. When it is necessary to obtain evidence, the copyright owner can

© Springer Nature Switzerland AG 2019
M. Qiu (Ed.): SmartCom 2019, LNCS 11910, pp. 320–329, 2019.
https://doi.org/10.1007/978-3-030-34139-8_32

detect the watermark information in the core product to prove its attribution, so as to achieve the purpose of copyright protection [3–5].

In order to prevent illegal users from pirating or forging IP cores at the behavioral level, Sengupta et al. [6] proposed a multivariate signature coding watermark generation technique existing in the Advanced Integrated Interval (HLS), which can improve the IP core reusability and security, although the watermark generated by the technology has the advantages of lower embedding cost, stronger author identification and lower hardware overhead, the technology needs to add more in the watermark embedding process. Additional constraints are used to represent the stored variables that enforce the interval graph. This scheme of key storage and key transmission through insecure channels poses certain risks for the security protection of IP cores. To this end, Abtioğlu et al. [7] have proposed an IP for FPGA platforms. Nuclear forgery protection method, in which they use the physical unclonable function (PUF) and the circuit in the device to generate a key, which solves the security problem of key transmission, and the feasibility of the method extremely depends on the reconfigurability of FPGA. Although this method can achieve high security and high randomness, the PUF mentioned in this method is designed based on some special scenarios, which will make it difficult to resist replay attacks and have security issues. In order to solve this problem, Zhang et al. [8] proposed a PUF-FSM binding method based on the protection configuration bitstream, and proposed a reconfigurable physical unclonable function (PUF) and finite state machine. The (FSM) combined locking scheme is used to defeat the replay attack. This method can effectively resist replay attacks and has the advantages of strong reconfigurability and low overhead. However, this method has unpredictable and usually high design and performance overhead characteristics. Cui et al. [9] proposed an ultra-low overhead watermarking scheme to protect IP cores. The scheme mainly enhances the flexibility of the local connection style by optimizing the scan design, and introduces the virtual scan unit by partial rewiring to achieve ultra-low overhead and characteristic of easy to detect, but this scheme has real-time and robustness characteristics of the bar is not high. In order to improve the robustness and real-time performance of the system, Liang et al. [10] proposed a method based on Hausdorff distance, which is used for identity verification of IC chips in IoT environment. LUT resources are used as a set of reconfigurable nodes in an FPGA. The method first embeds the copyright information into the selected unused LUT resources searched by the depth-first search algorithm, and then uses the Hausdorff distance matching function to reorder the random positions and then maps the positions to meet the specific constraints of the optimal watermark position. This team also proposed a method of hiding information in the core to achieve the purpose of proving original ownership [11]. This method introduces four methods based on core-core watermarking technology: FPGA technology, FSM technology, DFT technology and self-recovery dual core nuclear watermarking technology. This method mainly solves two problems: how to hide the information in the core circuit and how to authenticate the ownership of the core. The experimental results show that the method has the advantages of low power consumption and high watermarking resistance. Sengupta et al. [12] also proposed a novel multivariate signature coding method. The method is mainly applied to the process of embedding dynamic watermark information into the IP core, and optimizes the embedding cost of the watermark by the particle swarm optimization driving design based on the area delay constraint, thereby reducing the embedding cost, running time and reducing the storage hardware resource of the watermark system. However, its embedded capacity is limited and the real-time performance is not high.

It can be seen from the above research results that lots of IP watermark researches have been reported, but some problems still exist in previous methods, such as limited capacity and low watermark security. To this end, this paper proposes a reconfigurable dual IP watermarking algorithm based on the Shamir threshold scheme. Compared with the existing IP core watermarks, it is designed to improve the security and integrity of the watermark. The recoverable mechanism reduces the difficulty of design under the premise of ensuring security. At the same time, the method has the advantages of high security, large watermark capacity and recovery ability.

2 Recoverable IP Watermarking Scheme

The core watermark is a branch of the watermark technology to solve the problem of illegal theft in IP reuse. The recoverable IP watermark is embedded in the IP core to identify the copyright of IP core developer, which can more effectively prove its own copyright, and more decisively and powerfully judge the copyright infringement.

The watermark in this paper is designed as follows: Let first copyright information be Cr_1, the second copyright information be Cr_2. The encryption function is E and encryption key is ke. The watermark correlation function is denoted by F. The encrypted watermark information is respectively C_1, C_2. The watermark information are denoted by S_1, S_2. Let the embedded control key be kc, watermark embedding function be I, the watermark extraction function be A, the recovery function be R, and the watermarked IP carrier be T. The watermark will be transformed as follows during the preparation phase: $S_1 \leftarrow F(C_1, C_2) \rightarrow S_2$, where $C_1 = E(Cr_1, ke)$, $C_2 = (Cr_2, ke)$ are obtained by one encryption to obtain an encrypted watermark C_1, C_2, and then an association function is used to establish an association mechanism between the watermarks so that the information between the watermarks can be restored to each other. After the watermark is prepared, the watermark information S_1, S_2 after the encryption is associated and embedded in the reusable core T under the control of the control key kc, and the IP core product Ts containing the information between the watermarks is obtained, which is expressed by a mathematical expression: $Ts \leftarrow I(S_1, S_2, kc)$. When a copyright dispute occurs, the copyright owner can extract the watermark information in the reusable IP core $Cr_1' \leftarrow E^{-1}(A(kc), ke) \rightarrow Cr_2'$. If $Cr_1' = Cr_1$ or $Cr_2' = Cr_2$, the copyright of the IP core can be proven. If $Cr_1' \neq Cr_1$ and $Cr_2' \neq Cr_2$, the copyright cannot be proven. However, since the watermarks are mutually recovery, the correlation function F uses the Shamir threshold scheme to achieve mutual recovery. When C_1 in Ts is destroyed, the watermark information C_1, i.e. $C_1 = E^{-1}(R(S_2), ke)$, can be recovered by S_2, whereas C_2 is restored by S_1, i.e. $C_2 = E^{-1}(R(S_1), ke)$. Therefore, the watermark can protect the benefits of copyright owners to a greater extent.

The Shamir secret partitioning threshold scheme is an algorithm in cryptography, which can split a key into multiple sub-keys. The watermark generation in this paper depends on key reconstruction. It uses Shamir secret sharing scheme. The idea is as follows. The encrypted watermark information $c1, c2$ in the watermark is regarded as the secret $s(a_0)$ in the threshold scheme, and then the threshold principle based on Shamir key segmentation is respectively determined by $c1, c2$. The sub-keys c'_1, c'_2 are calculated, and then the sub-keys and partial watermark information are combined by a certain rule to form two new watermark information $s1, s2$. Since $s1$ contains the sub-key of $c2$ and $s2$ contains the sub-key of $c1$, both $c1$ and $c2$ can be restored respectively by $s2$ and $s1$. Therefore, a relational model between recoverable watermarks is established based on the principle of key reconstruction in the threshold scheme.

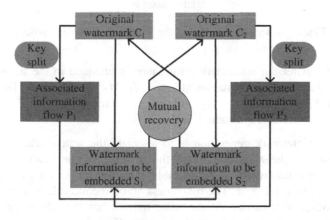

Fig. 1. Correlation between watermark information and watermark content recovery

3 Watermarking Algorithm Based on Threshold Scheme

3.1 Watermark Generation Algorithm

The generation of the digital watermark is divided into two parts: the preparation phase and the establishment of the association. In the preparation stage, in order to improve the confidentiality of the watermark information, the original watermark information is encrypted once. In view of the high sensitivity of chaotic sequence to the initial value of chaotic system and the high instability of chaotic sequence, the algorithm uses chaotic encryption technique to encrypt the original watermark information. In the second part, the key segmentation method in Shamir's secret partitioning scheme is used to establish the association between watermarks so that they can recover each other. The watermark processing method in this algorithm is consistent and does not distinguish. Specific steps are as follows:

1. Grouping. The original watermark information S is grouped into equal lengths to obtain a watermark information stream $M = \{m_i | i = 0, 1, 2 \ldots k\}$;

2. Encryption. The initial key *kh* is selected to initialize the chaotic system. The chaotic system generates the chaotic key sequence $K = \{k_i | i = 0, 1, 2, \ldots, k\}$, and the original watermark is encrypted by the function E. Finally, the encrypted watermark information stream M is obtained, that is, $C = E(M, K)$;

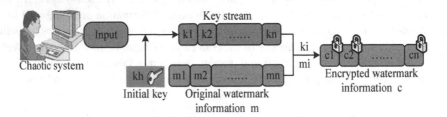

Fig. 2. Schematic diagram of the watermark generation process

3. Association. After the watermark information is obtained in the second step, two encrypted watermark information streams M_1, M_2 are obtained. The M_1, M_2 is associated $S_1 \leftarrow F(S1, S2) \rightarrow S_2$ with the correlation function F to obtain the embedded watermark information S_1, S_2.

The key of watermark generation is to associate the watermark. The correlation function F used in the association uses the principle of the Shamir secret sharing scheme. Since the watermark is recoverable, the implementation of the correlation function is described in Fig. 1. The robustness of the recoverable watermark is higher than that of other watermarks. At the same time, it has the advantages of stronger recovery ability and stronger anti-attack capability (Fig. 2).

3.2 Watermark Embedding Algorithm

The usual IP watermark embedding algorithm needs to convert the copyright information into the specific constraints before embedding. Then it is realized by using the development platform, or API provided by the electronic device manufacturer. To achieve resource searching and watermark embedding. The algorithm of this paper downloads the location information in the FPGA configuration file bitfile to randomly select the watermark location, and uses the unused LUT structure in the core watermark to add the identifier redundancy attribute information for watermark embedding. Based on the entire FPGA chip design process, we will use the corresponding hardware description language (VHDL) to write the corresponding behavioral level file, and the method of dual watermark embedding is used for the inserting watermark information S_1, S_2. The detailed steps are as follows:

1. Unused resource statistics. The unused LUT resources are searched to create an index table T for unused LUTs.
2. Generate an embedded location. In order to improve the transparency of the watermark, the algorithm embeds the watermark as close as possible to the used LUTs. We set the distance parameter L to find the LUT around the used LUT from

its distance L. If the LUT is in T, its position is recorded into the embedded position *Pos* sequence.

3. Watermark embedding. The watermark information is embedded in the corresponding LUTs in *Pos* sequence (Fig. 3).

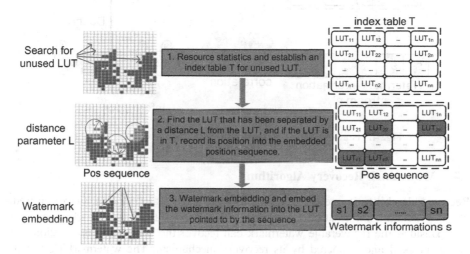

Fig. 3. Schematic diagram of watermark embedding process

3.3   Watermark Extraction Algorithm

When an IP core entering into the market is stolen by the malicious users, the corresponding watermark information can be extracted and decrypted to recover the copyright information, thus proving the identity of the IP core. The watermark extraction process is critical in the core circuit protection process. Figure 4 depicts the watermark extraction process in this paper. The specific steps are as follows:

1. Find. The LUT pointed to by the *Pos* position sequence reads and records the information in the LUT into the extracted watermark information stream S'.

2. Go to association. The extracted watermark information stream S' contains recoverable associated redundant information, which is only used for recovery. To obtain the correct watermark, it must be associated first. After the association is eliminated, the watermark information will become the encrypted information stream C' with only the watermarked information, i.e. $C' = F^{-1}(S')$, where F^{-1} is the decorrelation function.

3. Decryption. The original watermark information M' is obtained by decrypting C', that is, $M' = E^{-1}(C', K)$.

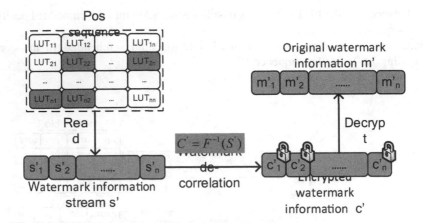

Fig. 4. Is a schematic diagram of the watermark extraction process

3.4 Watermark Recovery Algorithm

Recoverable ability is one of the characteristics of IP watermarking. Once the traditional watermark information is destroyed, the probability of watermark recovery is low. Besides, the recoverable watermark can recover the watermark information after being attacked and tampered by its recovery mechanism. The watermarking scheme based on the Shamir secret sharing model proposed in this paper can rely on the reconstructed key feature in secret sharing to achieve the recovery ability and security of the watermark. The process of recovery process is shown in Fig. 5.

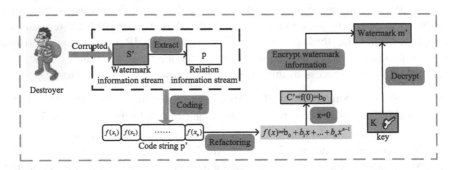

Fig. 5. Is a schematic diagram of the recovery process of the watermark

When the extracted watermark information has been tampered, the recovery mechanism between the watermarks is used to recover the impaired watermark information. The recovery steps are as follows:

4. Extract the associated information. The associated information flow P is extracted from the S' containing the associated redundant information flow.

5. Associate information coding. Re-encode the associated information stream P into a code string: $P' = \{f(x_i) | i = 1, 2, \ldots, k\}$.
6. Watermark information can be recovered. The k codes $f(x_i)$ in the re-encoded associated information stream p' are treated as sub-keys in the secret segmentation, and the equation $f(x)$ is reconstructed by the system of Eq. 1. Then let $x = 0$, the original watermark information M' can be recovered.

4 Experimental Results and Analysis

The IP cores used in the experiments were all from the opencores.org website [13], and we used our own designed core watermarking system to test with Xilinx ISE design tools, ModelSim simulation tools and Synplify synthesis tools.

4.1 Experimental Results

In the experiment, we can embed the IP watermark copyright information by the proposed method. The figure shows the layout effect of the IP carrier before and after embedding the watermark. When the attack of any two attack algorithms is broken, we can pass the above section. The method restores the IP core content embedded with the recoverable watermark information.

4.2 Resource Overhead

The additional overhead of the recoverable IP watermarking circuit mainly refers to the increased overhead of the circuit after the watermark is embedded, mainly including resource overhead and delay overhead. Taking the three testing circuits as example, the additional performance overhead of the core watermark circuit was evaluated and compared using the Xilinx Virtex II XC2V500 device. Where %R represents the percentage of embedded watermark information to unused resources.

Table 1. Resource overhead before and after watermark embedding

Core	Watermark capacity					
	32-bit watermark		128-bit watermark		256-bit watermark	
	Literature [10]	Ours	Literature [10]	Ours	Literature [10]	Ours
DES56	0.537	0.347	0.647	0.487	0.793	0.574
Audio	0.438	0.351	0.751	0.403	0.702	0.507
6081	0.442	0.366	0.766	0.464	0.832	0.529
AES	0.445	0.349	0.755	0.438	0.889	0.543

The analysis results show that the logic gates of different IP Cores are not the same, but the number of Slices used varies far from logic gates. From Table 1, we can clearly see that as the amount of watermark embedding and the number of resources occupied by the core design are increasing. This is due to the fact that once the recovery factor t is selected in the algorithm, the information needed to recover the corrupted watermark has been determined. According to the test results in the table, although the recoverable watermark requires more resources than the watermark in [10], the embedded watermark information capacity is twice the watermark capacity in the literature [10], and it has better robustness.

4.3   Anti-attack Performance Evaluation

In this paper, removal attack and passive attack methods are used to evaluate the anti-attack ability of the recoverable watermark. For different degrees of recoverable watermark information removal and destruction, we set the random position parameter value μ to 0.5 in the experiment.

Table 2. Comparisons between related works and ours

	Zhang et al.'s [8]	Cui's [9]	Liang's [10]	Ours
Security	Yes	Yes	Yes	Yes
Correctness	Yes	Yes	Yes	Yes
Anonymity	Yes	Yes	Yes	Yes
Random generation	Yes	Yes	Yes	Yes
Public verification	Yes	Yes	Yes	Yes
Fairness	Yes	Yes	Yes	Yes
Convenience	Yes	Yes	Yes	Yes
No online trusted third party	Yes	Yes	Yes	Yes
No pre-registration required	Yes	Yes	Yes	Yes
Participants legality	No	No	No	Yes
Support joint and individual e-lottery service	Support individual only	Support individual only	Support individual only	Yes

It can be known from the experiment in Table 2 that although our method is relative to the other two methods: the watermark embedding has a certain increase in the CLB resource occupancy rate, but the recovery ability of the proposed method after suffering attacks cannot be surpassed by the other two methods.

5   Conclusion

The recoverable IP core watermarking technology based on threshold scheme proposed in this paper. It realizes watermark recovery based on the key reorganization idea of threshold scheme. This algorithm makes full use of the advantages of large amount of information and good robustness of watermark. The self-recovery technology and chaotic encryption improve the robustness of the previous IP core watermark, and expand the embedded watermark information capacity in the process of watermark information embedding. From the experimental results: this solution does not cause large hardware overhead, and achieve good watermark recovery performance. It has a good application prospect. In the next step, we will consider using more attacks to test the security of this algorithm, and further study the effective embedding mechanism of recoverable core watermarks in different abstraction layers, thus further optimizing our algorithm.

Acknowledgements. This research was funded by the Fujian Provincial Natural Science Foundation of China (Grant 2018J01570) and the CERNET Innovation Project (Grant NGII20170411).

References

1. Liang, W., Xie, S., Li, X., Long, J., Xie, Y., Li, K.-C.: A novel lightweight PUF-based RFID mutual authentication protocol. In: Hung, J.C., Yen, N.Y., Hui, L. (eds.) FC 2017. LNEE, vol. 464, pp. 345–355. Springer, Singapore (2018). https://doi.org/10.1007/978-981-10-7398-4_36
2. Liang, W., Long, J., Cui, A., et al.: A new robust dual intellectual property watermarking algorithm based on field programmable gate array. J. Comput. Theor. Nanosci. **12**(10), 3959–3962 (2015)
3. Han, Q., Noura, H., Qiu, M., et al.: A user-centric data protection method for cloud storage based on invertible DWT. IEEE Trans. Cloud Comput., 1 (2019)
4. Anirban, S., Dipanjan, R.: Antipiracy-aware IP chipset design for CE devices: a robust watermarking approach hardware matters. IEEE Consum. Electron. Mag. **6**(2), 118–124 (2017)
5. Han, Q., Noura, H., et al.: All-or-nothing data protection for ubiquitous communication: challenges and perspectives. Inf. Sci. **502**, 434–445 (2019)
6. Anirban, S., Saumya, B., Saraju, M.P.: Embedding low cost optimal watermark during high level synthesis for reusable IP core protection. In: IEEE International Symposium on Circuits & Systems, pp. 974–977. IEEE (2016)
7. Abtioglu, E., Yeniceri, R., Govem, B., et al.: Partially reconfigurable IP protection system with ring oscillator based physically unclonable functions, pp. 58–65. IEEE (2017)
8. Zhang, J., Lin, Y., Qu, G.: Reconfigurable binding against FPGA replay attacks. ACM Trans. Des. Autom. Electron. Syst. **20**(2), 1–20 (2015)
9. Cui, A., Qu, G., Zhang, Y.: Ultra-low overhead dynamic watermarking on scan design for hard IP protection. IEEE Trans. Inf. Forensics Secur. **10**(11), 2298–2313 (2017)
10. Liang, W., Huang, W., Chen, W., et al.: Hausdorff distance model-based identity authentication for IP circuits in service-centric internet-of-things environment. Sensors **19**(3), 487 (2019)
11. Liang, W., Long, J., Zhang, D., Li, X., Huang, Y.: Study on IP protection techniques for integrated circuit in IOT environment. In: Di Martino, B., Li, K.-C., Yang, L.T., Esposito, A. (eds.) Internet of Everything. IT, pp. 193–216. Springer, Singapore (2018). https://doi.org/10.1007/978-981-10-5861-5_9
12. Sengupta, A., Bhadauria, S.: Exploring low cost optimal watermark for reusable IP cores during high level synthesis. IEEE Access **4**, 2198–2215 (2016)
13. OpenCores Web Site. http://www.opencores.org. Accessed 25 Jan 2019

Applications of Machine Learning Tools in Genomics: A Review

Joseph L. Fracasso and Md Liakat Ali[(⊠)]

Rider University, Lawrenceville, NJ, USA
mdali@rider.edu

Abstract. To overcome the challenges presented by the manual analysis of large datasets inherent to DNA sequences, machine learning (ML) tools are commonly employed due to their relative accuracy and ease of implementation. However, no consensus exists regarding the most broadly applicable and effective machine learning tool for performing multiple analysis on DNA sequences, with many researchers instead opting to utilize proprietary hybrids. Review determined that the modal techniques among the literature surveyed were support vector machines and neural networks, both existing in modified proprietary forms to best fit DNA sequence analysis. Analyses were principally focused on site specific activities which were then used to create inferences regarding the whole of the molecule. These findings suggest neural networks and support vector machines as verified by Bayesian statistics may be the optimal approach for analyzing long DNA sequences.

Keywords: Bioinformatics · DNA · DNA sequence · Machine learning · Neural network · Support vector machine

1 Introduction

Developments in medicine are inexorably linked to advancements in technology; as researchers are provided with more comprehensive tools, their capacity for developing and administering cures reasonably increases. Among the emerging fields in medicine facilitated by the rapid technological revolution of the information era is that of personalized medicine. A synthesis of the fields of genomics and computer science, personalized medicine aims to analyze the genetic code of an individual and in so doing identify potential disease risks, determine which treatments will be ineffective, and which will be effective [1].

This aforementioned information is all obtained from the machine learning mediated analysis of a DNA sequence obtained from the patient. DNA, or deoxyribonucleic acid, is the blueprint which informs all basal level activities in an individual, thus the smallest difference between any two sequences can induce profound differences. DNA sequences more specifically refer to the ordering of the four building blocks which make up DNA, the nitrogenous bases known as adenine (A), guanine (G), cytosine (C), and thymine (T). Sequences of DNA that dictate cellular actions are known as genes, and may exist in variable forms across individuals known as alleles. These sequences

M. Qiu (Ed.): SmartCom 2019, LNCS 11910, pp. 330–340, 2019.
https://doi.org/10.1007/978-3-030-34139-8_33

are interpreted by cellular machinery which calls for then may call for the synthesis of a molecule, or the activation or deactivation of another gene.

Elements of computer science are then incorporated to analyze these sequences with machine learning tools. Machine learning simply refers to the process by which a machine develops an understanding of a dataset from which it can then develop inferences about. At the most fundamental level, these inferences can refer to identifying common patterns across entries in a data set, from which researchers can then develop their own conclusions. In the realm of genomics, this principle equates to machines, with an input of a standard "labeled," DNA sequence, operating on a new DNA sequence, comparing its contents to the standard before finally labeling it accordingly-perhaps the machine develops an understanding that the promoter of a certain gene contains high quantities of the triplet GCT, thus when it next encounters a GCT sequence in the analyte DNA, it can then label that sequence as the previously identified or "known" promoter [1].

However, these machine learning tools may manifest in a variety of forms, from support vector machines to neural networks, to clustering algorithms, all of which have been the frequent subjects of inquiry for their applications in predictive genomics. Thus, there exists no dominant strategy and as such inquiry is divided among innumerable proprietary procedures, impeding comparison and progress in a developing field. It is the intent of this review to provide a summative review of the newest and most influential findings regarding these learning tools and the effectiveness of their implementation to determine which is the most efficient for machine learning based DNA sequence analysis based on parameters of applicability, accessibility, and accuracy. The methods and results of each study will be disseminated along with a brief evaluation corresponding to these aforementioned parameters, before concluding with an overall determination of the optimal strategy in accordance with this analysis.

2 Machine Learning Approaches in DNA Sequencing

Several universal techniques exist across all machine learning techniques when analyzing DNA sequences [1, 18, 19]. Fundamentally, all methods will be predicated on determining the significance of a given nitrogenous base (G, C, A, T) sequence given their respective bonding patterns. Differences then emerge in the presence or absence of a standard for comparison and the algorithms employed thereafter to formulate and evaluate associations between these sequences. Machine learning tools can thus be grouped into two general categories: supervised and unsupervised. Supervised approaches are provided with a standard for comparison, essentially definitions for certain sequences that determine their interpretation of DNA sequences, whereas unsupervised approaches are provided with no such definitions and develop their own via association.

In the case of the former, analysis begins with the previously selected DNA training sequence, applicable to the inquiry conducted and with appropriate labels for areas of interest, being transformed into a multi factored vector value. Next, this vector is functionalized by the selected machine learning tool within the four parameters of the nitrogenous bases, before finally being cross validated. The latter operates in loosely the same manner, but lacking a training sequence instead causes unsupervised approaches to rely on statistical analysis instead, developing definitions independently over multiple iterations [1]. Thus the general procedure for both techniques can be defined as information gathering, transformation, analytical cross checking, and validation.

3   Significant ML Studies and Their Results in DNA Sequencing

Pattern recognition is the principal mode of analysis for DNA sequences, providing different information depending on the perspective within which it is developed [18, 19, 20]. Busia et al. [2] propose a convolutional neural network for the alignment of 16 s RNA, a DNA analogue, with a standard sequence in order to determine its species of origin. Results were then compared to probabilistic Bayesian standards. Ultimately this method was found to be more accurate than widely accepted standards such as BLAST and BWA, within 2% of perfect memorization.

Yuen et al. [3] contends that conventional methods for distinguishing nucleotides in DNA sequencing are too nebulous and error prone and rectifies this with the implementation of empirical, electronic density of states data. The data are then extracted via principal component analysis, yielding vectorized principal components. These principal components are then used with the membership formula from the fuzzy c-means algorithm to determine probabilistically which nitrogenous base is present in a clustering method. Further verification is then obtained from the implementation of the Hidden Markov and Viterbi algorithms to distinguish nitrogenous bases from noise. This technique yielded classification of unlabeled DOS data with 91% accuracy.

Methylation sites in DNA can greatly influence the expression of the gene wherein they occur. To predict the location of these methylation sites, Bhasin et al. [4] proposed the use of a support vector machine using vectorized human DNA fragments as input to generate predictions regarding human methylation sites. Methylated and unmethylated CpG dinucleotide sequences were obtained from MethDB database. These sequences were broken and aligned into uniformly length fragments and were used to train the support vector machine. Five-fold cross validation was then used to evaluate the performance of this machine learning tool in completing this task, determining that this method was more effective when compared to artificial neural network, Bayesian statistics and decision trees.

A knowledge based neural network draws from standardized data to develop inference rules much like the other forms of machine learning previously mentioned. Noordewier et al. [5] applied this tool to predict and identify the bordering sites between *introns* and *exons* where splicing occurs, and whether that splicing site is an acceptor, donor, or neither. As such the neural network was provided with two information sets, one which labeled the center of a certain DNA fragment, and another which determines which of the three aforementioned categories the central piece corresponded to. After provisions of 3,190 examples, the network became able to generate weight based inference rules to address this splice junction problem. This knowledge based neural network approach was seen to outperform similar neural network approaches using similar example numbers. Down and Hubbard [6] presented a proprietary relevance vector machine, Eponine, a machine learning tool which determines the most applicable of a given set of basis formulas in a pruning process of comparing them to the assay data. However, to compensate for the size of DNA sequences relative to other data types, the algorithm was modified slightly and provided with randomly selected weight matrix data. The fundamental sampling transformations utilized were then to adjust the center of a distribution, adjust its width, adjust its weight in a DNA matrix, randomly construct a new DNA probability distribution and add it randomly to one end of the existing DNA matrix, and finally remove another column from the matrix. Promoters were most often identified as containing repeating TATA motifs at their center flanked by CG rich sites. Specificity was ultimately found to be greater than 70% for the determination of mammalian promoters.

Bzhalava et al. [7] have utilized next generation sequencing with the Illumina platform to generate metagenomic data that would be parsed to determine if they contained viral or other microorganism genomes. Analyte data undergoes rigorous editing to ensure relevancy through a number of systems before finally being analyzed using two algorithms, a BLASTn and HMMER3. BLASTn operated on an NCBI nucleotide database to align and close gaps between sequences, before finally taxonomically classifying them. Unknown sequences were then analyzed with HMMER3, based on the Hidden Markov models (HMM) for detecting viral DNA sequences. Data was then aggregated into a series of 1,000 random forests to determine the usefulness of coding portions of each sequence in identifying viral codons. Finally, these determinations were validated by an artificial neural network that created by-weight connections between identified sequences. Comparative accuracy was indeterminate [7]. With an indeterminate comparative accuracy, however, it is likely that this method should be developed further before consideration as a standardized procedure.

The evolution of a genome at a fundamental level is reliant on the completion of recombination such as those in meiosis. Liu et al. [8] proposed a pseudo nucleotide composition of vectorized dinucleotide sequences to prevent data loss in the transformation from sequence to vector, constraining information according to the parameters of neighboring nucleic acid residues, rank or tier of the sequence, and the weight factor of the sequence. Sequences were analyzed using a modified support vector machine implementing the RBF kernel and the regularization parameter and kernel width parameter to determine and predict sites of recombination. Optimizations were performed by 5-fold cross validation. Cross validation demonstrated an efficacy of 3.5–17.7% greater than other predictors. In Schietgat et al. [9], a proprietary system of random forests known as TE-Learner is proposed to identify transposable elements within a given order, classifying them at the superfamily level. The algorithm first selects sequences from the well documented Drosophila melanogaster and Arabidopsis thaliana species based on parameters provided by the characteristics of the given order.

Following this, the sequences are annotated and these annotated sequences are used as input for the aforementioned random forest algorithm which then determines if the sequence belongs to the specified order and accordingly assigns its superfamily. The random forest used operates with a first-order logic format to determine the probability that a given annotated sequence corresponds to the designated superfamily. It was determined that this technique yielded both better performance and runtime than comparable prediction techniques.

Zien et al. [10] proposes three modified support vector machine kernels for the determination of translation start sites in unlabeled DNA sequences. The machine was trained utilizing sequences obtained from GenBank as refined through the removal of introns and other purifications in a previous experiment. The first of the three kernel algorithms used was a sparse bit encoding scheme which gave each nucleotide a unique bit identity that would then be correlatively parsed by the SVM. The following kernel then allowed for similar functions, though with accommodations for local comparisons. The last of the three kernels utilized was a linear function that transformed the data into coordinate based information. Collectively these kernels were found to improve recognition by 26%.

Fang et al. [11] posits established methods of vector based analysis for DNA sequencing neglect important order reliant information. Sequence order retaining analysis has been effectively demonstrated for amino acid arrangements, but no such tool exists for DNA sequences, thus prompting further inquiry. Based on the genome analysis web server, pseudo k-tupler nucleotide composition, the proposed Python package presents a variety of 15 built-in physicochemical features, as well as user generated features to contextually analyze input sequences. In most instances, the machine utilizes the feature vectors of k-mers. Final outputs were compared in the tasting phase to known values and acceptable ranges of accuracy were determined to have been met.

Similar to Bhasin et al. [4], the principal concern of Angermueller et al. [12] is the prediction of methylation sites for the transcriptional changes they confer. This inquiry is distinguished then by the machine learning tool implemented and the input data utilized for training that tool. Input sequences of mouse embryonic stem cells as well as human and mouse cells were profiled utilizing genome-wide bisulfite sequencing and reduced representation, respectively. In place of an annotated training set, the proposed predictor, DeepCpG, instead both analyzes and refines models from unaltered sequence information by utilizing a deep learning neural network which operates within local sequence windows and neighboring sites of methylation. DeepCpG is capable of multiple assays, and features a CpG module, a DNA module, and a Joint module. The CpG module relies specifically on a gated recurrent network using vectors representing local methylation sites and their relative distances. The DNA module utilizes a convolutional neural network with positional weighted vector matrices as inputs in order to determine sequence motifs. The Joint module then concatenates the hidden vectors of the DNA and CpG modules and their interactions. The predictions of DeepCpG were found to be more accurate than established alternatives such as RF Zhang with every analyte and implemented module, with the greatest difference being 3.75% [12].

Vidaki et al. [13] too is concerned with a deterministic approach for the methylation status of DNA, and similarly leverages a unique methodology for creating and refining this approach, with the intention of evaluating methylation patterns for forensic science and determine the age of a blood donor or suspect. Input data consisted initially of CpG methylation profiles organized by general age groups which were then averaged and normalized within those groups. Researchers selected 45 age associated CpG sites from a 353 marker pool as given by previous inquiry, using these sites as inputs for the training and subsequent testing of multiple neural network architectures. A total of one hundred million generalized regression neural network architectures were tested by a network design tool with 50–70% of the potential 1156 cases (blood samples) being equivalently designated as verification and blind tests. The correlation and output error rates from the training, verification, and blind test datasets were then used to select the fifty most suitable architectures from each stage. The best performing architectures from this stage were then compared with fixed blind test cases but with unique training and verification datasets as per the previous stage in a method of advanced random sampling. The ten best of these architectures were then selected and subjected to another stage of testing with fixed training, verification and blind test data subsets, with the ultimate model being selected from this group. This final model was trained on a 60:20:20 training, verification, and blind test data set ratio, with predicted ages varying from true ages by an average absolute error of 3.8 ± 3.3, for a 2.93% increase in accuracy from other linear regression based models [13].

Guo et al. [14] were concerned with the development of a broadly applicable tool for the identification of nucleosome positioning within chromosomes in order to more efficiently predict and understand their regulatory effects and general interaction with major cellular processes. Complete genomic sequences annotated with the position of nucleosomes for humans, C. *elegans*, and D. *melanogaster* were collected and scored based on the propensity of DNA fragments within those genomes to form nucleosomes. The sequences were then transformed by the pseudo k-tuple nucleotide composition formula to correlate the sequences into by-weight tiers. A support vector machine with the radial basis function as the kernel to analyze the transformed data. As determined by jackknife cross validation predictions were found to be 79%–86.9% accurate between the assayed species [14].

As opposed to predicting the location of known functional sequence fragments, the inquiry of Quang and Xie [15] was instead occupied with determining the function of a given sequence. The authors highlighting the fact that over 98% of the human genome is non-coding and thus functionally poorly understood. As such, it was determined that the ideal machine learning tools to implement would be a proprietary combination of a convolutional neural network and a bi-directional long-short term memory network, referred to as DanQ (utilizing the same functional SNP priority framework from DeepSEA [16]). Input data was obtained from DeepSEA, separated into non-overlapping 200 bp bins, specific samples then consisted of 1000 bp segments centered on a 200 bp bin that aligned with a transcription factor binding peak as determined by chromatin immunoprecipitation. The data are then matricized, with each column corresponding to a nitrogenous base. In addition, distinct training, verification, and blind test datasets were obtained from DeepSEA, including reverse complements. Evaluation strategies also resembled that of DeepSEA with predicted probabilities being calculated as the average of reverse and forward probabilities. The RMSprop algorithm was then used to train two models, one of which utilizing the JASPAR motif database, which were then compared to a logistic regression model as a benchmark. It was then found that DanQ held a 50% improvement rate over other models in determining DNA sequence function.

Lee, Karchin and Beer [17] recognized the difficulties in accuracy and timeliness presented by analyzing complete mammalian genomes and thus proposed a machine learning tool to more efficiently provide predictions for these large datasets. Input data were analyzed by chromatin immunoprecipitation and divided into positive and negative examples to formulate a training set for a support vector machine. Varyingly sized k-mers were used as sequence features for the machine and weights of each sequence fragment were optimized to maximally distinguish between positive and negative classes. Using five-fold cross validation, it was ultimately determined that the proposed machine was capable of accurate prediction regardless of tissue type, k-mer length, or kernel used with regards to the detection of EP3000-and was even found to trainable to detect novel enhancers, including those of humans, though was in these cases, more tissue dependent [17]. The accuracy appears comparable to other techniques, with the only issues then being presented by the amount of transformations and training necessary for the accurate prediction of enhancers.

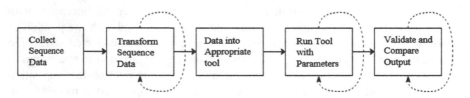

Fig. 1. A graphical representation of the generalized steps for the creation and validation of a machine learning tool for bioinformatics, with repeatable steps indicated by hashed arrows.

4 Discussion

Overcoming the tedium of manual DNA sequence analysis is made simplest by the implementation of machine learning tools that can stochastically interpret large datasets. These tools, with the recognition of standardized data or the mechanistic determination of their own standards can be made to label specific sections of DNA and create associations with those sections, the general process of which is displayed in Fig. 1. The intention of this article was to then demonstrate which specific machine learning tool is the most effective for the broadest range of tasks in sequence interpretation with a holistic review of primary literature, the general results of which can be displayed in Table 1.

Table 1. Aggregation of methods and assayed for reviewed articles in machine learning as applied to genomics.

Reference	Assay	Machine learning tools
Busia et al. [2]	Species of origin	Neural Network (NN)
Yuen et al. [3]	Density of states	Fuzzy C-means clustering, Hidden markov model
Bhasin et al. [4]	CpG methylation sites	Support vector machine
Noordewier et al. [5]	Splicing sites	Neural network
Down & Hubbard [6]	Promoter sites	Relevance vector machine
Bzhalava et al. [7]	Viral genome	HMM, random forests, NN
Liu et al. [8]	Sites of recombination	Support vector machine
Schietgat et al. [9].	Transposable elements	Random forest
Zien et al. [10]	Translation start sites	Support vector machine
Liu et al. [11]	DNA attributes	Pseudo k-tuple
Angermueller et al. [12]	CpG methylation sites	Neural network
Vidaki et al. [13]	CpG methylation sites	Neural network
Guo et al. [14]	Sites of nucleosome formation	Pseudo k-tuple, SVM
Quang and Xie [15]	Functional noncoding DNA	Neural network
Zhou and Troyanskaya [16]	Functional noncoding DNA	Neural network
Lee, Karchin and Beer [17]	Enhancer sites	Support vector machine

Ultimately it was found that while each study suggested a greater efficacy than existing alternatives, neural networks and support vector machines were the most commonly implemented techniques, as shown in Table 2, demonstrating the interest in neural networks that exists in the broader bioinformatics community with their majority percentages when compared the far smaller percentages of competing tools-with a difference of ten percent existing between neural networks and the second most common tool, support vector machines. These tools were universally modified to best analyze DNA sequences with specific kernels for labeling larger data sets or accepting different information and parameters (such as the aforementioned nucleotide bases, length of a sequence, or AT/GC content of an area), and made to produce labels and predictions for specific active sites in DNA molecules. This modality is suggestive of a dominant strategy in DNA sequence analysis that can inform the development of future machine learning tools, possibly through combining support vector machines and neural networks with verification from Bayesian algorithms.

Table 2. Frequency distribution of each machine learning tools used in reviewed articles.

Machine learning tools	Frequency
Neural network	35%
Support vector machine	25%
Relevance vector machine	5%
Random forest	10%
Pseudo k-tuple	10%
Hidden markov model	10%
Fuzzy c-means clustering	5%

The medical relevance of these models cannot be understated, with the greatest majority utilizing standard embryonic mouse or human genomic datasets, common assays across all biological fields. It is likely that with further investment and development, these machine learning methodologies could facilitate unprecedented advancements in bioinformatics and beyond, just as contemporary strategies have within recent years. Yet for the sake of learners and applications beyond medical sequencing, it is essential for the ideal standard approach to offer a unilateral applicability with accessible datasets and comprehendible frameworks, which may then be developed further for specialized inquiry. Thus, as demonstrated by the examined approaches, an ideal standardized sequence should offer a well-founded and simply written codebase with modular capabilities that can accept a variety of unaltered sequence data. These data should then undergo rigorous transformation, likely by bin separation, weight mapping and vectorization before utilization in a support vector machine or multi layered neural network framework. In either instance, frameworks should be generationally compared to produce a single ideal system, thus creating the most accurate, applicable and accessible tool possible.

5 Conclusion

The principle aim of this article is to broaden understandings of the applicability of machine learning tools for use in bioinformatics, in demonstrating the methods by which tedium can be eliminated from critical processes such as the sequencing and subsequent understanding of long DNA molecules. Review of current primary literature demonstrated that a variety of machine learning tools could be implemented for the purposes of analyzing DNA sequences with an even greater variety of assays, though most inquiry falls within the broader category of predicting the positions of certain sites of interest within the molecule utilizing pseudo k-tuple transformed data. Studies show that Support vector machines and neural networks are the most frequent machine learning tools used in genomics. Among those experiments that implemented these tools, the prediction of sites of specific activity were the most common assay, ranging from those of recombination, transcription, splicing, or methylation. Moreover, these tools were universally modified to conform to better fit their particular assay as opposed to being implemented in their standard forms, and were most often verified and optimized by statistical Bayesian analysis. The greatest challenges in assembling this review were presented by the specificity of the subject matter and scarcity of open access articles, thus causing potential shortcomings insofar as offering a limited review of the information on the potential of machine learning in genomics. Future work would then entail further primary research that would provide greater understanding of machine learning tool modality in DNA sequence analysis, enabling for inquiry in examining particularly long sequences of DNA with a combination of the modal tools.

References

1. Libbrecht, M.W., Noble, W.S.: Machine learning applications in genetics and genomics. Nat. Rev. Genet. **16**, 321 (2015)
2. Busia, A., et al.: A deep learning approach to pattern recognition for short DNA sequences. BioRxiv 353474 (2018)
3. Yuen, H., et al.: DNA Sequencing via Quantum Mechanics and Machine Learning. CoRR, abs/1012.0900 (2010)
4. Bhasin, M., Zhang, H., Reinherz, E.L., Reche, P.A.: Prediction of methylated CpGs in DNA sequences using a support vector machine. FEBS Lett. **579**(20), 4302–4308 (2005)
5. Noordewier, M.O., Towell, G.G., Shavlik, J.W.: Training knowledge-based neural networks to recognize genes in DNA sequences. In: Advances in Neural Information Processing Systems, pp. 530–536 (1991)
6. Down, T.A., Hubbard, T.J.P.: Computational detection and location of transcription start sites in mammalian genomic DNA. Genome Res. **12**(3), 458–461 (2002)
7. Bzhalava, Z., Tampuu, A., Bała, P., Vicente, R., Dillner, J.: Machine Learning for detection of viral sequences in human metagenomic datasets. BMC Bioinf. **19**(1), 336 (2018)
8. Liu, B., Wang, S., Long, R., Chou, K.-C.: iRSpot-EL: identify recombination spots with an ensemble learning approach. Bioinformatics **33**(1), 35–41 (2016)
9. Schietgat, L., et al.: A machine learning based framework to identify and classify long terminal repeat retrotransposons. PLoS Comput. Biol. **14**(4), e1006097–e1006097 (2018)
10. Zien, A., Rätsch, G., Mika, S., Schölkopf, B., Lengauer, T., Müller, K.-R.: Engineering support vector machine kernels that recognize translation initiation sites. Bioinformatics **16**(9), 799–807 (2000)
11. Liu, B., Liu, F., Fang, L., Wang, X., Chou, K.C.: repDNA: a Python package to generate various modes of feature vectors for DNA sequences by incorporating user-defined physicochemical properties and sequence-order effects. Bioinformatics **31**(8), 1307–1309 (2014)
12. Angermueller, C., Lee, H.J., Reik, W., Stegle, O.: DeepCpG: accurate prediction of single-cell DNA methylation states using deep learning. Genome Biol. **18**(1), 67 (2017)
13. Vidaki, A., Ballard, D., Aliferi, A., Miller, T.H., Barron, L.P., Court, D.S.: DNA methylation-based forensic age prediction using artificial neural networks and next generation sequencing. Forensic Sci. Int.: Genet. **28**, 225–236 (2017)
14. Guo, S.H., et al.: iNuc-PseKNC: a sequence-based predictor for predicting nucleosome positioning in genomes with pseudo k-tuple nucleotide composition. Bioinformatics **30**(11), 1522–1529 (2014)
15. Quang, D., Xie, X.: DanQ: a hybrid convolutional and recurrent deep neural network for quantifying the function of DNA sequences. Nucleic Acids Res. **44**(11), e107–e107 (2016)
16. Zhou, J., Troyanskaya, O.G.: Predicting effects of noncoding variants with deep learning–based sequence model. Nat. Methods **12**(10), 931 (2015)

17. Lee, D., Karchin, R., Beer, M.A.: Discriminative prediction of mammalian enhancers from DNA sequence. Genome Res. **21**(12), 2167–2180 (2011)
18. Ali, M.L., Monaco, J.V., Tappert, C.C., Qiu, M.: Keystroke biometric systems for user authentication. J. Signal Process. Syst. **86**(2–3), 175–190 (2017)
19. Gai, K., Qiu, M.: Reinforcement learning-based content-centric services in mobile sensing. IEEE Netw. **32**(4), 34–39 (2018)

Hierarchical Graph Neural Networks for Personalized Recommendations with User-Session Context

Xiang Shen[1]([✉]), Caiming Yang[1], Zhengwei Jiang[2], Dong Xie[1],
Yingtao Sun[1], Shuibiao Chen[1], and Bo Li[3]

[1] State Grid Shaoxing Electric Power Supply Company,
Shaoxing, Zhejiang, China
shx8022@163.com.cn, 13606751852@163.com.cn,
13606755005@163.com, 416024740@qq.com,
13957569100@163.com
[2] State-Grid Zhejiang Electric Power Co., Ltd., Beijing, China
jiang_zhengwei@zj.sgcc.com.cn
[3] Beihang University, Beijing, China
libo@act.buaa.edu.cn

Abstract. With the swift development of Internet and artificial intelligence, recommender systems have become more and more important as useful information has a risk of submerging in huge amounts of data or smart services always provide a behavior predictor to meet diversified user's needs. User-session based recommendations are commonly applied in many modern online platforms. Graph Neural Networks (GNNs) have been shown to have a strong ability to address the problem of session-based recommendation with accurate item embedding. However, there are a lot of application scenarios that have already provided user profiles. We propose a model based on Hierarchical GNNs for personalized recommendations, which evolves both item information in sessions and user profiles. The experiments on two industry datasets show the superiority of our model over the state-of-the-art methods.

Keywords: Graph Neural Networks · User-session based recommendation · Dropout · Personalized recommendation

1 Introduction

With a dramatic increase in the Web information environment, information overload has received wide social attention. In most of all online services, recommender modules have become essential components to help users relieve the pressure on information overload and obtaining interesting information from huge amounts of data. Recommender systems can be also used to increase personal comfort by suppling items or products orderly with gauge of historical activities or synergetic relationships of items or users. For example, recommender systems could automatically list items of interest, or give a suggestion of new discounts relevant to each other. Many recommender systems are working on the assumption that user identification, item label and past activities are

© Springer Nature Switzerland AG 2019
M. Qiu (Ed.): SmartCom 2019, LNCS 11910, pp. 341–348, 2019.
https://doi.org/10.1007/978-3-030-34139-8_34

available with the temporal variation. It is more importance to consider a framework with complex scenarios of information scarcity. The core and the most crucial link of recommender systems is to search a way of computing relevance degree of items, users, or user-items with or without temporal information. Temporal information is important as it could supply an evidence of when users take items into account. There is a fact that to compare with the items considered long ago, recent considered items are more likely to be taken. The temporal information with user's activity are recorded as sessions. A session is a group of interaction occurred in a given time frame. The time frame can be an hour, a day, several days, several weeks, even months or years.

Traditional methods of personalized recommendations usually provide functions by building up a user profile, such as user-user similarity based on past activities computed by collaborative filtering approaches [1] or latent factor vectors built by matrix factorization [2, 3]. There exists a problem of cold-start for recommendation approaches that need user past activities, and it is not rare that new accounts, unlogged users, or users without tracking information use recommender systems. Conventional recommender algorithms [4] have been applied to address the challenging problem of recommendations on session-based recommenders. RNNs (Recurrent Neural Networks) have been majority approaches with promising results in the research of session-based recommender systems [5–8]. There are some limitations in these aforementioned approaches, such as estimation of user representations without adequate user behavior in a session, complex transition among the distant items. To overcome the above limitations, SR-GNNs (Session-based Recommendation with Graph Neural Networks) [9] have been introduced to generate representations for graphs, which can be constructed directly from historical session sequences. Based on the session graph, it is easy to capture complex item transitions and make item embedding vectors with high quality. However, there is shortcoming that the user behavior in past session is non accessible, which might miss valuable information for the present session, in SR-GNNs.

In this paper, we provide a Hierarchical GNNs model for personalized recommendations, in which there are two layers of GNNs constructed to address the problems of both session-based recommenders and session-aware recommenders. The first layer of GNNs provides user identifiers and propagate information, which might give an improvement of recommendation accuracy, and the second layer of GNNs generates the recommendations coupled with the first layer. Extensive experiments conducted on two industry datasets demonstrate the effectiveness of our proposed approach over the state-of-arts.

2   Related Work

In this section, we review some related works on session-based recommender systems, including RNNs-based methods and GNNs-based methods.

Recurrent Neural Models. RNNs are often applied for capturing the feature of sequential data [10], which include image and video captioning, time series prediction and much more. Long Short-Term Memory (LSTM) [11] networks and Gated Recurrent Units (GRUs) [12] are two types of RNNs with powerful performance on various abovementioned tasks. In the work of [5], RNNs are first applied to session-based recommendations, which provide recommendations for new sessions by learning a one-hot representation from the clicked item-IDs in the current session. After that, several valuable works are proposed based on RNNs methods, such as proper data augmentation techniques [6], the fusion of sequential patterns and co-occurrence signals [7], and attention mechanism [8].

Graph Neural Networks. Neural networks have been exploited for capturing representation for graph-structured data, such as social network, knowledge bases and etc. In work of [13, 14], GNNs are proposed to operate on directed graphs by using a form of RNNs. GNNs have been applied for various tasks, such as script even prediction [15], situation recognition [16], and image classification [17]. Recently, SR-GNNs [9] have been employed efficiently for session-based recommendations. Different with [9], both session-based recommenders and session-aware recommenders are considered by applying a Hierarchical GNNs model.

3 The Proposed Method

In this section, we will provide the idea of our proposed Hierarchical GNN model, which consist of two layers of GNNs for personalized recommendation with user-context. Our model is based on SR-GNN model presented in [9], which aims to predict which item a user will click next based on current sequential session data. Different from SR-GNN, our work takes the evolution of the user interests over time into account, showing in Fig. 1. We describe our model by two parts, i.e. the architecture of hierarchical GNNs and learning process of supper parameters.

3.1 Architecture

As shown in Fig. 1, our HGNN model takes a user-level GNN (U-GNN) to model the user activity across sessions, and a session-level GNN (S-GNN) to model the global preference of common items from all sessions. Different from SR-GNN, at each time step, S-GNN and U-GNN make a joint decision to the result of computing recommendations. To SR-GNN, it is easier for our HGNN model to learn the user's preference on selection of item sequences. In [9], authors claimed that sessions could be represented directly by nodes involved in a session, then they focused on developing a method to learn long-term preference and current interests on items from sessions. In their situation, there doesn't exist the information of user activities across sessions. On the contrary, we have taken this factor into account, as there are a lot of information that user's based activities could reveal. For example, it is not hard to associate animations for toddlers with children, rather than a video of hot-pot making. However, the baby A may prefer Spider-Man than Superman, just contrary to the baby B. Therefore, if there are videos of Spider-Man and Superman simultaneously, the recommendation ranking of videos should be different for two babies.

In session-based recommendation, $V = \{v_1, v_2, \ldots, v_m\}$ stands for the set consisting of all unique items involved in all the sessions. The clicked sequence S_u is ordered by

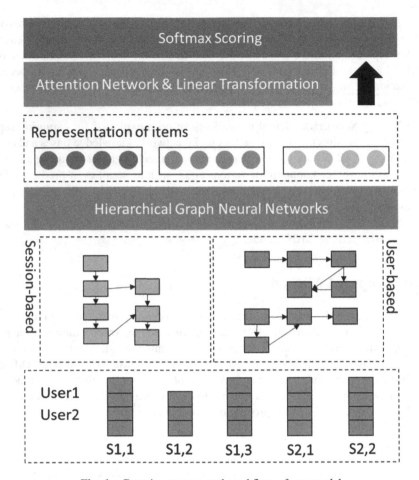

Fig. 1. Generic structure and workflow of our model.

timestamps from a session of the user U. In order to predict the next click, top-K values will be the basis of the candidate selection for recommendation. Same to [9], we embed every item into a unified embedding space and the latent vector of each item is learned via GNNs, and based on node vectors, each session can be represented by two embedding vector, which are composed of node vectors used in U-GNNs and S-GNNs.

3.2 Learning

In our S-GNNs, we take the same learning method for item embedding, and it is similar to obtain update functions for U-GNNs. It is different to obtain long-term preference and current interests of the input session after feeding all session graphs into GNNs. As in the workflow of our model, U-GNNs and S-GNNs will generate two independent local or global embedding vectors. To compute the hybrid embedding vector by taking linear transformation over the concatenation of four embedding vectors, including local and global embedding vectors obtained from U-GNNs and S-GNNs.

From our framework, when user is unknown our model would deteriorate to SR-GNN model, as the anonymous user makes U-GNNs same to S-GNNs. And we will test this part for our model. We applied the Back-Propagation through Time (BPTT) algorithm to train our model.

4   Experiments

In this section we describe our experimental setup and provide an in-depth discussion of the achieved results.

4.1   Datasets

Same to [9], we also evaluate the proposed method on two public representative datasets, including Yoochoose [18] and Diginetica [19]. The Yoochoose and Diginetica datasets are obtained from the RecSys Challenge 2015 and CIKM Cup 2016 respectively. The first dataset consists of a six-month stream of user clicks on an e-commerce website, and for the second one only transactional data is used.

As shown in Table 1, the most recent training sequences of Yoochoose are employed in the ratio of 1/128. In order to compare fairly with other methods, we drop sessions and items, which cannot meet session length greater than 1 or item occurrences not less than 5. Then there is a data-partition policy for generating training and test sets from the input sequence, with which the sessions of subsequent days and months (i.e. 30 days) are divided as test sets for Yoochoose and Diginetica respectively. Furthermore, to evaluate the performance of our approach, we filter out all anonymous users on the Diginetica dataset.

Table 1. The datasets used in experiments

	Yoochoose 1/64	Diginetica
Number of training sessions	184,929	184,701
Number of test sessions	55,898	6,473
Number of items	14,381	17,355
Number of users	NA	87,934
Average length	4.530	4.476

4.2   Evaluation metrics and parameter setup

There are two types of metrics taken for measuring performance of compared methods, including P@20 and MRR@20. These metrics are designed for the recommendation setting, as is often to make multiple recommendations for each user. P@20 (Precision), which is a popular measure of predictive accuracy, stands for the proportion of correctly recommended items amongst the top-20 items. MRR@20 (Mean Reciprocal

Rank), as the average of reciprocal ranks of correctly recommended items, takes the order of ranking into account. The number 20 means to set MRR to 0 once ranking exceeds 20. The larger the MRR value, the higher the ranking of correct recommendations in the top list.

To evaluate the performance of our proposed method, there are five representative baselines involved to comparisons, including POP, User-KNN, GRU4REC [5], NARM [20] and SR-GNN [9]. POP and S-POP recommend the top-N frequent items in the training set and in the current session respectively. GRU4REC employs RNNs to provide session-based recommendations by modeling the session sequences. NARM also applies RNNs to make recommendations, however it take attention mechanism into account for capturing user's sequential behavior and main purpose. SR-GNN exploits GNNs to model session sequences seamless with the ability of computing complex transitions of items.

Following previous method [9], the dimensionality of latent vectors $d = 100$ is established for both datasets. We initialize all parameters with a Gaussian distribution with a mean of 0 and a standard deviation of 0.1. In order to optimize these parameters, a mini-batch Adam optimizer is applied with the initial learning rate of 0.001. And we set the L2 penalty and the batch size to 10^{-5} and 100 respectively.

4.3   Comparison with other methods

We evaluate the performance of our proposed approach by making comparisons with several other session-based recommendation methods, where the result in terms of P@20 and MRR@20 is listed in Table 2.

Table 2. Comparisons of various methods over three datasets

	Yoochoose 1/128		Diginetica	
	P@20	MRR@20	P@20	MRR@20
POP	6.64	1.59	0.87	0.18
User-KNN	–	–	37.81	12.31
GRU4REC	58.54	21.87	29.31	8.12
NARM	66.91	27.31	48.45	15.91
SR-GNN	68.71	29.96	49.46	17.29
Ours	**68.73**	**29.97**	**50.11**	**17.79**

From the result listed in Table 2, it is obvious that our proposed approach is outstanding from other five methods in terms of P@20 and MRR@20 over three datasets. In the architecture of our proposed model, we not only consider the impact of items of common sessions, but also take user's preference as well. All these session sequences are integrated as graph-structured data seamless. The result also shows that neural network-based approaches outperform the traditional methods by adopting deep learning mechanisms. Furthermore, SR-GNN is so outstanding from GRU4REC and NARM because of capturing more complex and implicit connections between user clicks. To be more advanced, our proposed model takes consider of user session information as well as global session information.

5 Conclusions and Future Work

In this paper, we proposed a mode based on Hierarchical GNNs to address the problem of personalized recommendations with user-session context, which exploits two-layer GNNs by involving both session-based recommenders and session-aware recommenders. This method is able to capture temporal information by analyzing the user activity over sessions and the present session status, which means that our proposed method has an ability to acquire the knowledge hidden in the long-term dynamics of user sessions. Our proposed Hierarchical GNNs model outperform state-of-the-art session-based methods for personalized recommendation by taking experiments on Diginetica.

In future works, we have a plan to search the way of refining user representations by exploiting features of items and users.

Acknowledgement. The authors gratefully acknowledge the anonymous reviewers for their helpful suggestions.

References

1. Salakhutdinov, R., Mnih, A., Hinton, G.: Restricted boltzmann machines for collaborative filtering. In: Proceedings of the 24th International Conference on Machine Learning, ICML (2007)
2. Koren, Y.: Factorization meets the neighborhood: a multifaceted collaborative filtering model. In: Proceedings of the 14th ACM International Conference on Knowledge Discovery and Data Mining (2008)
3. Koren, Y., Bell, R.M., Volinsky, C.: Matrix factorization techniques for recommender systems. IEEE Comput. **42**(8), 30–37 (2009)
4. Koenigstein, N., Koren, Y.: Towards scalable and accurate item-oriented recommendations. In: Proceedings of the 7th ACM Conference on Recommender Systems (2013)
5. Hidasi, B., Karatzoglou, A., Baltrunas, L., et al.: Session-based recommendations with recurrent neural networks. In: ICLR (2016)
6. Tan, Y.K., Xu, X., Liu, Y.: Improved recurrent neural networks for session-based recommendations. In: Proceedings of the 1st Workshop on Deep Learning for Recommender Systems (2016)
7. Jannach, D., Ludewig. M.: When recurrent neural networks meet the neighborhood for session-based recommendation. In: Proceedings of the 11th ACM Conference on Recommender Systems (2017)
8. Li, J., Ren, P., Chen, Z., et al.: Neural attentive session-based recommendation. In: Proceedings of the 2017 ACM Conference on Information and Knowledge Management (2017)
9. Wu, S., Tang, Y., Zhu, Y., et al.: Session-based recommendation with graph neural networks. In: Proceedings of AAAI Conference on Artificial Intelligence (2019)

10. Lipton, Z.C., Berkowitz, J., Elkan, C.: A critical review of recurrent neural networks for sequence learning. CoRR, 1506.00019 (2015)
11. Hochreiter, S., Schmidhuber, J.: Long short-term memory. Neural Comput. **9**(8), 1735–1780 (1997)
12. Cho, K., van Merrienboer, B., Bahdanau, D., et al.: On the properties of neural machine translation: encoder-decoder approaches. In: Proceedings of 8th Workshop on Syntax, Semantics and Structure in Statistical Translation (2014)
13. Gori, M., Monfardini, G., Scarselli, F.: A new model for learning in graph domains. In: IJCNN, vol. 2, pp. 729–734 (2005)
14. Scarselli, F., Gori, M., Tsoi, A.C., et al.: The graph neural network model. TNN **20**(1), 61–80 (2009)
15. Li, Z., Ding, X., Liu, T.: Constructing narrative event evolutionary graph for script event prediction. In: Proceedings of International Joint Conferences on Artificial Intelligence Organization (2018)
16. Li, R., Tapaswi, M., Liao, R., et al.: Situation recognition with graph neural networks. In: Proceedings of IEEE International Conference on Computer Vision (2017)
17. Marino, K., Salakhutdinov, R., Gupta, A.: The more you know: using knowledge graphs for image classification. In: Proceedings of IEEE Conference on Computer Vision and Pattern Recognition (2017)
18. Yoochoose. http://2015.recsyschallenge.com/challege.html
19. Diginetica. http://cikm2016.cs.iupui.edu/cikm-cup
20. Li, J., Ren, P., Chen, Z., et al.: Neural attentive session-based recommendation. In: CIKM (2017)

Coattention-Based Recurrent Neural Networks for Sentiment Analysis of Chinese Texts

Lifeng Liu[1(✉)], Lizong Zhang[1], Fengming Zhang[1], Jianguo Qian[2],
Xinxin Zhang[1], Peidong Chen[1], and Bo Li[3]

[1] State Grid Shaoxing Electric Power Supply Company,
Shaoxing, Zhejiang, China
sytsytl51609@sina.com,
zlz951@163.com, zhangfm712@163.com,
13710208018@163.com, 13567556568@163.com
[2] State-Grid Zhejiang Electric Power Co., Ltd., Beijing, China
qian_jianguo@zj.sgcc.com.cn
[3] Beihang University, Beijing, China
libo@act.buaa.edu.cn

Abstract. Sentiment analysis aims to predict user's sentiment polarities of a given text. In this study, we focus on the sentiment classification task on Chinese texts, which are highly relevant in many online customer services for opinion monitoring. Recently, Recurrent Neural Networks (RNNs) perform very well on solving the classification problem of sentences. Compared with other languages, Chinese text has richer syntactic and semantic information, which leads to form an intricate relationship between words and phrase. In this paper, we propose a Coattention-based RNN for analyzing the sentiment polarities of Chinese short texts, in which the bidirectional RNN with the input word embedding is applied to learn representations of context and target, and coattention mechanism could obtain more effective sentiment feature. In the last, results on two public datasets demonstrate the superiority of our proposed methods over the state-of-the-art methods.

Keywords: Sentiment analysis · Chinese text · Recurrent Neural Networks · Attention mechanism

1 Introduction

In many online customer services where users are monitored whether they enjoy a gratifying chatting, the sentiment of user's attitudes behind talking texts could be obtained to reflect their service satisfaction. The goal lies in sentiment analysis or opinion mining is to reveal people's opinions, sentiments, emotions, appraisals, and attitudes towards entities such as products, services, individuals, issues, topics and their attributes [1]. The sentiment analysis is not only related to computer science, but also involves management science and social sciences such as marketing, communications, and finance, due to its influence over both business and society. The reason of this fact is that attitudes or opinions play dominant roles in our activities and behaviors, and our

© Springer Nature Switzerland AG 2019
M. Qiu (Ed.): SmartCom 2019, LNCS 11910, pp. 349–356, 2019.
https://doi.org/10.1007/978-3-030-34139-8_35

beliefs and perceptions of reality, and the choices we make, could be implicitly effected by others' worldviews and values. Large amounts of review texts which reflect our positive or negative feelings are posted towards different aspects of products and services we received.

The task of sentiment analysis is always redefined as a classification question of text on different levels. There are mainly three levels for sentiment analysis [2], i.e. sentence-level [3], document-level [4], and aspect-level [5]. The first two level tasks aim at revealing the whole sentiment orientation over the topic of the review or other entities. And the aspect-level task is highly relevant to characteristic or property of a specific entity. This paper focus on sentence-level sentiment analysis, which is a common task in the field of customer services. In our task, there are three categories according to the sentiment polarity, i.e. positive, neural and negative.

There are numerous techniques proposed to tackle various tasks of sentiment analysis including supervised and unsupervised approaches [6]. While supervised methods have been applied into various tasks of sentiment analysis by taking various supervised machine learning mechanisms and feature combinations [7, 8], unsupervised methods generally take advantage of sentiment lexicons, grammatical analysis, and syntactic patterns [9]. Deep learning techniques have emerged as a powerful toolkit, which have already found an increasingly wide utilization with state-of-art results in a lot of application domains such as computer vision, speech recognition and natural language process processing. Specially, there are evidences shown that deep neural networks are effective solutions for sentiment analysis in automatic feature extraction, such as CNN (Convolutional Neural Network) [10, 11], LSTM (Long Short Term Memory) [12–14], and attention networks [15, 16]. Different from most of research on sentiment analysis, of which the subject text is in English, our study is on the Chinese texts. Chinese is quite different from English in grammatical structure, meaning, expression and idioms. While English sentences tend to be longer with a need to be specific, Chinese prefer to use simple and short sentences to express rich and vivid information. Generally, Chinese texts are more complex and rely on context. Recently, RNN (Recurrent Neural Networks) [17, 18] has been proved that it can capture relationships of words, and have an ability of obtaining long/short-term dependencies by its gating mechanism. In our task, a Chinese sentence may embrace several targets with individual modifiers. When judging the total sentiment of a sentence, targets with uncorresponding modifiers could cause noises for each other. However, there are several works to exploit attention mechanism to learning context feature with target effectively for sentiment analysis [19–22].

In this paper, we propose a Coattention-based RNN model analyzing the sentiment polarities of Chinese short texts. Here, bidirectional RNNs are introduced, which can learn representations of context and target. To capture context features with quality for related targets, traditional attention mechanism which takes an average pooling method is inappropriate. Coattention mechanism is involved to address this problem by considering the attention representation for context generated from the target representation. We evaluate our approach on two public datasets, and results have shown our proposed architecture achieves superior performance on the task of sentiment analysis of Chinese texts.

After brief illustration of background and motivation, we elaborate our proposed approach in details. Then several experiments have been conducted to show the performance of our approaches. Finally, we close with the conclusion and future work.

2 Model

In this section, we describe the Coattention-based RNNs model in details for sentiment analysis of Chinese texts. To make our model work, there are four core components, which are word embedding, GRU networks, the coattention encoder and sentiment classifier in our framework, showing in Fig. 1.

2.1 Word Embedding

As the input of our model is Chinese sentences, there are two common choices to segment input sentences, which are by characters and by words. It is easy to segment and do subsequently encoding by using the by-character method, but there is an amount of effective information lost in such way. So we choose the by-word method, particularly employing jieba, to address the segmentation issue.

After word segmentation, we suppose that a clause consists of m words $[w_c^1, w_c^2, \ldots, w_c^m]$, and n nouns $[w_n^1, w_n^2, \ldots, w_n^n]$. To code these two types of sets, a word embedding matrix is pre-trained. Mapped from thus word embedding matrix, two embedding matrices are obtained for encoding the abovementioned word sets, $[e_c^1, e_c^2, \ldots, e_c^m]$ and $[e_n^1, e_n^2, \ldots, e_n^n]$.

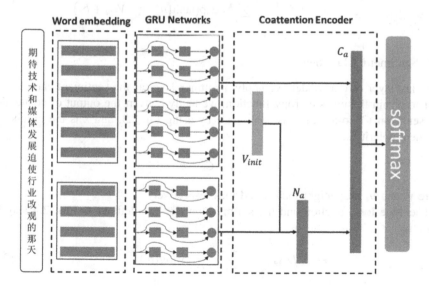

Fig. 1. The architecture of our framework

2.2   GRU Networks

In our model, a bi-directional GRU structure is employed by consisting of two GRUs, which follows progressive and inverse order of the input sequence. At each time step, the hidden states of the bi-directional GRU is the direct concatenation of the forward and backward outputs. Compared with a single-direction GRU structure, the bi-directional GRU structure is able to previous past and future information. To two above-obtained embedding matrices, there are two GRU networks to encode these input matrices and compute the hidden states for each word, respectively. We define these two encoding matrices as $C = [h_c^1, h_c^2, \ldots, h_c^m]$, and $N = [h_n^1, h_n^2, \ldots, h_n^n]$, respectively.

2.3   Coattention Encoder

In the coattention process, there are three steps:

(1) Encode clause's matrix to a vector V_{init} by using the average value of hidden states for each words;
(2) Attend to clause nouns based on V_{init}, and obtain N_a by applying Eq. 2.1;

$$N_a = \sum_{i=1}^{n} h_n^i \cdot \frac{\exp(\tanh(h_n^i \cdot v_n \cdot V_{init} + b_n))}{\sum_{j=1}^{n} \exp(\tanh(h_n^j \cdot v_n \cdot V_{init} + b_n))} \tag{2.1}$$

(3) Attend to clause based on N_a, and get C_a by applying Eq. 2.2.

$$C_a = \sum_{i=1}^{m} h_c^i \cdot \frac{\exp(\tanh(h_c^i \cdot v_c \cdot V_{init} + b_c))}{\sum_{j=1}^{m} \exp(\tanh(h_c^j \cdot v_c \cdot V_{init} + b_c))} \tag{2.2}$$

2.4   Sentiment Classifier

In the last layer of our model, we apply a softmax layer as the sentiment classifier. In order to obtain the cross entropy function, we firstly convert the output of coattention representation C_a to a k-dimensional space by using Eq. 2.3, and k is the number of sentiment polarities.

$$s = v_s \cdot C_a + b_s \tag{2.3}$$

where v_s and b_s are weight matrix and bias respectively.

Then, the loss function and the softmax function are defined as Eqs. 2.4 and 2.5 respectively.

$$Loss = -\sum_{0 < i \leq k} y_i log(p_i) \tag{2.4}$$

$$P_i = \exp(s_i) \Big/ \sum_{0 < i \leq k} \exp(s_i) \tag{2.5}$$

3 Experiments

In this section we describe our experimental setup and provide an in-depth discussion of the achieved results.

3.1 Datasets

We evaluate our model on two public datasets, which have been collected from online hotel reviews and Sina's Weibo data. The corpus of hotel reviews, named ChnSentiHtl, has 7, 767 reviews in total, consisting of 5, 323 positive reviews and 2, 444 negative reviews. The corpus of Sina's Weibo data, named SinaWeiboSenti, has 119, 988 reviews, including 59, 994 positive reviews and 59, 994 negative reviews. During training and test phases for sentiment prediction tasks, datasets are partitioned as shown in Table 1.

3.2 Evaluation Metric and Parameters

We employ accuracy as the metric for evaluating the performance of the approaches, which is define as Eq. 3.1.

$$Acc = \frac{Tr}{Tr + Fs} \tag{3.1}$$

Table 1. The partition of two sentiment datasets

	ChnSentiHtl		SinaWeiboSenti	
	Positive	Negative	Positive	Negative
Train	1, 000	1, 000	10, 000	10, 000
Test	1, 000	1, 000	10, 000	10, 000
Total	5, 323	2, 444	59, 994	59, 994

In Eq. 3.1, Tr is the number of reviews, which is correctly predicted by an approach, and Fs is the misprediction number. The accuracy refers to proportion of correctly predicted reviews over all reviews. As a rule of thumb, the higher accuracy scores the better approach performance. In this experiment, the average value of accuracy of each result is employed.

In our work, we use Word2vec vectors to initialize the word embedding, which are trained from web data. All weights are initialized with uniform distribution U(−0.01, 0.01), and all biases are set to zeros. We train the model with a SGD optimizer, and the learning rate is set to 0.05.

3.3   Comparison with Other Methods

We compare our proposed model with the existing methods, including SnowNLP [23], TF-IDF_XGBoost, and TF-IDF_SVM. SnowNLP is a mature NLP tool for Chinese text, including the function of sentiment analysis. TF-IDF_XGBoost/SVM is a method based on sentiment dictionary, in which TF-IDF is exploited for extracting representation features of input texts, and XGBoost and SVM are employed to classify the sentiment polarity. We evaluate the performance of these approaches on both ChnSentiHtl and SinaWeiboSenti, shown in Fig. 2.

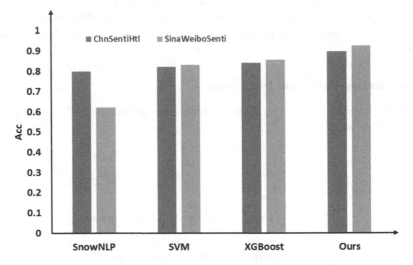

Fig. 2. The performance of compared methods on two datasets

To avoid over-fitting and balance the sizes of positive and negative samples, the method of random playback cross validation has been applied. We make five times of cross validation, and training set and test set do not intersect. More details are listed in Table 2. From results, it is not hard to know that our proposed method is outstanding from other methods on both the total dataset and polarity datasets.

Table 2. Comparisons of various methods on two datasets

	ChnSentiHtl			SinaWeiboSenti		
	Negative (%)	Positive (%)	Total (%)	Negative (%)	Positive (%)	Total (%)
SnowNLP	90.20	69.25	79.73	68.84	55.47	62.15
TF-IDF_ SVM	78.74	85.30	82.02	79.42	86.40	82.91
TF-IDF_ XGBoost	84.52	83.40	83.96	88.53	82.31	85.42
Ours	92.80	86.24	89.52	94.18	90.56	92.37

4 Conclusions and Future Work

This paper proposed a model based on Coattention-based RNNs for sentiment analysis of Chinese text, which takes the word embedding as input. It is important for this task to capture semantic and syntactic information by using word embedding during training. Bidirectional RNNs and Coattention mechanism are involved to learn representations of context and target with high quality. The proposed Coattention-based RNNs model significantly outperforms state-of-the-art methods by taking experiments on two public datasets.

In future work, we plan to consider taking an extensive structure to capture negations modifiers and learn unknown sentiment words and phrases in an acceptable way by exploring knowledge mapping and collaborative learning.

Acknowledgement. The authors gratefully acknowledge the anonymous reviewers for their helpful suggestions.

References

1. Bo, P., Lillian, L.: Opinion mining and sentiment analysis. Found. Trends Inf. Retrieval 2(1–2), 7–9 (2008)
2. Yang, C., Zhang, H., Jiang, B., et al.: Aspect-based sentiment analysis with alternating coattention networks. Inf. Process. Manag. **56**(2019), 463–478 (2019)
3. Long, J., Yu, M., Zhou, M., et al.: Target-dependent twitter sentiment classification. In: Proceedings of the 49th Annual Meeting of the Association for Computational Linguistics: Human Language Technologies (2011)
4. Balahur, A., Steinberger, R., Kabadjov, M.: Sentiment analysis in the news. Infrared Phys. Technol. **65**, 94–102 (2014)
5. Ma, Y., Peng, H., Cambria, E.: Targeted aspect-based sentiment analysis via embedding commonsense knowledge into an attentive LSTM. In: Proceedings of the 32nd AAAI Conference on Artificial Intelligence (2018)
6. Zhang, L., Wang, S., Liu, B.: Deep learning for sentiment analysis: a survey. Wiley Interdisc. Rev.: Data Min. Knowl. Discov. **8**(4), e1253 (2018)
7. Zhang, Z., Lan, M.: ECNU: extracting effective features from multiple sequential sentences for target-dependent sentiment analysis in reviews. In: Proceedings of the 9th International Workshop on Semantic Evaluation (2015)
8. Wagner, J., Arora, P., Cortes, S., et al.: DCU: aspect-based polarity classification for SemEval task 4. In: Proceedings of the 8th International Workshop on Semantic Evaluation (2014)
9. Liu, B.: Sentiment Analysis: Mining Opinions, Sentiments, and Emotions. The Cambridge University Press (2015)
10. Zhang, X., Zhao, J., LeCun, Y.: Character-level convolutional networks for text classification. In: Advances in Neural Information Processing Systems (2015)
11. Kalchbrenner, N., Grefenstette, E., Blunsom, P.: A convolutional neural network for modelling sentences. In: Proceedings of the 52nd Annual Meeting of the Association for Computational Linguistics (2014)

12. Qian, Q., Huang, M., Lei, J., et al.: Linguistically regularized LSTMS for sentiment classification. In: Proceedings of the 55th Annual Meeting of the Association for Computational Linguistics (2017)

13. Ruder, S., Ghaffari, P., Breslin, J.G.: A hierarchical model of reviews for aspect-based sentiment analysis. In: Proceedings of the 2016 Conference on Empirical Methods in Natural Language Processing (2016)

14. Zhou, P., Qi, Z., Zheng, S., et al.: Text classification improved by integrating bidirectional LSTM with two-dimensional max pooling. In: Proceedings of the 26th International Conference on Computational Linguistics (2016)

15. Lin, Z., Feng, M., dos Santos, C.N., et al.: A structured self-attentive sentence embedding. In Proceedings of International conference on learning representations (2017)

16. Yang, Z., Yang, D., Dyer, C., et al.: Hierarchical attention networks for document classification. In: Proceedings of the 2016 Conference of the North American Chapter of the Association for Computational Linguistics: Human Language Technologies (2016)

17. Dieng, A.B., Wang, C., Gao, J., et al.: TopicRNN: a recurrent neural network with long-range semantic dependency. In: Proceedings of International Conference on Learning Representations (2017)

18. Lipton, Z.C., Berkowitz, J., Elkan, C.: A critical review of recurrent neural networks for sequence learning. Comput. Sci. (2015)

19. Tay, Y., Tuan, L.A., Hui, S.C.: Learning to attend via word-aspect associative fusion for aspect-based sentiment analysis. In: Proceedings of the Thirty-Second AAAI Conference on Artificial Intelligence (2018)

20. Chen, P., Sun, Z., Bing, L., et al.: Recurrent attention network on memory for aspect sentiment analysis. In: Proceedings of the 2017 Conference on Empirical Methods in Natural Language Processing (2017)

21. Ma, D., Li, S., Zhang, X., et al.: Interactive attention networks for aspect-level sentiment classification. In: Proceedings of the Twenty-Sixth International Joint Conference on Artificial Intelligence (2017)

22. Wang, Y., Huang, M., Zhao, L., et al.: Attention-based LSTM for aspect-level sentiment classification. In: Proceedings of the 2016 Conference on Empirical Methods in Natural Language Processing (2016)

23. https://github.com/isnowfy/snownlp

Design and Implementation of Small-scale Sensor Network Based on Raspberry Pi

Honglei Zheng[1][(⊠)], Hong Guo[2], and Shimin Wu[1]

[1] College of Computer Science and Technology,
Wuhan University of Science and Technology, Wuhan, China
`derekzheng125@163.com`
[2] Hubei Province Key Laboratory of Intelligent Information
Processing and Real-time Industrial System, Wuhan, China

Abstract. With the development of modern technology, embedded technology has continued to develop. In the deep cooperation between embedded and wireless network technologies, the technology of sensor network has been born. The software system based on traditional wireless network cannot collect data in the real world. In some production environments, the embedded sensor network consists of a large number of sensor nodes, integrating sensing, acquisition, processing, and transceiving functions into an autonomous network system to achieve dynamic and intelligent collaborative sensing of the physical world. Based on the existing wireless sensor network system architecture, this paper designs and implements a small-scale sensor network system based on Raspberry Pi. After the software and hardware test of the sensor network system, the test results show that the system can complete the information collection and transmission, and has stability and synchronization to meet project requirements and stability requirements.

Keywords: Embedded · Sensing network · WiringPi · Websocket

1 Introduction

In today's wave of technology that promotes Internet+, traditional industries are beginning to seek cooperation with emerging Internet technologies to achieve industrial internetization. The traditional Internet network design can't exchange data with the real world, so the function is limited in some production and living environments, and the embedded sensor network can access a variety of sensor devices, integrating information collection and information processing functions. Forming an independent and complete network system to achieve the perceived synergy of the physical world [1].

The current mainstream embedded transmission protocol considers the power consumption and performance of the central control board. Most of them use low-rate network programming protocols to reduce the power consumption during transmission. With the performance of embedded chips, the Raspberry Pi class the high-performance development board has become more cost-effective, which can support high-complexity high-speed transmission protocols, and the number of access devices is greatly improved.

M. Qiu (Ed.): SmartCom 2019, LNCS 11910, pp. 357–365, 2019.
https://doi.org/10.1007/978-3-030-34139-8_36

Therefore, this paper mainly designs and implements a small-scale sensor network using the Raspberry Pi as the central control board. The Raspberry Pi is used to collect sensor information, and the information is sent to the server through the JSON transmission format after the information is collected and processed, and the instructions sent by the server are used to operate the hardware devices in the sensing system, thereby realizing stable data transmission and more. The type sensor accesses and automatically detects the reconnection after disconnection, which solves the problem that the device node goes to sleep after the network is accidentally disconnected. The sensor network has high stability and good synchronization, and has application prospect and value.

2   Related Technology

2.1   Sensor Network System

The basic sensor network system mainly includes a sensor node, a sink node, and a management node. The sensor data is transmitted hop by hop through the network, and is routed to the aggregation node through the multi-hop route in the self-organizing network, and the data is exchanged between the management nodes by using the Internet network.

(1) Sensor node. Mainly engaged in information collection and data processing tasks, processing power is general. At the same time, it receives other node data and cooperates with the task in the self-organizing network.
(2) Aggregation node. It is responsible for connecting the sensor network system to the external network. It is used as a gateway node for data exchange. At the same time, it accepts the management node command to monitor and control the sensor node. The aggregation node can also be an enhanced sensor node.
(3) Management node. The user of the sensor network system operates through the management node and accesses the hardware and software resources in the system. After the command is issued, the node is sent to other nodes through the node to manage the entire sensor network system [2].

Differentiated from the functional modules, the infrastructure of the sensor network uses the microprocessor minimum system as the core module, the sensing module is the functional module, including all access sensors in the sensor network, and the wireless communication module includes all network communication and data transmission. The processing module and the power module are responsible for powering the above three modules. The specific architecture is shown in Fig. 1.

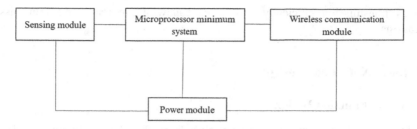

Fig. 1. Sensor network system structure

2.2 Websocket

Websocket is a full-duplex communication protocol first proposed by HTML5. The protocol is established on a single TCP connection [3], which makes the exchange of data between the client and the server easier. The protocol allows the server to take the initiative. Push data to the client. In the WebSocket API, the browser and the server only need to complete a handshake. The two can directly create a persistent connection and perform bidirectional data transmission. Through this fast data channel, the data between the server and the client. Transfer is more efficient [4]. The WebSocket protocol based on the HTTP 1.1 version can save server resources and bandwidth, and communicate in a stable and real-time manner (Fig. 2).

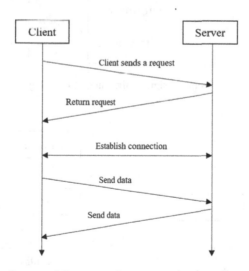

Fig. 2. Schematic diagram of the connection process between the server and the client

After the connection is completed, in the characteristics of the Websocket, the heartbeat mechanism is used to realize the long-lived keep-alive. The basic method based on TCP can be adopted, or a custom protocol can be adopted. The custom protocol has a smaller packet format and avoids the HTTP packet. Byte-level overhead improves transmission efficiency and saves bandwidth in real-world transmission applications.

3   Sensor Network Design

3.1   System Function Design

Nowadays, IoT devices are entering people's lives. The family Internet of Things makes people's lives more intelligent. People can use their mobile devices to control home appliances or get the data they need from their home sensor networks. The sensor network system studied in this thesis starts with the hardware part sensor network of the Internet of Things. It explores that one can send data to the server by the sensor, and the server can send instructions to the sensor node in the sensor network to the home. The system in which the device is controlled. With this system, the user can issue commands in the client of the mobile phone to operate the home device, and can select the device to view the data generated by the device at the set time point in real time. The overall architecture is shown in Figs. 3 and 4.

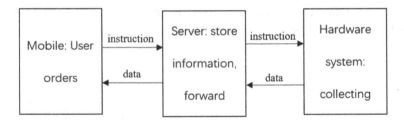

Fig. 3. Functional design of the Internet of Things system

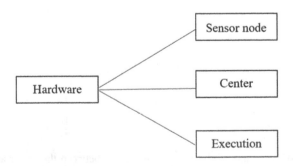

Fig. 4. Hardware system architecture

Cut into the sensor network part of this study, that is, the function design is: the sensor node reads the data and then reads it by the central control board, encapsulates it with the embedded JSON format, and uploads it to the data server by the central control board using the wireless network. After receiving the instruction information from the user, the central control board parses the received JSON information packet, thereby reading the operation state of the sensor node, and performing corresponding settings. The sensor network hardware system architecture.

3.2 System Architecture Design

The system service model includes a Raspberry Pi central control panel and a three-part access sensor node. The Raspberry pie card is used to control the hardware. The temperature and humidity sensor DHT11 is the sensor, which is responsible for collecting the temperature and humidity of the environment. Information, and IRGree Gree air-conditioning infrared control module, IOTWebsocket home decoration lights for the execution module, when the central control board receives the user instructions forwarded by the server, performs control settings on the actuator, all data processing, data transmission, control execution programs are integrated In the Raspberry Pi card board. The Raspberry Pi card and the server system complete the two-way transmission of data and instructions.

4 Implementation of Small-scale Sensor Networks

The development environment of the small-scale sensor network based on the Raspberry Pi is based on the Linux Debian family Rasbian operating system. Due to the performance limitation of the Raspberry Pi, part of the compilation work is compiled by configuring the cross-compilation environment on the PC side. After compiling, the Raspberry is compiled. Run the execution file.

4.1 Rasbian System Burning

The Raspberry Pi development board itself comes with 1G RAM, and the ROM needs to be inserted into the SD card. That is, the Raspberry Pi development board in the initial state does not have an operating system, and it needs to be burned by itself. The system can choose to minimize the version. The minimized version itself does not have a graphical interface. It is more used in the server. The system studied in this paper is used as the central control board. The system program will output the visualization data, so the research system selects the full version. As shown in Fig. 4. After the system is burned, it can be powered on after power-on. When booting, it will initialize the system through the initialization configuration file of the boot disk, and enter the system desktop after the initialization is completed. After the time zone, the American pinyin keyboard, and the network card are set through the terminal interface, you can use the Raspberry Pi card to program (Fig, 5).

Fig. 5. Rasbian complete system

4.2   Cross Compilation Environment Configuration

The Raspberry Pi is a card-type single-chip microcomputer, and its performance is limited. Therefore, the compilation of some code is performed by the PC. The executable file compiled in another system environment by one system is called cross-compilation [5]. In the development process of the sensor network system studied in this paper, in order to save resources and time, the Raspberry Pi development environment is configured in the PC-side UBUNTU18.04 system, and the Raspberry Pi official cross-compilation tool chain is used for configuration.

4.3   Websocket Long Connection Implementation

In the sensor network system studied in this paper, the Websocket protocol is used for information transmission, and the custom class of the system is packaged on the basic websocket-client class to achieve stable long connection and complete bidirectional information transmission to the server.

4.3.1   Heartbeat Mechanism

In the provisions of the Websocket protocol, the heartbeat mechanism is used to keep the long connection. In the two forms provided by it, the second mode is selected: the connection layer is customized based on the application layer. The custom connection package adopts the JSON format. When the client establishes a Websocket connection, it sends a JSON package to apply for a connection. After the server receives the key value, the server matches the verification value. If the verification is passed, the server sends a "HeartBeating" to simulate the heartbeat packet. After that, the server sends a heartbeat packet to the Raspberry Pi every 3 s. The customized heartbeat function of the Raspberry Pi is started every 6 s after receiving the heartbeat packet sent by the server. If it is within 6 s again, After receiving the heartbeat packet of the server, it determines that the connection between the two parties is stable. If it is not received, it determines that the current connection has been disconnected, and needs to call the reconnect module to re-initiate the connection.

4.4   Sensor Node Resolution

The sensor node uses DHT11 for information collection and continuously sends temperature and humidity information to the server. This system was developed using the Python language to programmatically read data from sensors. The encoding process is performed according to the timing diagram, using a single-bus bidirectional serial communication protocol, each time the acquisition is initiated by the start signal, and then the DHT11 sends a response to the Raspberry Pi and begins transmitting 40-bit data frames, with the high order first. The data format is: 8 bit humidity integer data plus 8 bit humidity decimal data plus 8 bit temperature integer data plus 8 bit temperature decimal data plus 8 bit check digit, the temperature and humidity fractional part defaults to 0, that is, the data collected by the Raspberry Pi is Integer, the check digit is 4 bytes of data plus the result of the lower 8 bits of data as a checksum. If the final result does not match the checksum, there is a problem in the data processing. In this research system, all data for verification failure is not sent to the server, and the data is defined as "BrokenData" in the Raspberry Pi.

4.5   System Function Test

After the development is completed, the system studied in this paper has carried out the final functional test. The following is a detailed step and a physical test situation diagram:

(1)   Start the server and listen for the specified Websocket port. The startup process is shown in Fig. 6.

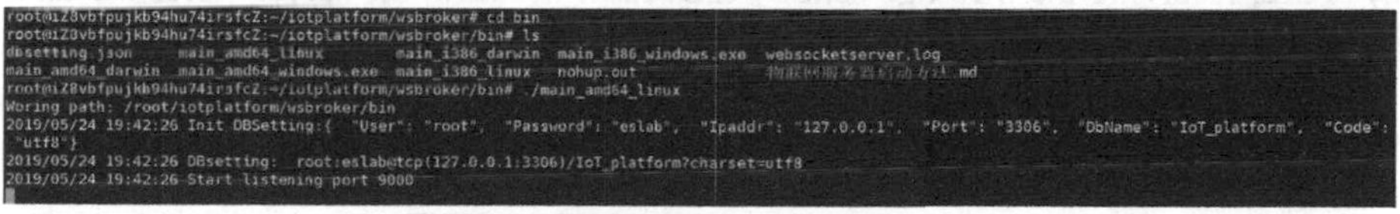

Fig. 6. Server startup

(2)   Power on the Raspberry Pi and connect peripherals such as the display via USB.
(3)   Connect DHT11 temperature and humidity sensor, connect with DuPont line, connect DHT11 VCC pin to Raspberry Pi pin 1, GND to Raspberry Pi pin 6, realize 3.3 V power supply of DHT11 sensor, data The pin is connected to the Raspberry Pi pin 7. The above Raspberry Pi pin connections are all based on the WiringPi pin position. The connection status is shown in Fig. 7.

Fig. 7. DHT11 and Raspberry Pi connection

(4) Run the program, the server verifies that the device ID is successful, and sends the heartbeat packet to the Raspberry Pi. After receiving the information, the Raspberry Pi prints the successful connection information on the external display and continues to print the connection. Heartbeat information to show whether the current connection status is normal.

(5) The Raspberry Pi sensor network system maintains a stable and long connection between the server and the server. The server continuously sends a heartbeat packet to the Raspberry Pi. The Raspberry Pi receives the heartbeat packet from the server and detects the connection status. The heartbeat information is printed on the external display, allowing the user to check whether the current system is running normally and print heartbeat information [6].

(6) After receiving the message sent by the sensor network, the server stores the data in the MySQL database. All databases of the system in the server are shown in Fig. 8.

```
mysql> show databases;
+--------------------------+
| Database                 |
+--------------------------+
| information_schema       |
| IoT_platform             |
| blog_app                 |
| bodydb                   |
| car_health               |
| chatroom                 |
| chinese_medical_network  |
| ios_Lab                  |
| light                    |
| mysql                    |
| performance_schema       |
| sys                      |
| vueblog                  |
+--------------------------+
13 rows in set (0.00 sec)
```

Fig. 8. Database design in the server

(7) After selecting the t_data data table, you can view the collection information of all sensing devices, including the device ID number, sensor data in JSON format, and data acquisition time. The specific data is shown in Fig. 9.

```
mysql> select * from t_data order by id desc limit 20;
+---------+-----------+---------------------------------------------+---------------------+
| id      | device_id | data_value                                  | create_time         |
+---------+-----------+---------------------------------------------+---------------------+
| 8441766 |      3000 | {"temperature": 28, "humidity": 46}         | 2019-05-24 02:57:52 |
| 8441765 |      3000 | {"temperature": 28, "humidity": 46}         | 2019-05-24 02:57:49 |
| 8441764 |      3000 | {"temperature": 28, "humidity": 46}         | 2019-05-24 02:57:46 |
| 8441763 |      3000 | {"temperature": 28, "humidity": 46}         | 2019-05-24 02:57:41 |
| 8441762 |      3000 | {"temperature": 28, "humidity": 47}         | 2019-05-24 02:57:36 |
| 8441761 |      3000 | {"temperature": 28, "humidity": 47}         | 2019-05-24 02:57:33 |
| 8441760 |      3000 | {"temperature": 28, "humidity": 47}         | 2019-05-24 02:57:30 |
| 8441759 |      3000 | {"temperature": 28, "humidity": 47}         | 2019-05-24 02:57:27 |
| 8441758 |      3000 | {"temperature": 28, "humidity": 47}         | 2019-05-24 02:57:24 |
| 8441757 |      3000 | {"temperature": 28, "humidity": 47}         | 2019-05-24 02:57:21 |
| 8441756 |      3000 | {"temperature": 28, "humidity": 47}         | 2019-05-24 02:57:16 |
| 8441755 |      3000 | {"temperature": 28, "humidity": 47}         | 2019-05-24 02:57:11 |
| 8441754 |      3000 | {"temperature": 28, "humidity": 47}         | 2019-05-24 02:57:08 |
| 8441753 |      3000 | {"temperature": 28, "humidity": 49}         | 2019-05-24 02:57:05 |
| 8441752 |      3000 | {"temperature": 28, "humidity": 50}         | 2019-05-24 02:57:02 |
| 8441751 |      3000 | {"temperature": 28, "humidity": 48}         | 2019-05-24 02:56:57 |
| 8441750 |      3000 | {"temperature": 28, "humidity": 49}         | 2019-05-24 02:56:54 |
| 8441749 |      3000 | {"temperature": 28, "humidity": 50}         | 2019-05-24 02:56:49 |
| 8441748 |      3000 | {"temperature": 28, "humidity": 52}         | 2019-05-24 02:56:46 |
| 8441747 |      3000 | {"temperature": 28, "humidity": 52}         | 2019-05-24 02:56:43 |
+---------+-----------+---------------------------------------------+---------------------+
20 rows in set (0.00 sec)
```

Fig. 9. Sensor data in the server database

4.6 Analysis of System Test Results

Based on the new network protocol technology, this paper proposes a design and implementation process of a small-scale sensor network system, and provides relevant theoretical basis as a support. On the basis of theory, through the analysis and combing of the application scenarios, the system has been designed for functional design, architecture design, and the overall operation process of the system. After the design is completed, actual development is carried out and basic robustness testing is performed. In summary, the sensor network system implements a full-duplex communication mode and guarantees a long-lived connection and disconnection reconnection mechanism to achieve the expected experimental goals.

References

1. Luo, S.: The development of the Internet of Things industry and the trend of technological innovation. Inf. Commun. Technol. Cont. Unit **12**(04), 4–8 (2018)
2. Gao, F., Wen, H., Zhao, L., et al.: Design and optimization of a cross-layer routing protocol for multi-hop wireless sensor networks. In: International Conference on Sensor Network Security Technology & Privacy Communication System, pp. 16–87. IEEE (2013)
3. Hou, L., Zhao, S., Li, X., et al.: Design and implementation of application programming interface for Internet of Things cloud. Int. J. Netw. Manag. 57–58 (2016)
4. Khan, I., Belqasmi, F., Glitho, R., et al.: Wireless sensor network virtualization: a survey. IEEE Commun. Surv. Tutorials **18**(1), 553–576 (2017)
5. Kamoshida, Y.: Simplifying install-time auto-tuning for cross-compilation environments by program execution forwarding. In: IEEE International Conference on Parallel & Distributed Systems, pp. 15–97. IEEE (2013)
6. Park, S., Kang, J., Park, J., et al.: One-bodied humidity and temperature sensor having advanced linearity at low and high relative humidity range. Sens. Actuators B (Chem.) **76**(1–3), 322–326 (2001)

Research on Template-Based Factual Automatic Question Answering Technology

Wenhui Hu[1], Xueyang Liu[1(✉)], Chengli Xing[2], Minghui Zhang[3], and Sen Ma[1]

[1] National Engineering Research Center for Software Engineering,
Peking University, Beijing, China
liuxueyang@pku.edu.cn
[2] SiChuan Tianfu Bank Co., Ltd., Nanchong, China
[3] Handan Institute of Innovation, Peking University, Handan, Beijing, China

Abstract. With the increase of people's demand for information retrieval, question answering system as a new generation of retrieval methods has attracted more and more attention. This paper proposes an automated template generation method based on remote supervision. In the process of generating template, in order to identify the keywords express the semantics of the problem, this paper designs an algorithm to mapping entity relationship to keywords by using pattern mining and statistical methods. This method implements automation of template generation, and makes the templates more accurate. For the template matching, by Deep-learning-based template matching algorithm, this paper use vector to represent words, and designs a tree-based convolutional neural network to extract features of the dependency syntax information. Building a neural network model for template prediction. Experimental results show that the above method can effectively improve the matching accuracy compared with the traditional template matching method.

Keywords: Question answering system · Knowledge graph · Template generation · Template matching · Neural network

1 Introduction

For major search engine developers, the greatest challenge they are facing is how to quickly and effectively extract the information people genuinely seek from the Internet. As a new generation of retrieval methods, the question answering system has become a heated issue. Compared to traditional search engines, its advantage lies in that with the natural language questions as input, it returns the exact answer of the question directly to the user. In the retrieval process of the fact-based question answering system, the main emphasis of research is the analysis of the semantics of questions. A feasible research direction is that it matches question input by users with problem templates in knowledge base, and deduces the query intention of the question in accordance with the template information, so the corresponding fact query statement can be generated and accurate answers from the knowledge base can be directly gained.

© Springer Nature Switzerland AG 2019
M. Qiu (Ed.): SmartCom 2019, LNCS 11910, pp. 366–375, 2019.
https://doi.org/10.1007/978-3-030-34139-8_37

Template-based automatic question answering process is as follow: the system analyzes the question when a new question is input. If the question itself has a nested or juxtaposed relationship, the system will decompose it into several sub-questions. By comparing the similarity between the question and the template in the template library, it can find out the most similar template. With the usage of the entity information in the question, the query statement corresponding to the template is completed and the exact answers to questions can be obtained directly from the knowledge base. The major difficulty for the template-based factual automatic question answering system is template generation and template matching [1].

In this paper, the entity relationship to keyword mapping algorithm is designed with pattern mining and statistics methods. Ultimately, it not only realizes the automatic generation of template, but also enables the mapping between words and relationships in the generated template more precise. The template matching algorithm based on deep learning is proposed in this paper: based on the word vector of the problem, the sentence dependency syntactic relationship is further considered, feature extraction of dependency syntactic relations is carried out with tree convolution neural network, and a neural network model for template prediction and its training method are designed. Experimental results show that compared with the traditional template matching method, the above method can improve the matching accuracy more effectively.

2 Relevant Research

In terms of template generation, vast majority of the question answering corpus template libraries of automatic question answering system are constructed manually. Question answering corpus is processed and question answering templates or rules are sorted out manually. For example, Fader [2], Lopez et al. [3] summarized the main forms of questions in English, and performed entity alignment with natural language expressions to generate problem template. With three kinds of artificial constructions, Bast and Haussmann [4] generated query template without relying on natural language expressions, which only instantiated the query template from the question corpus. Artificial template construction requires spending extensive amount of manpower and time, and question and answer templates are also very limited. Therefore, some scholars have proposed automatic template construction methods, question-answering templates are generated from question-answering corpus through question-answering corpus learning. Such as a template generation method based on expression and relationship matching proposed by Abujabal [5].

Essentially, the generated question template is still a question sentence manually or automatically, and it is only abstracted on the basis of sentence, and some specific elements are expressed in a sentence by type [6]. Therefore, it is still a sentence-to-sentence similarity calculation when matching the question with the template [7]. Sentence similarity is mainly reflected in the degree of repetition between words that constitute a sentence. Based on the current research situation, the calculation is mainly carried out in two directions: statistical-based method and word-sentence vector distance based method. The current mainstream direction for the research on sentence similarity is word similarity [8]. Some algorithms for calculating the global similarity of sentences by using word similarity are proposed based on the research of word similarity. Many scholars have put forward their own calculation methods in this respect. For example, Cranias et al. [9] first proposed the use of multilevel dynamic programming (Dynamic Programming) to calculate sentence similarity; Ding [10] proposed a method to calculate whether different sentences express the same semantics based on Latent Semantic Indexing; Carbonell and Goldsdein [11] of Columbia University proposed using Maximal Marginal Relevane to calculate sentence similarity; Nirenburg [12] proposed a similarity calculation method based on string matching: by calculating the similarity between words, the whole sentence similarity algorithm is obtained ultimately. Some algorithms achieve overall similarity by comparing character levels, such as famous string editing distance and MCWPA algorithm.

3   Question-Answering Template Generation

The template generation based on relational dictionary proposed in this paper is mainly divided into two steps, which are construction of relational dictionary with text corpus and generate question-answering template through question-answering corpus.

3.1   Construction of Relational Dictionary

In this paper, a text corpus-based relational representation method mining algorithm is proposed: an expression method of mining verbs and verb phrases from text corpus, mapping and associating the corresponding relations, and then obtaining the representation of the relations.

3.1.1   Mining of Relational Representation Method

In order to analyze phrases correctly, instead of counting individual words, the text corpus is analyzed with the method of pattern mining. The entity (entity-type, entity-type, phrase) is mined as an item set. The sentences in the text corpus are expressed as follows:

$$T(s) = \{(e_1, e_2, t) | e_1, e_2 \in E(s), t \subseteq I(s)\} \tag{1}$$

Where, $T(S)$ represents a set of items generated by sentence s, $E(s)$ represents the set of entities in sentence s, and $I(s)$ repents the set of important words in sentence s without entities and auxiliary words.

Due to the limitations of corpus, item set is not screened by threshold method; instead, the number of occurrences of an item set is used as its weight to indicate the probability of occurrence of the item set. The item set after statistics is integrated, if ($e1$, $e2$, $\{t1\}$), ($e1$, $e2$, $\{t2\}$), ($e1$, $e2$, $\{t1, t2\}$), and the occurrence times of the three are basically similar, then, it is considered that $\{t1, t2\}$ is a fixed combination of words, and only one item ($e1$, $e2$, $\{t1, t2\}$) is retained.

3.1.2 Mapping Related to Representation Method

In the process of pattern mining, item sets are expressed in the form of $(e1, e2, t)$. We need to query all the entities in $E(s)$, and obtain the sub-map $KG(s)$ of knowledge map. The phrases in each item set correspond to an edge in the sub-map of knowledge map, that is, a relationship in the knowledge map. Based on this, we can conclude that: phrase t is one way of representing this relationship, and from the relationship by querying from $e1$ and $e2$ and corresponding relationship between the representations, entity alignment is completed.

By entity alignment, the correspondence between relation and representation is obtained and recorded as "relation-representation method", that is: entries in the relational dictionary. At the same time, the possibility of calculating word frequency eliminates the wrong entries.

3.2 Template Generation Based on Relational Dictionary

3.2.1 Analysis of Question-Answering Corpus

In the pretreatment of question-answering corpus, the "Language Cloud" Language Technology Platform (LTP-Cloud) developed by Harbin Institute of Technology is used to carry out entity recognition, syntactic dependency and semantic dependency analysis on question-answer pairs in corpus.

For questions in question-answering corpus, word segmentation, entity recognition and part of speech tagging are carried out, and the method of syntactic tree is used to represent the structure of the sentence. Through word segmentation, the entity set $E(c)$ and the important word set $I(c)$ of the question-answering pair c are obtained.

The item set in $T(c)$ is queried in the relational dictionary, and possible representations in question-answering pairs c are identified. The knowledge map is queried through the entities contained in $E(c)$, the knowledge map is queried, and the sub-map of knowledge map containing all entities is obtained. The analysis of question-and-answer pairs has been completed.

3.2.2 Question Template

In order to make the correspondence between relation and representation as correct as possible, that is, select a set of edges to maximize the possibility (weight) of the occurrence of the set. This issue can be solved in two different ways: maximum weight bipartite matching and linear programming. In this paper, Kuhn-Munkres algorithm for maximum weight bipartite matching is used.

The corresponding relationship between words and relations in questions has been established when the entity alignment is complete. In order to translate questions into corresponding question-and-answer templates, questions need to be processed according to the dependency syntax tree of the question. Words that are less semantically related from the tree are removed to enable the remaining parts as concise as possible. Three types of words are retained: entity, interrogative pronouns and words in the representation method.

The additional information from the sentence are deleted under the circumstance that the above three types of words are retained, so as to simplify and template the question syntax dependency tree.

4   Template Matching Based on Convolution Neural Network

Template matching is the core of the question answering system based on semantic analysis. In this paper, the neural network-based deep learning method is used to calculate sentence similarity.

4.1   Word Vector Generation

In this paper, The GloVe model proposed by Stanford University is used to learn word vectors in text corpus to generate the corresponding word vector. After completing the training of GloVe model, calculate each word in the question with GloVe model, and replace the words in the dependent syntax tree with the corresponding word vectors in turn.

It must be noted that, the entity in the template is replaced with the corresponding entity type in the process of template generation. When word vector calculation is made on the words in question sentences, the same replacement is required to guarantee that the word vectors of the corresponding types are the same. Therefore, in the pre-processing, statistics for all the entity types in the corpus are made, and a fixed word vector for each type is given. When the corresponding entity appears in the question or template, replace it with the word vector corresponding to its type.

For question with N words, its dependency syntax tree has N + 1 nodes and N edges. With the exception of the additional Root nodes, each node corresponds to a word, and the node records dependencies on the edge of its parent node. Therefore, edge is considered being processed and converted its information to the current node.

Finally, the relation vectors of syntactic dependency labeling and word vectors are joined together, and a new vector is generated as the eigenvector of each word. The syntactic dependency and word vector are combined, and the information obtained is still called the word vector of the node. The original dependency syntactic tree is replaced by a tree structure with only node weights but all original information and unchanged morphology.

4.2   Construction of Tree-Based Convolutional Neural Network

In the Tree-based Convolutional Neural Network, the key problem that needs to be addressed is how to compare tree similarities under the condition of preserving tree structure information effectively. In this paper, a tree-based convolutional neural network is used to address these problems. The relationships among the layers of the tree are preserved in the process of convolution, convolution layer by layer, and the information of the whole tree is mapped to a vector in a multidimensional space. Finally, the eigenvectors are used for classification. The input of the neural network is a dependent syntactic tree after word vector substitution. The input dependency syntax tree is not fixed due to uncertainty in sentences. The output of the neural network is a distribution, representing the possibility of inputting questions belongs to each type of template.

The basic structure of tree-based convolutional neural network is as follows (Fig. 1):

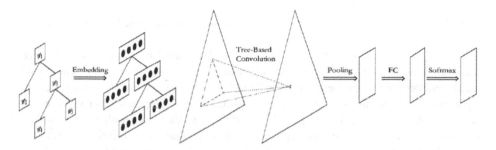

Fig. 1. Tree-based convolutional neural network structure

The network has four layers, in addition to the final full connection layer and the softmax layer, there are special convolution layer and pooling layer. A "continuous binary tree" is introduced to deal with the multi-fork tree in the syntactic tree.

4.2.1   Convolution Layer

Generally, the convolution layer of convolution neural network convolutes fixed size data by convolution kernel. However, in the tree structure, the process of convolution changes due to uncertainty in the shape of the tree. Convolution operations in tree structures need to be performed on each sub-tree separately, and the selection of convolution kernel depends on two parts: Firstly, the size of the convolution kernel. The length of the word vector of each node N_{vec} and the length of the eigenvector after convolution Nf determine the size of the parameter W_{conv} to be $N_{vec} \times Nf$. Secondly, the depth of the convolution kernel, that is, the depth of the window. Due to the special shape of trees, the depth of the window determines how many layers of sub-nodes are considered when convoluting a sub-tree.

When convolution is made on a sub-tree, and it is assumed that there are n nodes in the window, and their word vectors are: $v1, v2, \ldots vn$. The formula for calculating the eigenvector y is as follows:

$$\tanh\left(\sum_{i=1}^{n} W_{conv,i} \cdot v_i + b_{conv}\right) \qquad (2)$$

In the process of convolution, if the depth of the sub-tree is less than the number of layers of the window, the insufficient layers are supplemented by vector 0. After the convolution is completed, a tree constituted by eigenvectors with original syntactic tree structure is obtained.

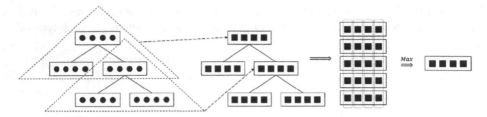

Fig. 2. Tree-based convolution and dynamic pooling of convolutional neural network

In tree-based convolutional neural networks, the input data is the syntactic tree obtained from the syntactic dependency analysis of questions. Different sentences lead to different tree structures; hence, the number of nodes in each window is also different. The number of nodes in the syntax tree requires corresponding quantities of W_{conv}, as the parameter. A "continuous binary tree" is introduced to solve this problem. Only W_{convt}, W_{convl}, W_{convr} are used as the parameters of the model, based on the location information of the node i, and linear combination of W_{convt}, W_{convl}, W_{convr} are used to express W_{conv}, i. The implementation of "continuous binary tree" will be described in Sect. 4.2.3.

4.2.2   Pooling Layer
When processed in the convolution layer, every node, including the leaf node, is convolved. It is integrated with the information of fixed depth sub-node. After processed in the convolution layer, a new tree has been created. However, the structure of the whole dependency tree has not changed, only the information stored by each node has changed from the word vector of a single word to the eigenvector containing sub-tree information. Similarly, the generation of tree structure is directly related to sentence length. Therefore, it is still unable to meet the requirement of fixed size and unable to pass directly as a parameter to the next layer of network. In this case, the dynamic pooling layer is needed to convert the tree structure into a fixed size input.

In this paper, the method used is to Max-Pooling all eigenvectors directly, and select the maximum value in each dimension as the result. N eigenvectors of length Nf are pooled into an eigenvector of length Nf. The right part of Fig. 2 is the process of tree-based dynamic pooling of convolutional neural network

4.2.3   Continuous Binary Tree
In many tree processing, there are multi-branch trees. For different nodes, the number of sub-nodes is also different. There are two ways to process such data: first one is to add same weights to all the sub-nodes. The second one is to endow different weights Wi according to the order of sub-nodes. In terms of the first method, the advantage is that it uses fewer parameters and has no limitation on the number of sub-nodes. The disadvantage is that it cannot reflect the different influence of different sub-nodes on the whole. In terms of the second method, it can effectively retain the relative order of information between sub-nodes, but in cannot determine the number of Wi due to the uncertainty of the number of sub-nodes. It will fail to process when the number of sub-nodes exceeds the expected tree. On the other hand, the number of parameters is directly related to the number of sub-nodes, the more sub-nodes, the more parameters,

so the training time and computational resources are also relatively large. Based on the advantages and disadvantages of the above two methods, a compromise approach has emerged: a certain number of parameters can be used, and Wi can be obtained with the linear combination of these parameters.

In this paper, three basic parameters Wl, Wr and Wt are used, the parameter Wi of node i is expressed by the linear combination of Wl, Wr and Wt, and formula is satisfied:

$$W_i = \alpha_i^t W_t + \alpha_i^l W_l + \alpha_i^r W_r \tag{3}$$

Where αit, αil and αir are calculated according to the relative position of node i:

$$\alpha_i^t = \frac{d_i - 1}{d - 1} \tag{4}$$

di represents the depth of node i in the current sliding window, and d represents the depth of sliding window.

$$\alpha_i^r = \left(1 - \alpha_i^t\right) \frac{p_i - 1}{n - 1} \tag{5}$$

pi represents the location of node i at the current layer, and n represents the total number of sub-nodes in the current layer.

$$\alpha_i^l = \left(1 - \alpha_i^t\right)\left(1 - \alpha_i^r\right) \tag{6}$$

The method of continuous binary tree can process arbitrary tree structure with fewer parameters in case of fewer parameters. It also has good adaptability for windows of any size and location.

5 Experiment

Test samples contain two pieces of information: questions and corresponding template numbers. Some of the samples are as follows (Table 1):

Table 1. Some samples of test data

Template number	Template	Question
1	Movie>/m. in md, <Character>. is/v, who/r, played/v	Who played Truman in *The Truman Show*?
2	<Movie>/n, director/n, is/v, who/r	Who is the director of *Leon*?
3	<Movie>/n, is/v. what/r type/n	Which year was *Blade Runner* released?
4	<Movie>/n. released/v: which/r, year/v	Which year was *Blade Runner* released?
5	<Person>/n, in/p-<Movie>/m. in/nd. play/v, who/r	Who did Marlon Brando play in the movie *The Godfather*?

Table 2. Test results of tree-based convolutional neural network

Data number	#1	#2	#3	#4	#5	Average value
Accuracy rate	0.732	0.741	0.707	0.725	0.779	0.7365

Training set and test set are needed for tree-based convolutional neural network. The samples were randomly grouped into {P1, P2, P3, P4, P5}. A total of five sets of data sets were constructed. Pi in group i was used as the test sample, and other data were used as training samples. The obtained results of five sets of data are as follows (Table 2):

In the sample data, 200 samples were randomly selected for test set. Several algorithms were tested and the obtained results are as follows (Table 3):

Table 3. Structural comparison of several algorithms

Algorithm	Evaluation standard				
	Hit@1	Hit@2	Hit@3	Hit@4	Hit@5
Word-based	0.653	0.663	0.663	0.67	0.675
Word-based (DP)	0.693	0.695	0.704	0.711	0.718
Word-base (DP+KM)	0.715	0.725	0.725	0.735	0.735
Tree-based CNN	0.721	0.726	0.731	0.738	0.74

Random represents the algorithm for randomly selecting templates; Word-Based represents the algorithm that directly calculates sentence similarity without component division; Word-Based (DP) represents the algorithm that directly calculates the maximum mean of rows and columns after the sentence components are divided according to the dependency syntax tree; and Word-Base (DP+KM) is word-based similarity calculation algorithm.

From the aspect of results, the partitioning results between convolutional neural networks and word-based are similar. It is speculated that most of the data in this experiment are simple factual questions, and the actual number of words in question sentences is basically less than 10 words. Furthermore, there are fewer templates with small differences. Therefore, the convolutional neural network is not capable for differentiation.

6 Conclusion

Aiming at the problem of template generation, this paper proposes an automatic template generation method based on remote monitoring, which not only realizes the automatic template generation, but also makes the mapping between words and relationships more precise. Aiming at the matching problem between question and template, a template matching algorithm based on in-depth learning is proposed. Based on the word vectors of the problem, the dependency syntactic relationship of the sentence is further considered, and the tree convolution neural network is used to extract the features of the dependency syntactic relationship. A neural network model and its training method for template prediction are designed.

Acknowledgement. Supported by the 2018 project Research and Application of Key Technologies on Online Monitoring, Efficient Operation and Maintenance and Intelligent Evaluation of Health Condition of Electrical Equipment' in state Power Grid Corporation (No. PDB17201800280), and Major State Research Development Program of China (No. 2016QY04W0804).

References

1. Chen, D., Fisch, A., Weston, J., Bordes, A.: Reading Wikipedia to Answer Open-Domain Questions. arXiv preprint arXiv:1704.00051
2. Fader, A., Zettlemoyer, L., Etzioni, O.: Paraphrase-driven learning for open question answering. In: Meeting of the Association for Computational Linguistics, pp. 1608–1618 (2013)
3. Lopez, V., Tommasi, P., Kotoulas, S., Wu, J.: QuerioDALI: question answering over dynamic and linked knowledge graphs. In: Groth, P., et al. (eds.) ISWC 2016. LNCS, vol. 9982, pp. 363–382. Springer, Cham (2016). https://doi.org/10.1007/978-3-319-46547-0_32
4. Bast, H., Haussmann, E.: More accurate question answering on freebase. In: ACM International on Conference on Information and Knowledge Management, pp. 1431–1440. ACM (2015)
5. Abujabal, A., Yahya, M., Riedewald, M., et al.: Automated template generation for question answering over knowledge graphs. In: International World Wide Web Conferences Steering Committee, pp. 1191–1200 (2017)
6. Berant, J., Chou, A., Frostig, R., et al.: Semantic parsing on freebase from question-answer Pairs. In: Proceedings of EMNLP (2013)
7. Bordes, A., Chopra, S., Weston, J.: Question answering with subgraph embeddings. Comput. Sci. (2014)
8. Joshi, M., Sawant, U., Chakrabarti, S.: Knowledge graph and corpus driven segmentation and answer inference for telegraphic entity-seeking queries. In: Conference on Empirical Methods in Natural Language Processing, pp. 1104–1114 (2014)
9. Cranias, L., Papageorgiou, H., Piperidis, S.: A matching technique in example-based machine translation. In: Conference on Computational Linguistics, pp. 100–104. Association for Computational Linguistics (1994)
10. Ding, C.H.Q.: A similarity-based probability model for latent semantic indexing. In: International ACM SIGIR Conference on Research and Development in Information Retrieval, pp. 58–65. ACM (1999)
11. Carbonell, J., Goldstein, J.: The use of MMR, diversity-based reranking for reordering documents and producing summaries. In: International ACM SIGIR Conference on Research and Development in Information Retrieval, pp. 335–336 (1998)
12. Nirenburg, S., Domashnev, C., Grannes, D.J.: Two approaches to matching in example-based machine translation. In: TMI, pp. 47–57 (1993)

A Novel Scheme for Recruitment Text Categorization Based on KNN Algorithm

Wenshuai Qin[1], Wenjie Guo[2], Xin Liu[1(✉)], and Hui Zhao[1]

[1] School of Software, Henan University, Kaifeng 475004, Henan, China
robots7@163.com, 124761323@qq.com, zhh@henu.edu.cn
[2] School of Computer Science and Technology, Beijing Institute of Technology,
Beijing 100081, China
bit_gavin@163.com

Abstract. With the rapid development of the Internet, online recruitment has gradually become mainstream. However, job seekers need to spend a lot of time to find a suitable job when there are a large variety of job information, which will seriously affect their efficiency, so it is necessary to carry out more detailed and efficient classification of the recruitment documents. Currently, common text classification algorithms include KNN (k-Nearest Neighbor), SVM (Support Vector Machine) and Naïve Bayes. Particularly, KNN algorithm is widely used in text classification for its simple implementation and accurate classification. But KNN algorithm has been criticized for its inefficiency in the face of large-scale recruitment. This paper improves the original KNN algorithm and proposes RS-KNN algorithm to achieve rapid refinement and classification of recruitment information. Experiments show that the improved algorithm has higher efficiency and less time consumption than the original algorithm.

Keywords: KNN · Text classification · Feature extraction · Job classification

1 Introduction

With the development of the Internet, a large number of recruitment information will be put on the third-party recruitment website every day [1]. Knowledge discovery through artificial intelligence techniques has become a mainstream in web-based applications [2,3]. Job seekers can get relevant recruitment information and log in to third-party recruitment websites. However, the recruitment information on the third-party recruitment website is complicated and confusing, which makes it difficult for job seekers to find jobs that suit them. So if there is a detailed classification of recruitment information in different fields, and can be quickly indexed and searched, searching functions will be improved the efficiency significantly [4,5].

Through many surveys, we found that most of the recruitment information is displayed in text format, so we use the text classification algorithm to classify

© Springer Nature Switzerland AG 2019
M. Qiu (Ed.): SmartCom 2019, LNCS 11910, pp. 376–386, 2019.
https://doi.org/10.1007/978-3-030-34139-8_38

the collected text. Text classification is a hot research field and the purpose of this research is to decide the class of text quickly and accurately with the help of classification algorithms. At present, KNN [6] algorithm, SVM [7], neural network [8] and Naïve Bayes algorithm are all applied to text classification.

By improving the original KNN text classification algorithm, the problem of low efficiency of KNN algorithm in the classification of recruitment information can be effectively solved, and the work efficiency of job seekers will be improved.

The main work of this paper includes the following three aspects:

(1) The principle of KNN algorithm is described, and the reason of low classification efficiency is analyzed. RS-KNN algorithm is proposed by improving KNN algorithm, which has better classification efficiency.
(2) The basic conditions are satisfied for classification experiments by preprocessing data, Chinese word segmentation, feature extraction, etc.
(3) The experimental results are obtained by comparing the KNN classification algorithm before and after improved, and the experimental results are analyzed.

The organizational structure of this paper is shown as follows:

Section 1 is the introduction. Section 2 introduces the background of KNN algorithm and points out the shortcomings of the application of the current algorithm in the recruitment text. Section 3 introduces the concepts involved in this paper. Section 4 introduces the improved KNN algorithm in details and the implementation of the improved algorithm. Section 5 shows the experimental results and Sect. 6 concludes the paper.

2 Related Work

Yuan [9] proposed a modified KNN algorithm based on the center. A semantic relationship between features is introduced based on the original KNN algorithm, Firstly, the sample set is clustered according to the semantic relationship, then the central document is generated, thereby the need for searching text is reduced, increasing the classification speed; Yang et al. [10] proposed an improved M operator and a symbol-based improved KNN algorithm to generate a strategy, which can effectively reduce the sample data set, reduce the computational complexity of the KNN algorithm, thereby improving the efficiency of the algorithm; Gu [11] proposed an improved particle swarm optimization KNN classification algorithm. The algorithm uses the random search ability of particle swarm optimization to perform global random search on the training document set. In the searching process, particle swarm skims over a large number of text vectors, eliminating the effects of individual particles.

At the same time, the interference factor is added to avoid local convergence of the algorithm, and the K nearest neighbors of the test sample are quickly found. The algorithm Bojanowski [12] proposed calculated the distribution of various texts in the vector space during the training process, and classified the text vectors according to the distribution positions in the sample space to narrow the scope. Next, K-nearest neighbor search improves the similarity calculation method, which can more accurately determine the high-dimensional and large sample sets of text vectors, which improves the inefficiency of KNN algorithm classification. Particularly, the traditional KNN algorithm acquires the consistent contribution of each feature, which means that some undifferentiated words can also affect the classification result. Yang et al. [13] proposed a feature weighted-based KNN text classification algorithm, which can solve this problem. It considers different contributions to the classification by giving weights to different characteristics, improve the important characteristics of weight, which can help to reduce the impact of undifferentiated words on classification results and improve the classification accuracy of the algorithm.

3   Concept

3.1   Web Crawler

The web crawler starts with the initial URL set, extracts all the links to the page, adds them to the URL set, repeats the loop until the termination condition, and gets the content rules on the page based on some content. The core principle of web crawlers is: through uniform resource locator address, Hypertext Transfer Protocol (HTTP) is used to simulate the way of browser requesting access to the web server, encapsulate the necessary request limits, get the permission of the web server, return to the original page and analyze the data [14]. By web crawler, we can quickly get the recruitment information on the major recruitment websites, and the obtained recruitment information can be used as the data set of our classification algorithm.

3.2   Text Preprocessing

In terms of word segmentation, there are some common methods such as string matching based methods, rule-based methods and statistics-based methods, but the matching speed is slow and the words that are not included cannot be matched. The algorithm based on the statistical method's principle is: the frequency at which contextually adjacent words appear together can judge the chance of generated word. Through the statistics of the joint frequency of the words appearing next to each other in the corpus, their mutual occurrence information is calculated. The mutual occurrence information reflects the close degree of the connection between Chinese characters. When the close degree is higher than a certain threshold value, the word group can be judged to form a word. The advantage of this approach is that it won't be limited by the text field to be processed and does not need a specialized dictionary. Based on chance theory, statistical segmentation abstracts the occurrence of Chinese character combination strings in Chinese context into a random process. The parameters of the random process can be obtained through large-scale corpus training. Popular

Chinese word segmentation packages include "paoding jieniu" word segmentation package (suitable for Lueene integration) [15], LingPipe (Java open source toolkit for open source natural language processing) [16], ICTCLAS and Python "jieba" module, etc. The participle of this paper USES Python's "jieba" module. The "jieba" module was good at splitting Chinese words. It can slice the sentences in the document accurately, and the word segmentation is very fast. It can also slice the long words, which can improve the recall rate.

3.3 Feature Selection

After getting the preprocessed text data, feature choice is required. Good feature choice can improve the performance of the model and help us understand the characteristics and underlying structure of the data, which plays an important role in further process of improving the model and algorithm. There are two functions of feature selection: One is reducing the number of features and dimensionality, so that the model will have stronger generalization ability; another is enhancing the understanding between features and eigenvalues. Currently, the commonly used methods for feature choice are CHI statistics [17], information entropy, mutual information (MI) [18], stop word removal and information gain (IG) and TF-IDF algorithms.

The core idea of TF-IDF algorithm is: if a certain word appears many times in a certain category of text documents, then it will be able to distinguish the category very well. Similarly, if there are many times in all categories of a certain word, this word cannot be distinguish very well. It uses the idea of statistics to test the importance of a certain word in a certain article. TF-IDF algorithm integrates word frequency factor and inverse document frequency, and then takes the product of term frequency (TF) and inverse document frequency (IDF) as the weight of characteristic words.

Term frequency weighting, also known as feature frequency, refers to the frequency of a term in a text document. In different categories of documents, the frequency of feature items will vary. Therefore, it is also possible to take the frequency information of feature items as the reference index of text classification. If the number of occurrences of a word in each category is similar, the ability of the word to distinguish that class is weaker. For the specific term t_i, the word frequency calculation formula is as Eq. (1),

$$tf_{i,j} = \frac{n_{i,j}}{\sum_{k=1}^{m} n_{k,j}} \tag{1}$$

where $n_{(i,j)}$ is the sum of the frequency of all the words in document d_j. Inverse document frequency (IDF) is a measure of the importance of a word in all text documents. The calculation formula of inverse document frequency is shown as Eq. (2) below,

$$idf_i = \log \frac{N}{\{|j : t_i < d_j|\}} \tag{2}$$

where N is the total number of documents in the data set $\{|j : t_i < d_j|\}$ Once we have the values of $tf_{i,j}$, we can evaluate TF-IDF. The calculation formula is shown in Eq. (3) below:

$$tfidf_{i,j} = tf_{i,j} \times idf_i \qquad (3)$$

3.4   KNN Algorithm Principle

KNN algorithm, also known as K nearest neighbor algorithm, is a mature algorithm in theory and relatively simple in machine learning. KNN algorithm does not need explicit and direct expression, and can infer the category of documents to be tested only according to the classification of training set documents. The core idea of KNN algorithm is: if most of the K nearest neighbor samples of a sample in the feature space belong to a certain category, then the sample also belongs to this category. The performance of KNN algorithm depends on the surrounding set of samples to be tested, which is suitable in the case of too much overlap within the class.

The specific classification process of KNN algorithm is: let the text vector $w = \{t_1, t_2, \ldots t_n\}$, where $t_i (i = 1, 2, \ldots n)$ represents the feature item of the text vector, and the training text set $S = \{C_1, C_2, \ldots C_m\}$, where $c_i = \{w_1, w_2, \ldots w_q\}$ represents the q text in class I in $S, i = (1 \ldots m)$. When processing the text W to be classified, the similarity between W and all samples in the training set S is first calculated, and then sorted from dozen to small to select K most similar texts. Then the sample number ki is counted, and finally the category of the text to be tested is determined by calculating the value of the discriminant function. At present, Euclidean distance and cosine distance are commonly used to express the similarity between samples. Given two texts, $d_i = (w_{i1}, w_{i2}, \ldots w_{im})$, $d_j = (w_{j1}, w_{j2}, \ldots w_{jm})$, where m is the feature dimension of the text. The Euclidean distance is expressed as:

$$D(d_i, d_j) = \sqrt{(w_{i1} - w_{j1})^2 + (w_{i2} - w_{j2})^2 + \cdots + (w_{im} - w_{jm})^2} \qquad (4)$$

Cosine similarity is expressed as:

$$Sim(d_i, d_j) = \frac{\sum_{k=1}^{m} w_{ik} w_{jk}}{\sqrt{\sum_{i=1}^{m} w_{ik}^2} \sqrt{\sum_{k=1}^{m} w_{jk}^2}} \qquad (5)$$

The advantages of KNN algorithm are: high classification accuracy; No training process required; A good classification efficiency in the case of a large number of samples. It also has the disadvantages as follows: it is expensive to calculate, For each text to be classified, the distance to all samples need to be calculated and sorted, and then the nearest K points will be calculated; When text

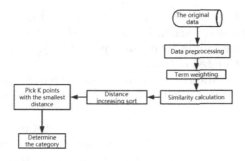

Fig. 1. Improved KNN algorithm flow.

is classified, the default weight of each dimension is equal, which will affect the classification accuracy.

4 Algorithm

In order to solve the problem of high time cost of KNN classification algorithm, the original KNN algorithm was improved in combination with the characteristics of recruitment text, so that it can be applied in the actual recruitment text classification with better classification efficiency. One of the shortcomings of KNN algorithm is its large classification time cost. When faced with a large number of recruitment texts, the efficiency of KNN algorithm will be relatively lower, so it is necessary to improve the KNN algorithm. This thesis starts with the reducing the number of the professional terms weights such as real estate, finance, development, sales, etc.

In general, the improved KNN classification algorithm process is: first, get the initial data, and then the data preprocessing, next, weighted terms selection, and then calculate the known categories of data set points and the distance between the current points, the weights of the same key calculated only once, next, sorted by increasing the distance and selection and the current K point distance minimum points, determine the type of first K points in frequency, finally, return the former K points frequency of the highest category as the current point prediction category. The process is shown in Fig. 1:

After the above analysis, the specific process of the improved KNN algorithm is as follows:

(1) Data preprocessing. Use the crawler to get the job text on the internet and preprocess the data.
(2) Select technical terms for weighting. After word segmentation and deletion of stopped words, the professional terms in the recruitment text can be easily obtained.

(3) Calculate the distance. The cosine formula is used for distance calculation. If a word with the same weight is encountered, it will be treated as the first word with the same weight by default, particularly, the word with the same weight will be calculated only once.

(4) Sort by increasing distance. After calculating the distance between the classified text and all samples, all distances are arranged in order from smallest to largest.

(5) Select the first K sample points with the smallest distance. When the order is good, the top K sample points closest to each other are selected for analysis to see which category these closest K sample points belong to.

(6) Identify the category. Judge which category the most recent K sample points belong to and divide them into this category. The RS-KNN algorithm proposed in this paper is implemented as follows:

Algorithm 1. RS-KNN algorithm

Input: Weighted data sets Train; The category of the data set Lables; K; Data sets of unknown classes that have been processed Test.

Output: Unknown class data set Test Corresponding classification label Category;

1: RS-KNN-Classify(Test,Train,lables,K):
2: **for** each $i \in Test$ **do**
3:     Calculate the distance between the sample to be tested and the known sample
4:     **if** The data set of the unknown category is the same as the feature word weight of the known category **then**
5:         continue;
6:     **end if**
7:     sort (distance); //Sort distances
8:     **return** sort(distance)[k]; //Returns the first k points closest to the sample point;
9: **end for**

Firstly, the weighted training set Train, category Lables, K value and the unknown data set Test were input. Then we traversed the unknown data set Test to calculate the distance between the text of each unknown category and the known sample. If the data set for the unknown category is the same as the data centralization value for the known category, skip and calculate the next word. Computing every unknown sample. Then sort by distance. The first K sample points with the smallest distance are selected to determine their categories.

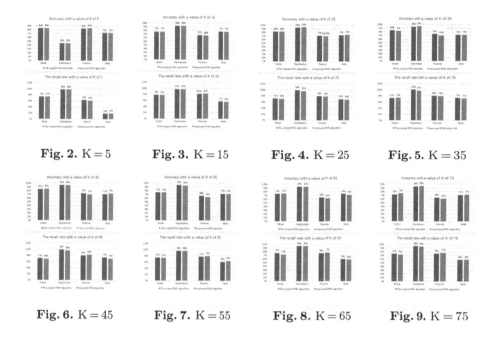

Fig. 2. K = 5	**Fig. 3.** K = 15	**Fig. 4.** K = 25	**Fig. 5.** K = 35
Fig. 6. K = 45	**Fig. 7.** K = 55	**Fig. 8.** K = 65	**Fig. 9.** K = 75

5 Experimental Setup and Result Analyses

The data of the improved KNN algorithm are from 6000 recruitment texts screened on the third-party recruitment websites, including finance, development, sales and real estate, with 1500 respectively. In the verification process, 70% of the data is used as the training data set and 30% as the test data set.

The improved algorithm is implemented by Python language. It runs on a machine with an operating system of Windows 10, a CPU of Core i7-7500u 2.7 Ghz and a hard disk capacity of 500G. The development environment is PyCharm.

The classification accuracy, recall rate and time consumed by the algorithm are used as evaluation indexes. Recall is the ratio of the number of text correctly classified by the classifier to the total number of such text in the test set.

In KNN algorithm, the selection of K value is very important. If the selected K value is too small, it cannot reflect the characteristics of the text. However, if the selected K value is too large, it can reflect the characteristics of each text, but it also brings too much noise, which will lead to the increase of text classification errors and affect the accuracy of the classification algorithm. As for the selection of K value, literature [19] believes that 2 of the training sample can achieve a better classification effect. The optimal K value verified by literature [20] is 10, while the optimal K value verified by literature [21] is 15, which indicates that the value of K cannot be determined by an exact percentage. Different text data sets need different optimal K values. Therefore, the K value of this experiment is set as 5, 15, 25, 35, 45, 55, 65, 75. The accuracy and recall rate of the algorithm are shown in Figs. 2, 3, 4, 5, 6, 7, 8 and 9 below:

With the increase of K value, the pairs of time consumed by the algorithm are shown in Fig. 10 below:

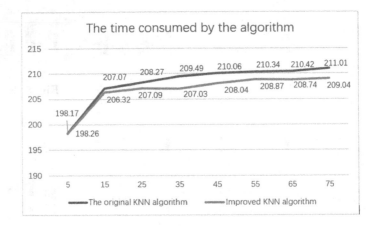

Fig. 10. Accuracy and recall rate of with different K values.

By comparing the experimental results in Figs. 2, 3, 4, 5, 6, 7, 8 and 9, we can find that the improved KNN algorithm has some reservations in classification accuracy. By compared with the original algorithm, in most cases, the accuracy can keep unchanged, when K is 5, in the financial sector classification accuracy of 1%, but the financial sector recall ratio decreased by 2%, with the increase of K value, all areas of classification accuracy is floating between 1% and 2%, recall rate is between 1% to 4%. When K value is 55, the improved KNN algorithm has the best classification effect. Observing 10, with the increasing of K value, the improved KNN algorithm and original KNN algorithm classification time is increasing, but the improved KNN algorithm compared with the original KNN algorithm is relatively small, consume time, when K is 35, the consumption of the improved KNN algorithm time with original KNN algorithm consumes less time for 2.46 s.

6   Conclusion

Aiming at the existing problems of the original KNN algorithm in the text classification of recruitment, this paper proposes the RS-KNN algorithm, which can reduce the influence of unfamiliar professional terms on the text classification results. Experimental results show that the improved KNN algorithm has better classification efficiency.

Acknowledgement. This work is supported by Postgraduate Education Innovation and Quality Improvement Project of Henan University, Henan University (SYL18020105).

References

1. Gai, K., Qiu, M.: Reinforcement learning-based content-centric services in mobile sensing. IEEE Netw. **32**(4), 34–39 (2018)
2. Gai, K., Xu, K., Lu, Z., Qiu, M., Zhu, L.: Fusion of cognitive wireless networks and edge computing. IEEE Wirel. Commun. **26**(3), 69–75 (2019)
3. Gai, K., Qiu, M., Zhao, H.: Energy-aware task assignment for mobile cyber-enabled applications in heterogeneous cloud computing. J. Parallel Distrib. Comput. **111**, 126–135 (2018)
4. Yin, H., Gai, K., Wang, Z.: A classification algorithm based on ensemble feature selections for imbalanced-class dataset. In: 2016 IEEE 2nd International Conference on Big Data Security on Cloud, pp. 245–249. IEEE (2016)
5. Yin, H., Gai, K.: An empirical study on preprocessing high-dimensional class-imbalanced data for classification. In: 2015 IEEE 17th International Conference on High Performance Computing and Communications, 2015 IEEE 7th International Symposium on Cyberspace Safety and Security, and 2015 IEEE 12th International Conference on Embedded Software and Systems, pp. 1314–1319. IEEE (2015)
6. Wang, Y., Chaib-draa, B.: KNN-based Kalman filter: an efficient and non-stationary method for gaussian process regression. Knowl.-Based Syst. **114**, 148–155 (2016)
7. Tong, S., Koller, D.: Support vector machine active learning with applications to text classification. J. Mach. Learn. Res. **2**(Nov), 45–66 (2001)
8. Lai, S., Xu, L., Liu, K., Zhao, J.: Recurrent convolutional neural networks for text classification. In: Twenty-Ninth AAAI Conference on Artificial Intelligence (2015)
9. Yuan, X., Sun, M., Chen, Z., Gao, J., Li, P.: Semantic clustering-based deep hyper-graph model for online reviews semantic classification in cyber-physical-social systems. IEEE Access **6**, 17942–17951 (2018)
10. Yang, K., Cai, Y., Cai, Z., Xie, H., Wong, T., Chan, W.: Top k representative: a method to select representative samples based on k nearest neighbors. Int. J. Mach. Learn. Cybern. **10**, 1–11 (2017)
11. Gu, S., Cheng, R., Jin, Y.: Feature selection for high-dimensional classification using a competitive swarm optimizer. Soft Comput. **22**(3), 811–822 (2018)
12. Bojanowski, P., Grave, E., Joulin, A., Mikolov, T.: Enriching word vectors with subword information. Trans. Assoc. Comput. Linguist. **5**, 135–146 (2017)
13. Yang, H., Cui, H., Tang, H.: A text classification algorithm based on feature weighting. In: AIP Conference Proceedings, vol. 1864, p. 020026. AIP Publishing (2017)
14. Heydon, A., Najork, M.: Mercator: a scalable, extensible web crawler. World Wide Web **2**(4), 219–229 (1999)
15. Goetz, B.: The lucene search engine: powerful, flexible, and free. JavaWorld (2000). http://www.javaworld.com/javaworld/jw-09-2000/jw-0915-lucene.html
16. Carpenter, B.: Lingpipe for 99.99% recall of gene mentions. In: Proceedings of the 2nd BioCreative Challenge Evaluation Workshop, vol. 23, pp. 307–309. BioCreative (2007)
17. Fienberg, S.: The use of chi-squared statistics for categorical data problems. J. Roy. Stat. Soc.: Ser. B(Methodol.) **41**(1), 54–64 (1979)
18. Bennasar, M., Hicks, Y., Setchi, R.: Feature selection using joint mutual information maximisation. Expert Syst. Appl. **42**(22), 8520–8532 (2015)
19. Wang, X., et al.: Research and implementation of a multi-label learning algorithm for Chinese text classification. In: 2017 3rd International Conference on Big Data Computing and Communications (BIGCOM), pp. 68–76. IEEE (2017)

20. Ma, Y., Li, Y., Wu, X., Zhang, X.: Chinese text classification review. In: 2018 9th International Conference on Information Technology in Medicine and Education (ITME), pp. 737–739. IEEE (2018)
21. Zhao, Y., Qian, Y., Li, C.: Improved KNN text classification algorithm with MapReduce implementation. In: 2017 4th International Conference on Systems and Informatics (ICSAI), pp. 1417–1422. IEEE (2017)

Machine Learning for Cancer Subtype Prediction with FSA Method

Yan Liu[1,2], Xu-Dong Wang[3], Meikang Qiu[1($\boxtimes$)], and Hui Zhao[4]

[1] Department of Computer Science, Texas A&M University Commerce,
Commerce, TX 75428, USA
yliu24@leomail.tamuc.edu, Meikang.Qiu@tamuc.edu
[2] Department of Radiation Oncology, UT Southwestern Medical Center,
Dallas, TX 75390, USA
[3] Department of Biochemistry, UT Southwestern Medical Center,
Dallas, TX 75390, USA
Xu Dong.Wang@utsouthwestern.edu
[4] School of Software, Henan University, Kaifeng 475004, Henan, China
zhh@henu.edu.cn

Abstract. Recent research demonstrates that gene expression based cancer subtype classification has more advantages over the traditional classification. However, since this kind of data always has thousands of features, performing classification is impossible by human beings without efficient and accurate algorithms. This paper reports an empirical study that explores the problem of finding a highly-efficient and accurate machine learning method on human cancer subtype classification based on the gene expression data in cancer cells. Several machine learning algorithms are well developed to solve this kind of problems, including Naive Bayes Classifier, *Support Vector Machine* (SVM), Random Forest, Neural Networks. Here we generate two prediction models using SVM and Random Forest algorithms along with a *feature selection approach* (FSA) to predict the subtype of lung cell lines. The accuracy of the two prediction models is close with a rate of more than 90%. However, the running time of SVM is much shorter than that of Random Forest.

Keywords: Machine learning · Feature selection · Support Vector Machine · Random Forest · Cancer subtype

1 Introduction

Machine learning technology, first paraphrased by Samuel, teaches computers to learn without being explicitly programmed and hence is one of the most exciting technologies actively being used in many more places today [1]. The major contribution of machine learning algorithms is to generate prediction models by learning from a large body of exiting data [2]. The ability to precisely classify observations is extremely valuable for various applications including finance, marketing, healthcare, fraud detection, and so on.

With the development of Deoxyribonucleic Acid (DNA) and Ribonucleic Acid (RNA) sequencing technology, a large number of biological data has been generated,

© Springer Nature Switzerland AG 2019
M. Qiu (Ed.): SmartCom 2019, LNCS 11910, pp. 387–397, 2019.
https://doi.org/10.1007/978-3-030-34139-8_39

which makes it possible to apply machine learning technology to biomedical research. In addition, the rapid growth of big data analytics also enables computer scientists and data scientists to mine the biological data and apply machine learning to solve some complex biomedical problems.

The applications of machine learning in biomedical sciences cover many fields, such as medical imaging analysis, diagnosis and gene expression analysis [3]. In 2016, retinal fundus images were analyzed with a deep learning model to detect diabetic retinopathy lesions. This model achieves an area under the *Receiver Operating Characteristic* curve (ROC) of 0.991 [4]. Among all the applications, disease classification is one of the major challenges, especially in the field of oncology, because disease classification is central to how we make diagnosis and treat patients.

Lung cancer is the leading cause of cancer deaths due to the late diagnosis. Based on histology, there are two major different types of lung cancer, Non-Small Cell Lung Cancer (NSCLC) and Small Cell Lung Cancer (SCLC). Knowing the cancer subtype is important because it affects the treatment options [5]. With the development of DNA/RNA sequencing technology, it is possible to know the molecular profile of each cancer patient. In this paper, we employ two machine learning approaches to predict lung cancer subtypes. Based on the personalized gene expression profiles from a large number of lung cancer patient cohort, our advanced cancer type classification model, FSA (feature selection approach), offers a unique mechanism to avoid the time waste when oncologists and doctors are suffering a complicated case of patient with an unknown lung cancer subtype. The model is a type of service tool which quickly and accurately turn data into diagnoses. The conceptual model pipeline of FSA is shown in Fig. 1.

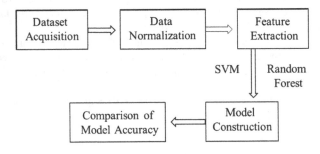

Fig. 1. Schema of the FSA design.

The main contributions of this paper are two folds: 1. We generate two prediction models using SVM and Random Forest algorithms along with a feature extraction approach to predict the subtype of 222 lung cell lines, including 124 non-small lung cancer cell lines, 39 small cell lung cancer cell lines and 59 normal lung cell lines based on their RNA expression data; 2. We also compare the prediction accuracy of models based on these two algorithms.

The results of this research provide theoretical supports that that SVM, along with a FSA, is a perfect classification algorithm for cancer subtype classification. Along with lung cancer, FSA may be able to be migrated and applied in multiple diseases, which requires further research for identifying and proving.

The structure of this paper is follows. We provide the rationale and background information about machine learning applications in disease classification in Sect. 2. Following the description of the model, an example about data processing and modelling is given in Sect. 3 in order to demonstrate the implementation of FSA in practice. The experimental results and analysis are represented in Sect. 4. The conclusions are given in Sect. 5.

2   Related Work

Throughout the history of medicine, disease classification is always one of the most primary and important factors which would determine how we treat patients. Human cancers are a large family of diseases and are classified by the location in the body where the cancer first developed, such as breast cancer, lung cancer and liver cancer. However, each primary cancer may have multiple subtypes [6]. Discovering cancer subtypes is helpful for guiding clinical treatment [7]. In the last decade with the development of human genome project, cancer biologists started to study how molecular subtypes of cancer may be useful in planning treatment and developing new therapies. As the cost of DNA sequencing continues decreasing, performing DNA/RNA sequencing of patient's tumor samples is possible. However, since tumor samples contain thousands of genes, deciding the genes which can be used to classify different types of cancer is a hard topic and almost impossible without computer's help.

Fortunately, with the development of machine learning and big data analytics, it is possible to employ these tools to discover cancer subtypes. There are two kinds of studies of cancer subtype classification. One study is to predict the cancer subtype based on the current knowledge [8]. In this kind of study supervised learning will be used to make prediction. Each sample will be labeled by its class and prediction models will be generated using the features, which are the gene expression data [2]. SVM learning is one of methods used in this kind of study. Compared to other methods SVM is very powerful at recognizing subtle patterns in complex datasets [9]. This kind of study may apply to clinical service, which may help pathologists to make decision.

The other study is to classify cancer subtypes only based on their gene expression data, but not the previous knowledge [10]. K-means and cluster models are always used in these studies [11]. The idea behind k-means is to divide N samples (cancer patients or cancer cell lines) into K clusters such that each sample belongs to the cluster with the nearest mean [11, 12]. This kind of study may lead to discovering new cancer subtypes, which will be especially important for basic medical research.

Although technically we can use machine learning methods to classify cancer subtypes based on the gene expression data, in fact it requires a lot of efforts before we can generate prediction models. One challenge is that each tumor sample or cancer cell line has thousands of genes (features). Deciding which features to use is extremely difficult. Feature selection is one core concept in machine learning, which may significantly impact the performance of the prediction model. Feature Selection is a process where you automatically or manually select those features which contribute most to your prediction models. Several feature selection algorithms have been reported. There are three major feature selection methods: Univariate Selection; Feature Importance; Correlation Matrix with Heatmap. Feature importance property of the model will generate an importance score of each feature of your data.

3   Data Processing and Modelling

A major part of machine learning is classification. The ability to precisely classify observations is extremely valuable for medical sciences. Classification of cancer subtype is very important for cancer therapeutics and cancer research. However, since gene expression data has a very large of features, usually more than 10,000, predicting cancer subtypes is extremely difficult using this large set of features. In this paper we propose a machine learning based approach along with a feature selection approach to predict the subtype of lung cancer cells. We followed the pipeline described in Fig. 1, acquiring the dataset, normalizing the gene expression values, selecting the most important features, and performing the prediction modeling. Two machine learning algorithms are used in this paper, SVM and Random Forest. After modeling, we measure the performance by ROC curve and the running time.

3.1   Dataset

The dataset was created by Dr. John Minna at UT Southwestern Medical Center at Dallas, and contains 222 observations, including 59 normal lung cell lines, 39 small cell lung cancer cell lines and 124 non-small cell lung cancer cell lines, and 18,696 features [13–15]. The gene expression was analyzed by gene microarray. The data was downloaded from www.ncbi.nlm.nih.gov/geo (accession no. GSE32036).

3.2   Data Normalization and Transformation

Normalization of RNA microarray data has proven essential to ensure accurate inferences and replication of findings. Various normalization methods have been proposed in high-throughput sequencing transcriptomic studies. In this each data item as a point in n-dimensional space (where n is number of features you have) paper average normalization is used to rescale intensities across multiple arrays and chips. This algorithm is an appropriate choice for experiments that employ a large number of arrays with differences in overall intensity. For average normalization, a scaling factor Si, is calculated by dividing the average intensity of the virtual array μv by the average intensity for all arrays in one sample μi

$$S_i = \mu^v / \mu_i \tag{1}$$

The bead-type intensities of all arrays in the experiment are normalized by S_i.

$$I_{pi(norm)} = I_{pi}S_i \tag{2}$$

Each probe is indexed by p and the number of probes ranges from 1 to n. Each array is indexed by i and the number of arrays ranges from 1 to m.

3.3   FSA (Feature Selection Approach) for SVM Modeling

Gene expression data has a large number of features, usually more than 10,000 features and is often linearly non-separable [16]. An appropriate nonlinear kernel to map the data to a higher dimensional space has been proven to be more efficient. Filter based approach is always used to select features. We rank each gene using kernel-based clustering method for gene selection [17], and then select genes based on their weights.

Algorithm: Feature Selection Approach (FSA)

Input: a data matrix X of gene expression and a vector l of class label.
Output: a vector W of weights of genes.

---

1.   Set x←individual gene expression in each sample;
     μ←the average gene expression of each sample
     σ←standard deviation
2.   Normalize the original data X with function (3)
3.   Calculate the cluster center of different class of genes in the input space;
4.   Calculate the dissimilarity between the genes and their cluster center of class;
5.   **for** $W_0 = 1/l$;
6.   Calculate the $(t+1)^{th}$ distance parameter $\Delta^{(t+1)}$ with function (4)
7.   Calculate $(t+1)^{th}$ weight $W^{(t+1)}$ of genes;
8.   Calculate $(t+1)^{th}$ objective $J^{(t+1)}$ with function (5);
9.   **if** $J^{(t+1)} - J^{(t)} < \Phi$ **then**
10. **end for**
11. Return $W^{(t+1)}$.

Normalize the original data X with Z score:

$$Z = (x - \mu)/\sigma \tag{3}$$

The tth distance parameter Δt:

$$\Delta^t = \alpha \frac{\sum_{i=1}^{C} \sum_{x_j \in C_i} \sum_{k=1}^{l} W_k^{(t-1)} \parallel \Phi(x_{jk}) - \Phi(v_{ik}) \parallel}{\sum_{k=1}^{l} (W_k^{(t-1)})^2} \tag{4}$$

The tth objective function $J^{(t + 1)}$:

$$J = \sum_{i=1}^{C} \sum_{x_j \in C_i} \Phi^2\left(x_j, v_i\right) + \sigma \sum_{k=1}^{1} W_k^2 \qquad (5)$$

Gene expression data with l genes and n samples can be represented by the matrix X. To eliminate the batch effect of multiple gene expression profiling experiments, we use Z-score to normalize the original data matrix by applying the function (3). The cancer classification was calculated as a supervised learning situation, by defining the cluster center. Then, a dissimilarity Φ between a sample gene and a cluster centroid could be defined using function (4).

Filter-based feature selection approach ranks all the genes independently by weighting each feature according to a particular method (Here we use an appropriate nonlinear kernel-based clustering method), then selecting genes based on their weights W.

3.4   (SVM) and Random Forest

SVM is a supervised machine learning algorithm used for both classification or regression problems. However, it is mostly used in classification problems. SVM plots each data as a point in n-dimensional space, where n is number of features of the data. Then classification is performed by finding the hyper-plane that differentiate the two or more classes. Most time there is no line that can separate the two or more classes in this x-y plane. SVM uses kernel functions, which take low dimensional input space and transform the data to a higher dimensional space. The transformation converts not separable points to separable points (Fig. 2). These kernel functions are mostly useful in non-linear separation problems. In this paper, we applied ksvm R package. ksvm uses John Platt's Sequential Minimal Optimization (SMO) algorithm for solving the SVM problem an most SVM formulations.

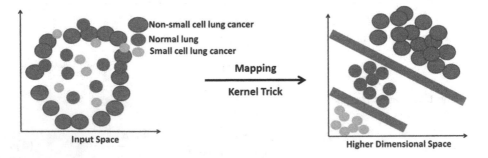

Fig. 2. The model of SVM

Random forest consists of a large number of individual decision trees. Each of them in the random forest spits out a class prediction and the class with the most votes becomes our model's prediction. Decisions trees are very sensitive to the data they are trained on. Random forest takes advantage of it by allowing each individual tree to randomly sample from the dataset with replacement, resulting in different trees, which is known as bagging. We use this algorithm because one of its advantages is that it can handle thousands of input variables without variable deletion. Our dataset has 18696 variables. When we use SVM model, we perform FSA, which is not necessary in this model.

3.5   ROC Curve

After modeling, we measure the performance. In machine learning, performance measurement is an essential task. When it comes to classification problems, we can use a ROC curve (Fig. 3). It is one of the most important evaluation metrics for checking a classification model's performance.

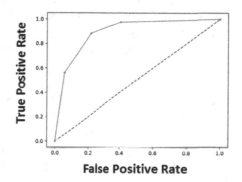

Fig. 3. ROC curve.

4   Results and Analysis

We use GSE32036 (described in the part of Dataset) to develop and examine the proposed methods. There are three known subtypes: normal lung, non-small lung cancer, and small lung cancer. According to the characteristics of this dataset, SVM and Random Forest models are extremely suitable for this small sample case with a large number of features. Before we generate the prediction models, we need to pre-process the dataset. All experiments are run using R language 3.6.1.

4.1   Experiment Setup

We computed the average expression of each gene in all observations and performed the Z score transformation. After the data was normalized, feature selection algorithm was performed to reduce the number of features. After feature selection processing, 6927 features were selection for SVM modeling. When generating SVM model, vanilla dot kernel function was used. When generating Random Forest model, ntree parameter was optimized to 500. In terms of supervised learning algorithms, all observations were pre-labeled to train the classifier as well as to evaluate the precision of the classification.

4.2   Results

The cross-validation method is used here to train and test the algorithms. Before training the two models, the dataset is randomly divided into training set (60%) and test set (40%). We repeat the experiments 10 times. Each time we perform the prediction with the two algorithms using the same training set and test set. The results are shown in Table 1. We list the actual subtype and the predicted subtype by two models.

Table 1. The prediction results of SVM and Random Forest

Actual			Predict (SVM)			Predict (Random Forest)		
Normal	NSCLC	SCLC	Normal	NSCLC	SCLC	Normal	NSCLC	SCLC
26	48	15	26	46	11	26	46	12
17	57	15	17	53	12	16	53	13
24	51	14	24	50	14	19	51	14
23	53	13	23	13	13	22	50	13
23	52	14	23	13	10	22	50	10
28	50	11	28	48	10	27	48	10
20	52	17	20	50	16	20	51	14
21	52	16	21	51	16	21	48	16
22	52	15	22	51	13	22	51	14
23	52	14	23	48	13	22	49	13

In Table 1, we randomly divide the data into training set and test set for 10 times. Each time we generate two models using SVM and Random Forest algorithms with FSA. Then we evaluate both models using test data. This table records the actual classification and the predicted classification by using these two models we proposed.

4.3   Analysis

In order to compare the precision of the two algorithms, we computed the accuracy rates. Figure 4 shows that in SVM model, the accuracy rates of normal lung cell group, NSCLC group and SCLC group are 100%, greater than 90%, and greater than 85% respectively. In comparison, in Random Forest model, these rates are greater than 90%, greater than 90%, and greater than 70% respectively. Apparently, Random Forest model is not as stable as SVM model. Therefore, in term of accuracy, SVM model is better than Random Forest model.

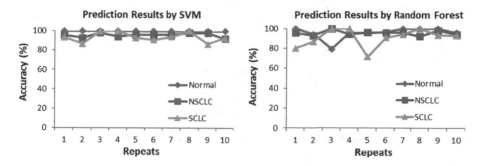

Fig. 4. Comparison of accuracy of SVM and Random Forest models.

In addition to accuracy, we also measure the running time used by the two models. We setup the system time before and after the experiments and compute the running time of the 10 experiments. Figure 5 demonstrates that the running time of SVM model is less than 10 s and the running time of Random Forest model is greater than 40 s.

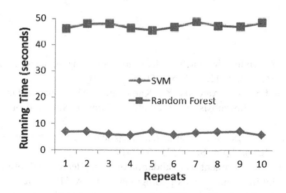

Fig. 5. Comparison of running time of SVM and Random Forest models.

As we demonstrate in Figs. 4 and 5, SVM generates better prediction results meanwhile it also uses less time. Therefore, we evaluate the performance of SVM model with FSA in the last part. ROC curve is used to evaluate the performance of the SVM model. Since ROC curve can only evaluate models of two classes, we remove the normal lung group and only evaluate the outcome of classification for SCLC and NSCLC subtypes. As shows in Fig. 6, Area Under the Curve (AUC) is 0.917 that means there is 91.7% chance that the model will be able to distinguish between NSCLC group and SCLC group.

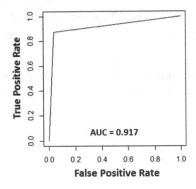

Fig. 6. The ROC curve based on the SVM model.

5 Conclusion

In summary, we generated two prediction models, SVM and Random Forest to classify the lung cancer subtype: normal lung, non-small lung cancer and small lung cancer. Both models led to a good prediction of three different cell types. The SVM model gave more accurate results and used shorter running time compared to the Random forest model.

References

1. Samuel, A.: Some studies in machine learning using the game of checkers. ii—recent progress. IBM J. Res. Dev. **11**, 601–617 (1967)
2. Kourou, K., Exarchos, T., Exarchos, K., Karamouzis, M., Fotiadis, D.: Machine learning applications in cancer prognosis and prediction. Comput. Struct. Biotechnol. J. **13**, 8–17 (2015)
3. Zemouri, R., Zerhouni, N., Racoceanu, D.: Deep learning in the biomedical applications: recent and future status. Appl. Sci. **9**, 1526 (2019)
4. Gulshan, V., et al.: Development and validation of a deep learning algorithm for detection of diabetic retinopathy in retinal fundus photographs. JAMA **316**, 2402–2410 (2016)
5. Inamura, K.: Lung cancer: understanding its molecular pathology and the 2015 WHO classification. Front Oncol. **7**, 193 (2017)
6. "what-is-cancer". https://www.cancer.gov/about-cancer/understanding/what-is-cancer
7. Jiang, L., Xiao, Y., Ding, Y., Tang, J., Guo, F.: Discovering cancer subtypes via an accurate fusion strategy on multiple profile data. Front. Genet. **10**, 20 (2019)
8. Wu, M., et al.: Prediction of molecular subtypes of breast cancer using BI-RADS features based on a "white box" machine learning approach in a multi-modal imaging setting. Eur. J. Radiol. **114**, 175–184 (2019)
9. Aruna, S., Rajagopalan, S.: A novel SVM based CSSFFS feature selection algorithm for detecting breast cancer. Int. J. Comput. Appl. **31**(8), 14–20 (2011)
10. de Souto, M., Costa, I., de Araujo, D., Ludermir, T., Schliep, A.: Clustering cancer gene expression data: a comparative study. BMC Bioinf. **9**, 497 (2008)

11. Kakushadze, Z., Yu, W.: *K-means and cluster models for cancer signatures. Biomol. Detect. Quantification **13**, 7–31 (2017)
12. Lloyd, S.: Least squares quantization in PCM. IEEE Trans. Inf. Theor. **28**, 129–137 (1982)
13. Wang, X., et al.: Subtype-specific secretomic characterization of pulmonary neuroendocrine tumor cells. Nat. Commun. **10**, 3201 (2019)
14. Borromeo, M., et al.: ASCL1 and NEUROD1 reveal heterogeneity in pulmonary neuroendocrine tumors and regulate distinct genetic programs. Cell Rep. **16**, 1259–1272 (2016)
15. Augustyn, A., et al.: ASCL1 is a lineage oncogene providing therapeutic targets for high-grade neuroendocrine lung cancers. Proc. Natl. Acad. Sci. U.S.A. **111**, 14788–14793 (2014)
16. Liu, S., et al.: Feature selection of gene expression data for cancer classification using double RBF-kernels. BMC Bioinformatics **19**, 396 (2018)
17. Chen, H., Zhang, Y., Gutman, I.: A kernel-based clustering method for gene selection with gene expression data. J. Biomed. Inf. **62**, 12–20 (2016)

Autonomous Vehicle Communication in V2X Network with LoRa Protocol

YauKa Cheung[1], Meikang Qiu[1($\boxtimes$)], and Meiqin Liu[2]

[1] Department of Computer Science, Texas A&M University-Commerce,
Texas, USA
{cyauka,meikang.qiu}@tamuc.edu
[2] College of Electrical Engineering, Zhejiang University, Zhejiang, China
liumeiqin@zju.edu.cn

Abstract. The weakness of short-range wireless signal and security issues will make a bad effect on the communication in *Vehicle-to-Vehicle or Vehicle-to-Infrastructure* (V2X). In this study, we proposed a system, based on *Long Range* (LoRa) protocol and *Long Range Wide-Area Network* (LoRaWAN), to reduce the latency of communication and minimize the data size in V2X networks. Through the experiment, it shows that the proposed system can enhance the overall performance and reduce the latency in V2X networks. Moreover, the security of transmitting data is increased.

Keywords: V2X · LoRa · LoRaWAN · Security · Latency · Communication · Autonomous vehicle

1 Introduction

The development of autonomous vehicle is a delicate topic in recent years. In order to better guide itself without human conduction, a bunch of sensors, *Internet of Thing* (IoT) and monitoring devices are installed in the self-driving vehicle. To better utilize the collected data, V2X is a great technology to let different self-driving vehicles to communicate with other cars and external system, like traffic lights, road stations and buildings nearby. However, short-range wireless signal, which is used in V2X technology, is highly restricted by distance and the connection and bandwidth will be reduced by weak signal. The risk of self-driving will be increased.

Regardless of how accurate the machine learning model or obstacle predictions are, if the autonomous vehicle can receive information earlier and be prepared to react to the prevention of the accident, the final result will be better. With the V2X vehicle networking technology, vehicles can acquire unknown parameters of the surrounding environment and the running status of nearby vehicles, and it provides early warning of possible dangerous scenarios. Therefore, the use of V2X car networking technology is conducive to improving traffic efficiency and avoiding traffic risks.

According to data released by Forbes and Bain & Company's latest survey, security, information technology/operational technology integration and unclear return on investment are the biggest obstacles to adopting the Internet of Things today. In the market, securing and integrating IoT networks are in the highest priority. The adoption

© Springer Nature Switzerland AG 2019
M. Qiu (Ed.): SmartCom 2019, LNCS 11910, pp. 398–410, 2019.
https://doi.org/10.1007/978-3-030-34139-8_40

of IoT in automotive industry will grow 37 times from 2014 to 2020. Moreover, it is expected that by 2021, additional IoT devices for vehicles in the US connected car market will reach $ 18.1B. IHS Markit believes that the installation of IoT devices and sensors will rise up from $27B in 2017 to $73B in 2025.

In Cooperative Intelligent Transport Systems (C-ITS), which is based on V2X, a safe connected cloud-based service is emphasized. Therefore, independent vehicles from different manufacturers are allowed to share real-time hazard information via the cloud service. It is highly possible to reduce issues of autonomous vehicle or accidents on the road by C-ITS [1]. However, the usage of V2X communication is still limited by different restrictions, such as the security issue in broadcasting harmful message [2].

Considering a scenario, if a car in front on the highway has an emergency, it will send a signal via internet connected device to C-ITS cloud [1]. Then, the information will be forward to the corresponding cloud service at vehicles behind that car. However, there is no 100% guarantee coverage of internet in reality, which means that it is possible that information cannot transmit to other vehicles.

Researchers now are focusing on different way to increase the security in this field [2]. We propose a method to simplify the connection and location prediction to enhance the efficiency and stability of communication.

Looking at Tesla, which is a great example for new generation IoT vehicle, it has 3G cell connection to the internet obstinately and includes Geolocation information. Meanwhile, the attitude and acceleration of car is detected by the sensors. The sensors detect and collect all data which generated by all devices, such as energy consumption, wheel position, brake and emergency baking position, climate system, seat position, rearview mirror, door handle, etc. Different from before, all the related data about the car will be shared with other systems, infrastructure and vehicles. Therefore, those information about high piracy [3] should be welly handled and processing in an efficient way.

Therefore, the demand on Internet accessing will rapidly increase. Manufacturers are mainly adding Long Term Evolution (LTE) for providing vehicle Internet connection. However, the latency and bandwidth of LTE are still two big challenges [3]. Furthermore, vehicles are high speed moving objects and possible to driving across different geographical areas.

While people discussing how to improve the performance of LTE. We are proposing a novel technology, LoRa protocol and LoRaWAN, to replace the LTE in the communication system. Based on the LoRa protocol and LoRaWAN, we redefine the way of communication for vehicles and IoTs in V2X. In order to provide better traffic prediction, machine learning is applied in route prediction algorithm [4]. Meanwhile, we suggest a simple way to predict and monitor the route. Based on the location of vehicle, the proposed system can predict the next closer gateways. The quick decision and stable connection will increase the overall performance in V2X network.

Despite various benefits brought by V2X communication in autonomous vehicles, the connection method still is one of the bottlenecks for improving the overall performance and safety in self-driving. In this paper, we are using LoRa protocol and LoRaWAN in V2X communication network instead of LTE and trying to provide another way to predict driving direction of vehicle and filter gateways, which are closer enough to self-driving cars. Moreover, based on the property of LoRa, we define a more efficient message format to transmit.

The structure of this paper is as follows: Sect. 2 is about introducing the background of LoRa protocol and LoRaWAN. The infrastructure of system design will be mentioned in Sect. 3. In Sect. 4, we define the packet message format for transmission. Then, the encryption of LoRa protocol will be introduced in Sect. 5. We define the problems and analysis the cases in Sect. 6 and then evaluate the experiment results in Sect. 7. Based on the results, discussion and conclusion are given in Sects. 8 and 9 respectively (Fig. 1).

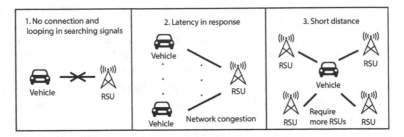

Fig. 1. Problems of LTE in V2X communication system.

2 Background

With the current development of autonomous vehicle, sensors, IoT and monitoring devices will generate lots of data. Those data will be exchanged and process in the whole transportation system. When a bunch of data, which includes location, vehicle status and other related conditions, is used for assisting self-driving, the latency of data processing and delay of exchange will increase. If the security of data transmission or early prediction of location can be achieved by changing communication methods, autonomous vehicles can focus on other topics. In this paper, we are going to implement LoRaWAN in V2X with LoRa protocol. The majority applications for the protocol of LoRa and LoRaWAN are in IoT, but new generation vehicles can be treated as product of combining IoT components.

2.1 LoRa

LoRa uses proprietary spread spectrum modulation that is similar to a derivative of Chirp Spread Spectrum modulation (CSS). This allows LoRa to trade off data for sensitivity with a fixed channel bandwidth by selecting the amount of spread used, which a selectable radio parameter is from 7 to 12. This expansion factor determines the data rate and determines the sensitivity of the radio.

In addition, LoRa uses Forward Error Correction coding to improve resilience against interference. LoRa's high range is characterized by extremely high wireless link budgets, around 155 dB to 170 dB. The data at the gateway use Frequency Shift Keying (FSK) to transmit. It is fully bi-directional communication.

2.2 LoRaWAN

The LoRaWAN defines the communication protocol and system architecture for the network, while the LoRa physical layer enables the long-range communication link. The LoRa physical layer is also responsible for managing the communication frequencies, data rate, and power for all devices. Devices in the network are asynchronous and transmitted when they have data available to send. Data transmitted by an end-node device is received by multiple gateways, which forward the data packets to a centralized network server. The network server filters duplicate packets, performs security checks, and manages the network. Data is then forwarded to the application server. The technology shows high reliability for the moderate load. It is bidirectional.

LoRaWAN is very useful technology in geolocation applications. It can reach up to 15 km in rural areas by the long-range feature. However, since the receivers are still sensitive in urban areas, it can only cover 5 km.

2.3 V2X Communication System

V2X communication system includes *Vehicle-to-Vehicle* (V2V), *Vehicle-to-Pedestrian* (V2P), *Vehicle-to-Infrastructure* (V2I), and *Vehicle-to-Network* (V2N). In the paper, we mainly focus on the V2V and V2I, which will be more important for self-driving system.

3 System Design

There are four components in the system: end-node, gateways, server and the application. End-node is connected sensors in the vehicle, which sends data by LoRaWAN protocol and the gateways are station to receive and transmit data in range. Server, *The Things Network* (TTN) used in the experiment, processes the forwarded packets from gateways. Next, TTN routes messages to the application to calculate the position.

3.1 End-node

The end-node is responsible for sending the data acquired from GPS receiver by LoRa module. The GPS module is used to check the geolocation and it coordinates will be transmitted over LoRaWAN as a payload in the packet. It sends uplink messages to the network server.

3.2 Gateway

The function of the gateway is routing the data received from the end-node to the server. In order to estimate and predict the location of self-driving vehicles, the calculation of receiving time of the packet from each gateway is needed to apply the algorithm.

The protocol between the gateway and the server is set in a binary file called "packet forwarder" that runs inside the gateway. There is no authentication of the gateway or the server, and acknowledgements are only used for network quality assessment, not to correct lost packets. This protocol only allows certain types of packets to be exchanged between the gateway and the server.

3.3   The Things Network

The function of TTN is handling decode of data from gateways and then transmitting to the application. It is important that the packets from the different gateways, with the same payload but with different times, arrived at the network server. The most relevant feature for the algorithm computation is the value of the time field in the JSON. If it receives the same data packet from several gateways, it will only process one of them and disregard the copies.

3.4   Application

Application mainly consists of database and program. The data obtained from TTN will be parsed and stored. Then it publishes device activations and messages.

4   Formatting Message

Data transmitted from End-node to the gateway will be simplified. Rather than sending all detailed information, we can mainly send important in numeric codes, which represent actions and situations. On the vehicle side, action will be much more important than other information (Fig. 2).

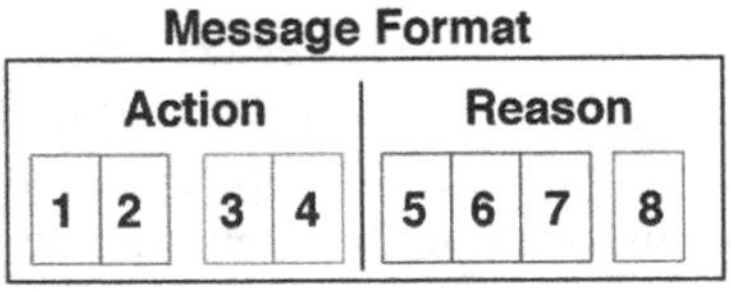

Message Format

Action				Reason			
1	2	3	4	5	6	7	8

Fig. 2. Defining the message format.

For the testing, we defined the 8-digit number string format to represent a message. Since we can categorize actions and statuses, vehicles can read the representing code and operate immediately.

We explain the format by the following example,

03 15 012 4

First two digits indicate action category. 03 means that vehicle has to stop. For next 2 digits, it means the value for that certain action. 15 is representing that the vehicle needs to stop after 15 miles, so autonomous vehicle can has longer buffer to slow down and adjust the speed. Then, 3 digits are used for illustrating the reasons. 012 is the traffic light. Finally, the last digit is supporting the reasons. In the example, the traffic light is red, which is 4, right now.

Therefore, autonomous vehicles can react and send control signals by just reading first four digits. For the edge computer, server, and applications are able processing other operations by last four digits.

5 Security

LoRaWAN utilizes security in two layers, TTN and application. TTN verifies the authenticity of the end-node. While the application layer ensures the operators in TTN layer, it cannot access to the application data.

There are two unique 128-bit session keys, one for TTN layer (NekSKey) and another for Application layer (AppSLey). The data is transmitted under LoRa protocol by radio wave. Even the radio waves themselves cannot be encrypted. The biggest advantage is that the CSS signal is low in power consumption and is not easily scanned and intercepted by other devices.

6 Defining Problem

6.1 Direction Prediction

In the current V2X communication system, the location of the vehicle will be very important. Direction prediction of the vehicle will affect which gateway the vehicle will communicate with.

The geolocation obtains the position received in Cartesian coordinates (x, y, z), where x is the latitude, y is the longitude and z is the height. The set of coordinates is useful for mathematical calculations and easier to manipulate (Fig. 3).

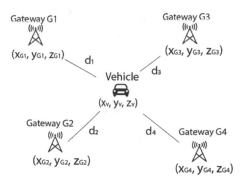

Fig. 3. Vehicle with LoRa gateways.

Assuming that the coordinates of the vehicle are (x_0, y_0, z_0) at time t = 0, then, at t = 1, the coordinates are (x_1, y_1, z_1). The application of Atan2 to calculate the direction of the vehicle driving and defining the direction is illustrated as following:

```
// enumerated counterclockwise, starting from east = 0:
enum compass {
    E = 0, NE = 1,
    N = 2, NW = 3,
    W = 4, SW = 5,
    S = 6, SE = 7
};
const string[8] headings = { "E", "NE", "N", "NW", "W", "SW",
"S", "SE" };
// actual conversion code:
float angle = atan2 ( vector.y, vector.x );
int octant = round ( 8 * angle / ( 2 * PI ) + 8 ) % 8;
```

The great-circle distance between two points, which identified by using GPS coordinates, is determined by using Haversine formula. That is the shortest distance over the surface of earth, which giving an as-the-crow-flies distance between the two points.

The Θ is the center angle between any two points on a sphere, where d is the distance and r is the radius of the earth.

$$\Theta = dr \tag{1}$$

The haversine formula is as follows:

$$hav(\Theta) = hav(\varphi_2 - \varphi_1) + \cos(\varphi_1)\cos(\varphi_2)hav(\lambda_2 - \lambda_1) \tag{2}$$

where φ_1 and φ_2 are the latitude of point 1 and latitude of point 2 respectively. And λ_1 and λ_2 are the longitude of point. Finally, we can get the versine of the angle (Fig. 4):

$$hav(\theta) = sin^2\left(\frac{\theta}{2}\right) = \frac{1 - \cos(\theta)}{2} \tag{3}$$

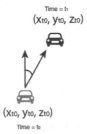

Fig. 4. Calculate the moving direction

After getting the direction of vehicle, we narrow down the number of nearby gateways. Then, the closer gateways can be ready transmitting packet back to the vehicle, by calculating the displacement (d) between vehicle and the gateway:

$$d = \sqrt{(x_v - x_g)^2 + (y_v - y_g)^2 + (z_v - z_v)^2} \tag{4}$$

Algorithm 1: Gateway Filtering by Vehicle Driving Direction

```
Input: coordinates of point 1 and point 2
Output: list of gateways G
1    Set ( x1, y1, z1 ) ← coordinates of point 1
2    Set ( x2, y2, z2 ) ← coordinates of point 2
3    Calculate moving direction with function atan2
4    Get stored gateway list
5    Set fg ← empty list for filtered gateways
6    For index in gateway list
7    Calculate the distance between point 2 and gateway
8    If distance is less than 6km then
9    Add the gateway to fg
10   End for
11   Return fg
```

6.2   Gateway Connection

We can filter those gateways and set how many closer gateways to be ready connect with the vehicle. Gateways is saved as: {G1:(22,23,3), G2:(89,783,8), …, G20:(22,140,8)}. Then, for example, G1, G3 and G7 will be allocation for transmission (Fig. 5).

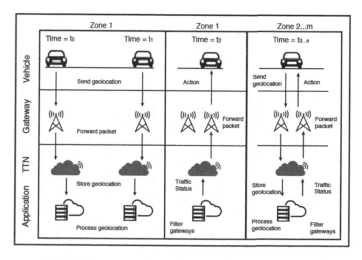

Fig. 5. Our approach to enhance V2X communication.

Case 1: Receive data in a zone.
Assuming there is a traffic light is red ahead in the zone. Next, the self-driving vehicle is entering the zone and will receive the alert message. The vehicle will slow down earlier before arriving that traffic light.

The TTN routes the message to the gateway. The vehicle will then receive the vehicle once it enters the coverage area of the gateway.

Case 2: Send data within a zone.
If a vehicle has an issue and needs to stop, instead of sending slower messages to far away gateways, the server would have let the vehicle to send a quick message to a nearby gateway. The message will include a few miles in front of the traffic lights needed to stop driving.

Case 3: Pass boundary between two zones.
Even though the autonomous vehicle is driving away from one zone and entering to another zone, we do not worry about that. Since the vehicle is using LoRa protocol, all the data will be sent to closer gateway. On the flip side, the filtered gateways will transmit message to the vehicle. Therefore, the situation of driving across the boundary between two zones is just same as in the same zone.

7 Evaluation

Our design for the evaluation will simplified to one vehicle with four gateways. In the experiments, we are mainly utilizing the LoRa protocol and LoRaWAN in V2X communication system to obtain the overall performance of connection. And then, verify whether the latency of data transmission can be reduced or not.

To evaluate the transmission performance, a gateway is installed inside an office. A car with the LoRa device was driving from time (t) = 0 min at starting point, office, and then driving back to starting point at T = 26 min. The route of the car is shown in Fig. 6.

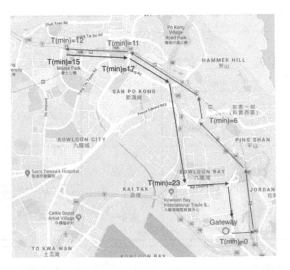

Fig. 6. The route of the LoRa performance test.

We sent five packets in every minute, and then calculate the received rate by:

$$Rate = \frac{Packet_{Received}}{Packet_{Sent}} \times 100\% \tag{5}$$

where $Packet_{Received}$ is the data stored in the TTN database and $Packet_{Sent}$ is data sent from end-node and vehicle.

As shown in Fig. 7, the results are shown. From t = 6 to t = 15, there are tall buildings between the car and gateway, so the rate dropped. Next, between time t = 12 and t = 17, the car was stopped for 3 min and then driving back. The rate dropped to 80% due to buildings and hill.

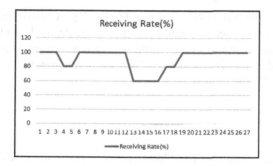

Fig. 7. Receiving rate

It was observed that even the receiving rate will affect the environment and the stability of LoRa is still good enough for using in V2X communication network. Moreover, it implied that the vehicles will not lose connection in V2X network and do not need to search network to connect.

For the latency, it includes transmission time on processing, queueing, and propagation. And the waiting time is due to cycling of regulatory duty. The transmission time is calculated by the formula; $T_{total} = T_{tx} + T_w$, where T_{tx} is the time for processing and propagation and T_w is waiting time. The waiting time is calculated by:

$$T_w = \frac{P_{busy,all}}{\left(\sum_{i=1}^{c} \mu_i + \lambda\right) \cdot 2} \tag{6}$$

where $P_{busy,all}$ is the Erlang-C probability that all servers are busy.

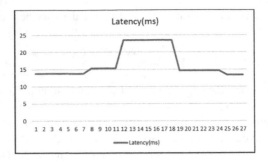

Fig. 8. Latency in the experiment

We can observe the results of latency in Fig. 8. We recorded the transmitting time and receiving time in milliseconds and corrected to one decimal number. While the car was driving far away from the gateway, the latency is increased. However, the latency is decreased after driving back to the gateway. The average time is 16.7 ms, which is acceptable latency for data transmission.

8   Discussion

In this paper, we mainly utilized the LoRa protocol and LoRaWAN in V2X communication system to enhance the overall connection performance. Meanwhile, the latency of data transmission also can be reduced. In the current V2X communication network, LTE has its own limitations and connection issues. By redefining the message format, we can diminish the packet size. Since we are following the format, which is the trade-off between transmission speed and content, the data and information will be limited.

Apart from the potential advantages brought by using LoRa in the whole V2X communication system, the cost will decreases by less gateways, which can cover wide area. The power consumption of LoRa devices are low, and the vehicles or gateways are able to save more energy than using LTE. The transmission parameters of LoRa protocol are defined by Adaptive Data Rate (ADR) scheme. The Spreading Factor, Bandwidth and Transmission Power are controlling the uplink of LoRa.

9   Conclusion

In conclusion, we presented the LoRa protocol and LoRaWAN and those technologies are implemented in V2X communication system to provide much more reliable connection between autonomous vehicles and infrastructures. The aim of this work is enhancing the performance of data transmission. In addition, the claims of avoiding the loss connection and reduction of latency are verified by our evaluations.

However, we are mainly focus on one autonomous vehicle in this paper. In real case, there are so many vehicles in the transportation system. Therefore, it is important to handle the load-balancing and decide how to weight the gateways. The future direction is continuously focusing on improving the communication performance in real urban V2X scenarios because the difficulty of route and direction prediction for vehicles will increase in urban area.

Acknowledgment. This work is supported in by the National Natural Science Foundation of China (No. 61728303) and the Open Research Project of the State Key Laboratory of Industrial Control Technology, Zhejiang University, China (No. ICT1800417).

References

1. Qiu, H., Noura, H., Qiu, M., Ming, Z., Memmi, G.: A user-centric data protection method for cloud storage based on invertible DWT. IEEE Trans. Cloud Comput. (2019)
2. Haidar, F., Kaiser, A., Lonc, B.: On the performance evaluation of vehicular PKI protocol for V2X communications security. In: Proceeding of IEEE 86th Vehicular Technology Conference (VTC-Fall) (2017)
3. Petit, J., Shladover, S.: Potential cyber attacks on automated vehicles. IEEE Trans. Intell. Transp. Syst. 16(2), 546–556 (2015)
4. Lv, Y., Duan, Y., Kang, W., Li, Z., Wangi, F.: Traffic flow prediction with big data: a deep learning approach. IEEE Trans. Intell. Transp. Syst. 16(2), 865–873 (2015)
5. Qiu, H., Qiu, M., Lu, Z., Memmi, G.: An efficient key distribution system for data fusion in V2X heterogeneous networks. Inf. Fusion 50, 212–220 (2019)
6. Kontzer, T.: Driving Change: Volvo's "Drive Me" Project to Make Self-Driving Cars Synonymous with Safety (2016). https://blogs.nvidia.com/blog/2016/04/06/volvo-safety-self-driving/
7. Wang, X., Mao, S., Gong, M.: An overview of 3GPP cellular vehicle-to-everything standards. GetMobile: Mob. Comput. Commun. 21(3), 19–25 (2017)
8. Abboud, K., Omar, H., Zhuang, W.: Interworking of DSRC and cellular network technologies for V2X communications: a survey. IEEE Trans. Veh. Technol. 65(12), 9457–9470 (2016)
9. Atallah, R., Khabbaz, M., Assi, C.: Vehicular networking: a survey on spectrum access technologies and persisting challenges. Veh. Commun. 2(3), 125–149 (2015)
10. MacHardy, Z., Khan, A., Obana, K., Iwashina, S.: V2X access technologies: regulation, research, and remaining challenges. IEEE Commun. Surv. Tutorials 20(3), 1858–1877 (2018)
11. Feng, Y., Hu, B., Hao, H., Gao, Y., Li, Z.: Design of distributed cyber-physical systems for connected and automated vehicles with implementing methodologies. IEEE Trans. Ind. Inf. 14(9), 4200–4211 (2018)
12. Li, L., Ota, K., Dong, M.: Humanlike driving: empirical decision-making system for autonomous vehicles. IEEE Trans. Veh. Technol. 67(8), 6814–6823 (2018)
13. Zhao, Z., Chen, W., Wu, X., Peter, C.Y., Chen, P.C., Liu, J.: LSTM network: a deep learning approach for short-term traffic forecast. IET Intell. Transp. Syst. 11(2), 68–75 (2017)
14. Lukosevicius, M., Jaeger, H.: Reservoir computing approaches to recurrent neural network training. Comput. Sci. Rev. 3(3), 127–149 (2009)
15. Guo, L., et al.: A secure mechanism for big data collection in large scale internet of vehicle. IEEE Internet of Things J. 4(2), 601–610 (2017)
16. Pacheco, J., Hariri, S.: IoT security framework for smart cyber infrastructures. In: IEEE International Workshops on Foundations and Applications of Self* Systems, pp. 242–247. IEEE, September 2016

17. Lloret, J., Tomas, J., Canovas, A., Parra, L.: An integrated IoT architecture for smart metering. IEEE Commun. Mag. **54**(12), 50–57 (2016)
18. Sornin, N., Luis, M., Eirich, T., Kramp, T., Hersent, O.: LoRaWAN Specification, pp. 1–82, January 2015
19. "LoRaWAN Network Server Demonstration: Gateway to Server Interface Definition," Semtech, Application note, pp. 1–19, July 2015
20. Augustin, A., Yi, J., Clausen, T., Townsley, W.: A study of LoRa: long range & low power networks for the Internet of Things. Sensors **16**(9), 1466 (2016)

Correction to: A Survey of Deep Learning Applied to Story Generation

Chenglong Hou, Chensong Zhou, Kun Zhou, Jinan Sun,
and Sisi Xuanyuan

Correction to:
Chapter "A Survey of Deep Learning Applied to Story
Generation" in: M. Qiu (Ed.): *Smart Computing*
and Communication, **LNCS 11910,**
https://doi.org/10.1007/978-3-030-34139-8_1

In the version of this paper that was originally published, the last name of the author
Sisi Xuanyuan was misspelt. This has been corrected.

The updated version of this chapter can be found at
https://doi.org/10.1007/978-3-030-34139-8_1

© Springer Nature Switzerland AG 2020
M. Qiu (Ed.): SmartCom 2019, LNCS 11910, p. C1, 2020.
https://doi.org/10.1007/978-3-030-34139-8_41

Author Index

Printed in the United States
By Bookmasters